ARIUS

ARIUS

Heresy and Tradition

• •

REVISED EDITION

Rowan Williams

William B. Eerdmans Publishing Company
Grand Rapids, Michigan / Cambridge, U.K.

© 1987, 2001 Rowan Williams

First published in 1987 by Darton, Longman and Todd Ltd
Second edition first published in 2001 by SCM Press

This edition published in 2002 in the United States of America by
Wm. B. Eerdmans Publishing Co.
255 Jefferson Ave. S.E., Grand Rapids, Michigan /
P.O. Box 163, Cambridge CB3 9PU U.K.

Printed in the United States of America

07 06 05 04 03   7 6 5 4 3 2

Library of Congress Cataloging-in-Publication Data

ISBN 0-8028-4969-5

To Christopher Stead
in gratitude and affection

Traditions, when vital, embody continuities of conflict.
Alasdair MacIntyre, *After Virtue*
(London 1981), p. 206

Contents

Contents

Part III Arius and Philosophy

Preface

This book has grown slowly and inexorably from what I had originally conceived as a couple of minor bits of research in the background of the Arian heresy, sparked off by an invitation from
Professor Henry Chadwick to review Rudolf Lorenz' important
work on the subject. As so often happens, what had seemed clear
points of reference faded away alarmingly as my studies advanced,
and the idea of writing a longer treatment of the whole area became
increasingly attractive, if only for the sake of clearing my own mind.
But since there has been a quite remarkable amount of new work
on Arianism in recent years, in this country as well as in the USA
and Europe, it also seemed to be a good idea to try and draw
together and assess where it had all led. In the event, there proved
to be many topics that could not easily be dealt with adequately in
the compass of this book. I have done my best to indicate where
there is 'unfinished business', or where I have adopted a contentious
conclusion that would need fuller defence than is possible here, in
the hope that there will be plenty of better and more energetic
scholars to pursue these issues as the discussion advances.

It is not exclusively an historical study. As the introduction will
make plain, there has seldom been a 'purely' historical treatment
of the Arian controversy. This work, like others, ventures some
reflections, mostly in the introduction and postscript, on the contemporary theological import of the issues discussed. The historian may
want to skip these sections, but I hope will not – there are some
questions here, I believe, of wider methodological relevance.
Equally, I hope that the theologically-minded reader will resist the
temptation to ignore the history, even (though this is asking a lot!)
the rather technical discussions of Arius' philosophical antecedents:
there is never, then or now, so purely theological a debate that it
can afford to bracket out the need for awareness of both social and
intellectual constraints on the language of controversy.

I gladly record my indebtedness to the many persons and institutions that have helped and supported me in the writing of this work. I have already mentioned the role played by Professor Henry Chadwick in starting me thinking on this subject: he has continued to be a source of support and constructive criticism throughout the period of writing. Professors Timothy Barnes and Charles Kannengiesser have also shown generous and friendly interest, and given time to the discussion of various questions; vigorous disagreements have never clouded amicable relations, and I have learnt enormously from both these colleagues. Like many others, I found my perspectives on the Arian issue were challenged and enlarged by the very fertile exchanges in the seminar on this subject at the 1983 Oxford Patristic Conference, and I must thank all my fellow-participants in that group. Dr George Dragas has been an invaluable source of information about, and frequently of copies of, contemporary Greek studies in the field, and I owe much to him in this and other ways. Canon Richard Young of Chicago and the Revd Philip Ursell of Pusey House, Oxford, kindly provided hospitality at crucial times during a sabbatical term. My former colleagues at Clare College, Cambridge, offered the help and support of an unusually friendly and open community of scholars; and the Faculty of Divinity at Cambridge, in particular the Patristic Seminar, gave me more than I can readily say. The dedication of this work expresses my debt to one colleague in particular, who has made very much his own the whole subject of Arian origins. His work, especially on the philosophical background to the controversy, has been one of those points of reference that have not faded; it has set me a standard of sympathy and exactness which I am aware of most of the time as only a distant goal. His careful and expert criticism has contributed greatly to everything that I have written in this field, and I have no doubt that the familiar cliché of acknowledgements is true – that this would have been a much better book if I had listened to him more often.

My wife has not only tolerated the invasion of our home by large numbers of third– and fourth-century figures in the shape of bloated mounds of books and papers over four years; she has helped to expedite their departure by typing the greater part of this manuscript with speed, accuracy and an impressive restraint in complaining, at the state of the footnotes in particular. I am very grateful. The staff at Darton, Longman and Todd have been their usual encouraging selves, and have once again greatly lightened an author's load by their advice and friendship.

At a time when there is so much renewed bitterness over doctrinal disagreements in my own and other churches, and so much unclarity over what might be involved in being 'loyal' to the tradition of the Church, it is important to be more aware than ever of the numerous and often elusive factors that help to form that tradition. My hope is that (to borrow David Tracy's terminology) the 'public' for this book will include those concerned for the Church's health and honesty, as well as the 'academy'.

ROWAN WILLIAMS

Oxford, November 1986

Preface to the Second Edition

Since 1987, research on the fourth century has continued to flourish. The present work has attracted its fair share of discussion in the past fourteen years; and, while there are many pages that would now need to be written otherwise and a good many areas in which I might want to approach a subject differently, it would be a very large task to revise the entire book. The generous suggestion from Alex Wright at SCM Press that a new edition might be possible has allowed me the opportunity to respond to various criticisms and to acknowledge weaknesses, as well as in some cases to offer further argument for what I still believe to be defensible positions. The appendix to the book, 'Arius since 1987' attempts to give a sketchy survey of some new moves in research as well as to engage with some commentators and critics. My hope is that this additional material will stimulate further debate and clarification. I am deeply grateful to all my colleagues who have taken the trouble to discuss the original work, to readers and students who still wish to tackle its subject matter, and to SCM Press for giving it a new lease of life. Whatever the very limited merits of the book, it should be clear that the questions both of substance and of method dealt with here are no less absorbing and significant now than when the work first appeared.

ROWAN WILLIAMS

Newport, Passiontide 2001

Introduction

Images of a Heresy

1

'Arianism' has often been regarded as the archetypal Christian deviation, something aimed at the very heart of the Christian confession. From the point of view of history, this is hardly surprising: the crisis of the fourth century was the most dramatic internal struggle the Christian Church had so far experienced; it generated the first credal statement to claim universal, unconditional assent, and it became inextricably entangled with issues concerning the authority of political rulers in the affairs of the Church. Later, it would become similarly entangled with the divisions between Roman and Barbarian in what had been the western empire: Rome was sacked by Goths who had adopted what was by then the non-imperial version of the Christian faith, and Arian rulers uncomfortably governed their conquered territories with the aid of Catholic, Roman civil servants. By the time that the great upheavals within the empire were over, Arianism had been irrevocably cast as the Other in relation to Catholic (and civilized) religion. Arius himself came more and more to be regarded as a kind of Antichrist among heretics, a man whose superficial austerity and spirituality cloaked a diabolical malice, a deliberate enmity to revealed faith. The portrait is already taking shape in Epiphanius' work, well before the end of the fourth century, and is vividly present in later accounts of the martyrdom of Peter of Alexandria, who ordained Arius deacon. By the early medieval period, we find him represented alongside Judas in ecclesiastical art. (The account of his death in fourth– and fifth-century writers is already clearly modelled on that of Judas in the Acts of the Apostles.) No other heretic has been through so thoroughgoing a process of 'demonization'.

1

This may be unsurprising – as I have said – given the range and depth of the issues involved in the crisis, political as well as theological issues. What is rather more surprising is the way in which the modern study of Arius and 'Arianism' has often continued to accept, consciously or not, the image of this heresy as the radically 'Other', projecting on to it whatever theological or ecclesiological tenets currently represent the opposition to a Christian mainstream in which the scholar and interpreter claims to stand. Of course, until relatively recently, not all that many Christians were prepared to deny or question that Nicaea and its (revised and expanded) creed were the indispensable criteria of orthodoxy; so, if one wished to justify a continuing adherence of some kind to Nicaea, even though one's own theology might be very significantly different from that of Athanasius and his supporters, Arius' views had to be represented as standing for some hopelessly defective form of belief. It is certainly not the case that scholars have engaged in deliberate sleight of hand here; but the combination of Nicaea's traditional and liturgical importance with the long history of what I have called the 'demonizing' of Arius is extraordinarily powerful. Anyone setting out to reconstruct the life and opinions of Arius has to reckon with this – and also to be aware of the temptation to correct the balance in a simplistic way by making Arius a theological hero. I am aware that, in some of what follows, I shall not have avoided distortions of one kind or another: my reading of the material suggests various patterns in the life of the Alexandrian church of the early fourth century strongly reminiscent of developments in contemporary Christian experience – conflicts about authority between the representatives of an hierarchical institution and the charismatic leaders of 'gathered' congregations, house-churches of various kinds, conflicts over the right theological use of Scripture, and so on; suspiciously contemporary questions. But the point at which an authentic and illuminating analogy turns into a Procrustean bed on which evidence is tortured is never very easy to identify. The reader as well as the writer needs warning here.

2

The point may be illustrated by looking briefly at a variety of scholarly treatments of Arianism in the last century and a half. The modern critical study of the subject really begins with Newman's justly celebrated essay of 1833, *The Arians of the Fourth Century*, a work many times reprinted, which exercised a formative influence on British scholarship in particular. Newman rightly claimed a degree of originality for his interpretation of the roots of Arianism: in an appendix on 'The Syrian School of Theology' added to the fourth (1874) edition (pp. 403–15), he noted the fact that, up to the 1830s, it had been customary to associate the Arian system primarily with Neoplatonism, whereas he had explained it in terms of the distinctive theological and exegetical positions of the Antiochene church. Earlier chroniclers had not, of course, ignored the ancient allegations that Arius was a follower of the doctrines of the Antiochene Paul of Samosata, and the likelihood that he had been a pupil of Lucian of Antioch, the exegete and martyr; but it is quite true that Platonic influences had been more emphasized. Cave's *Ecclesiastici* of 1683 alluded to the Neoplatonic principle of a hierarchy of hypostases as forming Arius' mind on the trinitarian issue; following Cudworth, Cave held that later Platonists deliberately accentuated the subordination of the second and third hypostases 'out of spite to Christianity, (to which the old Scheme [of Plato, and perhaps Plotinus]) did too near approach' (p. 44). Only at the end of a longish disquisition on this does Cave add that Arius had been predisposed to such views by his apprenticeship to Lucian, who taught, like Paul of Samosata, that Christ was 'a meer man' (p. 45).

This is not untypical of the approach to which Newman was reacting. In sharp contrast, the first twenty-seven pages of his essay deal with the Antiochene church, and, as has already been noted, he was later to add an appendix on 'Syrian' theology, a good deal of which reproduces some of the discussion in the *Essay on Development*. The philosophical background to Arius' views is barely touched upon in these opening pages, though the second chapter (pp. 28–42) postulates a close connection with the 'Sophists' – identified with practitioners of syllogistic disputation in general and the 'Aristotelic school' in particular (p. 32); this discussion is cast in very vague terms, being almost devoid of specific reference to authors or movements of the period, and blandly merges together a number of very diverse phenomena. But the first chapter is meant to set the tone of the whole work. Arianism is the child of Antiochene Christianity, which – as Paul of Samosata's teaching demonstrates

3

– is in thrall to Judaizing tendencies, in practice as well as in doctrine. The church of Antioch retains many traces of Jewish ritual observance and is the peculiar nursery of what Newman calls 'Humanitarian' views of Christ.

> I will not say [he writes (p. 20)] that the Arian doctrine is the direct result of a judaizing practice; but it deserves consideration whether a tendency to derogate from the honour due to Christ was not created by an observance of the Jewish rites, and much more, by that carnal self-indulgent religion, which seems at that time to have prevailed among the rejected nation.

'Jewish' ritualism is unable to see outward observance as the type of deeper truth, and so encourages the fallen mind's unwillingness to see more than what presents itself to the senses: thus it nurtures a low view of Christ, and a disputatious, rationalist temper, typical of the mind untutored by the heart. Naturally this is linked, as Newman seeks later on to show, with an impatience at the idea of mystery in theology and exegesis, a rejection of allegory, a refusal to read Scripture *within* tradition and an unintelligent adherence to the letter of the Bible combined with wooden syllogistic analyses of biblical language (pp. 236–44) – though the Arians can also, inconsistently, use allegory or metaphor when it suits them (pp. 244–8). In the appendix to the fourth edition, Newman made still more of the Antiochene devotion to the 'literal and critical interpretation of Scripture', the invariable connection between 'heterodoxy and biblical criticism', and the implicit denial of any real doctrine of inspiration by those rejecting allegory (1874, pp. 404–5).

The Alexandrian church is held up, in contrast, as the very exemplar of traditional and revealed religion (ch. I, s. III, passim). So far from Arianism being the product of an unhealthy Alexandrian flirtation with philosophical mystagogy, an adulteration of the gospel by Platonism (pp. 7, 26), it is the result of a systematic refusal of true philosophy, a refusal of the wisdom that pierces the material veil of things, in favour of shallow materialism. In true Alexandrian (or at least Origenian) style, Newman regards certain exegetical options as moral and spiritual in character and effect. Antioch's exegetical preference is no mere alternative within the spectrum of possible techniques: it is a spiritual deficiency.

One must charitably say that Newman is not at his best here: a brilliant argument, linking all sorts of diverse phenomena, is built up on a foundation of complacent bigotry and historical fantasy. However, setting aside for the moment the distasteful rhetoric of his exposition, it should be possible to see something of what his polemical agenda really is. *The Arians of the Fourth Century* is, in large part, a tract in defence of what the early Oxford Movement thought of as spiritual religion and spiritual authority. It works with a clear normative definition of Christian faith and practice, in which ascetical discipline goes hand-in-hand with the repudiation of Protestant biblicism (and Protestant rejection of post-scriptural development in teaching and devotion) and a commitment to the 'principle of reserve' a mystagogic approach to the faith in which deep mysteries could be concealed beneath simple forms and words and only gradually unveiled. Such a picture naturally supports a high view of priestly authority, and a low view of the rights of secular power in the Church. By 1874 Newman no doubt saw more need to underline the risks of the critical study of Scripture (the first chill draught from Germany was already making itself felt) than to labour the perils of old-fashioned Protestant literalism; hence the slight shift of emphasis in the Appendix. But the essential point is unchanged: allegory is necessary for spiritual religion.

Newman's version of the fourth-century crisis, then, rests upon a characterization of Arianism as radically 'other' in several respects. It is the forerunner of stolid Evangelicalism, Erastian worldliness ('carnal, self-indulgent religion'), and – by 1874, anyway – the new style of university theology. What unifies these diverse distortions of Catholic truth is their common rejection of mystical and symbolic readings of the world in general and Scripture in particular; they are all doomed to remain at the level of surface reality. And it is this 'Judaizing' tendency that provoked the early Church's worst crisis; let the modern reader take heed. Yet there are 'cheering and edifying' lessons to be drawn, as well as warnings.

Then as now there was the prospect, and partly the presence in the Church, of an heretical power enthralling it, exerting a varied influence and a usurped claim in the appointment of her functionaries, and interfering with the management of her internal affairs . . . [S]hould the hand of Satan press us sore, our Athanasius and Basil will be given us in their destined season. (p. 422)

5

This ringing exordium makes it abundantly clear that the 'Arians of the fourth century' are, in significant measure, those members of the nineteenth-century Church of England beyond the confines of primitive Tractarianism, those whose essential worldliness (even in the guise of devout biblicism) has left the Church a helpless prey to secular domination. At precisely those points at which his historical analysis seems eccentric, superficial and prejudiced, Newman shows his skills as a controversialist. Even more than in the fourth century itself, 'Arianism' is being created by abstraction from what it is not, and the importance of Newman's work is in its classical exemplification of this technique at least as much as in its contribution to serious scholarship (and probably more).

3

The same process is observable if we turn to Harnack's discussion of the nature of Arianism in volume II of the great *Lehrbuch der Dogmengeschichte* (4th edn, 1909; the English translation is from the 3rd edn, but the text of this section is substantially unchanged between the two editions). Like Newman, Harnack sees 'Aristotelian Rationalism' as the background of Arius' system and as typical of the school of Lucian (pp. 189–90; E.T. pp. 6–7); Lucian himself is described as heir to the tradition of Paul of Samosata, and synthesizing Paul's teaching with that of Origen (p. 187; E.T., p. 3). Harnack suggests a parallel between Antiochene theology of this sort and the earlier adoptionism of Theodotus: there too, according to Harnack, Aristotelianism combines with the critical study of Scripture to produce a theology stressing the humanity of Jesus at the expense of his integral divinity (pp. 189–90; E.T., pp. 6–7). However, the mixed legacy of Paul and Origen transmitted by Lucian leads to severe tensions in the thought of Arius. On the one hand we have an adoptionist picture of a Christ who 'is the Saviour, in so far as he has conveyed to us the divine doctrine and has given us an example of goodness perfectly realized in the exercise of freedom' (p. 220; E.T., p. 39); on the other, we are faced with a basically *cosmological* problematic, to which soteriology is irrelevant, the question of how to bridge the gulf between the transcendent God and the created order. Here the Son or Logos is brought in as a mediatorial figure of a straightforward Neoplatonic kind. The two

6

disparate elements are held together by the idea that the created mediator actually advances in status as a result of the incarnation (which thus becomes part of a trajectory of glorification, not a radical humiliation); but Arius' scheme is adulterated by a *mythological* version of adoptionism (involving the Logos, not Jesus) that leaves us finally with practical polytheism, two objects of worship (p. 220; E.T., p. 40).

In that Arius leaves no logical room for a pre-existent *Son* (for we must suppose the mediatorial Logos to be promoted to sonship in his post-incarnate state), he distances himself from Origen as much as from Nicene orthodoxy (p. 221; E.T., p. 40). The Logos who participates in the divine life, in however subordinate a role, and thus is able to unite creatures to God and bestow saving illumination upon them, is excluded on this showing: Arius and Athanasius together finally dismiss the Logos of Philo and the Apologists from the scene (p. 226; E.T., pp. 48–9). Both contribute to the elimination of hierarchical gnostic structures of thought from Christian theology, both make it impossible to base Christology upon cosmology. Yet Arianism and Nicene orthodoxy are by no means comparably acceptable versions of Christianity: Arius' teaching is novel, self-contradictory (p. 221; E.T., p. 41) and, above all, religiously inadequate. The combination of cosmology with veneration for a heroic teacher is characteristic of *Hellenism* (p. 222; E.T., p. 42); cosmology and morality fail to provide a vehicle for understanding that *fellowship* with God that is attained in and through Jesus, and, if Arianism had triumphed, it would have meant the end of authentic Christianity (pp. 222–3; E.T., pp. 42–3). Arianism lacks the vision of perfect unity through love, faith, feeling, that Harnack discerns in the theology of Paul of Samosata (p. 222; E.T., p. 43); it knows only an external obedience to God, in the Logos and the believer alike. Naturally this helps to provide a rationale for heroic asceticism, and it is this, combined with the polytheistic aspect of the system, that makes Arianism attractive to the Teutonic nations (p. 223; E.T., pp. 43–4). Athanasius is no closer to the Samosatene notion of union with God, but, at least, in his stress on the unity of *nature* between Father and Son and the ontological participation of believers in the divine life, he goes beyond the extrinsic model of union defended by Arius and preserves the idea of Christianity as 'living fellowship with God' (pp. 223–5; E.T., pp. 44–6). It is deeply paradoxical that true

7

Christianity should be saved by a theologian for whom the historical humanity of Jesus of Nazareth is of no interest at all: Athanasius salvages the gospel at a very high price – ultimately, as Harnack evidently believed, an unacceptably high price (pp. 223–4, 226–7; E.T., pp. 45, 48–9). Yet Arianism has 'no understanding of the inner essence of religion' (p. 227; E.T., p. 49), and the Church was right to reject and condemn it.

Harnack's lengthy 'evaluation' of the Arian and Athanasian systems is no less brilliant and no less eccentric than Newman's reading. Arius' teaching here has become a paradigm of that 'radical Hellenization' which, for Harnack, marks the whole post-biblical development of Christian doctrine. It makes certain necessary and correct *negative* moves (dissociating Christology from cosmology, emphasizing monotheism, 'demystifying' the divinity of Jesus), but destroys the possible advantage to be gained therefrom by retaining an hierarchical mythology, stressing morality and obedience at the expense of love and personal communion, and countenancing a practical polytheism; it thus leads to superstition and prideful asceticism. For Harnack, in fact, Arianism is the archetypal heresy in that it illustrates all the corruptions of Hellenized, Catholic Christianity (mythology plus moralism, the compromising of monotheistic faith, a sub-personal account of salvation, lacking in true interiority) without any of those features which have, historically, prevented Catholic Christianity from wholly losing sight of the gospel of Jesus of Nazareth – above all, the abiding commitment to the goal of *communion* with the divine life, however imperfectly and naturalistically this communion was understood. The 'otherness' of Arianism is the otherness of formalistic, moralizing religion. 'Protestant orthodoxy' or monkish Catholicism. The basic polarity between the spiritual gospel and the moralism that is always seductively close at hand is in fact spelt out by Harnack in the major essay on 'Presuppositions' which forms the second chapter of his first volume; in the light of this, the *classical* character of the Nicene crisis in Harnack's presentation becomes clearer still. Just as much as for Newman, the very nature of Christianity as a 'spiritual' religion is seen to be at stake.

4

Harnack is far more cautious than Newman in judging the root of all evil to be located in the school of Antioch, yet he too still sees Arian origins in terms of a fusion between syllogistic logic and biblical literalism, with an admixture of mythical cosmology. Again, like Newman, he sees the issue as essentially to do with the person and work of Christ. It was H. M. Gwatkin, in his *Studies of Arianism* (1882 and 1900), who seems first to have challenged the main lines of this consensus. We should *not* look to Antioch for the sources of Arianism; we have no ground for believing that Jewish influence was stronger at Antioch than at Alexandria; we cannot suppose that later Antiochene Christology, with its fervent devotion to Nicaea, is in any way an 'outgrowth' of Arianism (pp. 17–20). In a few brief paragraphs, Gwatkin effectively demolishes the greater part of Newman's picture, and sets a question mark against much of Harnack. However, like his predecessors, he continues to see Arianism as the result of irreverent philosophical speculation: it is 'almost as much a philosophy as a religion' (p. 20), 'measuring the heights of heaven with . . . puny logic, and sounding the deeps of Wisdom with the plummet of the schools' (p. 28). So far from being Jewish, it is essentially pagan in its elevation of a demigod to a central position of honour in its worship (p. 26), and, as such, it has an instant and facile attractiveness to half-converted heathens (pp. 30–1). But the essence of Arianism is its doctrine of the relation between God and the world, rather than its Christology in the strict sense. Arianism crystallizes the common Jewish, pagan and early Christian assumption that the spiritual dignity of the Godhead is to be defended by elaborating its absolute contrast to humanity (pp. 20–1); but the Christian doctrines of creation, especially the creation of human beings in the image of God, and redemption through divine involvement make it impossible in the long term to sustain such a strategy. Arius resolves the tensions in Christian thinking by a simple assimilation of God the Father to the remote and isolated absolute of Middle Platonism and of the Son to the creative demiurge. However, Arius' concern to remove all trace of emanationism and materialism from the relation of Father to Son leads to the idea of an arbitrarily willed generation of the latter, and a stress on his creaturely freedom.

> Here we get another view of the Pelagianism which is an essential element of the Arian system. Both schemes depend on the same false dualism of God and man, the same denial of the Christian idea of grace as a true communication of a higher principle of life . . . [T]he liberty of God is nothing but caprice, the freedom of man a godless independence. (p. 25)

The incompatibility of pure philosophical monotheism, belief in an absolute divine simplicity, with the revelation of the eternal divine love in the world's history goes unnoticed in Arianism, so that it fails to offer any hope of true communion with God (pp. 27, 31). It is this issue of the possibility of genuine relation between God and creatures that most preoccupies Gwatkin, and he returns to it at the very end of his work. Arianism failed because it lacked any notion of divine purpose working itself out in and through the material world, that notion which emerges with increasing clarity from evolutionary science: 'the theologian's problem is not so far removed from that of the historian or the zoologist, or any other man of science' (p. 273; and cf. pp. xi-xii of the Preface to the First Edition). Any system of thought, scientific or philosophical, that rules out in principle the manifestation of purposive love – supremely in Jesus Christ – cannot but perish. If we turn from Gwatkin's *Studies* to his Gifford Lectures of 1904 and 1905 (published in 1906), we find these themes elaborated at great length. There is a revelation in nature of divine power and wisdom (ch. III); but mere power is a meaningless definition of the divine. We need to understand the nature of the will that activates such power (vol. I, pp. 83–4), and that is revealed in 'the spiritual nature of man' as essentially moral (ch. IV). The *absolute* goodness of that moral will, however, can only be made known by specific historical revelation (ch. V), the nature of which is discussed in vol. II of the lectures, along with the history of its reception and interpretation. In the course of this survey, Arianism is briefly touched upon (ch. VI), to be characterized as a form of Deism, deficient in imaginative sensitivity to the nuances of metaphorical language, applying the bludgeon of common sense to the subtle metaphors of trinitarian language to produce a crude and contradictory system in which God is isolated and despotic – a kind of foreshadowing of Islam. In this respect, Nicene orthodoxy guarantees 'the political freedom of a distant future' (p. 112): 'God . . . will not deal with us as slaves

10

like a despot in heaven. And if we are free before God, we ought to be free before men' (p. 113). The series ends with a visionary evocation of the global synthesis of theological and scientific knowledge towards which the intellectual world is moving – a classic summary of the great heritage of Maurice, Westcott and others in Anglican thinking (pp. 323–30).

For Gwatkin, then, Arianism is 'Other' in that it makes impossible the distinctive vocation of Christian thought, which is to provide the religious framework for a triumphant evolutionary morality and philosophy; if the problem of Harnack's Arius is that he has not digested Ritschl, Gwatkin's Arius suffers from not having studied in late nineteenth-century Cambridge. Arianism as Gwatkin defines it could never have produced that beautifully and seductively integrated Anglican vision that briefly made the Church appear as the natural ally of welfare and enlightenment in the most advanced society (as it believed itself to be) in Europe. In that Gwatkin does not identify Arianism tacitly with any specific contemporary aberrations, he is better able than Newman and Harnack to cut through the tangle of slanted or distorted judgments in historical matters in which the earlier scholars had become enmeshed; *Studies of Arianism* is still a more useful guide to certain features of the history and background of Arian origins than the works of Gwatkin's great predecessors. But in its determination to 'read' the heresy as subversive of that particular Christian project to which Gwatkin was so passionately committed, its agenda is just as much of its time and place as Newman's and Harnack's.

5

One of Gwatkin's contributions to the development of Arian studies was, I have suggested, to shift some of the emphasis away from the supposed Christological focus of the heresy and towards the doctrines of God and creation. The analysis of Arius' doctrine as a variety of adoptionism looks a good deal less plausible in the light of Gwatkin's discussion. Nevertheless such an interpretation continued to be influential for many years, in Britain and on the continent of Europe. In fact, relatively little of real originality appeared in Arius scholarship in the first few decades of the present century. Seminally important work was of course done in the sorting-out of the chronology of the controversy, and in the isolation of a hard core of reliable primary documents by the great classical scholar Eduard Schwartz; even where more recent scholarship has disputed or overthrown his conclusions, the debt of all subsequent students to Schwartz's work remains very considerable. And it is his researches that lie behind the work of Hans-Georg Opitz, who, in the 1930s, published a very influential chronology of the beginnings of the crisis and a still indispensable (though frequently flawed and eccentric) edition of the primary texts, designed as part of a major edition of Athanasius' works; his sadly premature death in the Second World War left this project still in a fragmentary state, and Athanasius has yet to find a systematic editor or team of editors. But in the actual interpretation and analysis of the issues in the controversy, little was achieved in the pre-war period.

One notable exception to this judgment, however, is a brief but significant essay by Walter Elliger, published in 1931, 'Bemerkungen zur Theologie des Arius' ('Observations on the Theology of Arius'). Without naming his targets, Elliger argues that the consensus of earlier scholarship has radically misunderstood Arius, largely as a result of reading him through the spectacles of his opponents. With Gwatkin, Elliger maintains that Arius' own concerns were not primarily Christological: he is seeking to clarify the doctrine of God (p. 245). And lest he should then be accused of philosophical rationalism, Elliger continues, we should recognize that Arius' God is living and active, and that Arius speaks of him in tones of devotion and awe (pp. 245-7). What Arius has to say about Christology must not be abstracted from his primary religious concern, the unity and mystery of God; and we should also give him credit for resisting any kind of 'physical' or sub-personal doctrine of redemption (p. 248). In emphasizing the role of moral progress in the life of Christ, Arius stands close to Paul of Samosata (pp. 248-9). His inconsistency – a fatal one, in the event – is to seek to reconcile this luminously simple picture with a theology of the pre-existent Logos (a theology learned from Lucian); here he is least distinctive and interesting (pp. 241-50). But the heart of his theology is a moral and spiritual conception of God and of human salvation, and an account of union with God in terms of will and action. Our mistake is to try to interpret him in terms of a theology with which he is not at home, the Logos-theology he shares with his opponents. Once we have stopped looking at him from Athanasius'

12

perspective, we shall have a fairer picture of his strength. But this invloves a recognition that has wider import: we must acknowledge that the history of dogma is far more pluriform than conventional scholarship suggests (p. 251).

Elliger in fact does what he accuses others of doing: he reconstructs a good deal of Arius' theology from the testimony of his opponents and takes us back to the old adoptionist picture that Gwatkin had challanged. He seems to be engaging with Harnack on this question, attempting to show that Arius was, after all, a worthy successor to Paul of Samosata, and an acceptable hero for post-Ritschlian Protestantism. Elliger is, in effect, denying that Nicene orthodoxy has any kind of hermeneutical privilege in the study of patristics, and denying it more bluntly and openly than Harnack. Arius' theology must be judged in the degree to which it faithfully mediates authentic religious experience, and on such a criterion the judgment must be positive (p. 246). We still have here a covertly contemporary reading of Arius; but what is new is the refusal to 'demonize' Arius, the search for a genuine religious motivation in his teaching, and the open admission of the legitimacy (and unavoidability) of radical pluralism in doctrine and spirituality. In such ways, Elliger offers a striking anticipation of much more recent scholarship.

6

In Britain meanwhile various of Gwatkin's judgments were being taken up and developed at a more popular level. The association of Nicene orthodoxy with liberal democratic values had great appeal to those doctrinally orthodox Anglo-Catholics who espoused the 'Christian Socialist' position. The remarkable Conrad Noel, whose views were well to the left of Gwatkin's cautious reformism, published in 1909 a pamphlet on *Socialism and Church Tradition*, containing a startling paragraph on the Arian controversy. The issue:

> was held to be a life or death principle in democratic politics . . . The principle at stake, politically, was Democracy *versus* Imperialism; for the Arians held that God was a solitary being remote from the interests of men, a sombre emperor in the Heavens, who

had not been able to bridge the gulf between the heavens and the earth. Now, if this was so, they argued that such a solitary being was best represented upon earth by a solitary tyrant . . . The Catholic philosophers replied that the highest form of unity which could be conceived by us was the collective unity of the many and the one . . . The Catholic democrat seized upon the philosophic idea and translated it into politics. (pp. 7–8)

This spirited travesty was an influential element in the campaign of Anglo-Catholic Socialists early in this century to summon patristic authority to their aid. From the historian's point of view, it is at best a wild oversimplification, but it did raise a perfectly serious question about the correlation between dogma and politics in the fourth century: anyone familiar with Eusebius of Caesarea's writings to and for Constantine would be bound to recognize that there *were* those with anti-Nicene sympathies who saw hierarchical relation between God and the Logos extending downwards through the emperor to the rest of creation. The ambiguous political implications of strict monotheism in the late antique world were to be explored later in a seminal study by Erik Peterson, *Der Monotheismus als Politisches Problem* (1935), a work which continues to be discussed by patrologists and dogmaticians in Germany, and which has exercised a considerable influence on the theology of Jürgen Moltmann. But the alleged 'democratic' implications of Nicene orthodoxy have been sharply challenged by other scholars. Samual Laeuchli in 1968 attacked Barth's trinitarian theology for its loyalty to the Nicene confession, because that confession not only springs from but actually articulates and legitimizes a totalitarian and monolithic social schema (I shall return to this essay later; see below, n. 26 to the Postscript). More recently, the anthropologist Edmund Leach, in a paper on 'Melchisedech and the emperor' (delivered in 1972, published in 1983), has argued that Arianism represents an egalitarian and anti-authoritarian strand in early Christianity. The *identification* of the saviour with the substance of God serves to remove him from the human realm, so that salvation needs to be mediated by an authorized social and ecclesiastical hierarchy. The *separation* of the saviour from God implies the possibility of divine power being communicated directly to creatures in past and present alike, and this has revolutionary implications: Christ may be unique in degree, but he is sanctified and empowered by the same Holy Spirit as

14

inspires all the elect (pp. 75–7). The conclusion is that 'visible hierarchy among deities goes with egalitarian politics among men; isolated monotheism goes with hierarchical politics among men' (p. 83). This ingenious variation on Peterson's theme is supported by a complex argument from iconography, though it is historically as inaccurate and impressionistic as Noel's picture. But here again, a significant question is raised: does the subordination of Son to Father belong naturally with radical sectarian styles of Christianity, and is Nicene orthodoxy thus a betrayal of the millenarian detachment of the first believers?

This would need a long discussion in its own right; some hints at my own response may be found in the Postscript to this book. For the present, it is enough to note how Arianism can serve as a 'radical other' to Catholic faith even in the analyses of those not committed to that faith. Although in the fourth century the actual practice and organization of Nicene and non-Nicene churches was virtually indistinguishable, it is very tempting to suppose, with Leach, that anything that was *not* the hierarchical, legally-protected church of the empire must have been 'sectarian'; but this neat conclusion is spoilt by the fact that Arianism itself was intermittently the imperial faith. Granted all this, however, there is something to be said for the idea that the theology of Arius himself may have had *some* of the 'sectarian' resonances Leach suggests: more of this in I.C, below.

7

Gwatkin's charge that Arianism rules out a proper account of God's relation with creatures also has something of an 'afterlife' in G. L. Prestige's famous series of Bampton Lectures, *Fathers and Heretics* (1940). The lecture on 'Athanasius; or, the Unity of God' repeats a number of familiar points – that Arianism is crypto-pagan, poly-theistc (pp. 68, 91), rationalistic (p. 85), rendering true salvation impossible (p. 76); but Prestige, preaching in the first year of war (p. 90), attempts to provide a more clearly contemporary perspective. Arianism, by driving a wedge between God and the world, encourages human beings 'to look for salvation to sources other than the Lord of heaven and earth' (p. 91). It thus fosters reliance on secular schemes of welfare – the ideologies that have provoked the war –

or on degenerate forms of religious faith – vulgar Catholicism, with its dependence on saints and relics, or the 'polytheism' of (presumably) the kind of Calvinism 'that plays off the divine justice against the divine mercy' (ibid.). To be true to itself, to have a critical and regulative lodestone for its theology, and to be able to resist secular fashion, Christianity needed Athanasius and the Nicene faith. Gwatkin's critique here acquires a very slightly 'Barthian' tinge (not that Prestige was an admirer of Barth!); the sense of where the Christian centre is inevitably modified and sharpened by the experience of crisis in public life, and the image of Arianism shifts accordingly – towards the spectre of the idolatries engulfing Europe in bloodshed.

8

The post-war period has been astonishingly fertile in Arius scholarship. As the heat of confessional and ideological conflicts between and within Christian traditions diminished to some extent, a good deal more work was done that was not marked by any such blatant polemical interests as have emerged in the texts we have been examining. W. R. Telfer's historical researches, though often over-speculative, have prompted useful discussion; more recently, the work of Timothy Barnes has provided an exemplary standard of scholarly care and acumen in disentangling authoritatively much of the background to the Nicene controversy. Manlio Simonetti's studies of the theological and, more specifically, exegetical ambience of the controversy's origins have cleared up large areas where, hitherto, inadequate or biased accounts had predominated. In particular, his challenge to the facile 'Antioch *versus* Alexandria' scheme is of major significance. His paper of 1971 on Arian origins points out that we have no evidence at all either that there was a specific Antiochene school of exegesis before the late fourth century or that Arius was a consistent 'literalist' (later Arians certainly were not). Antioch was not theologically homogeneous, as far as we can tell, during this period: an 'Asian' theology of monarchian and adoptionist tendency, represented by Paul of Samosata, stands beside the Origenian pluralism of Lucian. Whatever Arius is, he is *not* in the former tradition. His alleged adoptionism is no more to be taken for granted than his literalism. This position is vigorously defended by Simonetti in his major work of 1975 on the history of the Arian crisis in general, and in substantial reviews, in 1980 and 1983, of the works of other scholars. Few experts in the field have so consistently resisted premature schematization of the material.

One other writer who has successfully done so is G. C. Stead. His discussion of the Platonic elements in Arius' thought (1964) remains an authoritative guide (though there are areas where it can be supplemented from other sources), and a 1978 paper on Arius' *Thalia* is probably the most thorough and judicious study in English of the subject. Although its conclusions about the metre of the work have been effectively challenged (see below, p. 285), it does much to establish the relative usefulness and trustworthiness of different blocks of quotations from or paraphrases of the work in Athanasius' polemical writings. Stead's contribution to the understanding of the background of Nicaea's *ousia*-language, in his *magnum opus* on *Divine Substance* (1977), should also be noted.

One of the strengths of Stead's 1978 paper is its refusal to follow the convention of ascribing a sort of religious or spiritual philistinism to Arius. The possibility that Arius was religiously serious, that he was genuinely concerned with salvation as well as with philosophy or cosmology, is, as we have seen, ignored by most earlier writers, except for Elliger, and is one of the most effective tools in the construction of 'Arianism' as a merely parodic Christianity. Perhaps the last work to insist on the total spiritual sterility and unreconstructed rationalism of Arius was Pollard's monograph of 1970; like this author's earlier articles it faithfully reproduces the Antiochene-Aristotelean-adoptionist portrait of the heresiarch. One such article provoked the well-known response of Maurice Wiles, 'In Defence of Arius' (1962), which, in addition to suggesting an Alexandrian background for Arius as an exegete, questions the assumption that Arius' position must be seen as 'unspiritual'. The former proposal, since it still takes Arius' literalism for granted was fairly decisively set aside by Simonetti in 1971 – in the sense that he sees no difficulty in making out Arius to have been well within the Origenian mainstream of Alexandrian exegesis. The latter point, reminding us that we do not have evidence sufficient to justify the denial of an Arian soteriology, remains perfectly valid.

But what sort of soteriology? Wiles confesses himself uncertain, but various attempts at reconstruction have been offered. If Arius is seen as an adoptionist, some of the difficulties may seem to be lessened – Christ becomes the exemplar of grace – assisted freedom in the creature – but complications remain. C. Mönnich, in an interesting and rather neglected paper of 1950, proposed a more nuanced version, drawing attention to the tradition that Arius had been involved in the early days of the Melitian schism in Alexandria, and thus had some history of involvement with a rigorist, sectarian group. There is evidence, says Mönnich (pp. 394–6), that Arianism had real appeal for monks and in areas (like Asia Minor) with a strong rigorist-ascetical tradition. Arius' thought builds on a common convention in early Christian thought of opposing form and matter, act and potency, God and the world; hence the idea of the Logos as active, motive power in the passive flesh of Jesus, with no admixture of compromised, feeble human freedom (pp. 399–404). The difference between this and Apollinarianism is that free will *is* still involved, but the free will of an unfallen creature, the Logos, attaining immutability (*ataraxia* and *apatheia*, like the Stoic sage) by consistent choice (pp. 406–7). Christ is the 'prototype of the divinized creature' (p. 407); but he is so as one in whom *human* liberty is non-existent, and the flesh is made the instrument of a superhuman will. Thus he is not an 'exemplar' in a straightforward sense: the ascetic, following Christ, has to lose the power of human choice in total submission to God (pp. 408–10). Christ is not the model of good moral behaviour, but the sign of what can happen (divinization) when there is a radical extirpation of sinful human will. The conflict thus becomes one about the means of salvation: Arius stands for the path of individual askesis, the Nicenes for 'the way of the church'. Heroism and grace stand opposed to each other, the 'pneumatic' and the 'catholic' models of discipleship. Athanasius and his followers naturally believe in asceticism, but an asceticism possible only through the grace of Christ – as the *Vita Antonii* makes plain from the Athanasian side (pp. 410–11).

Arius is here, rather as in Harnack's picture, the enemy of a true Reformed doctrine of grace, and Athanasius the champion of *sola fides*. This certainly brings soteriology into the heart of the debate, though it does so by some straining of the evidence both on Arius'

Melitian antecedents (and, indeed, the nature of the Melitian schism) and on the centrality of ascetic struggle and progress in Arius' view of Christ. However, it is a powerful argument, and succeeds in taking proper account of the tradition that Arius denied the existence of a human soul in the saviour. Its influence is evident – and fully acknowledged – in the most recent attempt to construct an Arian soteriology, the monograph by Robert Gregg and Dennis Groh on *Early Arianism* (1981). Here the alleged adoptionism of Arius is emphasized very heavily: the Arian Christ is conceived in Stoic terms as one who undergoes moral advancement (*prokopē*) by a betterment in his will (pp. 15–24); his obedience is the prototype for our own, the disposition that leads to adoption as children of God (pp. 28–30). It is in this context that we must understand Arian assertions about the Logos' mutability: it is his solidarity with us in the process of choosing and growing in virtue.

> Elected and adopted as Son, this creature who advanced by moral excellence to God exemplified that walking 'in holiness and righteousness' which brings blessing on all children of God who would do likewise. In this sense, and with this idea of salvation intended, the Arians preached their Christ and in that very preaching summoned believers to hope for and to strive for equality with him. (p. 65)

Mönnich's point about the appeal of this to ascetics is taken up in a chapter arguing in detail that (as Mönnich implies) the *Vita Antonii* ascribed to Athanasius deliberately sets out to 'capture' Antony for the Nicene camp, 'bringing his heroics under the control of this [Nicene] scheme of grace' (p. 150). A possible threat to episcopal authority from what Mönnich calls the 'pneumatic' wing of the Church is thus neutralized. As the final chapter of Gregg and Groh's book explains, the issues at stake are practical and political: to opt for the model of an heroic redeemer divinized by virtuous will is to opt for a Church in which the transmission of wisdom by a qualified teacher is central (pp. 163–4); to opt for the saviour's immutable divinity is to accept the fixed categories of episcopal orthodoxy. The vagaries of individual wisdom and sanctity are not enough to sustain the Church in the traumatic days of persecution, when there is change and decay all around, betrayal and back-sliding. The immutable Christ transforming our *nature*, not our will

19

alone, through the objective sacramental life of the apostolic Church – this is what the believer needs in troubled times (pp. 181–2).

Much emphasis is placed on the role of exegesis in all this, especially exegesis of Hebrews, though not too much is made of 'literalism'; the authors are wary, too, of postulating too straightforward a link with Paul of Samosata (pp. 165–8). But the book still operates, as various reviewers pointed out, with the categories imposed on Arius by his opponents. Simonetti's review of the work in 1983 pointed out its neglect of the cosmological side of Arius' thought and of Arius' repeated and vehement insistence on the radical *difference* between the Son and other creatures: 'early' Arianism (as opposed to what has come to be called 'neo-Arianism' in the middle of the fourth century) is not distinctive because of its voluntarism or adoptionism. Others, such as S. G. Hall, noted somewhat slanted interpretations of Arius' Greek. Eric Osborn, in a witty essay in 1984 ('Arian Obedience: Scouting for Theologians') granted *some* force to the idea that the controversy was partly about grace and ethics, but concluded that, if Arianism was indeed a moralistic pietism of this sort, it is inimical to the gospel. 'This account . . . might explain its appeal to the imperial establishment and to perennial pietism, and is therefore worth noticing as we pass the seventy-fifth anniversary of the Boy Scout movement' (p. 56). Gregg and Groh's view has already been influential in the writings of other patristic scholars in the USA particularly, but a full response to the quite damaging criticism of Simonetti and others has yet to appear.

In this version of the controversy, we see a further transmutation of the Arianism-as-Other theme, this time into the categories of institutions and authority. Mönnich's hints about pneumatic and catholic ideals are developed into a contrast between a 'transactional universe' in which categories of will, choice and relation determine the style of Church life and a world of defined substances, divine and other, whose relations are specified in authorized forms once and for all. As in Leach's study, it remains possible to see Nicenes and non-Nicenes in terms of polar opposition, even where Nicaea and its supporters are equally under suspicion; though Gregg and Groh are careful (p. 29) not to offer a one-sidedly 'modern' Arius, or a demonized Athanasius.

And in fact their focus upon differences in attitudes to authority may have some mileage, as I shall argue in what follows. R. Lorenz's major monograph of 1978, *Arius judaizans?* sketched out (pp. 119–22) a picture of Arius as teaching a new version of (orthodox) Alexandrian *gnōsis*, the wisdom of inspired saints. This suggestion has some connection with the book's other main contention, that Arius is presenting a residually but significantly Jewish-Christian theology of the angelic, high-priestly mediator, given that Alexandrian *gnōsis* has such close affinities with Hellenistic Jewish wisdom, though Lorenz perhaps overstates the likelihood of real links here. Origen's doctrine of the mediatorial, mutable but perfect, soul of Christ is, for Lorenz, the means whereby the tradition is passed on to Arius; but it is doubtful whether Origen's doctrine owes that much to Jewish influence. Simonetti, in 1980, criticized many aspects of Lorenz's case, notably a certain lack of historical perspective (such as allows Lorenz to see Arius as synthesizing really radically opposed theological styles, Lucian's 'Origenism', so-called, with Paul of Samosata's adoptionism), and provoked a lengthy and heated rebuttal from Lorenz in 1982. However, the points made about *gnōsis*, about Arius' closeness to – for example – Clement of Alexandria, should stand. They are further reinforced by an important and, in many respects, highly controversial paper by the Athanasian scholar Charles Kannengiesser, delivered in 1982, arguing that Arius is propounding a more autonomously 'scientific' hermeneutics than his opponents, a style more at home in a community of conscious intellectuals – that is, though Kannengiesser does not use the term, a *gnōsis*.

This is less vulnerable to the charge of simplistic polarization because it allows for the fact that an Arius of such a kind would have stood in a long theological tradition in his own church. We are still in the business of identifying something of the *spiritual* impetus of Arius' teaching, in terms of what he wished to conserve against episcopal innovation; a great deal of recent work seeking to understand Arian spirituality has, not surprisingly, helped to demolish the notion of Arius and his supporters as deliberate radicals, attacking a time-honoured tradition. In this connection, it is worth mentioning two more recent essays which go some way towards suggesting that the Nicene solution in certain respects blocked out some legitimate concerns of Christian devotion. Wiles and Gregg, writing in 1985 on Arius' supporter Asterius, or rather, on the homilies ascribed to him, conclude that Asterius (together, by implication, with others) wished to guarantee the idea of a divine

saviour who truly shared the conditions of a suffering humanity –
a genuinely *incarnate* redeemer. R. P. C. Hanson, in the same volume
(a collection of papers on Arianism from the 1983 Oxford Patristic
Conference), agrees, adducing substantial evidence from later Arian
literature: 'Arian thought achieved an important insight into the
witness of the New Testament denied to the pro-Nicenes of the 4th
century, who unanimously shied away from and endeavoured to
explain away the scandal of the Cross' (p. 203). The paradox is,
though, that this insight is held at the high price of postulating 'two
unequal gods'; only Nicaea can actually do justice to a doctrine
that the Nicene Fathers would have rejected – the self-sacrificing
vulnerability of God. A similar point is eloquently made in a brief
but searching discussion by A. C. McGill in his book, *Suffering: A
Test of Theological Method* (1982). The God of Arius remains, at the
end of the day, defined by his own self-sufficiency: the God of
Athanasius allows for the presence of dependency, even 'need' in
the divine life, and so challenges any notion that God is *essentially*
unilateral domination (pp. 70–82). Polarities again; but McGill's
account is not meant particularly as an historical one. It puts the
unavoidable question of what the respective schemes in the long
term make possible for theology; and the answer to that question,
from a theologically acute historian of doctrine like Hanson, may
indeed lead to the odd conclusion that the Nicene fathers achieved
not only more than they knew but a good deal more than they
wanted.

10

We have come a fair way from the harsh polemic of Newman,
though the shadow of Arianism-as-Other still haunts modern
discussion. I do not think this need paralyse efforts at interpretation,
however. 'Arianism' *was* that which 'Catholicism' rejected or left
behind, and there is some usefulness in seeking to understand it in
these antithetical terms: nearly all the readings I have mentioned
contribute some real insight to the continuing discussion. But a
fundamental question of method remains, which may perhaps be
illuminated by a discussion in another academic field. Johannes
Fabian's book, *Time and the Other: How Anthropology Makes its Object*
(1983), maintains that western academic anthropology works with

the implicit notion of a 'normative' time in which the scholar stands, as opposed to the distant or 'other' time in which the objects of study exist – they are, for example, 'primitive', that is, are located in our terms at a distant point in our time-track. The problem of relation *now* with persons and groups who are in fact 'co-eval' with us is thus avoided: a self-contained object is created for contemplation (see especially the remarks on the image of Bali, pp. 134–5), and there can be no confrontation that radically challenges the observer. If Fabian is right, the creation and imposition of 'normative' time is a device for avoiding the relativization of one's own position (and thus the possibility of change): because – surely – our past is decisively and undeniably *not* where we now stand, what can be relegated to the past is not to be listened to seriously. Against this, Fabian asserts: 'Tradition and modernity are not "opposed" (except semiotically) . . . What are opposed . . . are not the same societies at different stages of development, but different societies facing each other at the same Time' (p. 155).

This should give the historian of doctrine pause. '"Arianism" *was* that which "Catholicism" rejected or left behind', I wrote in the last paragraph. True: but that can be taken to mean that there is a single normative time in which Christian thought develops, the 'time' of Catholic doctrine, for which various deviations and errors are decisively *past*. Fabian's point is that 'normative time' confuses spatial distinctness with temporal: tribe X is distant from us now, and so is also distant from us in developmental terms. What I am suggesting is that the converse also holds: such-and-such a heresy is an undeveloped, arrested, inadequate form of belief, distant in *developmental* terms from present orthodoxy; so it is 'over against' us *now*, an 'other' in respect of present doctrinal priorities.

The distortions this produces are less practically damaging than the effects of a pre-critical anthropology (the happy, if usually unconscious, ally of Eurocentric politics and economics), but they are serious enough. They encourage a simplistic and conflict-free account both of the history of Catholic orthodoxy and of its present character and requirements; they foster that sterile dialogue of the deaf that prevails in so much present discussion between doctrinal 'conservatives' and 'liberals'. We cannot, of course, help telling the story of doctrinal controversy, in full awareness of the way in which the very forms of a history seen as *doctrinal* history pressing towards the idea of a normative time culminating in *my* or *our* present, has important lessons for us. We need to give full weight to the fact that 'Arians' and 'Catholics' were conducting a debate within a largely common language, acknowledging the same kind of rules and authorities. We need to see how 'Arian' and 'Catholic' were coeval as Christians engaged in the definition of the very idea of normative faith, and to see how diffuse this struggle was and (often) how unclear its boundaries (hence my inverted commas for 'Arians' and 'Arianism'). We need to grasp how deeply Arius' agenda – and the rather different concerns of most of his followers – entered into what was to become orthodoxy in the process of the controversy. And if this can to some extent be achieved, we shall be clearer about what in our supposedly straightforward doctrinal 'present' is owed, negatively and positively, to Arius.

The effort to understand Arius and his followers, so far as possible in their own terms, is beset with difficulties, since nearly all our primary material is already fixed in the polarities I have described. Nevertheless the attempt is still worthwhile: to follow through the inner logic and problematic of Arius' thought and that of the later enemies of Nicaea is to discover what it is that 'orthodoxy' has to take on and make its own – to discover the 'Arian' problematic as formative of what we now utter as orthodox. The same could be said of other early Christian deviations: modern scholarship has become increasingly aware of how the very vocabulary of orthodox theology is shaped by borrowing and reworking the terms and images of dissident groups, Valentinian, Messalian, Pelagian, Origenist. To understand such processes is to experience orthodoxy as something still future (to become 'coeval' with the debate, at some level); which means that a briskly undialectical rhetoric today of 'conserving' and 'defending' a clear deposit of faith may come less easily to us. The long-term credibility and sustainability of the Nicene faith may have something to do with the degree to which it succeeds – usually more or less unwittingly – in subsuming and even deepening the Christian concerns of the teachers it set out to condemn. A picture of doctrinal history along these lines is perhaps more constructive than a reiteration of imagined absolute oppositions – the implication being that, in any doctrinal conflict, theologians are not likely to know with total clarity what the doctrinal (and concrete ecclesial) forms will be that will succeed in most comprehensively holding the range of proper and defensible Christian interests involved in the conflict. There is no absolute *locus standi* above the struggle; there is, ideally, a continuing conversation that must be exploratory and innovative even when it is also polemical. Orthodoxy continues to be *made*. 'Loyalty' to how the Church has defined its norms must contain a clear awareness of the slow and often ambivalent nature of the processes of definition if we are to avoid supposing that the history of doctrine is not really *history* at all and that contemporary 'right belief' has no connection with or conditioning by a specific past and present. That this need not involve a wholly relativist view of doctrinal truth will, I hope, be clear in what follows, and is made more explicit in the Postscript. But what the articulation of doctrinal truth concretely *is* can be traced only through the detailed reworking and re-imagining of its formative conflicts. That, surely, is the strictly *theological* point of studying the history of doctrine.

Part I

Arius and the Nicene Crisis

A

Arius before Arianism

1 ORIGINS

Epiphanius tells us[1] that Arius was born in Libya: and a number of other small pieces of evidence tend to bear this out. Arius' two most consistent episcopal supporters in later years were Secundus and Theonas,[2] bishops respectively of Ptolemais (or 'the Pentapolis', in some texts)[3] and Marmarica: Ptolemais was the chief city of western or 'upper' Libya, the older Cyrenaica, whose five major coastal settlements gave the district its familiar name of the Pentapolis; Marmarica or 'lower Libya' (sometimes *Libya sicca*) was the desert area between Cyrenaica and the *fines Alexandriae*, the border of the urban area of Alexandria at the western end of the Mareotis.[4] Diocletian's reorganization of the empire established the distinction between the 'two Libyas' as a matter of nomenclature but there is no secure evidence as to whether this was also an administrative division. Whatever the truth of this, it sounds as though Secundus and Theonas may have been effectively metropolitans of the Libyan districts;[5] and when Philostorgius, the Arian historian, lists other bishops sympathetic to Arius,[6] the first four are from some of the other cities in the Pentapolis. In fact, we know of no Libyan bishops opposing Arius; given a certain amount of Libyan resistance to the claims of the Alexandrian see over its western neighbours,[7] it would not be surprising if a Libyan cleric in trouble with the bishop of Alexandria commanded more or less unanimous support from his homeland.

The same picture is suggested in a letter from the Emperor Constantine to Arius, written around 333.[8] Arius had been given permission to return from exile to his 'native territory' (unspecified) in 327 or 328,[9] and Constantine writes as though Arius is currently in Libya. Evidently Arius is enjoying widespread popular support, since Constantine shows signs of panic at the idea of a schism. A little earlier (331 or 332), we find Athanasius visiting Libya,[10] and the emperor's letter clearly suggests that it was becoming a very troubled area from the point of view of the Alexandrian see. Once again, the whole pattern makes excellent sense in terms of partisanship for a local celebrity against intrusive foreign prelates.

If Epiphanius is to be relied on as regards Arius' place of birth, is he also to be trusted when he describes Arius as an 'old man', *gerōn*, at the time of the outbreak of the controversy?[11] Here we have no collateral evidence, though Constantine's letter of 333 contains a passage[12] describing, in most insulting fasion, Arius' wasted and lifeless appearance – a passage which certainly fits a man well-advanced in years. The widespread consensus that puts Arius' birth in the 250s[13] has no definite foundation in the texts of the fourth and fifth centuries, but it seems safe to assume that he was not a young man when the crisis broke. If he was ordained presbyter by Bishop Achillas, as several sources claim,[14] and if the Nicene regulations about the minimum canonical age for such ordinations reflect earlier practice, he was at least thirty in 313. All in all, a date for Arius' birth some time before 280 is most likely; assuming that Epiphanius has an authentic tradition behind what he writes, we can probably push this date rather further back, but without any hope of certainty.

The only clue we have as to Arius' education is the single word *sulloukianista*, which occurs in his letter to Eusebius, bishop of Nicomedia, appealing for help in the first years of the controversy. Historians have generally taken 'fellow-Lucianist' pretty literally, and assumed a period of study with the martyr Lucian of Antioch. Ever since Newman,[15] this has produced some very questionable reconstructions of Arius' intellectual background;[16] but in fact – yet again – we can be certain of very little. Lucian's own theology has to be reconstructed from hints and allusions (and there is also a credal statement used by the synod of Antioch in 341 which was alleged to have originated with Lucian);[17] he cannot be taken as representative of an Antiochene 'school' of theology or exegesis (he taught in Nicomedia for some of his career at least);[18] and it is in any case not clear that we should assume from the one word in Arius' letter that he had actually been Lucian's student. Wallace-Hadrill notes[19] that Arius is not named by Philostorgius in his lists[20] of Lucian's pupils, and supposes that the Lucianists formed a coherent political and theological grouping quite independently of Arius. Certainly, if Philostorgius is to be believed, there were real theological divergences between this group and Arius,[21] and the later 'neo-Arians'[22] of the mid-century traced their theological ancestry back to the Lucianists rather than Arius. This is not entirely conclusive: Philostorgius is not by any means a reliable source, and we need not, in any case, assume that he ever means to give a full list of Lucian's pupils. But the anti-Nicene theological tradition evidently preserved the memory of a certain distance between Arius and some of his allies; it cannot be taken for granted that Arius was a *disciple* of Lucian in the sense that others such as Eusebius of Nicomedia claimed to be, even if he had attended lectures by the martyr. 'Fellow-Lucianist' may be no more than a *captatio benevolentiae* – laying claim to common ground with potential supporters; or it may rest on the fact that Arius *had* studied, in Antioch or Nicomedia, with Lucian. It is very doubtful whether it tells us much about what lies behind Arius' utterances in terms of theological formation.

Likewise, although he is described as a skilled dialectician,[23] we cannot with confidence reconstruct a philosophical education. If he was (as has been argued)[24] indebted to certain currents in revived Aristotelianism and Iamblichus' version of Neoplatonism, he could have encountered such teaching in Syria around 300, when Iamblichus himself was teaching at Antioch and Apamea.[25] Iamblichus' teacher Anatolius was probably the Alexandrian Christian Aristotelian described with some veneration by Eusebius;[26] he ended his life (we do not know exactly when, but probably in the 270s) as bishop of Laodicaea, and seems to have been caught up at some point in the struggle against Paul of Samosata. A tempting candidate for the role of Arius' mentor he is still regrettably a shadowy figure: no evidence connects him directly with the heresiarch, and we should have to push the date of Arius' birth a good way back into the 250s to make any personal contact possible. Links with Anatolius and his celebrated pagan pupil, a period of studying philosophy in Syria – these are intriguing possibilities, but no more.

Whatever the nature and extent of his putative earlier travels, the Arius who at last emerges into clear historical light at the end of the second decade of the fourth century is firmly anchored in Alexandria, presbyter of an important church and a popular

31

preacher with a reputation for asceticism. Epiphanius' pen-portrait[27] is worth reproducing:

> He was very tall in stature,[28] with downcast countenance[29] – counterfeited like a guileful serpent, and well able to deceive any unsuspecting heart through its cleverly designed appearance. For he was always garbed in a short cloak (*hēmiphorion*) and sleeveless tunic (*kolobion*); he spoke gently, and people found him persuasive and flattering.

The sleeveless tunic is reminiscent of the *exōmis* worn both by philosophers and by ascetics: Philo[30] mentions that the contemplative Therapeutae of his day were dressed thus. Arius' costume would have identified him easily as a teacher of the way of salvation – a guru, we might almost say. It is not surprising that Epiphanius also notes[31] that he had the care of seventy women living a life of ascetic seclusion, presumably attached to his church. What we do not know is precisely how long Arius had occupied this influential post; as already noted, he is said to have been ordained by Achillas, and, according to Theodoret,[32] Achillas' successor Alexander gave him authority to 'expound the Scriptures in church'. So we can perhaps trace Arius' public career back as far as 313, and assume that, for most of this decade, he ministered at the church which Epiphanius calls 'Baucalis'[33] – a respected cleric of some seniority, with a high reputation as a spiritual director. Before 313, nothing is clear; however, one story surfaces in the middle of the fifth century which has been widely believed, and, before going any further, it is necessary to look briefly at this. It is the allegation made by Sozomen[34] that Arius was involved in the most serious internal disruption of Egyptian church life prior to the controversy over his own teaching: the schism initiated in 306 by Melitius, bishop of Lycopolis.

2 THE TROUBLES OF THE ALEXANDRIAN CHURCH I: THE MELITIAN SCHISM

In February 303, Diocletian initiated what was to prove the most serious and sustained persecution the Christian Church had so far endured. In the eastern part of the empire and in Africa, martyrdom became common; though in the West, Diocletian's colleague Maximian and Maximian's junior coadjutor Constantius, father of Constantine, did virtually nothing to further the persecution in their territories.[35] When, in 305, Diocletian abdicated in favour of his fanatically anti-Christian second-in-command, the Caesar Galerius, the situation in the East deteriorated further from the Church's point of view. Galerius' protégé Maximin was given the rank of Caesar and put in charge of Egypt and Syria (the civil diocese of 'the East', Oriens); under his supervision, the persecution continued with hardly any interruption[36] until 313, when Licinius seized power in the eastern empire. These eight years were a costly time for the Church in Egypt, in more senses than one.

Several bishops suffered in the persecution (though some such as Apollonius of Lycopolis in the Thebaid publicly apostatized);[37] and the prolonged imprisonment of a bishop would create obvious problems for his diocese. It seems that the bishops lost little time in devising a system whereby certain of their responsibilites were delegated to 'visitors' in case of an emergency:[38] these visitors would have seen to it that poor relief continued to be administered, and it is possible, though very far from certain, that (if they were presbyters) they also had some responsibility for the maintenance of preaching or catechesis.[39] Probably at some point late in 305 or early in 306, four Egyptian bishops, Hesychius, Pachomius, Theodorus and Phileas, wrote from prison to their confrère, the newly-appointed bishop of Lycopolis (Apollonius' successor),[40] to complain that he had entered their dioceses and performed ordinations, contrary to established law and custom. If he should argue in his defence that there is a grave pastoral need to be met, this is far from the truth: there is no shortage of authorized visitors (*circumeuntes et potentes visitare*) – and, in any case, it is for the people of the diocese themselves to make representations to their bishops if they think they are being neglected. The sole circumstance in which such behaviour might be permitted would be if the bishop of Lycopolis had received a direct commission from the bishop of Alexandria;[41] and this would only be possible in the event of a diocesan's death and a subsequent interregnum. Melitius of Lycopolis has not consulted with the imprisoned bishops, nor, it appears, has he referred the alleged problems of the orphaned dioceses to Peter of Alexandria: he has ordained unsuitable and factious persons (for how could a peripatetic bishop judge the suitability of candidates in an unfamiliar diocese?), and caused grave divisions in the churches.

Peter, we gather, was absent from Alexandria, in flight or in hiding; later legend[42] has him travelling beyond the imperial frontier in Mesopotamia, and spending long periods in Syria, Palestine and 'the islands' (Cyprus?), but the implications of the bishops' letter are that he can be reached without too much difficulty. At this particular point, anyway, he is most unlikely to have been outside Egypt. This is reinforced by the fragment of narrative that follows the bishops' letter in the codex (from the Chapter Library at Verona) which preserves the text:

> After he had received and read this letter, he [Melitius] did not reply nor did he visit them in prison, nor did he go to blessed Peter: but when all these bishops, presbyters and deacons had been martyred in the prison in Alexandria,[43] he immediately entered Alexandria. There was a man called Isidore in the city, a regular troublemaker, eager to be a teacher [*or:* eager to run his own faction];[44] and also a certain Arius, who had an outward appearance of piety, and he too was eager to be a teacher. When they had discovered what Melitius wanted and what it was that he required, they lost no time in joining up with him (being envious of the authority of blessed Peter); and – with the result that Melitius' aims became publicly known – they pointed out to him where the presbyters to whom blessed Peter had delegated the power to visit the districts of Alexandria were in hiding. Melitius notified them [sc. the presbyters] of a charge against them,[45] excommunicated them,[46] and himself ordained two persons, one to work in prison, the other to work in the mines.[47]

It seems as though the complaint is that the episcopal deputies are not doing their job: Isidore and Arius are able to tell Melitius that the 'visitors' themselves have gone into hiding, giving Melitius an *occasio* for suspending them. The ordinations cannot have followed immediately: Egyptian Christians were first transported to the Palestinian mines in 307 or 308, so at least one of Melitius' new presbyters is unlikely to have received his orders in 306. This presupposes that Melitius stayed in Alexandria for several years – as we should deduce from the letter of Peter to his flock which immediately follows this narrative fragment in our collection. Peter writes as if Melitius is still in the city, having ordained a number of 'prison chaplains' and broken communion with Peter's own delegates.[48] If this reading is right, Melitius saw a pastoral need not only in the dioceses of the Nile Delta in general, but among the prisoners in particular, and was concerned that there should be those among the presbyters whose main job it was to minister to them – which would fit with the remark in the passage quoted about his activities following on a general slaughter of the clergy who happened to be already in custody.[49] It may be also that he regarded some of the clergy left in the prisons as, for some reason, disqualified from administering the sacraments.

This raises the question of whether there is any truth in Epiphanius' version of the schism (probably derived from Melitian sources),[50] in which the real issue between Peter and Melitius (who is described as a kind of archbishop, second in rank to Peter) is the treatment of those who lapsed under persecution. Melitius is represented as objecting to Peter's canons on this matter, during a period when both bishops were in prison together. Since the canons we possess[51] date from Easter 306, when Melitius was almost certainly at liberty and Peter was probably in hiding or abroad, Epiphanius' circumstantial tale cannot be true as it stands. Later Melitians, who certainly described themselves as 'the church of the martyrs',[52] may have thought it in their interest to depict the schism as a dispute of the familiar kind about penitential rigorism in the Church. Peter's canons are fairly lenient, though hardly scandalously so, and their publication may have offended Melitius, and removed any remaining scruples he may have had about usurping the bishop's office in Alexandria: it would not be surprising if he were a rigorist, especially in the light of his predecessor's apostasy at Lycopolis.[53] However, we can be confident that this was not the main cause of the schism, since it is perfectly clear that Melitius was active before the spring of 306. A dispute over the canons sounds like an *ex post facto* justification for his behaviour. Nor is it even clear that Melitius himself was *ever* in prison in Egypt.[54] If we largely discount Epiphanius, and translate the notoriously difficult *in carcere et in metallo* of the Verona text as I have suggested, and not as implying that Melitius is himself in custody, we are left with a straightforward picture of Melitius as an *episcopus vagans* taking full advantage of the disorder of the Church in the Delta between 306 and 311 to establish a firmly-rooted rival jurisdiction, unhampered by the attentions of the persecutors. Peter's concern, as shown in his letter to Alexandria, is far more intelligible if Melitius is supposed to be at large in the Delta for a substantial period than if he is conducting ordinations from his own cell (let alone in the distant Phaeno mines). And Athanasius' rather absurd accusation[55] that Melitius had been deposed for apostasy among other unspecified crimes would be a little more surprising if Melitius were generally known in Egypt to have suffered as a confessor – though Athanasius is never a fanatically accurate controversialist. Epiphanius *may* – through his connections with Melitian communities in Palestine – have access to a genuine memory that Melitius spent some time in the Phaeno under Maximin. But the Palestinian communities need not owe their genesis directly to Melitius himself.

The point that chiefly concerns us, however, is whether the Arius of the sketchy narrative quoted above is the heresiarch himself. Sozomen's outline of Arian origins[56] unambiguously presupposes this identification, and adds further circumstantial detail. Arius is a supporter of Melitius' 'innovations' who subsequently is reconciled with Peter and made deacon by him; however, when Peter excommunicates Melitius and denies the validity of Melitian baptism, Arius objects, and – we are left to presume – is deposed or excommunicated. He succeeds in making his peace with Achillas after Peter's death, is restored to his orders and later ordained as a presbyter. This story is again reproduced with still further elaboration, in an eighth-century Latin version of the *passio* of Peter:[57] the earlier (perhaps sixth century) Greek original[58] had already related how the imprisoned Peter refused to restore Arius to communion, foreseeing in a prophetic dream that Arius would divide the whole church, but had rather bizarrely represented Arius as already under censure for *heresy*.[59] The intelligent Latin translator, aware that this could not be right, filled out his version with detail from elsewhere,[60] assimilating the course of events roughly to Sozomen's account. It has been argued[61] that, in this reworking, he made use of an Alexandrian dossier of synodical and related material in which are contained the documents concerning Melitian origins already quoted – a dossier perhaps drawn up originally as a 'Jubilee Book' to celebrate Athanasius' fortieth anniversary as bishop of Alexandria in 368. This book, it appears, or substantial portions of it, travelled to Carthage in 419, in response to a request for information about the Alexandrian texts of the canons of Nicaea and

Serdica, and finally found its way into the rather disparate collection of canonical and narrative pieces preserved in the celebrated Verona Codex LX. Specifically, the attempt has been made to show that this book *in its full form* was the source for the additional detail in the Latin *passio* about Arius' Melitian phase, since the translator does not mention Sozomen as a source, and none of the other recognizable supplementary sources named carries an adequately complete version of the story: the one otherwise unidentifiable source, a Latin *libellus* containing much material on Athanasius, would then have been the Jubilee Book itself, in a rather fuller Latin version than that surviving in the Verona codex. And if all this is granted, Sozomen's story is independently confirmed, and the identification of the Melitian Arius with the Arius of the later controversy becomes overwhelmingly probable.

This ingenious case must, unfortunately, be regarded as far from proven. We simply do not know how much more narrative the 'Jubilee Book' contained, but we do know that the letter of Peter excommunicating Melitius followed immediately on the narrative section mentioning Arius; there is no room for a reconciliation with Peter and a later breach when the bishop rules against Melitius. There *may* have been further documents confirming the excommunication and rejecting the validity of Melitian baptism, but this is pure speculation. In fact there are no elements in the Latin *passio* that *could* not have come from Sozomen: the redactor obviously knew of Sozomen's low reputation as an historian,[62] and may have been reluctant to mention him for this reason. So, although it is highly probable that the *libellus* used by the Latin translator was indeed the Jubilee Book, we cannot confidently assert that it provided him with a full and circumstantial account of Arius' schismatic adventures, independently corroborating Sozomen. We cannot even know for sure that the translator had any more of the Jubilee Book before him than we have, as no other identifiable fragments survive,[63] though one or two details[64] do suggest that he may have been familiar with documents not preserved in the Verona codex.

The identification thus rests solely on Sozomen's authority; and it must confront the monumental objection that no writer before Sozomen so much as hints at it. Alexander of Alexandria[65] angrily describes Arius' arrogantly divisive behaviour without adding that it is not the first time this has been in evidence; Athanasius[66] describes the obstinacy of the Melitians and their tactical alliance with the anti-Nicene party without any suggestion that this was what might have been expected in the light of the earlier history of Melitius and Arius; Epiphanius too[67] has an account of the Arian-Melitian rapprochement after Nicaea, but the only previous link that he mentions is a tradition[68] that Melitius was the first to denounce Arius' heresy to Alexander (some[69] have seen in this Melitius' delayed revenge for Arius' desertion). It is hard to believe that any of these could have refrained from mentioning a connection potentially discreditable to both groups of adversaries; and Alexander and Athanasius at least were in the best possible position to know Arius' record.

It is just conceivable that the Alexandrian bishops fail to mention this because of embarrassment at the stance on Melitian baptism allegedly taken by Peter: Arius' objections would have been vindicated by the Nicene canons, which prescribe rebaptism only for unequivocal heretics (followers of the 'unitarian' theology of Paul of Samosata).[70] And, as far as we can tell, the position of the great Dionysius of Alexandria in the mid-third century was inimical to a uniformly rigorist policy towards baptism outside the Catholic fold.[71] Batiffol long ago pointed out[72] that Sozomen's story was not particularly creditable to Peter in the light of subsequent practice and policy; and it would certainly be a striking fact if he so dramatically rejected the views of the greatest and most authoritative of his predecessors. However, Athanasius and Alexander would not have needed to go into details: the mere fact that Arius' past had been ecclesiastically murky would have sufficed. Interestingly, the Latin redactor of the *passio* omits all mention of a controversy over baptism, and has Arius simply objecting to the excommunication of Melitius' party: why could not a fourth-century writer have been similarly selective?

In fact, no source other than Sozomen (once again) suggests that the validity of Melitian baptism was ever at issue; had it been, we should expect the Nicene canons to pronounce on it, as they do on Novatianist and Paulinian baptisms and Melitian ordinations.[73] It begins to look as though this detail of the story at least derives from quarters eager to discredit Peter and whitewash the memory of Arius. Sozomen is heavily dependent in this section of his history on the Arian chronicler Sabinus of Heraclea,[74] about whose reliability Socrates has some hard things to say;[75] it seems highly probable that Sabinus is the ultimate source of the identification of the two Arii. Sabinus was writing in the 370s: he is likely to have known the Jubilee Book and it is indeed quite possible[76] that he composed his *Synodikon* as a counterblast to the Athanasian anthology which was beginning to circulate in the eastern Mediterranean. If we assume that he knew Arius to have been a deacon under Peter, the mention of a schismatic *lay* Arius[77] in Peter's reign would suggest a rupture of some kind: Arius must have been reconciled with Peter before his ordination. The further refinement of a subsequent break and reconciliation, culminating in presbyteral ordination by Achillas is a bit more puzzling. It may be pure invention; but, at the risk of over-ingenuity, we might perhaps imagine a further letter or letters from Peter in the Jubilee Book[78] immediately preceding some notice of his martyrdom, which, like Alexander's encyclicals against Arius, carried a list of those excommunicated along with their ringleader – a list including the name of *Arius quidam*. Add to this a (Melitian?) tradition that Peter had at some point rejected Melitian baptism, and you have all the materials for a story that – from an Arian or Melitian point of view – is flattering to Arius and unflattering to his bishop: Arius appears as the defender of genuine Catholic and Alexandrian tradition.

The coincidence of two troublesome churchmen named Arius in Alexandria during the same period is hardly greater than the fact that Arius (the heretic) had an associate of the same name.[79] But for Sabinus, the identification must have seemed irresistibly obvious: and at a time when Arians and Melitians were allies, the picture of an Arius supporting Melitius against Peter would serve a useful political purpose. The Catholic historian Socrates ignores this story, recognizing that, as Sabinus tells it, it is a rather double-edged weapon; the less intelligent Sozomen seizes upon it to discredit Arius. The rather confused tradition of Peter's excommunication of Arius then finds its way into the Greek *passio;* and, finally, the author of the Latin version makes an impressive attempt to reconstruct a full narrative. He uses Theophanes and Cassiodorus to correct some chronological and other errors in the Greek, and finds in them[80] the outline of the tradition of Arius' Melitian episode; he turns to the Jubilee Book (if this is indeed his *libellus*) for further information about Melitian origins (he knows the letter of the imprisoned bishops to Melitius, and, apparently, one or more letters from Peter to them);[81] and at last, perhaps aware of the same puzzles that Sabinus faced (Arius is ordained by Peter, yet appears as a layman, both in 306 or thereabouts, and in a list of excommunicates in 311), he checks Cassiodorus against his sources and comes up with Sozomen's story, which he proceeds to reproduce in splendidly vivid and dramatic form.

So the Melitian Arius, beloved of several modern scholars,[82] appears to melt away under close investigation. The only thing emerging from this jumble of unreliable tradition that looks at all like a fact is the assertion that Arius was ordained deacon by Peter: if this was recognized as well-established recollection in the fourth century, it would explain a good deal of what I have proposed as the later development of the story. Probably we can also take it that Arius was indeed ordained presbyter by Achillas,[83] as all the historians agree in describing him as already a presbyter on the succession of Alexander. Two texts record one final piece of tradition about Arius prior to the outbreak of the controversy: Theodoret[84] and Philostorgius[85] state that he was a candidate in the episcopal election of 313. According to Theodoret, Arius' defeat by Alexander was a contributory factor in his later delinquencies; according to Philostorgius, Alexander owed his victory to the fact that Arius was prepared to transfer to his rival the votes that had been cast for himself. In literary terms, these narratives are independent; both are nakedly propagandist versions of a tradition, which, however, neither of them is likely to have invented *ex nihilo*. Disappointed ambition as a stimulus for heresy is a theme found elsewhere (Tertullian[86] tells a similar tale about the Gnostic Valentinus); but, as with the Melitius story, we should expect Alexander or Athanasius to make some capital out of such a fact. And if Philostorgius' version is true, might not Arius himself or his allies have had a word to say about Alexander's ingratitude, in their protests about the bishop's treatment of the heresiarch? It seems most likely that a 'disappointed ambition' story grew up in Catholic circles as part of a conventional explanation for Arius' behaviour, and that Philostorgius, not confident enough to ignore this, attempted to rewrite the record in Arius' favour. However, it is not clear that we can be absolutely certain that all this is pure legend: our sources agree in representing Arius as an extremely popular figure a few years later, and it can hardly be thought impossible that he should be thought suitable for episcopal election. We are left with yet another of those tantalizing possibilities hovering on the margin of what we can securely know of Arius.

3 THE TROUBLES OF THE ALEXANDRIAN CHURCH II: BISHOPS AND PRESBYTERS

The church of which Alexander became bishop in 313 does not seem to have been a particularly harmonious body. In addition to the Melitian problem, there were evidently difficulties with an ultra-ascetic group associated with a certain Hieracas (or Hierax) of Leontopolis:[87] Hieracas questioned the resurrection of the body, held that Christians should practise celibacy, and also denied that baptized children would have an opportunity of entering heaven if they died in infancy, as they had done nothing to deserve salvation. His strange views on the Holy Spirit are recorded by Epiphanius,[88] and Arius lists him[89] among the trinitarian heretics whose views he repudiates. One further, rather intriguing, fact mentioned by Epiphanius[90] is that Hieracas was fluent in Coptic as well as Greek, and wrote extensively for a non-Greek speaking public: a point which should lead us to tread very carefully in attempting to correlate schism or heresy with ethnic tensions.[91] Hieracas has some affinities with Origen, as Epiphanius notes, so that a deep gulf at this date between sophisticated Greek-speaking speculative thinkers and simple Coptic faithful is unlikely.[92] How serious a threat the 'Hieracite' movement was to the Egyptian church we cannot tell: the dearth of fourth-century reference suggests that it was a small and localized group, which probably never spread beyond the Delta. Its interest is in the evidence it provides, not only for theological bilinguality, but also for the survival, in close proximity to normative Catholic circles, of gnostic or 'Encratite' views, and for the authority accorded to extra-canonical literature: Hieracas made significant use of the Jewish-Christian apocalyptic fantasy, the *Ascension of Isaiah*.[93] In other words, it was quite possible in the early fourth century for a Christian group not far from Alexandria to take for granted a number of profoundly 'un-Catholic' things: the authority of a gifted teacher, an exemplary spiritual hero,[94] could operate in such a group quite without reference to the authority of bishop or canon.

The case of Hieracas focuses in a particularly sharp way some of the difficulties Alexander faced in Alexandria itself. The bishop of Alexandria occupied at this date what may seem a highly paradoxical position in the Egyptian church: on the one hand – as our evidence has already hinted – he more closely resembled an archbishop or even a patriarch than any other prelate in Christendom. The letter of the four imprisoned bishops to Melitius speaks of Peter as something more than a mere senior confrère: the plain implication of the text[95] is that he has the right to appoint 'commissaries' in vacant sees; and there is a fair amount of evidence[96] that he normally consecrated other Egyptian bishops, and perhaps even nominated them. At least from the time of Dionysius,[97] he was addressed as *papa*, and other bishops in Egypt refer to him as their 'father'.[98] On the other hand, within Alexandria itself the bishop was surrounded by powerful and independent presbyters, supervising their own congregations: there is already something like a 'parochial' system, with the bishop as president of a college of near-equals. Dionysius still writes[99] to his 'fellow presbyters' in the mid-third century. A rather confused tradition long survived that, until the accession of Athanasius in 328, the bishop was consecrated by the Alexandrian presbyteral college and not by any other bishop; and although the evidence is unclear, such a practice would by no means be surprising.[100] Despite his unique powers in the rest of Egypt, the Alexandrian pope remained, in his own city, a *primus inter pares*.

We have no evidence as to the origins of the 'parochial' system in Alexandria, although references in Eusebius[101] to the 'churches' and *paroikiai* (which more commonly means 'dioceses') of Alexandria go back to the early third century. The city was, in any case, split into five districts,[102] with very clear physical dividing lines;[103] and it is possible that this encouraged a plurality in Christian leadership from an early date. However, the names we possess of the various Alexandrian churches do not easily fit into the geography of the separate sectors, and the distribution of presbyters and churches was probably more haphazard. Epiphanius tells us[104] that Alexandria had an unusually large number of churches in his day, in addition to the episcopal basilica, the Kaisareion,[105] and gives the names of nine – the churches of Dionysius, Theonas, Pierius, Serapion, Persaea, Dizya, the Mendidion, Annianus and Baucalis – adding that this is not a complete list. The later *passio* of Peter refers[106] to a shrine on the site of St Mark's martyrdom in the

'Boukolia' district, eastward of the new harbour area which extended beyond the mole leading out to the Pharos, probably near the north-eastern necropolis; this may be identical with Epiphanius' 'Baucalis'.[107] We also hear in the *passio*[108] of a church dedicated to the Mother of God built by Peter, somewhere in the region of the western necropolis. Athanasius refers[109] to a church called *Kyriou* – or, more likely, *Kyrinou* – but gives no clue as to its whereabouts, or its date or origin. The great church of St Michael, on the edge of the Jewish quarter, had been a temple of Saturn; we are told[110] that it was turned over to Christian use during the episcopate of Alexander (probably only after 324). Most other churches of which anything is known are substantially later in date.

Epiphanius' 'Mendidion' is an anachronism in a list of *early* fourth-century churches: Athanasius consecrated this new church in the old forum area in August 370,[111] to relieve the long-felt overcrowding in the older church of Dionysius nearby.[112] The church of Theonas may originally have been built by the bishop whom it commemorates, but was certainly rebuilt (again to relieve overcrowding) by Alexander:[113] it seems to have been in regular use for larger gatherings before the building of the Mendidion and the conversion of the former temple of Augustus, the Kaisareion, into a basilica.[114] It was known as the church of the Mother of God by the sixth century,[115] and may be identical with the shrine mentioned in the *passio* of Peter: the statement that he built it need not be taken too strictly (he may have extended or adapted an existing building; or the assertion may be purely legendary). If, as the *passio* indicates, Peter was buried near this site, this would help to explain the importance of the church under Peter's successors; its enlargement by Alexander may have been connected with an attempt to establish it as a pilgrimage centre, a shrine for the 'crown' of the Egyptian martyrs.[116] Earlier bishops had been buried near the *martyrium* of Mark on the other side of the city.[117] If the identification of Boukolia with Baucalis *is* correct, Arius could have been custodian of the relics of Alexandria's protomartyr and patron; a fact which would, no doubt, further have complicated his relations with the bishop and reinforced his prestige in the local church. But this is very uncertain: we have no firm information about the origins of the cult of St Mark in Alexandria, and the whole legend and cultus may date from after 300.[118] What is perhaps more likely is that the Boukolia church began as an oratory in or near what had become a mainly Christian area of the eastern necropolis; there is no particular reason to doubt that a number of bishops were buried at this site, and the church would thus still have been a place of some significance.

The other names in Epiphanius sound like house-churches. 'Annianus' is probably the same as the Annianus mentioned by Eusebius[119] as Mark's successor; if a house-church identified by this name was known to be the oldest continuously used oratory in the city, this might have been the source of a tradition that the first 'sub-apostolic' bishop was called Annianus. Of 'Serapion',[120] 'Persaea', and 'Dizya', we know nothing at all. 'Pierius' is an interesting case: almost certainly, it was the meeting-place of a congregation led by the Pierius who was head of the catechetical school in the late third century.[121] There is reason to believe[122] that he apostatized under persecution; yet he appears as a saint and martyr in later tradition.[123] It has been plausibly suggested[124] that the existence of a church under his name fostered the mistaken belief that he was a martyr commemorated by the building.

The plurality of churches in Alexandria suggests that the beginnings of Christianity in the city were piecemeal and various – no single primitive congregation under its Catholic bishop. This picture is reinforced by such evidence as we have of the prevalence in and around the city of gnostic influences and the survival in 'respectable' circles of extracanonical literature.[125] The 'catholicizing' of the church was evidently well under way by the end of Demetrius' episcopate (233),[126] but the survival of numerous independent congregations evidently continued to pose problems. The assigning of regularly ordained presbyters to the local congregations probably goes back to the time of Demetrius,[127] and may have been an attempt to cement a rather fragile unity between the *paroikiai*. But the events of the early fourth century show the inadequacies and risks of this system. The presbyters – as has been noted – were not docile diocesan clergy but members of a collegiate body. It is not entirely surprising that we should come across disputes between bishop and presbyters over the respective limits of their authority.

Problems were no doubt intensified by the after-effects of persecution. We have seen that Bishop Peter's flight from the city and the impotence or incompetence of his presbyteral commissaries created a vacuum which Melitius was only too eager to fill. In response to this unhappy legacy (and we should not forget the long interregnum that followed Peter's martyrdom), Alexander seems to have embarked on a campaign to consolidate the church around the bishop. Both Socrates[128] and the Emperor Constantine[129] represent Alexander as initiating discussion on a vexed theological and exegetical topic and attempting to give some sort of lead himself; indeed Constantine implies that Alexander demanded specimen exegeses from the presbyters, presumably to reassure himself that they were orthodox. The details and date are, as usual, obscure; what is clear is that Arius finally emerges into something like full historical light at this juncture. He and Alexander publicly repudiated each other's theologies, and, although there is no suggestion that Arius wholly rejected the bishop's authority, a tangible schism gradually developed: Alexander complains[130] of separate conventicles of Arius' supporters meeting for worship in the city – probably breakaway groups from churches whose presbyters continued to support the bishop.

We do not know how many of these there were. Of those named by Epiphanius as 'parish' presbyters, two appear in the lists of Arius' supporters;[131] and if the 'Achillas' who was initially closely associated with Arius[132] is the head of the *didaskaleion* described in laudatory terms by Eusebius,[133] the pro-Arius faction in the presbyteral college was impressively weighty. However, Epiphanius plainly implies that there were sharp rivalries between the presbyters themselves, and that their followers already constituted distinct parties: if this is true, it would be wrong to see Arius as the figurehead of a *general* presbyteral revolt against Alexander's 'papalism'. And the subscriptions to Alexander's culminating pronouncement against Arius[134] testify that the overwhelming majority in the presbyterate – including, presumably, at least some of the parish priests, as well as the presbyters attached to the bishop's offices or working outside the city boundaries – continued to support the bishop.

The most conspicuous odd man out is the celebrated Colluthus. Alexander[135] states that Colluthus used the crisis provoked by Arius as an excuse for initiating or maintaining some kind of schismatic activity: the most satisfactory interpretation of this not very clear text is that Colluthus was already presiding over independent congregations in the city (and Epiphanius[136] claims that his supporters described themselves as 'Colluthians' at the period prior to the Arian crisis), but exploited the troubled situation brought about by Arius and Achillas to justify his continuing in schism.

45

From later testimony by Athanasius,[137] we learn that Colluthus had at some point begun to ordain his own clergy – a painful reminder for any Alexandrian bishop of the persisting problem of Melitius. Colluthus obviously considered himself to be a bishop; Alexander's remarks suggest that the presbyter was dissatisfied with Alexander's leadership, and especially with his handling of Arius and Achillas. This implies that Colluthus represented an opposite theological extreme to Arianism (some kind of monarchianism?), for which Alexander's views would be almost as suspect as Arius'. The bishop's supposed unorthodoxy would disqualify him from his office, which would devolve upon a fitter candidate – probably the presbyter next in seniority.[138]

Arius and Achillas did not go this far (and, accordingly to Alexander, disapproved strongly of Colluthus' handling of ecclesiastical funds);[139] but they had in Colluthus the precedent for resisting an episcopal authority believed to be heretical. As the last few pages have been designed to show, neither Colluthus nor Arius was doing anything that the history of the Alexandrian churches would not have led us to expect. The beginnings of Arianism lie, as much as anything, in the struggles of the Alexandrian episcopate to control and unify a spectacularly fissiparous Christian body – and thus also in a characteristic early Christian uncertainty about the ultimate locus of ecclesiastical authority itself (we shall be coming back to this issue in I.C. below). Alexander, as his letter to Alexander of Byzantium about the local troubles amply shows, felt himself threatened with the virtual disintegration of the Alexandrian church into a bundle of mutually hostile sects.

As we shall see,[140] Colluthus' eventual reconciliation and submission to Alexander was made possible through the decisive and final rejection of Arius and his party by the bishops and clergy of Egypt. Repeated and uncompromising episcopal denunciations of the Arian faction must have made Colluthus' position less and less defensible; the fact that he was allowed to continue as a presbyter in good standing[141] does suggest, however, that he demanded a price for his return to Catholic obedience, a kind of canonical safe-conduct in return for his eagerness to join in the excommunication of Arius' faction. The years between the outbreak of the controversy and the Council of Nicaea evidently saw a good deal of hard work in Alexandria, aimed at uniting the church against a single common enemy. The solid anti-Arianism of the majority of the Alexandrian

Christians for the rest of the century owes something to this period as well as to the efforts and the personality of Athanasius.

At this point, it is necessary to turn to the very complex questions arising out of the uncertain chronology of events during these years. Our primary evidence consists in a number of relatively brief and and sometimes very fragmentary documents surviving for the most part in dossiers and chronicles of much later date. The standard collection of documentary sources made by Hans-Georg Opitz[142] remains indispensable; but it does not provide a fully consistent and satisfactory chronology for either the pre– or the post-Nicene period. Absolute precision is impossible, given that we have so few external fixed points against which to check conclusions, but the documents give us a reasonable amount of internal evidence; and their intrinsic interest amply justifies a close inspection of their contents.

B

The Nicene Crisis: Documents and Dating

1 THE CONTROVERSY TO 325

Recent scholarship has generally accepted the order and dating proposed by Opitz for the documentary remains of the early days of the crisis.[1] Opitz begins his collection with the very well-known and well-attested letter of Arius to Eusebius of Nicomedia, and places it around 318; this is then followed by a fragment of Eusebius' reply, a letter of Eusebius of Caesarea to Euphration (or Euphrantion) of Balanaeae, an *ad clerum* fragment of Alexander of Alexandria (319), and the important *henos sōmatos* encyclical of Alexander, with its long list of signatures (also 319). Opitz assigns the Bithynian synod mentioned briefly by Sozomen, and the 'credal letter' to Alexander written by Arius and his followers to 320 or thereabouts. Eusebius of Caesarea's letter to Alexander follows, Eusebius of Nicomedia to Paulinus of Tyre and some fragments of a letter of Paulinus himself are placed in 320 to 321, around the supposed time of Eusebius of Caesarea's Palestinian synod. Various brief pieces quoted much later by Athanasius[2] take us to 322, and the immensely long letter (*hē philarchos*) of Alexander to his namesake of 'Constantinople'[3] is dated 324, along with the remains of a further encyclical allegedly signed by a large number of bishops from Egypt and elsewhere. Constantine's letter to Arius and Alexander Opitz assigns to October 324 (at Nicomedia).

Leaving aside for the moment the other documents of the pre-Nicene stage of the controversy, we shall need to examine the contents of and possible relations between these pieces in some detail. Opitz' order implies a narrative something like the following. Arius' formal excommunication and deposition by an Alexandrian synod was followed promptly by his appeal to Eusebius of Nicomedia – and perhaps to other potentially sympathetic prelates such as the Palestinian Eusebius. Both Eusebii at once involved them-selves in campaigning for Arius' reinstatement, and the *henos sōmatos* represents Alexander's counter-move. Presumably Arius and a number of his supporters had by now left Egypt; and, encouraged by the support of the Bithynian bishops, they wrote from Nicomedia to present their case to Alexander. The epistolary battle developed rapidly, and pressure from Nicomedia led to a further synod in Palestine supporting Arius; and finally, Alexander, exasperated by the constant appeals of Arius' episcopal allies, issued a series of letters (or several versions of one letter?)[4] spelling out the exact nature not only of Arius' heresy but of his behaviour and that of his supporters in Alexandria. It is possible that Arius had actually returned to the city by this time, as the letter of Constantine to Arius and Alexander jointly[5] seems to have been taken by Ossius of Cordova on his mission to Alexandria and the East.[6]

Unfortunately we possess virtually no external fixed points by which to check the plausibility of this reconstruction. Constantine's appeal to the parties to compose their differences must in fact date from the very end of 324 or the early months of 325: he set out on his tour of the East in November 324,[7] and, in the letter, he tells the quarrelling clerics that the cause of his turning back before completing his planned visit to Egypt was his deep distress at the condition of the Alexandrian church.[8] He was back in Nicomedia by February 325:[9] to allow sufficient time for Ossius' travels in the Levant and the synods at which he was present in Egypt and Syria, we should have to suppose that the letter was written on Constantine's journey back – or perhaps in Syria, when the emperor was on the point of returning. The evidence taken overall suggests composition in Antioch around Christmas 324 (we shall return later on to the chronology of subsequent events leading up to the council); this is the only date which we can rely on with even moderate confidence. Much would be illuminated if we knew for certain the date of Licinius' edict[10] prohibiting episcopal meetings, as this would provide a *terminus a quo* for some at least of the events in question; but we can only be sure that it occurred later than the public breach between Constantine and Licinius in 321. Eusebius' history might be read as implying that the anti-Christian enact-ments of the eastern Augustus actually followed on the beginnings of the war with Constantine, and so date from the spring of 324. This is not possible;[11] but the fact that Licinius undoubtedly used anti-Christian legislation as a weapon of retaliation against Constantine's earlier aggression would support the view that these measures belong to the critical period of summer 323.[12] If so, the information is not all that helpful: the prohibition of synods may have been in force for no more than about sixteen months.

So we are left to determine the order of our documents almost entirely on internal evidence. One such piece of evidence which has generally been regarded as significant is the role of Colluthus:[13] the *henos sōmatos* carries his signature, at the head of the list of subscribing presbyters, while the *hē philarchos* speaks, with strong feeling, of his schismatical activities.[14] This seems clear enough; and, if we follow Opitz, Alexander's bitter complaints in *hē philarchos* that Arius and Achillas are forming separate congregations in Alexandria and that certain bishops are uncanonically supporting their views and activities might follow very intelligibly on the encouragement given to the heretics by the Palestinian synod (placed by Opitz in 321/22) to assemble (*ekklēsiazein*) their followers and to continue acting as presbyters.[15] If *henos sōmatos*, then, antedates this move in Palestine, the Bithynian synod must be placed around the same time as the encyclical's composition – probably not earlier (Alexander does not refer to anything other than individual activity on the part of Nicomedian Eusebius), but representing the climax of that growing pro-Arian agitation of which Alexander complains. Working back from a 319/20 date for *henos sōmatos*, we arrive at the traditional date of c. 318 for the beginnings of the crisis. Although all these dates are approximate, they provide a reasonable narrative structure into which the remaining letters and declarations may be fitted with fair plausibility.

However, this widely-accepted structure is in fact fraught with difficulties. First of all, there is the matter of Colluthus' activities. *Hē philarchos* not only describes him as a schismatic, who apparently justified his rupture with Alexander on the grounds of the bishop's tolerance of Arius;[16] it also claims that *Arius'* setting up of separatist congregations was prompted by disgust with Colluthus.[17] This is (as we have seen) a very tangled web. But if *henos sōmatos* is given its usual date, it is the culmination of a series of measures against Arius and is roughly contemporary with Eusebius' Bithynian synod; it thus post-dates Arius' excommunication, expulsion and appeal to Nicomedia. Why should Colluthus *after* all this complain about Alexander's tolerance? As noted already, some have suggested[18] that Arius and his supporters returned to Alexandria after *henos sōmatos*, encouraged by the sympathy of Palestine and Bithynia, and only then embarked on the course described in *hē philarchos*. This is possible: Colluthus might have been protesting at the fact that Arius had been permitted to return. But it is a rather awkward reading of *hē philarchos:* it leaves unexplained the absence of reference both to the synod of 'nearly one hundred bishops' which, according to *henos sōmatos,*[19] confirmed Arius' excommunication, and to the activities of Eusebius of Nicomedia.

Next, there is the problem of interpreting the decision of the Palestinian bishops (Opitz 10). If this synod's permission to Arius to officiate as a priest is a licence for him to act in *Alexandria*, a very eccentric view of canonical propriety on the part of Eusebius Pamphilus and his colleagues is implied; but if it is a licence to form 'émigré' congregations in Palestine, it has no relevance to the situation described in *hē philarchos*, and cannot offer any sort of help in dating the latter.

Thirdly, we have noted that, in *hē philarchos*, Alexander complains about the support given to Arius by three unnamed bishops in Syria,[20] yet is silent about the far more damaging campaign being waged at the supposed time of writing by Eusebius of Nicomedia – a relatively near neighbour of the recipient of the letter. And, in *henos sōmatos*, Eusebius is described as 'eager to renew his former malevolence' (*palaian gar autou kakonoian . . . ananeōsai boulemenos*):[21] this is an odd remark, since we know of no reason for hostility between Alexander and Eusebius prior to the outbreak of this controversy, and a brief interruption in the course of (say) 319 in the flow of Eusebius' polemical output would hardly seem to justify the implication here of a fairly prolonged silence. Again, Alexander describes the Arians as eager to provoke persecution at a time of peace – a very odd remark if the letter was written in 323 or 324, at the time of Licinius' anti-Christian legislation. Finally, in regard to *henos sōmatos*, there is the difficulty posed by the accounts offered of Arius' teaching. As has often been remarked,[22] the list of Arian errors in *henos sōmatos* is closely related to comparable catalogues in the writing of Athanasius,[23] increasing the considerable probability of this letter's having been drafted by the hand of Athanasius as secretary to Alexander; it bears little direct relation to what is said in *hē philarchos*, and suggests that the writer of the letter has read Arius' *Thalia*.[24] If *henos sōmatos* dates from 319/20, Arius must have

51

composed the *Thalia* very soon after his excommunication and expulsion from Alexandria; in which case, the verses would have been circulating freely by 324, and it is surprising that *hē philarchos* shows no knowledge of them, and makes no use of what Athanasius at least regarded as a damning witness against Arius and his party.[25]

There are a few other, less serious, difficulties. Regarding the 'credal letter' to Alexander, for instance, the unlikelihood has been noted[26] of Arius travelling through Syria and Asia with an entire ecclesiastical entourage including his two episcopal supporters from Libya. This is *perhaps* not quite so implausible as it sounds, since Epiphanius and Athanasius give us to understand that Arius' followers were driven out of the city as well as the heresiarch himself; and Alexander's letters assume that others apart from Arius are liable to present themselves for communion in the churches of Syria and Asia. It is also possible that the list of subscriptions to the letter[27] has undergone some revision: the presence of the Mareotic presbyter Pistus[28] at the end of the list is curious, as is the fact that the names of the two bishops stand after those of the priests and deacons. A copyist aware of the notoriety of the Libyan bishops may have sought, by adding their names, to bring the list into complete conformity with that given in *henos sōmatos*,[29] and may also have felt that Pistus (later consecrated by Secundus and, for a time, Arian bishop in Alexandria)[30] deserved a mention in view of his later prominence. So the problems raised by the list of signatories are not insuperable. However, it is surprising that the text makes no complaint about excommunication or ill-treatment, but simply sets out a series of propositions which Alexander is invited to recognize as identical with his own public teaching. The text makes slightly better sense if placed earlier in the controversy, before the first major synodal condemnation; the obvious context for it would be either as a response to Alexander's demand for clarification[31] when Arius was first delated for heresy, or as a submission to be read out at the synod itself. If so, this letter is the first actual Arian document we possess. It might be pointed out that Athanasius in *de synodis* places it after his extracts from the *Thalia;* but Athanasius is not giving a strictly chronological record, and this witness cannot be decisive against the theory of an earlier date.

What then of Alexander's two letters? *Hē philarchos* presupposes[32] that a synodical decision has been taken against Arius and Achillas, though it is not clear whether the meeting in question was a 'home synod' of the city of Alexandria and its environs or a full episcopal session. The former seems more likely, as Alexander would probably have mentioned the fact if the entire Egyptian episcopate had taken part in the proceedings. Again it is not wholly clear whether the separatist congregations organized by Arius and Achillas are active in Egypt or outside it (or both). It sounds very much as if Arius and his supporters are travelling beyond the borders of Egypt (*Epecheirēsan de peridromais* . . .)[33] at the time of writing, and Alexander may well be objecting to the existence of Arian *ecclesiolae* outside his jurisdiction; but the opening paragraphs of the letter suggest that some kind of dissident activity had preceded the synodical condemnation.[34] Foreign episcopal support is already forthcoming for the heretics, and Alexander specifically mentions[35] the encouragement given by three unnamed Syrian prelates. Since Arius, writing to Eusebius of Nicomedia, mentions six bishops of the province of Oriens anathematized by Alexander,[36] one or more of the three Syrian delinquents may be among them: almost certainly, Eusebius of Caesarea and Paulinus of Tyre were two of those whom Alexander had in mind. Arius, then, has been corresponding with the Syrian episcopate both before and since the synod; and, since Alexander refers[37] to the dissidents having persuaded some bishops to write in their support, Eusebius of Caesarea's letter to Alexander *may* belong to the period preceding *hē philarchos* (though we are told that several other of his letters to Alexander were known; and this text may be a good deal later). So too, if the exiles are forming separate congregations, the Palestinian synod permitting this must already have taken place. Sozomen[38] describes Arius as having initially approached Eusebius Pamphilus, Paulinus, and Patrophilus of Scythopolis for this permission; so that Patrophilus is most probably the third of the Syrian bishops complained of by Alexander.

The failure of *hē philarchos* to mention Eusebius of Nicomedia, as already noted, implies that Sozomen's narrative, which places all these proceedings *after* the Bithynian synod, is open to some doubt. The picture we have so far reconstructed is of Arius and his supporters establishing a fairly firm base in Palestine (perhaps in Caesarea, that haven of Alexandrian exiles) in the immediate aftermath of their condemnation. If (as Barnes has argued)[39] Arius' associate Achillas is indeed the master of the Alexandrian *didaskaleion* so warmly spoken of by Eusebius[40] – if, that is, we suppose him not to be the same person as the Achillas who succeeded the martyred Peter as bishop – this Achillas would have guaranteed for Arius a friendly hearing in Caesarea; but the identification is not completely secure. Nevertheless it is safe to say that Palestine and some parts of Syria welcomed the Egyptian exiles; and therefore it is from Palestine that Arius writes to Eusebius of Nicomedia. As this letter suggests, he has had time to consolidate his support: he can speak confidently of the virtual unanimity of the bishops of the Oriens in favour of his views. Evidently he has not yet travelled or canvassed beyond Syria: the approach to Nicomedia marks a new departure. This follows Epiphanius' narrative reasonably closely, though Telfer is right to be sceptical (on the basis of the documentary evidence) as to whether Arius ever actually travelled to Nicomedia itself.

When and why was such a new departure made? This is not easy to answer. Eusebius had been attached to the court of Licinius for some considerable time, and would therefore have been a person whose favour was worth cultivating. However, he can hardly have been particularly influential during the period of Licinius' harassment of the church between summer 323 and autumn 324 – when, indeed, Eusebius' position must have appeared pretty ambivalent to many Christians in the East. There are insuperable difficulties[41] in placing Arius' approach to him in the months following Constantine's victory; nor is it likely that it immediately followed Eusebius' translation to Nicomedia, as the letter mentions his successor at Berytus, Gregory, as having been condemned by Alexander along with Eusebius Pamphilus,[42] presumably some little time prior to the writing of the letter. However, if Eusebius had *fairly* recently moved to the imperial capital, his former colleagues in Syria might well encourage Arius to look to his powerful patronage. And the likeliest reason for this search for a new ally is a new offensive by Alexander: *hē philarchos* is an obvious candidate. A letter to the bishop of Byzantium designed to warn the churches around the Bosphorus against a heresy beginning to spread into Asia[43] would indeed have roused Arius' Palestinian sympathizers to cast around for help.

No doubt Eusebius' response from Nicomedia was encouraging;[44] and (if Athanasius is to be believed)[45] he urged Asterius the Cappadocian sophist, who had, like himself, been a pupil of Lucian of Antioch,[46] to tour Asia and Syria speaking in support of Arius.

However, since *henos sōmatos* represents Eusebius as having recently returned to the fray after an interval of inactivity, we must suppose that he had other pressures to contend with for a time – most probably the difficulties occasioned by Licinius' policies in 323–4. This suggests that the renewal of activity on Arius' behalf followed Licinius' defeat and Eusebius' alliance with the interests of Constantine; but it is impossible to say whether the Bithynian synod mentioned by Sozomen[47] occurred before mid–323 or after Constantine's victory. Sozomen says that the synod led to a general barrage of letters in support of Arius to Alexander and others; and if the synod was held soon after the defeat of Licinius, this requires a very rapid sequence of activity in the last months of 324. This is not impossible; but Alexander's failure to mention any recent synod called by Eusebius is a factor weighing against it. In any case, though, *henos sōmatos* fits extremely well into the period after the fall of Licinius: Eusebius is free to campaign openly, he is confident of his influence in Church affairs,[48] and is eager to consolidate this influence further;[49] Alexander is impelled to give as authoritative a statement as he can of his side of the argument.

If *henos sōmatos* is indeed a document of this very late stage of events before Nicaea, a possible solution to the question of Colluthus suggests itself. At the time of *hē philarchos*, Colluthus is obviously under censure, and a cause of considerable anxiety to the bishop. However, although those who had received ordination at his hands continued to trouble the Egyptian church,[50] Colluthus himself apparently returned to Alexander's communion as a presbyter: Athanasius tells us[51] that Colluthus, 'having made himself out to be a bishop, was subsequently commanded to be a simple priest [once more] by the general sentence of a synod, delivered by Ossius and the bishops with him'. This is undoubtedly the meeting held early in 325, when Ossius arrived in Alexandria with Constantine's letter. Was *henos sōmatos* approved by the Alexandrian clergy on this occasion? If Colluthus had just been reconciled to his diocesan, there would be some point in having his signature as presbyter leading the list of subscriptions, as a prominent public declaration of loyalty. The Alexandrian church was not in a mood to comply with Constantine's demand for unity in the terms he had laid down; but a declaration of complete solidarity with Alexander, following the settlement of a long-standing and troublesome schism, might have seemed to the synod at least a gesture in the direction of what the emperor wanted. Colluthus' signature is thus an important political counter in the attempt not to alienate Constantine in the crucial months of Ossius' mission.

There are no other significant considerations arguing against a late date for *henos sōmatos*, and, as we have seen, a certain amount of internal evidence points in the same direction. Such a reversal of the traditional order of Alexander's two great letters, together with what may be gleaned from *hē philarchos* in particular about the circumstances of writing, offers the skeleton of a narrative for the early development of the Arian crisis rather different from that commonly accepted, but (I hope) making slightly better sense of some of our evidence. One immensely important document, of course, has yet to be placed: the *Thalia*. But before we turn to look at that in detail, let us summarize the tentative conclusions so far reached about the course of events into which Arius' manifesto should be fitted.

At no point do we possess any exact dates for our pre-Nicene fragments, and it is therefore impossible to date with any precision the outbreak of the controversy; indeed, as we have already seen,[52] it is hard to say what it is that should be regarded as the concrete beginning of 'Arianism'. However, assuming that the pace of events was fairly brisk once it had begun, it seems reasonable to date the first Alexandrian synod which condemned Arius and his supporters to around 321.[53] The synod will have considered and rejected both the credal letter of the dissidents and (possibly) certain letters supporting Arius from some of the Syro-Palestinian bishops mentioned in the appeal to Eusebius of Nicomedia.[54] Arius and his eleven[55] supporters probably remained in the city for a time, generating the riotous conflicts described in *hē philarchos;* but eventually, either through general pressure from the church, or as a result of the intervention of the secular arm to restore order,[56] they were obliged to leave. They found a welcome in Palestine, and received formal permission from a synod (321/2?) to meet as a congregation: despite their deposition in Alexandria, the presbyters exercised their normal functions, probably in the name of whatever Palestinian bishop had sponsored them. In the months following, Alexander observed their influence spreading, and was already beginning to receive letters from their supporters. Alarmed at the prospect of a further extension of their activities, he wrote to a senior prelate as yet unaware of these alarums and excursions, the bishop of Byzantium; and he also, according to Theodoret,[57] wrote to his allies in Syria, Philogonius of Antioch and Eustathius of Beroea. This in turn disturbed Arius' partisans; they urged him to approach Eusebius of Nicomedia (perhaps with half an eye already to the possibility of secular intervention to reinstate Arius).[58] Arius did so, emphasizing his agreement with Eusebius' erstwhile colleagues and continuing friends in Palestine, and received a friendly reply. Eusebius' energetic championship of Arius, and probably also the circulation of Alexander's letter or letters,[59] prompted further approaches to the bishop of Alexandria; Asterius now enters the lists as a further defender of Arius. By early to mid–323 the dispute is at its height: Alexander may have convened a further synod at this point (probably the synod of 'almost one hundred bishops' mentioned in *henos sōmatos*),[60] a full-scale meeting of Egyptian and Libyan bishops (with some prelates from other districts?). If the Syrian fragments of a conciliar *tomos* published by Opitz as Urkunde 15[61] are authentic, they probably come from the synodical letter of this meeting; the large number of signatures reported (though not reproduced) suggests that the non-Egyptian bishops present were encouraged to circulate the document further and obtain more subscriptions. The incomplete list we have concludes with the name of Philogonius of Antioch, who seems to have been supported by a good number of Syrian and Palestinian bishops – which suggests that many of Arius' initial supporters were wavering.[62] Eusebius of Nicomedia evidently thought it necessary to call on his friends in Syria to bestir themselves: only Eusebius Pamphilus was unflagging in his zeal.[63]

Licinius' measures in 323 prevented any further decisive actions, though they probably did little to stem the flow of correspondence. When peace returned to the Church, Eusebius of Nicomedia celebrated with a synod in Bithynia (doubtless designed to attract Constantine's attention) and a further flurry of letters. Constantine began to take an interest in the affair: whether or not the troubles in Alexandria were the real reason for his premature return from the East is uncertain;[64] but he was sufficiently concerned to despatch Ossius to Alexandria in the winter of 324/5. By the time Ossius reached the city, news of the Bithynian synod and evidences of its effects in the shape of yet more letters had also arrived: Alexander was offended and intransigent. However, he welcomed Ossius' authoritative assistance in restoring some sort of unity to the Egyptian church by the regularization in synod of Colluthus' position (as noted already, the fact that Colluthus was not deposed entirely from the ordained ministry no doubt owed something to his willingness to anathematize his old enemy, Arius),[65] and probably also by the deposition of the Libyan metropolitans, Secundus and Theonas, who had supported Arius. Either at the synod or (more probably) shortly after its formal conclusion (there are no episcopal subscriptions to *henos sōmatos*), the encyclical letter of Alexander and his clergy was issued, the letter of a 'home synod' only. Ossius no doubt informed Constantine promptly of these developments; but the emperor had already determined on further action. Ossius would have received notice, on his arrival (late March 325?) in Antioch, of the imperial decision to call a general council.

At Antioch, Ossius presided over a further synod[66] which confirmed the election of Eustathius of Beroea to succeed Philogonius (who had died in December 324; the intervening months had been turbulent).[67] The election (and the activities of the synod) confirms that, for whatever reason, the majority of bishops in the Oriens were now firmly behind Alexander: their synodical letter (again surviving in Syriac)[68] was sent to Alexander of Byzantium, among others, and included a suspended sentence passed on the dissentient bishops at the synod (Eusebius Pamphilus, Theodotus of Laodicea and Narcissus of Neronias).[69] Their case was to be referred to the newly-announced synod to be held at Ancyra; the change of venue (to Nicaea) must have followed very swiftly.[70]

This gives the following order for Opitz' main documents (his proposed dates are given in brackets):

Urkunde 6; Arius' credal letter, c. 321 (320).

Urkunde 10; the decision of the Palestinian synod, c. 321 (321/2).

Urkunde 14; *hē philarchos*, 321/2 (324).

Urkunde 1 and 2; Arius to Eusebius of Nicomedia and Eusebius' reply, 321/2 (318).

Urkunde 15; the *tomos* of the episcopal synod at Alexandria, early 323 (324).

Urkunde 8; Eusebius of Nicomedia to Paulinus of Tyre, 323 (320/1).

Urkunde 5; the Bithynian synod, 324 (320).

Urkunde 17; Constantine's letter, Christmas 324 (October 324).

Urkunde 4b; *henos sōmatos*, January/February 325 (319).

Urkunde 18; synodical letter from the Antiochene Council, March 325 (325)

The remaining pre-Nicene documents can be fitted in in various ways; the evidence is not sufficient to justify any dogmatism. Eusebius Pamphilus' letter to Euphration (Opitz, no. 3, dated 318/19) could be an indirect riposte to *hē philarchos:* Alexander[71] stresses the coeternity of Father and Son (*aei parontos tou huiou*), and discusses[72] the significance of calling the Son an *eikōn* of the Father (the image of the eternal must be eternal itself); Eusebius vigorously denies the co-existence (*sunuparchein*) of Father and Son, and argues[73] that prototype and image must be distinct *pragmata*. But most of this is the common currency of the debate: the letter might belong to a slightly earlier phase,[74] though it makes fair sense to regard it as part of a wider response to Alexander's fresh denunciation. The fragments from letters to Alexander by Athanasius of Nazarba and the presbyter George (Opitz' 11 and 12, c. 322) are very likely to come from this phase. Alexander complains explicitly of Arius' numbering or 'including' the Son with other creatures,[75] and Athanasius of Nazarba asks[76] what is so very wrong about 'including and numbering' Christ as one of the sum of all things. George's letter may likewise relate to Alexander's specific point about the logic of the language of paternity: the bishop maintains[77] that the Son must be eternal if the Father is eternally Father, and George objects[78] that a human son *comes to be* the son of his father, so that the father must exist prior to the son.

As already noted, Eusebius Pamphilus' letter to Alexander (Opitz' 7, c. 320) may be earlier than *hē philarchos*. Unlike the letters we have just been considering, it is fairly unspecific and relies heavily on Arius' credal letter. However, as Opitz observed, it exhibits one or two apparent verbal parallels with *henos sōmatos*.[79] There is thus a possibility of its being a 'last-minute' response to the encyclical, designed to state a case for the defence before the opening of the Nicene synod. If so, it is part of the hasty and anxious reaction of Arius' Syrian supporters to the disastrous verdict of the synod of Antioch, a reaction traceable in the fragment of a letter by Narcissus of Neronias printed by Opitz as no. 19.

This leaves only Alexander's letter to the clergy of Alexandria and Mareotis (4a), the fragment of a letter written by Paulinus of Tyre (9), the letter of George to the Arians in Alexandria (13), and the record of Alexander's correspondence with Pope Sylvester (16). The first of these is normally and almost certainly correctly associated with *henos sōmatos*,[80] and suggests that the encyclical is indeed a reprise of earlier condemnations: the introductory *ad clerum* is presumably meant to bring the *local* church up to date on the number and names of recent defections to the Arian party, while the body of the encyclical assumes that the dissidents named there have been away from Egypt for some time, and is directed to those likely to have dealings with them. Paulinus of Tyre's letter is almost impossible to date in its fragmentary condition; it may again represent part of the general response to *hē philarchos*, but there is no firm evidence even for its being pre-Nicene. George's letter to the Arians still in Alexander's jurisdiction seems to pick up Alexander's phrase in *hē philarchos*[81] stating that the Son is *ek tou ontos patros*, when he suggest to Arius' followers an acceptable interpretation of the bishop's doctrine that the Son is *ek tou theou;* and so it is likely that it belongs in the same period as his letter to Alexander himself. Finally, there is Alexander's letter or letters to Sylvester, recording the excommunication of eleven clerics; Liberius, who preserves this record,[82] appears to date the correspondence *ante ordinationem Athanasii*. This may be an unreliable memory,[83] but it may also mean that Alexander's letters to the pope were known not to have been drafted by Athanasius as Alexander's secretary – or, possibly, that lists of clerical subscriptions to letters from Egypt at this date lacked the name of Athanasius. In either case, a date around the time of *hē philarchos*, or even earlier, is indicated. Athanasius would have been in his early twenties at this time; and if the later canonical regulations[84] about the minimum age for ordination as deacon were in force already, he would not have been admitted to the diaconate before 322–3, which would fit well with the general picture proposed here. However, this must remain uncertain.

This revised chronology for Opitz' documents does not suggest any very revolutionary changes in our understanding of the heresy itself; but a few points of interest do emerge. Firstly, if *hē philarchos* is as early as I have suggested, it is a more significant document than has sometimes been recognized. It provided a quarry of controversial points to be exploited by Arius and his supporters, and certain features of its phrasing and theology thus helped in sharpening the focus of the controversy. We shall return in a later chapter to a closer examination of the theology of this letter. Secondly, if

60

Eusebius of Nicomedia's entry into the debate occurred at a somewhat later stage than is commonly supposed, the role of Eusebius Pamphilus becomes correspondingly more significant; as a good deal of recent research[85] has indicated, Eusebius of Caesarea's adherence to the Arian cause was not a matter peripheral to his general theological style and commitment. Thirdly, if we are right in supposing that Eusebius and his colleagues in Palestine allowed Arius and others to function as presbyters in their territory, we have a very dramatic and specific contemporary case underlying the fifteenth and sixteenth canons of Nicaea,[86] which prohibited the clergy from moving between dioceses. Canon 16 in particular envisages the case of a presbyter or deacon moving of his own will from the church of his normal obedience and being 'received' by another church, that is, accepted into communion and, probably, recognized as a cleric[87] by another bishop. As observed already, the canonical decisions of Nicaea are not always so far removed as we might think from the main doctrinal debate. It is noteworthy that the Palestinian synod apparently allowed the Alexandrian refugees to act as presbyters in the Alexandrian style, independently convening and presiding at services. It would be a mistake to read too much into this; but a Eusebius who could approvingly report the doctrinal interrogation of prominent bishops by learned presbyters on more than one occasion,[88] and whose language still suggests a fundamental continuity between episcopal and presbyteral office[89] is likely enough to have shared the historic Alexandrian bias towards the idea of a presbyter exercising a kind of 'episcopal' authority as teacher and congregational president. How much this attitude helped to provoke the hostility of episcopal colleagues in the Oriens, we cannot say; but Athanasius' description[90] of the resentment aroused in Syria by the behaviour of Asterius in teaching publicly – and uninvited – in churches when he was not even in holy orders of any kind doubtless reflects increasing episcopal suspicion of independent teachers or preachers. The recognition of a foreign teacher (even one who was a presbyter) as authorized to expound the Scriptures publicly in Christian assemblies called at his own initiative, combined with the freelance propaganda of Asterius, must have been (at least) disturbing to the Syrian bishops, and cannot have endeared Arius' Palestinian friends to them.

2 THE *THALIA*

It remains for us to look at the questions posed by Arius' *Thalia*.[91] It cannot strictly be considered as 'a' document in the Arian case, since we do not possess a single complete and continuous text; and the interpretation of many passages in the extracts we do possess remains a matter of vigorous controversy.[92] It is more than usually artificial in this instance to separate chronological from doctrinal discussion, but a fuller examination of the theology of our extracts must wait until a later chapter, while in the pages that follow we shall simply attempt to locate the text within the framework so far worked out. The only explicit chronological statement we have about the work is that of Athanasius nearly forty years later.[93] After summarizing the original teaching of Arius and recording his excommunication by Alexander, he continues: *all' ekblētheis kai epitribeis Areios para tōn peri Eusebion sunethēken heautou tēn hairesin en chartē(i) kai hōs en thalia(i) . . . graphei men polla.* This has proved difficult to translate successfully. The traditional rendering[94] took *ekblētheis* and *epitribeis* together as referring to Arius' troubles in Alexandria, and assumed that *para tōn peri Eusebion* meant 'while with the Eusebians'; but Telfer[95] long ago pointed out the difficulties with this reading, and he has been followed by more recent scholarship (notably Kannengiesser).[96] However, Telfer's own hypothesis, that the text indicates a temporary but serious breach between Arius and his allies (so that *ekblētheis* and *epitribeis* refer to Arius' rejection by the *Eusebians, para tōn peri Eusebion*) has not found wide acceptance, although it makes good grammatical sense. Less grammatically easy,[97] but historically more plausible (would we not find some hint in Catholic polemic of a breach in the opposition camp at this crucial moment?), is the translation 'After his excommunication, Arius, under pressure from the Eusebian party, committed to writing a summary of his heresy . . .' A further possibility is to take *para tōn peri Eusebion* as meaning 'from the Eusebian camp', perhaps (less probably in the light of certain considerations about the theology of the text), 'from the Eusebian point of view'; or, more speculatively, building upon a sense of *para* well evidenced in Athanasius' writings,[98] 'at the prompting of', or 'arising from the agency of the Eusebians'. This would mean taking *para tōn peri Eusebion* with *sunethēken* rather than with the two opening participles (which would refer back to Arius' treatment by Alexander). Such a reading is attractive, though the nakedly causal use of *para* in such a context is undoubtedly awkward.

Whatever the precise interpretation of the phrase, the gist of it is clear enough in all the suggested versions: the *Thalia* was composed with the encouragement of *hoi peri Eusebion*. But who are these 'Eusebians'? Occasionally Athanasius fails to make clear which of the Eusebii he has in mind;[99] but on the whole 'Eusebius' alone seems to refer to Eusebius of Nicomedia – as has normally been assumed in this instance. Eusebius Pamphilus was a less important figure to Athanasius, and he is commonly identified as 'of Caesarea'. If Nicomedian Eusebius is indeed meant here, those 'with' him must include his neighbours and colleagues, Theognis and Maris, and perhaps other Bithynian bishops. But the phrase as regularly used by Athanasius[100] refers rather more widely to Eusebius' theological allies, and so would include figures like Asterius, Leontius (who eventually became bishop of Antioch), Anthony of Tarsus and others. As far as we can reconstruct a coherent picture from Athanasius and the fifth-century historians (including Philostorgius), the group described as *hoi peri Eusebion* is roughly the same as the group identified as pupils of Lucian of Antioch.[101]

The *Thalia* was thus produced (if we are to trust Athanasius)[102] as a fairly direct result of Arius' new contacts with the Lucianist circle after 321 or 322. It is difficult to be any more precise, but there are some indications that its composition occurred some time after the original link was made. We have already observed the difficulty of assessing Arius' claim to be a 'Lucianist'; and Philostorgius notes[103] that there was a significant theological disagreement between Arius and the Lucianist party over the question of whether God could be known by creatures (including the Son). Philostorgius sees in the Lucianists the ancestors of the Eunomian or 'neo-Arian'[104] position which affirmed that God in his grace made himself entirely accessible to created minds. Now the surviving fragments of the *Thalia* bear out with some force Philostorgius' characterization of Arius' position. According to Athanasius,[105] Arius taught that the Son knows the Father only as we do; comprehending (*katalabein*) the Father is as impossible for him as for all other creatures. If this fairly represents what Arius believed and taught, the *Thalia* could hardly be described as a 'Lucianist' document.

However, if we use not only Athanasius' fragmentary report and paraphrase in the first book of his *contra Arianos* but also the long poetic extract in *de synodis*, the problem may be capable of resolution. The *de synodis* text stresses that although God remains unknowable we are enabled to have at least some 'negative' knowledge about him because of the Son.[106] God remains invisible to all, yet manifests himself in the created glory of the Son;[107] and the Son himself beholds the Father in the measure and manner proper to him, but still imperfectly.[108] The *Thalia* may thus be emphasizing that a consistent apophatic attitude to God as he is in himself does not rule out a genuine belief in revelation: the totally transcendent God is not incapable of bestowing the grace whereby the Son and, on account of him, other creatures also 'see' the invisible Father, grasp the fact of his utter mystery and otherness. Such an emphasis would be intelligible in a work designed to reassure the Lucianists of its author's basic orthodoxy without betraying any fundamental principles or insights.

On this account, Arius' initial warm reception by Eusebius of Nicomedia would have been followed by a period in which Eusebius' attempts to rally his circle around Arius met with some hesitation. Lucianists, and perhaps others (Palestinians influenced by the Origenian tradition like Paulinus of Tyre), were not completely happy about endorsing Arius' views. The Alexandrian synod of 323 may in its anathemas have mentioned doctrines unacceptable to the Lucianists;[109] or, more probably, reports of Arius' public teaching and preaching in Palestine may have puzzled or offended some potential allies. So it is plausible to think that Eusebius of Nicomedia and his circle, disturbed by Alexander's mobilization of the Egyptian and Syrian episcopates in support of a theology deeply inimical to the Lucianist tradition, urged Arius to produce an extended statement of his beliefs which might clarify the ground on which the theological battle would be fought. *Hoi peri Eusebion* were anxious as to whether, in supporting Arius, they might not be endorsing a heresy as serious as that of Alexander himself.

Whether or not the *Thalia* proved reassuring, it was just sufficiently uncontroversial to prevent the fragmentation of the anti-Alexandrian party. It is important not to exaggerate the divisions among the 'Arians' at this date. Philostorgius is unquestionably oversimplifying the issues, from the perspective of someone committed to a Eunomian theology. If we turn from the *Thalia* to Eusebius of Nicomedia's letter to Paulinus of Tyre, for instance, we find some reference to the incomprehensibility of God;[110] but it is also noteworthy that Eusebius seems to avoid saying directly that the Son cannot know the Father, and seems more concerned to emphasize that neither we nor the angels can know the *archē* of the Son,[111] and that the Son's nature is inexpressible – like that of the Father whose likeness it is.[112] We should not, then, ascribe to the earlier Lucianists the full-blown revelational optimism of Eunomius; but it is likely that theologians formed in a tradition which concentrated on the idea of the Son as perfect image of God[113] would have found *too* drastic a doctrine of the Father's remoteness from the Son uncongenial. The *Thalia* is a strongly-worded piece of apophatic theology, but it does not belong in a different universe of thought from that inhabited by Eusebius and Paulinus; whereas it is clearly distinct from the systems of Aetius and Eunomius. We have no knowledge of later Arian use of the *Thalia*, and the paucity of information about it in orthodox historians suggests that – in contrast to some of the letters we have already discussed – it never formed part of a regular dossier on Arianism, at least after 360 or thereabouts; which suggests that it was not to the fore in the debates of the mid-century, and represented a theological style no longer acceptable in Arian circles.

The only possible exceptions to this silence about later use of the *Thalia* is a passage in Athanasius' letter to the Egyptian bishops.[114] After describing with scorn how the anti-Nicene party of the 350s attempted to escape the imputation of Arianism he points out that the leaders of the party are undeniably people who have benefited from the patronage of Eusebius and his allies. The anti-Nicenes have produced a creed against which the Egyptian and Libyan bishops must be warned:[115] they have undertaken to pass judgment on dogmatic issues, and, despite their own confusion and contradictions, they have put forward 'a *Thalia*' as a canon of faith. This hardly suggests a use of the original *Thalia*, or even a revised edition of it, since we have just been told that Athanasius' opponents are eager to dissociate themselves from the memory of Arius. Presumably, Athanasius' point is that any creed put out by this group is in fact equivalent to Arius' own original composition from the point of view of Nicene orthodoxy.

However, the idea of a revised *Thalia* published in the 350s has lately been defended by Kannengiesser.[116] He argues that the verse extract reproduced in *de synodis* 15 is closer in language and theological concern to the debates of this decade than to the earlier days of the controversy,[117] and proposes that we have here a revision produced by a 'neo-Arian', perhaps even Aetius himself.[118] This seems highly unlikely, if we consider the disagreements between the school of Aetius and Arius himself; it is just possible if we take the remark in Athanasius' *ad episcopos Aegypti* quite literally and imagine a theologian associated with Acacius of Caesarea (the leading anti-Nicene bishop of the day) producing such a work. However, if this is what happened, Athanasius' use of the text in *de synodis* is hard to explain. He may (as Kannengiesser suggests)[119] wish to present Acacius as a new Arius indistinguishable in heretical intent from the old; but this presupposes that his readers will recognize the text as coming from Acacius or someone of comparable contemporary prominence. Otherwise the use of the text in a controversial work is rather pointless. But this seems to run counter to the *professed* purpose of Athanasius in the second section of the *de synodis*, which is to exhibit the essential continuity of Arianism from first to last: beneath a deceptive appearance of variety, all non-Nicene formularies of belief really lead back to the naked 'blasphemies of Arius'. Indeed Athanasius' purposes are far better served by the use of a genuine text of the *Thalia* which will be an embarrassment to those anti-Nicenes who would prefer to forget about Arius himself. In so far as there are difficulties over the theology of this extract, they are to be resolved not by treating it as a pseudepigraph but by a greater flexibility in assessing what could and could not have been said or thought earlier in the century.

The theology of both sets of *Thalia* extracts will be discussed in detail in II.B on the assumption that Athanasius in *de synodis* gives us a substantially authentic text. However, we are no nearer dating the *Thalia* with any precision in the years of the controversy's first phase. The most that can be concluded on the basis of the preceding discussion is that the work was composed in Palestine[120] in order to guarantee support from Lucianist theologians and other rather reluctant parties. Given that it must have been written after the first opening of negotiations with Eusebius of Nicomedia, and probably after the 'synod of one hundred', a date in the summer or autumn of 323 is most likely, though whether earlier or later than Eusebius' letter to Paulinus (a part of the same campaign of consolidation and reassurance) it is impossible to say.

3 NICAEA AND AFTER

At Antioch early in 325, the bishops supposed that the 'great and holy synod' was to meet at Ancyra;[121] but further letters from the Emperor were probably already on the way, moving the meeting to Nicaea. If the letter attributed to Constantine (surviving only in Syriac) and published by Opitz as no. 20 in his collection is authentic, the reasons for this change had to do chiefly with convenience and the pleasantness of the climate of Nicaea; Barnes, however, notes[122] that the spring of 325 was a period of some considerable political unrest, a period in which Constantine would not have wanted to be more than a few hours journey from his capital (Ancyra would have been the best part of three days away, nearly two days, perhaps, for a good courier). The bishops were allowed to travel by the imperial postal service, the *cursus publicus*, and were entertained in Nicaea at the emperor's expense. How many attended is a matter of much uncertainty: Eustathius of Antioch (who was probably one of the presidents of the council)[123] estimates that there were rather more than 270 bishops present, but admits that he did not bother to check; Athanasius, having at first[124] settled for around 300, rounded up the figure to the familiar symbolic 318 late in life.[125] Recent research[126] has been less generous, and detailed examination of such lists as we do possess has failed to yield more than about 200 names. The contradictions may be partly explicable by exaggeration (though Eustathius was in a good position to estimate the numbers) or by the late arrivals, early departures, and irregular attendance at sessions, in the time-honoured tradition of councils, episcopal and otherwise. It is fairly likely at least that a good many more than 200 were present.[127] Eusebius of Caesarea's estimate[128] of about 250 is probably as near as any.

Philostorgius[129] records the names of twenty-two bishops sympathetic to Arius at the council. If this list is reliable, Arius' support was still quite strong: one bishop in ten, in a council full of people with no very deep theological commitment one way or the other, is a promising base to work from. However, the list bristles with problems: one of those named had been dead for some years,[130] two had subscribed to the condemnation of Arius at Antioch,[131] four appear elsewhere as anti-Arians,[132] and certain bishops known to have been Arian sympathizers do not appear.[133] Astonishingly, Melitius of Lycopolis is listed. One of the more interesting features of the list is the presence of six bishops from Libya – four from the Pentapolis, in additon to their metropolitan, Secundus, and his colleague from 'lower Libya', Theonas. Obviously there is some solid foundation for the presence of a good many of these names, several of which are familiar from elsewhere – the Bithynian triumvirate of Eusebius, Theognis and Maris, for instance, and the group of Syro-Palestinians and Cilicians prominent in the early stages of the struggle; altogether, about thirteen names seem well-established, two are impossible, the rest uncertain, but, for the most part, wildly unlikely. Since Sozomen says[134] that seventeen bishops supported Arius at the opening of the council, Philostorgius' catalogue must be regarded as being of very limited use, though not wholly untrustworthy.

Scholarly controversies over the conduct of the council proliferate, to such a degree that we cannot hope to examine them all in detail.[135] What is important for our present purpose is to note that it became evident very early on that the condemnation of Arius was practically inevitable. Eustathius[136] describes how a credal document of some sort written by 'Eusebius' (which one?) was presented, repudiated and torn up in the presence of the whole synod, at an early stage in the proceedings.[137] Theodoret, in additon to reproducing this story, mentions[138] a formulary drawn up by a number of Arian bishops (neither of the Eusebii is named) which was likewise presented and torn up, apparently rather later on. This may be the statement of faith objecting to the use of *homoousios* mentioned by Socrates;[139] if so, it belongs in the stage of debate immediately following the first proposal of the final form of the synodical creed – by which time Arius' party must have known that their cause was hopeless. They can only have been motivated by the desire to register as strongly as possible their incredulous indignation at the fact that a Christian assembly could sanction the blasphemously materialistic implications of the *homoousion*.[140]

At what point did the word *homoousios* become a matter of debate? Arius repudiates one possible meaning for it in his letter to Alexander[141] and another in the *Thalia* as reported in *de synodis*.[142] Ambrose[143] records a fragment from a letter of Eusebius of Nicomedia (no. 21 in Opitz)[144] read at the council, which opposes the sense of *homoousios* attacked in the *Thalia*: ' "If", he [Eusebius] said, "we do indeed call the Son of God uncreated [*increatum*, no doubt representing *agen(n)ēton*] as well, we are on the way to confessing that he is *homoousios* with the Father." ' And Ambrose adds that, when this was read at the council, the bishops decided to include the word in the creed, seeing how strongly the Arians disliked it. This is certainly an oversimplification; but if it refers to a genuine letter of Eusebius, the chances are that it was this document which was torn up early in the sessions (despite impressive arguments from Stead, it does still seem probable that the Eusebius referred to by Eustathius is the bishop of Nicomedia, not Eusebius Pamphilus). This confirms the view that *homoousios* (and similar expressions such as *ek tēs tou patros ousias*) was already being discussed in the years leading up to Nicaea: it did not spring fully-armed from the head of Constantine (or Ossius) at the council itself. Ambrose may not be correct in implying an instant decision by the bishops on hearing Eusebius' views, but he is probably right in so far as Eusebius' statement marked out the ground on which the debate would be fought. Eusebius of Nicomedia, like Arius himself, had rashly begun by stating what his party regarded as non-negotiable. It is very clear from Athanasius' *ad Afros*[145] that the council was increasingly concerned to find a formula to which Arius' supporters could never agree: on Ambrose's account, Eusebius had effectively solved its problem in advance[146] – though, in the event, only the heroically consistent Secundus and Theonas held out against it to the last.[147] Philostorgius' story[148] of Ossius and Alexander of Alexandria agreeing in advance that the term should be employed is unlikely to be true, as they will not have known before the opening of proceedings exactly where Eusebius and his party would take their stand, or which of many uncongenial expressions would prove to be wholly unacceptable.

Eusebius Pamphilus skilfully represents his own role in the council as an eirenic one; indeed, his accounts of proceedings in both the *Vita Constantini*[149] and the letter to his church at Caesarea[150] suggest that no very violent disagreement persisted beyond the first session. It is now generally thought unlikely that Eusebius' creed, as he reports it for the Caesarean church,[151] really formed the agreed and uncontroversial basis for the council's final definition: Eusebius' text is strongly slanted towards pluralism, distinguishing between the 'real' separate subsistences of the three persons of the Trinity, an emphasis which has disappeared in the conciliar creed; and the number of additional controversial phrases in the latter suggests a far more protracted process of debate and redrafting than Eusebius relates. However, his pleasantly complacent picture may have some truth. Evidently, if he did propose a text, it was rejected as inadequate. Athanasius sketches[152] the process whereby *ek tou patros* and *theos alēthinos* were pressed on the Arians for acceptance, and describes how they were able to find ways of making such language amenable to their heretical views; Eusebius' creed fits well into this process. Whether it is his own composition or a baptismal creed of Caesarea, it is ambiguous in just the crucial areas Athanasius mentions – the meaning of *ek theou*, of 'continued' or continuous'[153] (as opposed to strictly *eternal*) existence, of *alēthinos* as applied to the Son's being and Godhead. It was becoming plain that the hardest sticking-point was, after all, *homoousios*, and the frustrated and impatient drafters[154] at last produced something like the final text. At this point, the opposition made their last passionate protest, as Socrates tells us. But the negotiations were not yet over, for, according to Eusebius' account in his letter to the church at Caesarea,[155] Constantine defended the decisive word against just the doubts raised by the authors of the protesting memorandum; and, judging from the final vote, most of the remaining dissidents were persuaded. If Constantine's defence was the result of coaching by Eusebius, the bishop of Caesarea could rightly claim to have been an architect of the virtual unanimity of the council. Clearly, Constantine's points in support of the *homoousion* are points which Eusebius accepts: his own defence of the conciliar creed largely repeats what he has attributed to the emperor.[156] It looks as though Eusebius had performed the considerable *tour de force* of working out an interpretation of *homoousios* just about acceptable even to Eusebius of Nicomedia and his circle: Constantine was persuaded simply to say what the world did *not* mean, and, on those terms, the Lucianist resistance finally collapsed. Eusebius Pamphilus' manifest sense of a diplomatic triumph having been accomplished was not misplaced.

In its letter to the Egyptian and Libyan churches,[157] the council recorded its condemnation of Arius' views and Arius' person: he was excommunicated and probably degraded from the presbyterate; and Secundus and Theonas shared his fate.[158] All three, together with at least one of Arius' Alexandrian colleagues, the deacon Euzoius,[159] were exiled by Constantine at the conclusion of the council. This dual punishment, ecclesiastical and civil, was not only an ominous precedent: it sowed the seeds of endless bitterness and confusion in the years that followed, since, although the emperor could rescind his own legal decisions, he could not on his sole authority reverse ecclesiastical rulings. The two systems were to be seldom in step after 325.

According to Philostorgius,[160] Arius (and presumably Euzoius) and the Libyan bishops were exiled immediately at the end of the council after refusing to subscribe the creed and its anathemas. The fate of Arius' other chief defenders is less easy to sort out. Eusebius of Nicomedia, Maris and Theognis were variously described as having signed the Nicene decrees and then changed their minds, having signed with mental reservations or private emendations of the text, and having refused to sign from the first. Socrates[161] assumes that Eusebius and Theognis were exiled at the same time and for the same reason as Arius, Sozomen[162] claims that Eusebius and Theognis signed the creed, but not the deposition of Arius, and were removed from their sees fairly promptly by Constantine, Theodoret[163] has only Secundus and Theonas exiled at the close of the council, but offers a rather garbled account of the fate of Eusebius some chapters further on.[164] Philostorgius gives the most detail, although it is doubtful how much is to be relied on: Eusebius, Theognis and Maris were prepared to sign a text containing *homoiousios* rather than *homoousios*, and so escaped immediate censure;[165] three months later, they approached the emperor and announced that they had signed only from motives of prudence. Their repentance was rewarded with exile to Gaul.[166]

Philostorgius' narrative in its present form is not very plausible. The introduction of *homoiousios* as a compromise term belongs to a later date,[167] and the sudden *prise de conscience* of the three bishops sounds like an attempt to give an acceptable Arian gloss to the embarrassing fact that Constantine had suddenly turned against the Bithynian champions of Arianism. Philostorgius, or his source, was evidently trying to make sense of the two equally awkward facts that the Bithynians had signed the creed and that, none the less, they suffered exile for their beliefs. However, the hard core of fact is certainly the report that they were not exiled immediately. Athanasius[168] clearly implies that their condemnation was distinct from that of the clerics anathematized at the council. This is also presupposed in the most authoritative document we possess on the exile of Eusebius, Constantine's own letter to the Nicomedian church.[169] Constantine gives vent to some strong feelings about

Eusebius' previous closeness to Licinius, accusing him of conniving in the martyrdom of bishops by the late emperor of the East, and of plotting against and insulting himself. Eusebius left Nicaea, it seems, under a cloud,[170] his case suspended while he did penance of some sort (a temporary prohibition against exercising his orders rather than a deposition?): the emperor indicates[171] that Eusebius begged him to intervene personally on his behalf to prevent him losing his office altogether. However, the bishop had not changed his views, and, when certain Egyptian dissidents[172] were summoned to the capital to answer for their contumacy at a meeting of their native hierarchy under the imperial eye, Eusebius and Theognis presumed to defend them (and receive them to communion?);[173] consequently, Eusebius and Theognis have been deposed and banished, and their churches are invited to elect new bishops.

This suggests that Sozomen is right in saying that Eusebius and Theognis refused to subscribe to the anathemas of the council, and were saved from disgrace only by their signing of the creed (and this is exactly what the two bishops themselves say in their letter petitioning for restoration).[174] They were then put under discipline for some set period;[175] and presumably their ill-judged support of the Egyptians occurred before their penance was completed. The occasion of their delinquency was almost certainly the meeting described by Eusebius Pamphilus[176] as following closely on Nicaea: continuing dissension in Egypt led Constantine to recall the Egyptian bishops for further discussion, after which (in true Eusebian style) all was harmoniously settled, and the emperor endorsed the bishops' decisions. Bearing in mind the number of Libyan bishops claimed as Arian sympathizers by Philostorgius, it may have been some of these who were involved, and whom Eusebius tried to assist.[177] The imperial deposition of bishops would have had to be sanctioned by a synod, of course, and a meeting of Egyptian prelates would hardly have the authority to remove bishops of another province; however, the canons of Nicaea had made formal provision[178] for the calling of provincial synods twice yearly, and Eusebius and Theognis must have been canonically removed from their sees at such a synod of the Bithynian clergy (Constantine's letter to the Nicomedian church tells its recipients that they must now proceed to elect a new bishop, and a synod would in any case have had to meet to effect such an appointment).[179] So we can conclude that the recall of the Egyptian bishops to the capital was followed almost immediately by a *local* synod (late in 325) of the kind envisaged by Nicaea, called to deal with the consequences of the imperial sentence against Eusebius and Theognis (and, apparently, a number of inferior clergy regarded as adherents of their party):[180] Maris of Chalcedon, although he had evidently shared his colleagues' reservations about the Nicene anathemas, is not mentioned as suffering the same fate, except in Philostorgius' account.[181]

The institution of twice-yearly provincial synods has often been overlooked by historians seeking to clarify the extraordinary complexities of the course of events between Nicaea and the death of Arius.[182] There is no need for an undue multiplication of quasi-ecumenical councils to account for the numerous doctrinal and political shifts of these eventful years: most of the matters in question have to do with precisely those processes which the Nicene system was designed to facilitate – the review of cases of excommunication and the election of new bishops. The chaos of the period owes much to the fact that there was no very obvious way of guaranteeing general acceptance for such local decisions – with the possible (extra-canonical!) exception of imperial pressure.

So when we read later that[183] Arius was recalled from exile and given an opportunity to clear himself, it is not to be taken for granted that this was the act of another large-scale synod. Socrates, Sozomen and Gelasius[184] give versions of the letter sent by Eusebius and Theognis to an episcopal meeting some time after their exile. They protest (though mildly) that they have had no formal trial, note that Arius (in whose guilt they have never believed)[185] has been restored by the same synod, and express their anxiety that their own silence may be taken as proof of their guilt. They very carefully state that their faith is the same as that of the other bishops, and that they have examined the implications of the *homoousios* and are now committed to preserving the peace of the Church and avoiding heresy – which is a neat evasion of the question of whether they actually *accept* the formula.[186] They petition for the same clemency to be shown to them as to Arius. This letter has often been taken to be addressed to a 'second session' of the Council of Nicaea,[187] or at least some major gathering which reversed the Nicene decisions;[188] but there are difficulties in such a reading. The plain implication of the letter is that the synod addressed is the same synod that condemned the two exiled bishops; and since they were not *deposed* at Nicaea, the council addressed cannot have had the same personnel as Nicaea. Again, it is rather difficult to imagine a council is session for a long enough time to cover all the events involved: Arius is recalled and readmitted to communion, news of this is sent to Eusebius and Theognis, probably in Gaul, they write and ask to be summoned to the council to make their defence, and, according to Socrates[189] and Sozomen,[190] their petition is accepted and their episcopal successors are removed from office. Even if the synod did not summon the exiles to defend themselves in person, this still requires an uncomfortable amount of coming and going. It is not impossible that all this should have occurred; but I think it rather more likely that the context is several *successive* meetings of the provincial synod of Bithynia. After Arius' readmission, Eusebius and Theognis would have written to the *next* meeting to request a hearing at the session after that.

But how had it come about that Arius could be so soon restored? The end of 325 was a low point for the Arian-Lucianist group, but events in 326 dramatically redressed the balance. That forthright and consistent opponent of Arianism, Eustathius of Antioch, had become involved in a quarrel with Eusebius of Caesarea soon after Nicaea,[191] and, when Constantine's aged mother visited the East late in 326, Eustathius made some tactless or critical remark about her which provided an opening for his Palestinian enemies to mount an attack. Accused of heresy and immorality, as well as of disrespect for the imperial family, Eustathius was deposed by an Antiochene synod and exiled by Constantine, probably in 327.[192] A number of bishops who shared Eustathius' theological preferences[193] were also ejected at the same synod, on a variety of charges.

This was clearly an auspicious moment for reopening the question of Arius' fate. Constantine wrote to Arius in November of 327[194] summoning him to court at Nicomedia, and expressing surprise that he had not come earlier. This suggests that the Antiochene synod had, formally or informally, extended an invitation to Arius to clear his name before the emperor, but that Arius (sensibly) waited for some official signal before presenting himself. Rufinus[195] seems to be the source of the story that the emperor's sister Constantia in her last illness introduced her Arian chaplain to Constantine; after Constantia's death, this presbyter encouraged the emperor to believe that Arius' faith was no different from that of Nicaea: and the result was the surviving letter to Arius. The story is almost certainly legendary in its details, but may reflect a memory that members of the royal house had some sympathy with the anti-Nicenes; Constantia, after all, had been close to Eusebius of Nicomedia, who had joined her in interceding for the life of her husband Licinius.[196] If there is any truth in this, family pressure joined with ecclesiastical encouragement in prompting Constantine to give Arius a second chance in the winter of 327.

Arius and Euzoius returned from exile and presented a rather non-committal creed to the emperor and his ecclesiastical advisers: it speaks of the Son as 'begotten from [or out of] the Father before all ages', but is silent about the *homoousios*. Evidently, however, it satisfied Constantine, who wrote to Alexander,[197] pressing him to accept Arius and Euzoius back in Alexandria; and (if the reading proposed above of the letter of Eusebius and Theognis is correct) it was successfully presented to the local Bithynian synod, which readmitted Arius to communion. The exiled bishops petitioned for restoration a few months later, at some point in the first half of 328, and were back in their sees by the late summer or autumn. This, incidentally, suggests that Philostorgius (or his epitomizer) is right in saying that Eusebius and Theognis returned from exile after 'three whole years'.[198] The Arian historian then goes on to describe a major council (of 250 bishops) held at Nicomedia after Eusebius' return, at which a new creed was promulgated and Eustathius and Alexander of Alexandria were deposed. This is obviously, for the most part, fantasy: Philostorgius seems to be conflating several meetings. The synod which deposed Eustathius has taken on some of the features of the Tyre-Jerusalem synod of 335 which accepted Arius' confession of faith,[199] and perhaps the Antiochene 'Dedication' synod of 341, with its various non-Nicene approved creeds. The figure of 250 bishops is most probably an attempt to claim equality of numbers with Nicaea as recorded by Eusebius of Caesarea.[200] The core of truth, if any, is no doubt some record that the returned Eusebius lost no time in calling a synod[201] to confirm Arius' restoration and (possibly) formally to anathematize the views associated with Eustathius and Alexander (who had firmly refused to comply with Constantine's request).

By this time, however, Alexander had died (on 17 April 328),[202] and his successor had been elected, though in the face of strong opposition.[203] At the end of the summer of 328, the new bishop of Alexandria, Athanasius, and the rehabilitated bishop of Nicomedia embarked on an ecclesiastical civil war which did not relax for a moment up to the death of Eusebius in 341. The Bithynian synod of late 328, under Eusebius' chairmanship, must have been the source of the renewed appeal to Alexandria for Arius' restoration as recorded by Socrates and Sozomen.[204] Once again, this was supported by the emperor,[205] and once again the request was refused. Athanasius was threatened by Constantine and Eusebius with harsh retribution for his disobedience, but he remained adamant. It seems to have been at this point that the Melitian schismatics in Egypt reverted to an open hostility to the 'Catholic' episcopate which they had not shown in the last days of Alexander.[206] By 330, they had made a tactical alliance with the Arians,[207] and gained the patronage of Eusebius of Nicomedia;[208] a concerted campaign to have Athanasius disgraced and removed began, a campaign which was to dominate church affairs in the Levant for over a decade. The details of the accusations laid against Athanasius, and his defence, are not our immediate concern here, however; what matters from the point of view of Arius' biography is that the struggle against Athanasius increasingly obscured the cause of the unfortunate heresiarch in the years between 328 and 335.

We do not even know where he spent this period. Constantine's letter inviting Arius to court promises him the chance to return to his 'native land' if all goes well;[209] and it is likely enough that he was in Libya for some years.[210] Secundus (and Theonas?) must have returned from exile at some point before the death of Constantine,[211] and Athanasius often speaks as if their restoration had been part of the great Eusebian campaign of the years after 328. In 331 or 332[212] Athanasius (who seems to have made a policy of visiting troubled areas under his jurisdiction early on in his episcopate)[213] went to Libya Pentapolis; and it has been plausibly suggested[214] that his aim was to bring pressure to bear on the Nicene side in episcopal elections. If Arius himself was in Libya, such an explanation is still more likely; with the return of his oldest and most faithful allies, Arius was assured of a welcome. However, there is no evidence that any effort was made during these years to restore him to communion in Alexandria after the uncompromising refusals of Athanasius in 328. Arius evidently came to feel that his friends at court had forgotten him, and took the bold step of protesting directly to the emperor in 332 or 333. He asked in desperation what he was to do if no one (in Egypt?) was prepared to take the initiative in receiving him,[215] and proffered yet another confession of faith,[216] apparently employing a highly ambiguous formula stating that the *logos* of God's substance was *anarchos*.[217] The surviving fragments of this letter suggest a man at the end of his tether.

Arius' mistake was to emphasize the numerical strength of his support, especially in Libya.[218] Rightly or wrongly, Constantine assumed that Arius was threatening a schism,[219] the one thing which all the imperial efforts were designed to avoid. The emperor wrote, probably in 333,[220] an open letter to the heresiarch and his supporters which is extraordinary in its venom and abusiveness, dubbing Arius an 'Ares', a god of war,[221] who seeks to create strife and violence, and quoting the Sibylline Oracles[222] on the divine judgment threatened for Libya on account of the Libyans' sins against heaven.[223] Arius' creed is dissected and found to be incompatible with Nicaea;[224] and when the emperor has finished refuting his theology, he turns[225] to sneering at Arius' wasted and ascetic appearance. Clerics and laity who break the peace of the Catholic church by continuing adherence to Arius are assured of legal retribution.[226] The letter suggests a very confused situation in Libya. Arius, though restored to communion in another province and permitted to return (by imperial decree) to his own province, has still not been synodically rehabilitated by an Alexandrian decision. Not surprisingly, his allies in Libya have assumed that he is to be regarded as 'in good standing', in the light of the imperial reprieve. Arius appeals to the emperor, on the grounds of this *de facto* restoration by a majority in Libya, to bring pressure to bear on Alexandria to allow a formal restoration. But Constantine – no doubt mindful of the Donatist troubles – sees in this the creation of a separate church, and thus withdraws from Arius' sympathizers the privileges of Catholic Christians. It sounds as though Arius had, in effect, asked the emperor what alternative he and his supporters had but to act as if they were back in communion with the Church at large until the emperor formally compelled the churches to ratify this.[227] It is probably an anachronism to think of anything like a self-consciously 'Arian' church in Libya emerging or being envisaged at this date; but Arius was accustomed from earlier experience to acting on the decisions of friendly local churches rather than waiting for a volte-face in Alexandria. Even so, his letter was evidently written out of long-standing bitterness and impatience with the Egyptian church which he had served faithfully and which had excluded him for nearly thirteen years. Arius is caught in the cross-currents of uncertainty about the workings of a church unexpectedly and unpreparedly having to adjust to a situation in which its unity and doctrinal consistency have for the first time become matters of public and political concern.

Constantine's concern was dramatically shown in the edict which accompanied his reply to Arius,[228] associating Arius' supporters with Porphyry, the great pagan critic of the Church, and ordering that Arius' works be treated like those of Porphyry: they are to be burnt, and anyone who does not surrender copies in his possession is to be executed. This edict – apart from its depressing foretaste of varieties of intellectual fascism through the centuries down to our own day – explains, to some extent, why Arius' written works survive in such fragmentary form, why they are not available for quotation even by later Arians (or perhaps *especially* by later Arians: it would be far easier for quotations to survive – as they have done – in works dedicated to their refutation).

The emperor had concluded his letter to Arius by inviting him once again to make his defence in person at court; and Arius evidently did so, with unexpected success – success, that is, to the extent that he was encouraged to present his case to a major episcopal gathering in 335, when Constantine convened a synod for the dedication of the church he had built in Jerusalem. According to Socrates,[229] sixty bishops were involved, though it is not clear on what basis invitations were issued: obviously the Syro-Palestinian and Cilician bishops would be present, and we know too that Eusebius of Nicomedia, Theognis and Maris were present, together with two new and youthful recruits to the Arian episcopal camp, Urascius and Valens from Illyricum.[230] The bishops were instructed to meet at Tyre first, to settle once and for all the (by now very numerous and serious) accusations against Athanasius. They set up a commission to investigate the charges, a commission consisting of Athanasius' worst enemies, including the omnipresent Bithynians; the commission reported back to a second session at Tyre after the dedication festival at Jerusalem in September 335. Their report was predictably hostile; and they delivered it to a synod which had apparently, at Jerusalem, admitted Arius and Euzoius.[231]

According to Socrates, the emperor had intimated to the bishops that he was satisfied with the orthodoxy of the two petitioners; and Sozomen[232] adds that he invited the synod to examine their credal statement. Sozomen clearly believes that this statement was that printed by Opitz as no. 30; but this is more likely to belong to the first stages in Arius' rehabilitation in 327, as we have assumed above. Socrates speaks of a 'recantation', which is not an obvious description of the surviving credal letter, and the fragments of Arius' confession of 332/3 suggest that Arius was prepared by this stage to concede (at least in ambiguous formulations) some things which he had still held to in 327. However, it is possible that the supposedly earlier letter is indeed that presented at Jerusalem; in which case the synod showed remarkable flexibility in admitting a statement of faith which makes no concessions to Nicene language – indeed, takes no notice of it at all.

Whatever the details, Arius was accepted in September 335, and the bishops wrote from Jerusalem to Athanasius in Alexandria informing him of their decision, and appending a copy of the emperor's recommendation[233] – which, they emphasize, is based on personal interviews with Arius and his followers. They claim, unconvincingly, to believe that Athanasius will be only too pleased by this restoration of Christian unity and tranquillity. In fact, Athanasius did not immediately receive this letter, having (by the end of October) made his way in secret to Constantinople to appeal in person to the emperor[234] – a stratagem which turned out disastrously for him, as it led ultimately to the first of his exiles, in November 335. The Alexandrian church was left in chaos. When Arius arrived in Alexandria (probably as Socrates states,[235] after Athanasius' exile, considering the volatile siutation there), rioting broke out; and he was refused communion.[236] Constantine summoned him back to the capital,[237] apparently holding him responsible for fomenting discord; but Athanasius' enemies were in the ascendant at court, and Arius suffered no further penalty. Constantine continued to regard him as orthodox.

No immediate action on Arius' behalf was taken in the early months of 336; but the position of the Nicene party continued to worsen. Marcellus of Ancyra, a prominent scourge of the anti-Nicenes, had refused to participate in the dedication festivities at Jerusalem when he realized that Arius was to be admitted to communion.[238] Various indiscreet statements in his polemical tracts (especially those directed against Asterius) were inconclusively discussed at the second session of the Council of Tyre,[239] and the Eusebian party were thus able to point to accusations of heresy against Marcellus, as well as his insult to the emperor in refusing to participate in the dedication at Jerusalem, when they reported to Constantine.[240] The emperor had recalled the synod for a further session in the capital, to deal with the problem of Athanasius, but the majority of the exhausted bishops went straight home from Jerusalem.[241] This left the field open for Eusebius and his allies, who not only succeeded (as noted already) in securing Athanasius' banishment, but also induced the emperor to summon a further synod to deal with Marcellus[242] – probably a synod of bishops from Marcellus' own province of Galatia and the neighbouring province of Bithynia.[243] The aged bishop of Constantinople understandably took exception to the calling of a synod in his diocese at which he had no canonical status;[244] he was also well aware that the intentions of those chiefly responsible for the synod were not friendly to his own position as a strict Nicene. His protests fell on deaf ears.

The new synod met in the summer of 336 and deposed Marcellus for holding the heresy of Paul of Samosata;[245] the Bithynians seem to have decided to exploit the opportunity of embarrassing Alexander of Constantinople still further by pressing him to receive Arius into communion – presumably with the spoken or unspoken threat that the synod would not be averse to another heresy trial before it disbanded. Arius was examined by the emperor, and, to Constantine's evident surprise, declared his assent to the creed of Nicaea.[246] Athanasius reports[247] that Arius read a statement of his belief but kept concealed about his person a fuller and more unequivocally 'Arian' confession; this enabled him to swear solemnly that he held *ex animo* to 'what he had written'. Socrates repeats this story,[248] but, judicious as ever, admits that it is hearsay only: all he is sure of, from an examination of Constantine's correspondence, is that Arius bound himself by an oath. The emperor ordered Alexander to admit the penitent heresiarch to communion.

Arius may have been genuinely repentant; but it sounds as though he was, rather, struggling to find a peaceful compromise. He may, like Thomas Cranmer in his miserable last days, have thought that the humiliation of a doubtfully honest recantation was a necessary price to pay for dying in communion with the church of his baptism; or he may have been the fraud and perjurer Athanasius believed him to be. The former alternative is perhaps the more plausible as well as the more generous judgment. Whatever the truth of this, the story immediately disappears into the sphere of melodramatic semi-fiction. According to Athanasius,[249] it was a Saturday when the emperor ordered Alexander to admit Arius (at the liturgy on the following day). Faced with this ultimatum, Alexander (accompanied by Athanasius' friend, the presbyter Macarius) withdrew to the episcopal church (Hagia Eirene) and prayed that either he or Arius might die before morning. Arius meanwhile, smitten by 'the necessities of nature', retired to a public lavatory, and died, apparently from some kind of internal haemorrhage or rupture.[250] The emperor and the city were duly shocked and edified.

This story is not without its difficulties. On the one hand, Athanasius relies on the presence of an eye-witness; on the other, in his letter to Serapion on Arius' death (written around 340),[251] he admits that some considerable uncertainty prevails as to whether or not Arius died in Catholic communion – an admission rather hard to square with the extremely public and dramatic events which he goes on to relate. Socrates, as we have noted, alludes to letters of Constantine on the subject, and it seems likely enough that the emperor did indeed regard Arius' sudden death as a judgment; but Sozomen (relying probably on the Arian Sabinus at this point)[252] reports that opinions varied and that some even believed Arius to have been killed 'by magical arts'. Athanasius himself says[253] that Arius was buried by Eusebius of Nicomedia and his colleagues – which does not suggest that he was universally looked on as an impenitent heretic cut off in his perjury.[254] On balance, we have no reason to doubt that Arius' death was embarrassingly sudden, and that the Nicene party were able to ascribe it to the effect of their fervent intercession; but whether it occurred with quite the convenient timing (and in quite the symbolically appropriate manner) described by Athanasius must be less certain. There must have been sufficient of an interval after the interview with Constantine for the story that he *had* been received by Alexander to circulate with some plausibility.

Conclusion

Arius' death, like most of his life, is surrounded by uncertainties, and is yet at the same time an unmercifully public affair. His life and death were not easy material for a conventional hagiography, and (if we can judge by Philostorgius) he was never unequivocally a hero for the parties associated with his name. However, this is not so puzzling a fact as the modern student is inclined to make it. 'Arianism' as a coherent system, founded by a single great figure and sustained by his disciples, is a fantasy – more exactly, a fantasy based on the polemic of Nicene writers, above all Athanasius. Some anti-Nicenes may, in the early days, have been happy with the name of 'Arians',[1] as a designation of their theological preferences – not their ecclesiastical allegiance; but it is most unlikely that they would have been content with such a name for long after Nicaea. 'Arianism' was neither a church nor a 'connection', in its own eyes. 'Arians' thought of themselves, naturally enough, as Catholics; or, more accurately, the very wide spectrum of non-Nicene believers thought of themselves as mainstream Christians, and regarded Athanasius and his allies as isolated extremists[2] – though increasingly they also looked on the more aggressive anti-Nicenes (Aetius, Eunomius, and the like) as no less alien to the mainstream of Catholic tradition. It was not just ecclesiastical protocol which made the bishops at Antioch in 341 declare, by way of preface to a non-Nicene confession of faith, that they were not 'followers of Arius; for how could we as bishops be followers of a presbyter?'[3] They meant exactly what they went on to say, that they had accepted Arius as orthodox, but did not look on him as a factional leader, or ascribe any individual authority to him. It is because this is the case that Athanasius' controversial energies, especially in *de synodis*[4] and (as Kannengiesser has recently and expertly shown)[5] *contra Arianos* I and II, are dedicated to building up the picture of his enemies as uniformly committed, explicitly or implicitly, to a specific set of doctrines advanced by Arius and a small group of confederates like Eusebius of Nicomedia and Asterius the Sophist.

Nicene apologists thus turn 'Arianism' into a self-conscious sect – as if the boundaries of Catholic identity were firmly and clearly drawn in advance. But the whole history of Arius and of Arianism reminds us that this was not so, and, indeed, that the fact that it was not so was one of the major elements in the controversy. Of course, the Christian Church had become fairly well-accustomed in the second century to reflecting upon its identity and its boundaries; yet the conventions then established were not universally or unambiguously fixed. Against the gnostics, 'Catholic' critics maintained their commitment to a church in which authenticity and acceptability of teaching could be measured by some *publicly* available standard. Ignatius, Irenaeus, Tertullian and others fix this standard (with varying emphases) in terms of a determinate number of sacred texts as interpreted within those churches which can demonstrate continuity of teaching with the first apostles of Christ – a continuity normally focused in the unbroken succession of presiding teachers from the apostles.[6] However, the career of Origen throws into sharp relief many of the loose ends left by the controversy with gnosticism. Normally the authoritative teacher is the bishop, even for Origen;[7] but there is no clear way of resolving the tensions set up when a bishop's ruling works against a teacher who believes himself to be (and is believed by others to be) a faithful exegete of the sacred text in the Catholic Church. Origen touches on the question in a famous passage from his second homily on Numbers:[8] *ordo* in the Church is above all a spiritual issue; there must be a true correspondence between institutional authority and spiritual stature. The truly spiritual person, 'free enough from worldly habits to search out all things and to be judged by no one', may sometimes occupy a lower clerical rank, while the selfish and stupid occupy the *cathedra doctoris* (which may mean either presbyteral or episcopal office, or, less probably, that of a licensed catechist).[9] The implication is clear enough: like the apostle, the inspired teacher is entitled to rely on his own (scripturally grounded) authority when confronted with an unspiritual cleric seeking to decide for him what he shall do or say.

As von Campenhausen observes,[10] this is a 'pietist' critique of episcopal authority, not a wholesale denial of it; we do not end up with a non-hierarchical Church, but with a dual system of hierarchy.[11] Episcopal authority had emerged originally as something closely bound up with the role of charismatic teacher,[12] and it presented considerable difficulties when apparently divorced from charism or sanctity. The relevance of this for practical problems about penitential discipline is obvious: here are the roots of Cyprian's struggle with the *confessores* who had so dramatically acquired the repute of holiness. After all, it was in the matter of penitential discipline that the early Church was most directly challenged to define its boundaries and determine its identity. The basic paradox remained a sharp one: how could a person who did not embody (and so, in a sense, classically *express* or *articulate*) the identity of the Christian community as a community of inspiration and holiness presume to *define* that identity in an active and juridical manner? Episcopal authority as a disciplinary office was fraught with these tensions.

Yet it is clear that episcopal authority even as a teaching office was equally problematic. Catholic apologetic in the second century is not concerned with the individual bishop's *positive* teaching so much as with the fact that he is 'structurally' safeguarded from error as president of a self-continuous body with readily-available doctrinal norms.[13] What then of the case of a bishop whose 'structural' credentials are in peccable offering controversial or offensive readings of the scriptural text which is the field in which he is called to exercise his authoritative charism? As Cyprian suggested,[14] he is, in the first place, answerable to the judgment of his fellow bishops; but, in circumstances in which he attempts to require conformity to his dubious teaching from his own church, the question of what right that church might have to resist his teaching is not readily decidable in institutional terms. A church accustomed to the 'dual hierarchy' notion might well expect to raise up individual teachers convinced of their right and *obligation* to resist an heretical bishop; and the long-range recourse of such dissenters would be appeal to a wider consensus of 'true teachers', episcopal and otherwise.

In the Alexandrian church, we have to do not only with an environment in which this sort of response would be predictable, but also (as noted above) with one in which 'monarchical' episcopal authority over against the presbyteral college was ill-defined. The presbyter licensed to expound Scripture in virtue of his ordination and commission to a specific congregation was exercising an authority significantly like that of a bishop;[15] and as a membe: of the group which (it seems) corporately consecrated the bishop,[16] he would not have seen this authority as *dependent* upon that of the bishop. In other words, ecclesial practice in Alexandria reinforced the traditional Origenian view of parallel hierarchies. And when Arius resists Alexander's attempt to make the presbyters answerable to the bishop for the doctrinal probity of their preaching, he turns to those in and beyond Egypt who understand the tradition in which he is working. He is supported by his immediate colleagues, and perhaps by the head of the *didaskaleion*, by Eusebius of Caesarea, a man deeply committed to the ideal of 'school' tradition looking to a charismatic master, and by Eusebius of Nicomedia as a 'Lucianist', and so again a 'school' theologian. His first episcopal allies are men who have had the experience of learning from the wise and inspired; and the *Thalia* is addressed implicitly to all who share such an experience:

> According to the faith of God's chosen, those with discernment of God,/His holy children, imparting the truth and open to God's holy spirit,/These are the things I have learned from the men who partake of wisdom,/The keen-minded men, instructed by God, and in all respects wise./In such men's steps I have walked, advancing in thoughts like theirs,/A man much spoken of, who suffers all manner of things for God's glory,/And, learning from God, I am now no stranger to wisdom and knowledge.[17]

Arius had learned from the *theodidaktoi*, as others have learned from Pamphilus or Lucian, and he makes an implicit claim to be himself a teacher in this kind of succession. Part of his tragedy is that (even among his allies) the tradition of such school-centred Christianity is a dying one. *De facto*, the controversy becomes a matter of episcopal politics. Arius was an anachronism, asking that the Constantinian Church resolve its problems as if it were the federation of study-circles presupposed by the profoundly traditional Alexandrian language of the *Thalia*.[18] Of course Arius – like Origen – addressed himself to a wider Christian public, and, if we are to believe Philostorgius,[19] was a skilful popular propagandist; but the *Thalia* prologue shows very clearly where he believed the pulse of Christian life to be. He asks to be judged by those whose spiritual experience corresponds to his own, and who understand the proper liberty of speculation that belongs to the *theodidaktos*.

Whether this would ever have been a realistic request is doubtful. A theologian like Origen might receive international acclaim and recognition of his teaching authority,[20] but this did not prevent his ordination from being declared invalid in Alexandria by his relentlessly hostile bishop Demetrius.[21] The difference between the cases of Origen and Arius is that, whereas in the early- to mid-third century[22] it was possible to live with unresolved disciplinary or canonical disagreements,[23] by the second decade of the fourth century the visible harmony and uniformity of the church had become, as observed above, a question of public and legal interest. It was a development which both sides in the controversy were eager to exploit in their own interest. Arius had asked for recognition from other churches and for pressure to be applied to his own church so that his deposition might be reversed; but whoever first encouraged Constantine to take an interest in the debate must have had some idea of repeating the successful activation of secular power against heresy that had occurred in the case of Paul of Samosata,[24] this time with a greatly increased advance likelihood of success. Catholic unity could at least be enforced by law, the law of a (more or less) Christian ruler.

Thus the history of Arius illuminates from one specific perspective the great shift in Christian self-understanding which we associate with the age of Constantine. We are witnessing a new development in Christian reflection on the boundaries and the definition of the Church. Pre-Nicene Christianity had been obliged to live with a certain degree of organizational mess because of its chronic inability to sort out a single policy for resolving conflicts between institutional authority of a clearly public kind and personal authority, acquired by a particular kind of experience (suffering in persecution, study with a saintly teacher)[25] and exercised in a direct and individual way within a group of adherents. Episcopal authority itself had its roots precisely in the *experience* of tradition, the continuity of teaching; yet it was one step removed from the authority of the *theodidaktos* in that it operated fairly strictly within the sacramental context. That is to say, it represented a focus of unity in a common *practice* of worship, centring upon the presence of the symbolic token of continuity and self-identity, the apostolically-validated bishop,[26] rather than a focus in the *personality* of the teacher or the distinctive *ideas* of a school. If we call these two approaches the 'Catholic' and the 'Academic' (in the classical sense)[27] respectively, it seems that Arius, like his great Alexandrian predecessors, is essentially an 'Academic'; and, like those predecessors, he might have survived tolerably well in a different ecclesiastical and political climate. However, both his friends and his enemies pressed for a 'Catholic' solution to the problem, a solution in terms of episcopally agreed rulings about the limits of admission to communion. The early years of the controversy show the impossibility of this kind of resolution through the mechanism of local synods; imperial authority intervenes to make possible a universal, 'ecumenical' solution, in accord with Constantine's own goal of homogenizing his potentially chaotic empire.

By this means, the 'Catholic' model of the Church comes to be allied with the idea of a monolithic social unit and the policy of religious coercion. Initially it had served to guard the church against the fissiparous tendencies of a 'school' Christianity, to keep the criteria of Christian identity a matter of public visibility rather than privately 'inspired' decisions taken in the intense atmosphere of the group of pupils around a charismatic master. Its credibility had depended a good deal upon its own incorporation of the appeal to a tradition of teaching and its exercise of a teaching ministry. As such, it could serve as a precarious but fairly acceptable means of holding diverse 'Academic' groups in loose unity, as well as affirming that being Christian was not exclusively a matter of belonging in a philosophical study circle. But in the larger cities of the empire, bishops were increasingly detached from the context of teaching, increasingly engaged in administering charities, building and maintaining churches, negotiating disciplinary issues with their colleagues:[28] in Rome, Carthage and Alexandria in the third century, bishops were vulnerable to the protests of the charismatic 'parallel' hierarchy of teachers and confessors, protests based on the fact that the bishop himself could no longer credibly be presented as a *theodidaktos* simply in virtue of his office in the Church. He was liable to make disastrous judgments about discipline, blurring the moral boundaries of the Church and compromising its purity, liable to excuse flight in persecution, liable to introduce false teaching or suppress true, acting out of envy for the God-instructed élite. Callistus, Cyprian and Demetrius were bishops who carried little conviction with their 'Academic' and ascetical brethren; and Eusebius' contemptuous portrait of Paul of Samosata[29] depicts the nemesis of a certain sort of episcopacy from the standpoint of a scholar heavily committed to 'Catholic' continuities, yet formed in a 'school' environment, a man who believed in the proper unity of the two models. He could take up the cause of Arius precisely because of his belief that bishops were in certain circumstances answerable to the judgment of charismatic teachers when they failed to act themselves as *theodidaktoi*.

How is this to be harmonized with the appeal to secular authority to resolve disputes over the things of God? The fact of central importance in understanding this is that Eusebius Pamphilus and many others did not regard Constantine's authority as secular. On the contrary, the emperor was a God-inspired man, a true philosopher,[30] a teacher who directs his flock to heaven, and causes 'schools of holy learning'[31] to be set up. Church conflict is resolved by the virtual redefinition of the empire itself as a 'school' gathered around a charismatic royal teacher. No longer does the Church have to define itself as a pure and self-continuous community over against the world; the whole *oikoumenē* now has its 'bishop' and pastor.[32] As the visionary caught up in the contemplation of the Logos,[33] the emperor has the right, like any authoritative teacher, to examine and criticize and, where necessary, discipline or expel his pupils – language and ideas clearly visible in, for example, Constantine's correspondence with Arius.[34]

Thus the paradox of the early fourth-century Church is that the tension between 'Catholic' and 'Academic' in the church's life, a tension sharply highlighted by the Arian struggle, was dealt with, at least in some quarters, by a 'Catholic' polity (one centring upon episcopally administered sacramental discipline, using the sanction of excommunication from the church at large) enforced by a lay authority conceived in quasi-Academic terms (using the sanction of exclusion from the group of intimates, reinterpreted as legal exile and banishment from the imperial presence).[35] In theoretical terms, this rapidly proved to be no solution at all: imperial inspiration was as blatant a case of institutionalized charisma as episcopal authority had been, and conflict was as sharp as ever. None the less, one of the effects of the breakdown of Eusebius' synthesis was to reinforce episcopal authority within the Church: an Athanasius, resisting the (in his eyes) fatuous religious claims of a Constantius, could be presented as an inspired leader of God-directed spiritual discernment. The Catholic (Nicene) bishop, indifferent to the threats and blandishments of unspiritual authority, confident in his apostolic legitimacy and his obedience to the holy and inspired universal synod of 325,[36] could retrieve a good deal of the aura of the *theodidaktos* teacher. It was Catholic prelates like Basil of Caesarea and Gregory of Nyssa[37] who promoted again the language of Christian teaching and Christian (specifically ascetic) life as 'true philosophy' – a language originally at home in the 'Academic' world of Justin, Clement, Origen and Eusebius.

Part of what made this possible was another significant new fact. The 'school' tradition of Origen and Arius was increasingly at odds with the trend of urban Church life in the Levant by the end of the third century, and it does not seem to have possessed the inner resources to survive in its classical form. Origen's status had a lot to do with his deserved reputation as a master of the life of prayer; to belong to a school with such a master was to learn a whole form of life, a set of disciplines, imaginative and physical, disposing the human being for the discovery of the Logos and union through the Logos with its ground and source.[38] Yet Lucian of Antioch, remembered as an exegete of colossal stature, does not seem to have been remembered as a master of the spiritual life;[39] and Arius likewise, despite his impeccable credentials as an ascetic and his great popularity with ascetics,[40] is presented to us as primarily a teacher of ideas and an interpreter of Scripture. That aspect of the Origenian tradition which conceived the 'school' as a community of religious discipline was to reappear initially in circles very far from those in which Origen himself had been at home. The monastic movement had its roots in the Egyptian peasantry, and Antony the Great is unlikely to have been familiar with Origenized Platonism. Yet his biographer (if not Athanasius himself, certainly a committed Athanasian)[41] depicts him as confidently employing the *lingua franca* of late classical philosophy and refuting both Arians[42] and non-Christian philosophers with ease and fluency.[43] His is the true philosophical life. Much has been written about the similarities between the *Vita Antonii* and the conventions of the classical sage's biography;[44] but perhaps what is most significant is the implicit alliance between this new 'philosophy' and the interests of the Catholic episcopate.[45] Very generally speaking, Arianism failed to capture the ascetic movements of the fourth century;[46] and in this respect, what was left of the 'school' tradition out of which Arianism had first come regained its vigour in a firmly Catholic and monastic setting.

The strengthening of the bonds between the monastic world and the eastern episcopate in the fourth and early fifth centuries has been well chronicled and discussed.[47] There were certainly interruptions in this harmony, notably the Origenist and the Pelagian crises; but these were not so much divisions between bishops and monks as disagreements within the ascetic movement itself. On the whole, monasticism performed the important job of restoring the charismatic spiritual authority of bishops, and, for a time, effectively reunited catholic and charismatic approaches to Church life, providing an interior foundation for the courageous resistance to imperial pressure of Athanasius, Basil, and a good many more. Yet the 'monasticizing' of bishops could lead to the politicizing of monasticism, the deployment of monastic shock troops in episcopal controversies (as encouraged and orchestrated by the fifth-century bishops of Alexandria); there seems no final escape from the manifold ambiguities surrounding the exercise of power in the Christian Church.

The career of Arius, a meeting-point for some very diverse currents in the story of the Church, rightly compels us to attend (theologically as well as historically) to these issues of limits and power in the religious group. Relative pluralism, with a regular ritual focus, and an agreed set of texts as a basis for teaching and exploration, was appropriate to a Church which lacked any notion of itself as a single *institutional* unit, and whose communications were necessarily private and piecemeal. Before Constantine, the Church was simply not in a position to make universally binding and enforceable decisions. From Nicaea onwards the Church decided, and communicated its decisions, through the official network of the empire; it had become visible to *itself*, as well as to the world, in a new way. And to those concerned with enforcing agreed decisions, whether for the sake of the empire's unity like Constantine or for the sake of theological integrity like Athanasius (and perhaps Eusebius of Nicomedia), the independent and actually or potentially recalcitrant 'school' group was inevitably redefined not merely as a sect, but as a body outside the framework of civilized society. The Church's new 'visibility' meant that the wrong sort of Christian group was regarded pretty much as the Church itself had been regarded by the pagan empire, as something subversive of the sacred character of social life.

The Constantinian synthesis was in the long run destructive of both the 'Catholic' and the 'Academic' senses of the Church in most of the Christian world; as the existence of the monastic movement already implied, the tension between institutional unity and 'open' (i.e. publicly transmitted) tradition (with its risks of authoritarianism and formalism) on the one hand, and holiness, purity, and highly personalized guidance (with its risks of élitism and introversion) on the other was not to be wiped out by the Church's metamorphosis into the guardian of legally sanctioned ideology. In what we have come to call the 'post-Constantinian' era, this tension is no longer avoidable; and we may perhaps learn from the story of the early Church that we are wrong to expect it to be resolved in terms of the *victory* of one model. Recent patristic scholarship[48] has been much preoccupied with the relation of gnosticism to 'episcopal' Christianity, and eager to point to the non-theological motives (especially to do with power) in the Catholic repudiation of gnostic groups. It is part of a general, and not unhealthy, suspicion of history written by the winners, the 'government line'. But this reaction can fall into the opposite trap of supposing the apparently suppressed style of Church existence to be the lost ideal – a modern version of the long-standing tendency to rely on a 'myth of Christian beginnings'.[49] The historian may happily bypass much of this, observing only the paradigmatic character of certain crises like the one we have been examining in this part. The theologian who continues to locate her- or himself in the active history of Christian speech and imagination has a longer job, and has also a responsibility to do more than idealize lost patterns of life. We are not exempt from the task of examining and *evaluating* the byways of early Christian thought and experience in the light of the point which the story has reached now. In plain terms: Arius may stand for an important dimension in Christian life that was disedifyingly and unfortunately crushed by policy or circumstance and yet may stand in other ways for a theological style doomed to spiritual sterility. Some of this sort of evaluation will be attempted later in this book. But the necessary prelude to such a discussion is to stick to the particulars of history for a little longer, and explore what can be uncovered of Arius' intellectual concerns, their background and import.

Part II

Arius and Theology

A

The Theology of Arius

We have only a handful of texts that can confidently be treated as giving us Arius' own thinking in his own words; apart from these, we are wholly dependent upon the reports of his enemies. And, as intimated in Part I, such reports, especially in the writings of Athanasius, have to be handled with caution – not total scepticism, indeed, but with the recognition that, divorced from their own original literary context, they are, in the works in which they are now found, very far from presenting to us the systematic thought of Arius as he himself saw it. In other words, we can never be sure that the theological *priorities* ascribed to Arius by his opponents were his own, even if his *statements* are transmitted correctly. On the other hand, we should be equally cautious about totally rejecting those allusions to Arius' theology which correspond to nothing in his own undoubted works – simply because the latter are so limited and fragmentary. All this is an unsatisfactory basis for studying Arius' thought, but, short of dramatic new documentary discoveries, it is the only basis we are likely to have. As Kannengiesser justly observes,[1] we can only rely on refinements of interpretative technique and literary criticism to advance our understanding, and our conclusions are accordingly provisional and partial.

The complete texts that can be ascribed more or less directly to Arius are only three in number: in the chronological order proposed in Part I, they are (i) the confession of faith presented to Alexander of Alexandria (Opitz, 6), signed by Arius and eleven supporters (excluding the two bishops, whose signatures are of doubtful authenticity), (ii) Arius' letter to Eusebius of Nicomedia, (iii) the confession submitted by Arius and Euzoius to the emperor in 327, or just possibly, 335. Although the fragments of the *Thalia* are in some respects our most important evidence for constructing a 'profile' of Arius as an independent thinker, we shall begin by looking at these slightly less distinctive texts, so as to understand first how Arius presented himself to different kinds of 'public' (with decidedly different degrees of sympathy!).

The two statements of faith differ notably in style. The letter to Alexander is elaborate, even diffuse, a statement which explicitly claims to be within a tradition shared with its recipient and potential audience. This claim is strongly reinforced when the letter is compared with the synodal creed of the Antiochene Council of 325:[2] both begin with a list of divine predicates, strongly emphasizing God's transcendence and inaccessibility, but also his providential goverance of the universe; both describe God as Lord of 'the Law, the Prophets and the New Covenant'.[3] The Christological sections (understandably) diverge sharply for the most part, yet coincide in a number of positive points: the Son of God exists *alēthōs* (though Antioch slants this to mean also that he is called 'Son' *alēthōs*),[4] and is, like the Father, 'unchangeable, inalienable' (*atreptos* and *analloiōtos*), yet not *agennētos*.[5] Other parallels are sparse; and it is noticeable that Arius refers more to the tradition of teaching of the Church, Antioch more to the Scriptures – probably for tactical reasons in both cases. Arius is defending his status as a teacher in the Church, who has 'learned' not only from teachers of the past but from the bishop[6] – a polite concession to Alexander's view of episcopal authority. Antioch is opposing a group who insist on the scriptural logic of their position. All in all, however, it is very plain that a common set of conventions underlies both documents; and Luise Abramowski, in her pioneering study of these texts, is probably correct in locating them within a broadly 'Origenian' framework and relating them to the theology expressed in the confession of faith ascribed to Origen's pupil, Gregory Thaumaturgus.[7]

In contrast, the creed submitted to Constantine, though not wholly unrelated to this framework, is bald and brief. The Son is said to be 'produced' by the Father (*gegenēmenon* or *gegennēmenon*? probably the latter, as it would have been acceptable to Arius *and* his opponents; but the distinction is still only loosely drawn)[8] 'before all ages', and all things are said to be made through him. Arius and Euzoius affirm that the trinitarian faith rests on Scripture (the dominical command to baptize in the name of Father, Son and Spirit, Matt. 28:19), and that they wish nothing more than to be in all respects loyal to Scripture and the faith of the Catholic Church, avoiding 'unnecessary issues and disputations'.[9] This confession is almost entirely colourless in terms of the debates that had divided eastern Christianity in the century or so leading up to it; its vocabulary is strikingly un-Alexandrian, and it has only a few phrases in common with the creed proposed at Nicaea by Eusebius Pamphilus. It has some points of contact, though there are significant divergences even here, with the second creed of the Dedication Council at Antioch in 341 – the text alleged to have originated with the martyr Lucian. Of this latter creed, more will be said later.[10] In any event, the document presented to Constantine tells us almost nothing about the distinctive views of Arius, except perhaps for reminding us of his strong commitment to belief in three distinct divine hypostases, existing *alēthōs*.[11] Parts of the text, especially the final section, may well derive from a formula of more western type, encountered by Arius in his Illyrian exile.

As for the letter to Eusebius, this is largely couched in negative terms, as a repudiation of Alexander's views, and those of Alexander's allies in Palestine and Syria. It is inadmissible to say that God and his Son 'co-exist':[12] God must *pre*-exist[13] the Son. If not, we are faced with a whole range of unacceptable ideas – that the Son is part of God, or an emanation of God, or, worst of all, that he is, like God, self-subsistent.[14] The Son exists by God's free will, brought into existence by him before all times and ages and existing stably and 'inalienably'.[15] The logic of this position – which quite eludes Alexander – is simple: God alone is *anarchos*, and the Son has an *archē*.[16] Since the Son is what he is, the firstborn and only-begotten, he cannot be made out of anything else (nothing but God pre-exists him); but he is not a portion of God, who is a simple, spiritual reality; and thus he must be made, like all creation, out of nothing.[17]

The letter concludes with the well-known apostrophe to Eusebius as *sulloukianista*, 'fellow-Lucianist', a word whose precise meaning we have already seen to be unclear.[18] What *is* clear is that the document represents a basis upon which Lucianists might be expected to unite. Just as the letter to Alexander states Arius' common ground with a certain kind of Origenian theology, this text defines what is or might be shared with Lucian's pupils. Thus, once again, neither text in isolation tells us everything about Arius' distinctive theological characteristics; yet, as we compare these letters with what we know from other sources of both schools of thought appealed to by the heresiarch, the contours of Arius' own reflection appear more sharply. First, however, we shall attempt to sketch the twofold consensus on which he relies.

(i) God alone is self-subsistent, *agennētos;*[19] he is immaterial, and thus without any kind of plurality or composition; he is subject to no natural processes, no emanation or diffusion of his substance.[20]

(ii) He is entirely free, rational and purposive.[21]

(iii) He initiates the creative process by freely bringing the Son into being, as a subsistent individual truly (*alēthōs*) distinct from himself;[22] he does this 'before all ages',[23] yet there is a sense in which the Father exists prior to the Son, since the Son is not eternal, that is, not timelessly self-subsistent.[24]

(iv) By the will of God, the Son is stably and unalterably what he is, a perfect creature, not just 'one among others';[25] he is the 'inheritor' of all the gifts and glories God can give him, but, since this is the effect of God's sovereign will, the Father's glory and dignity is in no way lessened by such a gift.[26]

(v) Although the role of the Holy Spirit is not spelt out, the Catholic faith is defined as belief in three divine subsistents (*hupostaseis*).[27]

It should be clear from this catalogue that God's freedom of will is a theme of central importance in such a theology. Anything which could possibly compromise it is carefully and explicitly excluded. God is the *sole* source of all, and has none beside him,[28] so that his will is uniquely sovereign; his will is not to be restricted by anything that smacks of material or temporal limitation, or by any natural 'inner dynamism' compelling God to go forth in creation beyond his own perfection. Yet he is a loving and self-revealing God, made known in the scriptural history and caring for what he has made;[29] his freedom and sovereignty are exercised in *grace*, the grace first given to the first of creatures, his only and beloved Son.[30]

Turning from these documents to the *Thalia* extracts, a rather more complex set of issues arises. Athanasius twice presents us with fairly long reports of the contents of this work, in *contra Arianos* I.5 and 6 and *de synodis* 15; but it is not clear how exactly these passages are related to each other. The *contra Arianos* text (A) begins with seven metrical lines, designed to illustrate the frivolity of a man who could write of theology in a metre associated with lascivious

98

comedy,[31] and then proceeds to give a list of theological propositions, sometimes introduced with 'he says', or 'he presumed to say', or some similar form of words. These propositions cannot, for the most part, be construed as metrical – which could mean either that the *Thalia* was a mixture of prose and verse or that Athanasius is paraphrasing. The sequence is briefly interrupted with a reference to 'other works' by Arius' supporters, alluding to an argument which we know from elsewhere[32] to derive from the writings of Asterius. In contrast, the *de synodis* version (S) is entirely metrical, though not very regularly so, and corresponds in metre with the extract with which A opens;[33] it reads continuously, without interjection or comment by Athanasius; and in style and vocabulary it is highly distinctive,[34] 'elevated', rhetorical, almost incantatory. Like the extracts of A, it does not purport to be a complete text,[35] but it is presumably meant to be as representative as possible of the distinctive tenets of its author. It is impossible to determine whether it read continuously in its original context: there are several apparent breaks or changes of direction in the argument, suggesting that there may be substantial omissions; but bearing in mind the often diffuse and recapitulatory style customarily used by polemicists of the period, we cannot be dogmatic about this.

Taken all in all, A is difficult to treat as reliable quotation[36] (apart from the opening lines), though we should not exaggerate the degree of possible distortion. And S, despite what we have noted in Part I about its linguistic and theological peculiarities and the doubts lately raised as to its authenticity, still has a good claim to be treated as direct quotation. The theology of the *Thalia* is *not* completely obscure to us. If my earlier suggestions are correct,[37] we are still dealing with something in the nature of an apologia, but one in which Arius has been given the opportunity to expound what really are his own individual insights at reasonable length, and with some degree of confidence. We should expect the *Thalia*, then, to take us a little further towards the core of Arius' theology than the remains of his 'diplomatic' correspondence. Before further discussion, however, it may be as well to set out these texts *in extenso*, as we shall be examining their contents and relationships in some detail.

A

(For the opening lines, see p. 85 supra. The numbering of points in what follows is my own.)

[The ridiculous witticisms he hammers out in this work, witticisms that ought to be shunned by all, full of irreverence as they are, are things like these:]

(i) God was not eternally a father. There was [a time] when God was all alone, and was not yet a father; only later did he become a father.

(ii) The Son did not always exist. Everything created is out of nothing (*ex ouk ontōn*), all existing creatures, all things that are made; so the Word of God himself came into existence out of nothing. There was [a time] when he did not exist (*ēn pote hote ouk ēn*); before he was brought into being, he did not exist. He too had a beginning to his created existence.

(iii) For – so he says – God used to be on his own (*monos*), and his Word and Wisdom did not yet exist. But then God wanted to make us; and only then did he make some kind of being (*hena tina*) that he dubbed Word, Wisdom and Son, so that through him he might make us.

(iv) So: there are two 'Wisdoms', he says, one that is proper to God and exists together with him (*idian kai sunuparchousan*), and [the other] the Son who has been brought into being in this Wisdom; only by participating in this Wisdom is the Son called Wisdom and Word. 'Wisdom', he says, 'came into existence through Wisdom, by the will of the God who is wise'.[38] Likewise he says that there is another Word in God besides the Son, and the Son, participating in this Word is, once again, called Word and Son by grace-and-favour . . . [The reference to Asterius follows]

(v) . . . Like all others, the Word himself also is subject to change (*treptos*); he goes on being good as long as he wants to, by his own free will. And then, when he wants to, he too, just like us, is able to change his ways, because he is changeable by nature. For it is because of this, he says, that God, knowing in advance that he would be good, gave him this glory of his in anticipation, the glory he afterwards had as a human being on account of his virtue. So it was because of his actions, which were known in advance to God, that God made him become the kind of being he in fact is.

(vi) Again, he has presumed to say that the Word is not true God (*theos alēthinos*). He may be called 'God' but he is not '*true* God'. It is only by participating in grace, like all others, that he too is called by the name 'God'. All beings are, in respect of their substance (*kat' ousian*), alien to God and unlike him (*xenōn kai anomoiōn*); and so too the Word is entirely different from and unlike the Father's substance and property (*idiotētos*). He is 'proper' to (*idios*) [the class of] made and created things and it is to this that he belongs.

(vii) On top of all this, as if he had become a pupil (*diadochos*) of the devil himself in recklessness, he stated in the *Thalia* that the Father is thus invisible to the Son, and that the Word can neither see nor know his own Father clearly and exactly (*akribōs*), but what he knows and what he sees he knows and sees in proportion to (*analogōs*) the measure of his own capacities – just as we know according to our own proper capacity (*kata tēn idian dunamin*). For not only (he says) does the Son not know the Father clearly and exactly, since he lacks comprehension (*katalabein*), but also the Son himself does not know his own substance (*tēn heautou ousian*).

(viii) [And he says that] the substances (*ousiai*) of Father, Son and Holy Spirit are separate in nature, alienated and cut off from each other, foreign to each other and having no participation (*ametochoi*) with each other. As he himself put it, 'they are in substance and in splendour wholly unlike each other, infinitely (*ep' apeiron*) unlike.' So, as regards likeness of glory and of substance, the Word, he says, is quite other than the Father and the Holy Spirit. In words such as these did that godless man express himself. He claimed that the Son is a distinct being in himself and has no kind of participation in the Father.

S[39]

1   . . . So God himself (*katho estin*) is inexpressible (*arrētos*) to all beings.

He alone has none equal to him or like him, none of like glory. We call him unbegotten (*agennēton*) on account of the one who by nature is begotten;

We sing his praises as without beginning because of the one who has a beginning.

5　We worship him as eternal because of him who was born in the order of time (*en chronois*).

The one without beginning established the Son as the beginning of all creatures (*archēn . . . tōn genētōn*),

And, having fathered (*teknopoiēsas*) such a one, he bore him as a son for himself.[40]

He [the Son] possesses nothing proper to God, in the real sense of propriety (*kath' hupostasin idiotētos*),

For he is not equal to God, nor yet is he of the same substance (*homoousios*).

10　God is wise in the sense that he is the teacher of wisdom (*sophias didaskalos*).

A full demonstration that God is invisible (*aoratos*) to all,

Invisible to what is made through the Son, invisible to the Son himself:

I shall say in plain words how the Invisible is seen by the Son –

It is in [or by] the power by which God himself can see, [but] in his own degree,[41]

15　That the Son endures the vision of the Father, as far as is lawful [. . . ?]

Or again: there exists a trinity (*trias*) in unequal glories, for their subsistences (*hupostaseis*) are not mixed with each other. In their glories, one is more glorious than another in infinite degree (*ep' apeiron*).

The Father is other than the Son in substance (*kat' ousian*), because he is without beginning.

You should understand (*sunes*) that the Monad [always] was, but the Dyad was not before it came to be.

20　At once, then, [you see that] the Father is God [even] when the Son does not exist.

So the Son, not existing [eternally] (*ouk ōn*) (since he came into being by the Father's will),

Is God the Only-Begotten, and he [lit.: this one – the Holy Spirit?] is different from both.[42]

'Wisdom' came into existence through Wisdom, by the will of the God who is wise,[43]

And so it is thought of (*epinoeitai*) in countless manifestations
(*epinoiais*), spirit, power and wisdom,

25   God's glory, truth, image, Word.

You should understand (*sunes*) that he is thought of too as
radiance and as light

The Higher One (*ho kreittōn*) is able to beget an equal to the
Son,

But not one more renowned, higher or greater than he.

By God's will (*theou thelēsei*) the Son is such as he is, by God's
will he is as great as he is,

30   From [the time] when, since the very moment when, he took
his subsistence from God (*ek tou theou hupestē*);

Mighty God as he is, he sings the praises of the Higher One
with only partial adequacy (*ek merous*).

To put it briefly: God is inexpressible (*arrētos*) to the Son,

For he is what he is for [or to, or in] himself, and that is
unutterable (*alektos*),

So that the Son does not have the understanding (*suniei*)
that would enable him to give voice to any words expressing
comprehension (*tōn legomenōn kata te katalēpsin*).

35   For him it is impossible to search out the mysteries of the
Father, who exists in himself (*eph' heautou*);

For the Son does not [even] know his own substance,

Since, being a son, he came into actual subsistence (*hupērxen
alethōs*) by a father's will (*thelēsei patros*).

What scheme of thought (*logos*), then, could admit the idea
that he who has his being from the [a?] Father (*ton ek patros
onta*)

Should know by comprehension (*en katalēpsei*) the one who
gave him birth?

40/   For clearly the one who has a beginning (*to archēn echon*) is in

41   no way [in a position] to encompass in thought or lay hold
upon the one without beginning as he is [in himself] (*hōs
estin*).

The differences in *tone* between these two versions is especially
striking. Athanasius' brief sentences, underlining the negative points
being made, reduce Arius' thought to the simplest of terms, spelling
it out with relentless explicitness; while the S text balances negations
with affirmations of the Son's dignity, and generally avoids the neat

103

and condensed arguments of A. Even when S apparently undertakes to set out an argument (11), what follows is still loose in form and rhetorical in style. A gives the impression at several points of elaborating a remark so as to bring out unacceptable implications or rephrase it in less emollient terms. Thus the 'only later' of A (i) is a fairly obvious deduction from S4, 5, 19–22, 40–41, but is expressed in such a way as to imply change in God, and to suggest that his fathering of the Son is a pretty peripheral matter. What S expresses (20) by saying that the Father's divine status is independent of the existence of the Son, A puts in terms of 'fatherhood' being incidental to the divine nature. The point may be the same, the emphasis is different. Again A (viii) piles up a series of very negative-sounding terms to describe the distinction of the divine hypostases, a distinction which is far more neutrally defined both in S (16–18) and in the purported quotation from Arius in A (viii) itself. And in A(iii), *hena tina*, 'a certain being', 'some sort of thing or other', is almost certainly a deliberately contemptuous paraphrase. A(ii), (v) and (vii) contain equally obvious glosses: the Son is repeatedly assimilated to the level of other creatures, and the phrases 'like us' and 'like all others' recur. The Arius who wrote to Alexander[44] that the Son was a 'perfect creature, yet not as one among the creatures (*hen tōn ktismatōn*), a begotten being (*gennēma*), yet not as one among things begotten (*hen tōn gegennēmenōn*)' is eager to avoid any suggestion that the Son is simply 'like all others' – though some of his supporters were less careful.[45] Athanasius is again being reductive: if a creature, then a creature in the same sense that we are creatures; what other sort of creaturehood is there? This is to be a significant aspect of the bishop's polemic elsewhere in *contra Arianos*.[46]

The theme of the Son's likeness to us relates to a further question of considerable difficulty regarding the relation of A to S, and of orthodox reports of Arius' teaching in general. A(v) has no parallel in S, nor any in Arius' letters. Yet not only A but the two encyclicals of Alexander emphasize very strongly that Arius taught a mutable Logos,[47] whose divine dignity is a reward for his unswerving spiritual fidelity; and Athanasius is obliged, in *contra Arianos*[48] to reply to Arian exegesis of a number of texts that speak of some sort of 'promotion' or apotheosis for the Saviour. S7 has traditionally been seen as a basis for this sort of accusation; but it has rightly been pointed out[49] that, although this line is none too easy to interpret, it is most unlikely to mean that God 'adopted' the Son in the sense Alexander has in mind in *hē philarchos*. It is possible to treat the whole of A(v) as a deduction by Athanasius on the basis of the Son's creatureliness: if a creature, then mutable; if mutable, then capable of moral/spiritual advance or regress. Or: if God's Son by grace not nature, them *made* to be God's Son; if made to be God's Son, then made so in the same sense that we hope to be – by an act of adoption, which we receive as a result of faithful and virtuous living.[50] However, given the attention Athanasius expends on the exegetical issues connected with this, it cannot be a problem wholly generated by anti-Arian polemic. The total lack of allusion to any sort of adoption in Arius' own undoubted works, however, must make it doubtful whether the theme was central to his concerns, as has so often been maintained. A fuller discussion will be undertaken later in this section, when we turn to the consideration of sources and influences for Arius' thought.

Comparing both A and S with Arius' letters, we may observe a great deal of overlap: God is alone *agennētos* and *anarchos*, his freedom is stressed (with four allusions in S – 11, 21, 23, 29, 37 – to the begetting of the Son at the Father's *will*), his priority to the Son and essential independence of the Son is clear, as is the Son's existence *alēthōs*, as a true, distinct hypostasis, who receives all the grace he is capable of receiving, indeed, all the grace a creature *could* receive (S28); and the Catholic faith involves belief in three hierarchically ordered divine subsistents. What is most *distinctive* in the *Thalia*, however, is the theme that dominates both A and S, the absolute unknowability of the Father. Nothing in Arius' letters directly corresponds to this, nor does anything in the fragments we possess from Arius' supporters. Eusebius of Nicomedia writing to Paulinus stresses that the mode of the Son's generation is *akataleptos*,[51] and that the Son is created in perfect likeness to the 'inalienable and unutterable'[52] nature of the Father, but this difficult text (already discussed briefly above)[53] does not affirm the *Son's* ignorance of the Father. Arius' position, however, depends upon the argument spelt out at the end of S: the Son's ignorance is a logical consequence of his createdness. The Son is dependent, and thus his mode of being is quite other than the Father's; how can he comprehend a mode of being which is not like his?

This raises the related question of what Arius meant by his denial of the Son's knowledge of *his own ousia*.[54] In the context of S, this seems once again to relate to the Son's mode of being: he is willed into existence by the Father, and cannot therefore have that 'perspective' on his own substance which his creator possesses. This may be a rather condensed way of saying that a creature cannot know itself as God knows himself, that is, eternally and necessarily: or (as I have suggested elsewhere)[55] it may be an affirmation that no creaturely self-knowledge can be knowledge of an *ousia*. We shall be returning later on to the question of Arius' relation to the traditions of Alexandrian theology and to the philosophical debates of his age, and it is in this context that I believe we can best make sense of this – at first puzzling – notion. In the context of the *Thalia*, however, the function of the doctrine seems to be to underline yet again the fact that the Son is by nature a creature, living and operating as creatures do. It is not a gratuitous derogation from the Son's dignity, but an explanation of the fact that he stands in need of grace if he is to perform the function for which God has brought him into being. It is 'by God's will [that the Son] is as great as he is' (S 29).

We are returned once more to the theme of God's gracious will. Having created the Son, he ensured the Son's closeness to himself by giving him all the glory he is able to receive *and* by bestowing upon him some sort of participation in the divine intellect. This seems the best reading of S 14,[56] and it accords with the implication of other passages: S10, for instance, suggests a contrast between the sense in which God is *sophos*, as source of wisdom, and the sense in which any creature may be so (as participating in the wisdom emanating from God); and S23 points in the same direction, on either of the possible readings of the line. Thus the Son is by God's will granted what we must presume to be a unique degree of knowledge of God: it is logically out of the question that anything that is not God should understand 'by comprehension' what it is to be God, the divine *ousia;* but this does not mean that creation is totally cut off from God, since God is a self-revealing being. 'Because of the one who has a beginning', we know and worship a creative, active, loving deity, since we see the effects of his creative love in the glory of the Son.

The incomprehensibility of God in the *Thalia* is not therefore an isolated or arbitrary dogmatic affirmation; it is a necessary consequence of God's being what he is, *uniquely* self-subsistent. And it is that very self-subsistence which renders him unconditionally free, to create and reveal as and when he wills. All that limits his self-communication and self-revelation is the irreducible difference between him and his creation; but what he *can* give, he does give. If my previous analysis of the *Thalia* as an apologia addressed to the Lucianists is correct, the purpose of this dialectic between transcendence and revelation within the Trinity itself is to persuade a rather suspicious audience that a stress upon the unknowability of God did not imply any questioning of the reality of his gracious manifestation in history. We may recall Arius' emphasis in his letter to Alexander upon the divine goodness and providence, and upon the importance of the Scriptures of old and new covenants. There were those in the fourth-century Church who associated strongly apophatic statements about the divine with gnosticism – Basilides' 'non-existent' God,[57] the Valentinian Christ exhorting the aeons to be content with such *katalēpsis* as they possessed (that is, the knowledge of God as *akatalēptos*).[58] Some of those who made this connection were to be found in 'neo-Arian' circles later in the century,[59] and their theological forebears were no doubt to be found among those whom Arius sought to win over by the *Thalia*. As in his letter to Alexander (and in the creed submitted to Constantine) Arius presents himself as essentially a *biblical* theologian. There is a good deal to be said about Arius' relationship with late classical philosophy; but we misunderstand him completely (as we misunderstsnd Origen) if we see him as primarily a self-conscious philosophical speculator.[60] Like his Alexandrian predecessors, he presses philosophy into service to establish on a firm basis what revelation teaches; and revelation, for Arius, was the revelation of a supremely free and active God. To understand his liberty, it was necessary to affirm his freedom from created intellection, his unconditioned nature, and his absolute uniqueness. Such philosophical points as Arius deploys are used precisely to safeguard this central concern.

All of which serves as a reminder that Arius was by profession an interpreter of the Scriptures, and that (according to Constantine at least)[61] the controversy began in the discussion of a disputed passage in the 'divine law'. Some[62] have taken this very much at face value, and have concluded that a disagreement about that fundamental crux, Proverbs 8:22, initiated the crisis. Perhaps such a text did indeed form the subject of a specific clash early on; but it would be a mistake to look for one particular focus. It is clear from Alexander's *hē philarchos* and from Athanasius' *contra Arianos* that Arius and his supporters were interested in a large number of texts, from Old and New Testaments alike. Those who have insisted[63] that the Arian controversy is essentially about hermeneutics are right – not least because, as Simonetti remarked,[64] the history of theology itself, particularly patristic theology, is a history of exegesis (and so its crises are crises for the *principles* of exegesis).[65]

Unfortunately, however, we have very little evidence for Arius' own exegesis (though rather more for that of some of his supporters). We cannot be completely certain that all the texts dealt with by Athanasius in the *contra Arianos* were used by Arius himself, though some of them must have been. Alexander[66] mentions that Arius *cum suis* appealed to texts (in the gospels?) which presented the incarnate Word as weak or ignorant: these no doubt included some of the passages considered in the latter part of *contra Arianos* III.[67] Likewise Alexander alludes to the Arian use of Proverbs 8:22, and Eusebius of Nicomedia's letter to Paulinus quotes it directly. Athanasius[68] has a long discussion of Psalm 45:7–8 ('You have loved righteousness and hated iniquity; therefore God, your God, has anointed you with the oil of gladness above your kindred'), and this too is mentioned by Alexander as one of the texts in dispute. One text barely touched upon in *contra Arianos*,[69] but noted briefly in *de decretis*[70] and given a position of some significance in *hē philarchos*[71] is Isaiah 1:2 ('I have begotten and raised up sons, and they have rebelled against me'); again, this appears in Eusebius' letter to Paulinus,[72] along with reference to Deuteronomy 32:18 ('You have forsaken the God who begot you') and Job 38:28 ('. . . who gave birth to the drops of dew?'). Arius himself, in his credal letter,[73] notes three ambiguous scriptural expressions: 'from him' (*ex autou*, Romans 11:36), 'from the womb' (*ek gastros*, Psalms 110:3), and 'I came out from the Father and have come' (*ek tou patros exēlthon kai hēkō*, John 8:42). The second of these was evidently in use in Alexander's circle,[74] and was perhaps used by Dionysius of Rome[75] in his correspondence with Dionysius of Alexandria (though the authenticity of this material has been called in question);[76] at any rate, it seems to have been part of a standard Old Testament catena in Alexandria. Two final examples of early Arian polemical exegesis may be added: Athanasius of Nazarba's reference[77] to the 'hundred sheep' of the parable in Luke 15:3–7, and Asterius' notorious attempt[78] to show that 'power of God' is a term of loose and general application in Scripture. However, since these are explicitly associated with specific works of specific authors, they are not likely to have been part of Arius' own repertoire of exegetical arguments.[79]

It appears probable, then, that the passages on which the theological disagreements between Arius and Alexander first focused were: Psalm 45:7–8, Proverbs 8:22, Isaiah 1:2, and a number of unspecified New Testament texts. As Simonetti has argued,[80] John 14:28 ('The Father is greater than I') is unlikely to have been among them: Alexander[81] and Athanasius[82] both use it to make an anti-Arian point (if 'greater' – not 'better' or 'higher'[83] – then not different in *kind*), and the same argument reappears in Victorinus.[84] Only later is it thought necessary to refer this saying only to the incarnate condition of the Word. The initial debate was not about the rightness or wrongness of hierarchical models of the Trinity, which were common to both sides. More plausible candidates would be some of the passages mentioned by Athanasius – Philippians 2:9–10 (in conjunction with Psalm 45:7–8),[85] Hebrews 1:4 and 3:1–2,[86] Acts 2:36,[87] Romans 8:29,[88] and perhaps the gospel texts of *contra Arianos* III – John 3:35, 10:30, 12:27, 14:10, 17:3 and 11, Matthew 11:27, 26:39, Mark 13:32, Luke 2:52 (though this is *very* doubtful), and several more referred to in passing. Taken as a whole, these citations had apparently been used by Arius and his followers to establish three basic theological points:

(i) The Son is a creature, that is, a product of God's will;
(ii) 'Son' is therefore a *metaphor* for the second hypostasis, and must be understood in the light of comparable metaphorical usage in Scripture;
(iii) The Son's status, like his very existence, depends upon God's will.

One thing which should be noted immediately is that none of this exegetical material, as described or implicitly characterized by Arius' enemies, really supports the idea that Arius was a 'literalist'.[89] It is not literalism to take the Psalms as spoken *in persona Christi* or to identify the 'Wisdom' of the Old Testament with Christ. As for the interpretation of the New Testament, we have no idea of how Arius might have treated gospel narrative or parable (though Athanasius of Nazarba was clearly no stranger to allegorical readings);[90] if he assumes that the language of Acts, Philippians or Hebrews about the exaltation of Christ means that Christ receives his glory at the Father's will, we can see quite plainly from the letters and the *Thalia* that he did *not* understand this in the crude terms of an apotheosis of the man Jesus at a point in time. Athanasius' objection to Arius' exegesis is not that it is negligent of a 'spiritual sense', that it is 'Judaizing' in character,[91] but that it is arbitrary, *kata ton idion noun:*[92] it is based on a private or individual reading of the sense (*nous*) of the text. Once again we return to the issue of authority in the Church: Arius is accused of teaching, on his own authority, an interpretation of Scripture at odds with the mind of the Church. It is not that there is an established 'ecclesiastical' reading[93] of the controversial passages that Arius deliberately spurns; Athanasius clearly has to work very hard to develop an alternative exegesis to that of his opponents. The point is, presumably, that Arius' interpretations are 'private' in so far as they undermine the actual faith and practice of the Catholic Church: Alexander[94] and Athanasius[95] both appeal to the fact that Christ is worshipped as divine, Athanasius challenges the Arians[96] to make sense of the baptismal rite on their theological presuppositions. Arius' readings are thus *de facto* divisive. *Lex orandi lex interpretandi* is Athanasius' governing rule; but Arius – once more echoing Origen – evidently believes that, so long as the fundamental *regula fidei* is not disturbed, scriptural elucidation by duly qualified teachers may provide a critique of popular religious practice, or, at least, may oblige the initiate, the mature Christian, to reinterpret such practice when he or she is involved in it.[97] The background of the exegetical debate is that tension between 'Catholic' and 'Academic' models of the Church outlined in our first section.

We may suppose, then, that Arius began from an awareness that Church practice, and perhaps popular preaching, had left a good many theological loose ends in the early years of the fourth century.[98] His objections (in the credal letter to Alexander) to the misuse of texts describing the Son as 'coming out of God' strongly suggest that Alexander's circle had been citing such passages in support of their contention that the Son existed in continuity of substance with the Father, Arius, in effect, insists upon taking proof-texts like these in the wider context of what Scripture says about Father and Son, and indeed what the mainstream of Christian theology had asserted about the immutability, incorporeality and self-subsistence of God – 'the faith we have inherited from our forefathers and have also learned from you, holy father'.[99] Assertions like those of Alexander and his supporters reflect a careless and unthinking hermeneutic, unwilling to grapple with the substantive doctrinal problems raised by the scriptural witness as a whole to the relation of God with his Son. Assuming, as Arius did, that the Church's teaching of God's unique and immaterial nature is non-negotiable, a necessary corollary of believing in the scriptural God at all, then – just as with statements apparently contradicting or compromising God's incorporeality[100] – all that is said about the begetting of the Son must be interpreted in the light of this central belief. If anyone is disposed to see here the dominance of a philosophical or rationalistic motif over the data of revelation, they should bear in mind that, for *all* the writers of the early Church, that freedom from time, matter, fate and chance expressed in the classical philosophical attribution of negative predicates to God (immateriality, immutability, and so on) was self-evidently the only way to make sense of scriptural data – which themselves, in any case, witnessed *expressis verbis* to a God whom 'no one had seen at any time', whose purposes did not change, immortal and unapproachable.[101] Athanasius is at one with Arius here: the difference between them has to do with the role in theology of unsystematic traditions of belief and behaviour – what Basil the Great[102] was later to call 'dogma' as opposed to 'kerygma'. It is not *primarily* a disagreement about the god of the philosophers *versus* the god of Abraham, Isaac and Jacob (this is a tension as sharply felt in Catholic as in heterodox writers), and the *Thalia* (whatever Athanasius may say) is unmistakably a hymn to the living God of scriptural narrative.[103]

Arius' aim is to develop a biblically-based *and* rationally consistent catechesis. This is why he is interested in questions of usage, metaphor and genre in his exegesis. He is confronted with a bewildering complexity of conventions in Scripture for naming the mediator between God and creation, and he seeks to reduce this chaos (and the consequent chaos of theology and preaching) to some kind of order. Thus, there are texts (like Proverb 8:22) which affirm that the mediator is created by God's will, and there are texts (like Psalm 110:3) which, *prima facie*, imply a 'natural' continuity between God and the mediator, and texts throughout the New Testament as well as the Old describing the mediator as 'Son', and the relationship of the mediator with God as one of being begotten or brought to birth. How do we know which kind of language

111

has priority? By the fact that the latter, taken literally, is plainly inconsistent with what the *whole* of Scripture and tradition teaches about the nature of God. And such a conclusion is borne out by the further fact that metaphorical uses of the language of 'sonship' and 'begetting' can be found elsewhere in Scripture (Isa. 1:2). The metaphor of 'sonship' applied to the mediator's relation to God is *controlled* by the scriptural witness to a God distinct in essence from all contingent being, a witness articulated in passages like Proverbs 8:22. If God is a God who creates of his own free and gracious will, all other things depend upon that will: there is no other, quasi-physical, kind of dependency-relationship. Thus when in Scripture we encounter the metaphor of sonship in such a context, we must be aware that the 'core' element of the metaphor cannot, in the nature of the case, be the semantic field that covers kinship, biological continuity,[104] membership of the same genus, and so forth; it must be the narrower field of familial intimacy, a dependency expressed in trust or love – the field evoked for us when *we* call God 'Father'.

Kannengiesser is right[105] to call this a 'learned' or 'scholastic' catechesis, in so far as its argument is based upon a set of governing principles strictly applied, prior options about what controls the reading of the text – as opposed to what he terms the 'narrative' or 'anthropomorphic' exegesis of Athanasius. I should prefer to describe Athanasius' approach as *inductive*, an exegesis which is no less concerned than that of Arius with rational consistency, but is wary of foreclosing its options, and more inclined to allow the metaphor of 'sonship' to establish its own core area in relation to all the other clusters of imagery used to characterize the mediator's status, in Scripture and in worship. The effect of this is to challenge the primacy of any one mode of speaking about the mediator (such as that represented by Proverbs 8:22) in isolation, and to raise the question of whether *all* dependency *vis-à-vis* the ultimate source, the Father, must be the result of an anthropomorphically conceived act of divine choosing:[106] what if the will to produce the dependent reality of creation is intelligible only if the divine life is first conceived as itself an act of giving and responding, which is *free*, in the sense of being utterly unconstrained, yet *natural*, in the sense of not being the effect of a punctiliar act of conscious self-determination?[107]

Athanasius' hermeneutic would require a separate treatise to do it justice, and it is thus briefly sketched here simply in order to highlight what is, in contrast, characteristic of Arius' mode of proceeding. We.have observed how Arius deals with the variegated scriptural material about the Son's relationship to the Father, and how his conclusions are supported by allusion to the metaphorical nature of sonship-language elsewhere in Scripture. This leaves the third point noted above as a major theme of Arian exegesis to be investigated – the question of the Son's status, his 'promotion' at God's will. We have already remarked that it is very difficult to harmonize what Athanasius and Alexander say about Arius' views on this subject with what we have of Arius' own writings; and what, if anything, in the *Thalia* corresponded to Athanasius' summary in A(v) cannot be determined. However, the problem is somewhat illuminated by the fact that both Alexander and Athanasius associate the crypto-adoptionist views they ascribe to Arius with the heretic's exegesis of Psalm 45:7–8. Athanasius reports[108] that the Arians, in interpreting both this passage and Philippians 2:9, laid much stress on the *dia touto* and *dio*, 'therefore', in the texts. They did not, apparently, use these expressions directly in support of a simple exaltation-theology (Christ as a creature promoted because of virtue); despite the persuasive arguments of Gregg and Groh,[109] we have to be cautious in ascribing to Arius the exemplarist doctrine of salvation that might be implied in such a scheme, and to be mindful of the fact that Arius himself is *not* speaking of Christ as a human being rewarded for his probity.[110] According to Athanasius, the points made in the Arian exegesis of the psalm were (i) that the *dia touto* implies a reward, and a reward implies voluntary choice (*proairesis*) and thus mutability; and (ii) that exaltation *para tous metochous sou*, 'above your kindred' or 'fellows' implies that the Son is a member of the class of things created[111] (that is, *metochos* is being taken in the common classical and Septuagintal sense of 'colleague' or 'partner' or 'joint possessor').[112] Thus Arius' reading of this psalm was closely connected with some fairly central themes in his theology – the createdness of the Son, and the fact that he does not by nature possess any of the divine attributes.

If Arius really restricted himself to raising only these two points in commenting on Psalm 45 and Philippians 2, it may well be that he was as uneasy with the rhetoric of exaltation and apotheosis as were his critics. Arius' scheme depends upon the fact that God bestows power and glory upon the Son from the beginning, so that *de facto* the Son is *atreptos kai analloiōtos;* if this were not so, the Son would not have the role he has as *archē tōn genētōn,* as *sophia,* as the manifester of God's glory. There can be no chronological element in the virtue-and-reward scheme implied in Psalm 45. Again, it seems as if Arius is attempting to sort out a set of confusing and apparently contradictory data in Scripture; and again Proverbs 8:22 represents the central controlling principle. There are passages, like those in Psalm 45 and Philippians 2, which might superficially be read as suggesting a change of status for the Son (just as there are those which, at the other extreme, might imply that the Son is 'part' of God); yet to read them in this way is to overlook those more fundamental witnesses that depict the Son as creative Word and Wisdom and the image of the Father's glory from before the world was made. Arius is, in fact, faced with a considerable dilemma: the Son cannot have his godlike glory and stability by nature, and so must be given them; but if he is given them, the implication must be avoided that there is some sort of change in his status – that there is a time when he is not Wisdom and Word (cf. S 29–30). On the other hand: as a creature the Son is mutable, and as a rational creature he is mutable according to his choice (*proairesis*); and what is to be avoided here is the suggestion that God overrules the Son's freedom by his premundane gifts and graces. It is a peculiarly acute form of the classical dilemma about grace and freedom, and Arius' solution is no better or worse than most efforts that have been made by theologians through the ages. Reconstructing Arius' views from Athanasius' condensed and hostile summaries, we can conclude that Arius argued (i) that the Son, in his pre-incarnate state and in his life on earth *voluntarily* 'loved righteousness and hated iniquity'; that is, he fully and properly exercised his creaturely freedom according to God's purpose in creating rational beings, by contemplation, virtue, and praise of God; (ii) that such an exercise of rational freedom is normally what fits us for transfiguring grace, the 'glory' of familiarity with God, so far as any creature can be familiar with the unapproachable mystery of the Father; (iii) that God, in endowing the Son with this dignity of heavenly intimacy from the very beginning of his existence, is therefore acting not arbitrarily but rationally, knowing that his firstborn among creatures is and will always be worthy of the highest degree of grace, a perfect channel for creative and redemptive action, and so a perfect 'image' of the divine, wholly transparent to the Father.[113]

This may sound rather tortuous: it is understandable that Athanasius[114] should relentlessly press his opponents to admit that a disjunction between nature and grace must amount to a belief that the state of grace represents an *advance* from the state of nature, and thus a change; or that some of Arius' presumably less sophisticated or less cautious supporters were persuaded to say that the Son was capable of falling away from his state of virtue and glory.[115] However, it makes as much sense (in its theological context) as Athanasius' exegesis of these awkward passages – awkward for Arius as well as for Athanasius, if we take the theology of the *Thalia* at face value.

It is possible that Arius engaged with these 'adoptionist' texts quite deliberately because of their actual use by other theologians (of a Sabellian or Paulinian cast of mind), or because of dissatisfaction with a tradition of partial, evasive or ambiguous interpretation which encouraged such exploitation of the passages by heretics. If so, Arius cannot be seen as advancing, on his own initiative, a provocatively adoptionist doctrine; rather he is attempting to 'capture' the imagery of adoption or exaltation for orthodox theology (as he conceives it), once again by a rigorous reading of certain texts in the light of a central controlling principle. And, here as elsewhere,[116] part of Athanasius' polemical technique is to show that Arius' 'solution' to a theological *aporia* leads him inexorably towards the position he most wants to avoid – in this instance, the Christological doctrines associated with Paul of Samosata.

However, a fuller elucidation of this demands a fuller discussion of Arius' relationship to earlier Christian theology. We have seen so far that Arius is anxious to present himself as a defender of traditional orthodoxies, a teacher in a reputable succession, and that he is likely to be deliberately in dispute with other writers in his exegesis. A great many attempts have been made to locate him in one sort of tradition or another; but it is perhaps a mistake to look for one self-contained and exclusive 'theological school' to which to assign him, even the elusive 'school of Lucian of Antioch'. It is more helpful to look at his intellectual context, not to discover a set of sources for his ideas, but to understand better his theological agenda: what made *these* particular questions, terms or texts important for such a man at that particular time? His enemies first[117] associated him with Paul of Samosata and with Judaizing tendences in Christology; later on, after the reputation of Origen had been virtually ruined in the Church, Arius was regarded by some as an Origen *redivivus*.[118] Some more modern scholars[119] have been much preoccupied with the question of whether Antioch or Alexandria should be seen as his spiritual and intellectual home, assuming that the alternatives of Paul of Samosata or Origen represent a reasonably accurate statement of the options. Others[120] have been rightly sceptical of this rather facile antithesis. Nevertheless, it is convenient to divide the study of Arius' antecedents into – broadly speaking – examination of Alexandrian and non-Alexandrian traditions – granted that there will be overlap between the two, and that neither is systematic or homogeneous. There should at least be no danger of seeing Arius as a slavish follower of theological convention, Alexandrian or otherwise, if the analysis of his thinking in this section makes any sense of our texts. His claim to be a traditionalist must be examined and assessed, but we should not forget that he is a thinker and exegete of resourcefulness, sharpness and originality.[121]

B

Alexandria and the Legacy of Origen

1 PHILO

Perhaps the most extreme statement of Arius' purely Alexandrian roots is Wolfson's conclusion that Arius was responsible for 'a reversion to the original view of Philo' on the Logos, after the aberrations of a modalism which deprived the Logos of real subsistence;[1] Arius, like Philo, believed that the Logos had two phases of existence, as a quality of the divine essence and then as a separate being created by an act of divine will. This interpretation depends, of course, on assuming that Philo *does* teach a 'two-stage' doctrine of the Logos (comparable with that of several of the second-century apologists).[2] Wolfson lays much stress on a rather limited number of Philonic texts[3] that speak of the Logos as the totality of the noetic creation, the ensemble of intelligible things: in so far as this is 'outside' the mind of God, 'Logos' must designate something other than God in such a context.[4] And in this sense the Logos is 'firstborn' and 'oldest of creatures',[5] a reality distinct from the *agennētos* God.[6]

It is very doubtful indeed whether we can confidently ascribe so sharply defined a picture to Philo. Despite the numerous expressions implying that the Logos is a being in its own right (not least those passages in which Philo speaks of the Logos as *theos*),[7] there is actually very little that suggests a 'creation' of the Logos by an act of will. The nearest Philo comes to this is a remarkable parallel to the view Athanasius ascribes to Arius[8] – that God brings forth the Logos because he has decided to create the world. Philo's version[9] is that God, 'having willed to create this visible world', first 'sketches out' or 'models' the realm of ideas, the *kosmos noētos*, of which the material creation is the image, and which a later passage[10] clearly identifies with the Logos. The phraseology certainly seems to imply that the Logos exists at God's will in so far as its subsistence in the

117

form of a 'world of ideas' depends upon a prior decision to create the world of particulars,[11] to which end the noetic world is an instrument.[12] But this does not necessarily justify a conclusion like Wolfson's. Philo is clearly concerned to deny that there is anything *outside* God that has a part in creation, or any motive for creation other than God's free will,[13] and so it is necessary for him to insist upon the dependence of the world of ideas on God; but on the other hand, the *kosmos noētos* is the 'shadow' or image of God,[14] reflecting what is eternally in him, not the product of an *arbitrary* act of will unrelated to the divine nature. God wills to create according to his own nature, and so 'sets out' the content of his divine reason[15] in the form of a paradigm for the world. It could be said, then, that, for the purpose of creation, the 'immanent' Logos becomes the agency by which a multiple universe, which is none the less maintained in orderly, intelligible form, is constituted as possible and actual. But this is to say that God's reason becomes active and formative according to his choice, and his choice is effected according to what his reason allows – not that a separate agent or even a self-contained repository of ideas is created by God's will in the same sense that the contingent world is created.

Philo's language is, of course, consistently personalist and mythological: the Logos is an 'archangel',[16] a 'priest' and 'prophet',[17] a 'viceroy' (*huparchos*),[18] and so on. It has been persuasively argued, however,[19] that Philo deliberately adopts the conventions of Alexandrian Jewish mythology concerning an angelic helper for the creator, with the overall aim of *demythologizing* such a picture by relating it to what is for him the fundamental issue of how God is known by rational spirits. Language about a 'second power' or 'second God' functions to define what Sandmel has called[20] a point of 'intersection' between God and the created mind: the Logos is that in virtue of which we can begin to know God through the rational structures of the world which are accessible to the *nous*. Of course, what makes Philo more than a 'routine' Platonist is his conviction that this knowledge depends upon God's initiative, not only in creation, but in the inspiration of Scripture (that is, the Torah), and in the gifts bestowed on the soul in contemplation and meditation on the Law.[21] The Logos might indeed be called the principle of *grace* in God, 'disposing gifts',[22] filled with 'immaterial powers',[23] those powers through which God is known to us – supremely, the two powers that 'attend' God like the cherubim on each side of the ark,[24] forming, with God, the trinity of angels that appeared to Abraham at Mamre[25] – the creative power and the kingly power (by which creation is sustained and organized). It should be noted that the Logos is *above* the two primary powers, and so closer to the divine being as such:[26] it is the *archē* of existent things, and their 'seminal substance' (*spermatikē ousia*),[27] but, when it is being considered over against the multiple forms of God's providential involvement in the world (the *dunameis*), it is clearly *not* separable from the one God. It is God himself turned towards what is not God.

Consequently, it is not surprising that Philo's language about the Logos is confusing. As a kind of 'boundary' (*methorios*) between God and what has come into being (*to genomenon*), the Logos is neither *agenētos* nor *genētos*[28] (as can be seen, Wolfson's use of this passage distorts Philo's careful paradox). Yet, as containing and *activating* God's capacity to relate to a contingent world, the Logos is 'eldest of those things that have received generation'.[29] The Logos is a 'place in the midst' (*tō(i) mesō(i)*): thus, to be 'in' the Logos is not to be in God *simpliciter*, but rather to be in a position to grasp the real transcendence of God and his incomprehensibility to the created mind.[30] In this sense, the Logos is the teacher and healer of the mind; but to see the Logos as such is only to see the shadow (*skia*) of God.[31] The mind that has been truly purified receives the grace to see both the *agenētos* and its *skia;* thus Moses receives his knowledge of the heavenly tabernacle directly by God's power, but Bezalel knows it only from the 'shadow', that is, from the rational image in the mind of Moses, who himself sees both image and *paradeigma* – both the Logos as shrine of the eternal ideas, and the simplicity of God which is beyond the multiplicity of ideas.[32] The final goal, it seems, is to see the Logos 'in' God, to grasp that for God to be God is *more* than for God to be the first principle of the universe; and to pass beyond the awareness of this gulf (seeing God 'in' the Logos) to direct union with or 'nourishment' by God in his simplicity,[33] 'beyond form and beyond sight'.[34] We progress from contact with God in his *dunameis*, awareness of him as relating providentially to creatures, to seeing that God *acts* thus because he *is* thus: there is eternally in him a foundation for his communication with rational souls, a 'place' for the world as an ordered system designed to lead created spirits back to him. But, having thus seen and understood God as Logos, as turned towards the world, we are then confronted with the fact that this 'turning' does not exhaust the divine being, which in itself is immeasurably more than the ensemble of rational structures, and are drawn towards the final and unfathomable mystery of God as God. Whether Philo had a doctrine of 'mystical union' in any strict sense remains debatable;[35] but (despite the logical difficulties involved in such a position) he *does* seem to have believed that there could be a relation to God other than in his world-related aspect as Logos. Perhaps the mere recognition of the inexhaustible depths of divine simplicity, and a willingness to forget any apprehension of God as *defined* by his relation to creatures is all Philo means (in which case, he very strikingly anticipates that pattern summed up in the western Christian tradition by the language of *The Cloud of Unknowing*).

It is not that Philo has any simplistic doctrine of an advance from things we do understand to things we do not, a crude reason-faith dichotomy. On the contrary, the knowledge acquired by the righteous soul is, throughout its development, something other than conceptual mastery. We must begin with self-knowledge,[36] but this is not a knowledge of the soul's or mind's *substance*. Like the eye, the mind beholds other things, not itself, and Adam, though he names the beasts, does not name himself.[37] It is a knowledge of the nothingness of contingent existence, a kind of self-despair:[38] the knowledge of God begins in an awareness of the distance between God and creatures, not in the forming of a concept of one's own spiritual essence. Likewise, as we learn to know God through his *dunameis*, we do *not* learn the definition or essence of these powers,[39] nor do they tell us the proper name (*kurion onoma*) of God. As we have seen, when the spirit comes to be fully 'in' the Logos, it apprehends only the incomprehensibility of what is beyond; and the true name even of the Logos cannot be uttered.[40] God alone perfectly knows (*ēkribōse*) his own *phusis*:[41] his *kurion onoma*, as perceived by the soul that is leaving multiplicity behind, is *ho ōn*, 'He Who Is',[42] but this 'most generic' of designations[43] does not, of course, express positively what it is to be God.

The word 'God' poses some problems: in itself, it does not name God as decisively as *ho ōn*, and seems, in Philo's eyes, to relate more specifically to God qua creator. Thus *theos* may designate the Logos[44] or even the creative *dunamis* as opposed to the regal *dunamis* (which is called *kurios*);[45] but when applied to these 'shadows' it is used *en katachrēsei*, 'in a transferred sense', and without the article. *Ho theos* means God in his own mysterious being, *theos* God as purposive and active in respect of creation. Philo is far from clear in spelling out this distinction: strictly one would suppose that even *ho theos* would be inappropriate for God in himself, in so far as the name is by definition linked to providential involvement.[46] However, even God beyond all his relations with the world is, as we have seen, source and 'container' of the creative ideas, and does not act against his nature in making and preserving the world. Philo's problem is intrinsic to his whole scheme of thought: it must not be supposed that the manifest, even visible or audible *theos* of Scripture is identical with the incomprehensible self-existent God; yet that which is manifest in revelation is nothing *other* than the true God. The same tension is apparent in Philo's varying use of words like *monas* and *archē. God* is the ultimate unity of things, the monad that is seen when we press 'even beyond the *duas*'[47] (*duas* here may mean the duality of the two powers, or, more probably, the Logos as the beginning of multiplicity, God knowing himself as object to himself, and so initiating the process of generating a world);[48] and God *archē . . . geneseos*.[49] Yet in his own essence he is above *monas* and *archē,*[50] and the Logos more properly bears these titles.[51] Philo seems to share the Neopythagorean distinction between two kinds of primal unity, corresponding to the first and second 'hypotheses' of Plato's *Parmenides;* the unity of transcendent existence in and for itself, pure simplicity and self-subsistence, and the unity of all things in ultimate rational harmony, the reducibility of things to formal dependence upon a single principle.

Philo's fundamentally strict monotheism[52] and his concern to stress the free and gracious initiative of God necessarily involve him in asserting unbroken continuity between God's nature and his activity, and so between God's unity *in se* and his unity considered as principle of all things: the Logos cannot be the issue of God's free choice precisely because it is God as he is, God in his integral being, who freely acts to bring the world into being. God as one in and for himself is already the God who is *archē* in respect of creation: the terminological unclarity over *theos, monas* and *archē* serves as a reminder that God never becomes anything other than himself as he creates, yet is not exhausted and defined or determined by creation. Philo is obliged by his concept of a free and self-revealing God to resolve as far as possible the different levels of cosmic unity found in the *Parmenides* and the Neopythagoreans into a single principle, the divine act flowing freely from the unknowable yet loving divine nature: the plurality which poses no problems for an hierarchical or emanationist cosmology has to be heavily qualified in a more personalist scheme. It is noteworthy too, in this connection, that Philo's God is not 'beyond being', like the One of the *Parmenides*,[53] but is being itself. Creation shares in what God supremely possesses;[54] yet it does so simply because of God's will. Although it is correct to say that, for Philo, time begins with creation,[55] the fact that creation is not eternal justifies the loose and paradoxical statement that 'there was a time when it was not' (*ēn pote chronos hote ouk ēn*).[56] It exists because God decides to share his life: its continuity with him does not mean that it is naturally *part* of him.

This has been a rather long and laboured digression, but its purpose will, I hope, be clear. Wolfson's simple account of Arius' relation to Philo will not do; yet, at many points, there are real and striking correspondences. Indeed it could be said that the sole crucial point of distinction is what Wolfson believed to be their common ground – the doctrine of an individually subsistent Logos, distinct from the Father. What is metaphor to Philo is literal description for Arius. But apart from this, we can identify at least three areas of shared concern. First there is the interest in divine freedom and grace, signalized in Philo by the insistence on a beginning for creation and on the mind's need to be raised up by God. Second, there is the idea of the Logos as essentially a mediator of God's *gifts*, multiply reflecting the divine simplicity. Thirdly there is the austerely apophatic tone, stressing the difference between knowing God in his gifts and knowing him as he is; the notion of the Logos as revealing both the continuity and the gulf between God and his gifts; and the correlation of our incapacity to form a concept of our own *ousia* with our incapacity to know God's 'essence' (Philo's position on this last question must surely bear out the interpretation already proposed of Arius' denial that the Son knows his own *ousia*).[57] The distinction between 'proper' and 'transferred' uses of *theos* belongs to Athanasius' polemic, rather than what we know of Arius' own work, but Philo's use of the terminology is suggestive; the same is true of the parallels in speaking of the Father's self-knowledge.[58] As we turn from Philo to Arius, we recognize that we are still faced with the same *kind* of debate.

Recognizing this should not, of course, mislead us into hastily concluding that Arius was an assiduous student of Philo. What all this shows is, rather, that Philo mapped out the ground for the Alexandrian theological tradition to build on, and that Arius' theological problematic is firmly within that tradition. Philo is attempting to utilize side by side two equally powerful models of 'saving knowledge': on the one hand stands a tradition that stresses ascent, purification, the mind's stripping away of the illusions of sense-experience to arrive at rational and ideal harmony; on the other, a tradition resting upon the sovereign freedom of a personal God to manifest himself in a creation that is not necessary to his own life. For the former, the human mind can arrive at a point of unification or simplification where it confronts the unconceptualizable self-identity of reality as such – 'the One', 'the truly existent', *ontōs on*, or that which is 'beyond being and mind'. The problem that arises is how what is by definition related to (or relative to) nothing but itself is connected with the unity the contingent mind can attain and 'stand' in: the problem which, for later Platonists, turned on the nature of the gulf between ultimate unity and intelligence, and which generates the enormously important doctrine that the ideas, the structures of rational harmony, are internal to intelligence itself, *not* what intelligence beholds outside itself, in the One. In what sense is there continuity, participation, between these first and second principles, and so between 'reality as such' and concrete *realities*?[59]

In contrast to this emphasis on the ascent of the mind, the 'revelationist' tradition sees the human mind as being activated by an initiative from beyond itself; and since that initiative is wholly free, it does not *need* a mechanism of mediation through an hierarchically ordered cosmos. All language that suggests a real plurality of continuous levels of being (beyond the simple duality of material and immaterial or intelligible, inevitably taken for granted by someone like Philo) is ultimately metaphorical: the gulf is between the freedom of the creator and the total dependence of everything else. Yet here the problem arises of how God is to communicate to the created mind except through created and limited words or images. In this context, the problem becomes one of keeping separate God and the created 'projections' by which he communicates, while recognizing that he is still truly present in his words.

Both traditions are ultimately apophatic; both therefore, produce the paradox that the means by which God becomes known both is and is not God. Philo, who is not a particularly systematic thinker, is not attempting to resolve these two schemes into a single comprehensive theory, but to deploy two kinds of metaphor and rhetoric in the service of what is essentially a single vision of spiritual development. To look for a clear definition or identification of the Logos in his writings would be as fruitless as (to borrow a Wittgensteinian example)[60] to try to define an expression without drawing a face, or to describe a contrapuntal piece of music without playing the melodies. Here we are dealing with relations in which the terms define yet do not exhaust each other. The paradox of something that 'is and is not God' is only disturbing if that something is indeed accorded an identity of its own – which is precisely the early Christian problem. That which is neither *genētos* nor *agenētos*, neither simply temporal nor eternal as God is eternal, part of the divine life, yet existing for the sake of creation, *theos* but not *ho theos*, *archē* yet derived from a higher principle – if this is not just the deliberately 'frozen' and hypostasized area of relation or intersection between God and the universe, but *a* being, the paradoxes threaten to become flat contradictions. Alexandrian theology follows Philo in wishing to deploy two languages at once, but is haunted by the difficulties for *both* languages of a Logos who can subsist as a human individual, and who is to be seen as relating personally, as 'Son', to the source of all things. In this sense at least, Philo may help us to understand Arius, for whom the logical stresses of the Alexandrian Christian tradition finally proved intolerable: without wholly discarding the vocabulary and framework of metaphor going back to Philo, Arius attempts to cut the Gordian knot produced by those of his forebears who have taken Philo for granted.

2 CLEMENT

Prominent among these is Clement. In spite of some disagreement over the exact degree to which it is right to call Clement a 'negative theologian',[61] there is no doubt at all that he wishes to stress, as much as does Philo, that God is *by nature* remote from us: by nature we are 'alienated' from him, unrelated in *ousia*, *phusis*, *dunamis*, *oikeia*, related only as the 'work of his will'.[62] God must – and does – draw near to us in mercy for us to know him: *we* cannot draw near to him, 'for how might the *gennētos* have drawn near to the *agennētos?*'[63]

He is uncircumscribed and unlimited,[64] incapable of being rightly (*kurios*) named,[65] although we may form some notion of God as we accumulate words that express his almighty *dunamis*.[66] Only the Logos, who, says the apostle, is 'in the bosom of the Father', can reveal God.[67] St John 'calls what is invisible the unutterable the "bosom of the Father": and some, for this reason, have called it "depth" (*buthos*), as if it were something unattainable and unfathomable (*anephikton te kai aperanton*), encompassing and engulfing everything'.[68] Faith in God is not something we possess by nature, as some of the Gnostic teachers seem to be saying: it is our free and conscious response to God's free self-revelation.[69]

This self-revelation occurs in and through the Logos: without the Logos, it is possible to attain some 'feeble' awareness of God's power and works, not his *ousia*;[70] but only the Christian's 'God-instructed' (*theodidaktos*) wisdom can bring us to the depth of God's own being.[71] The Logos is supremely the teacher (*didaskalos*) of wisdom, instructing – in diverse ways – the whole universe:[72] it, or he, is the Father's counsellor, in his role as Wisdom, the *dunamis* and *energeia* of the Father,[73] the primary 'organizer' or 'administrator' of the universe, who guarantees providential care for even the tiniest portion of the whole;[74] he is High Priest[75] and *arche* of all other principles, activated by the will of the Father.[76] Indeed, he can be called the *thelema* of the Father, as in the beautiful appeal to the human race which Clement puts into the mouth of 'the one great High Priest of the one God his Father'[77] in the final pages of the *Protreptikos;*

> I long, I long to endow you with this grace, granting you the blessed heritage of immortality; and I freely give you reason (*logos*), knowledge of God, I freely give you what I myself perfectly am. This is what I am, this is what God wills, this is *sumphonia*, this is the *harmonia* of the Father, this Son, this Christ, this Word of God, the arm of the Lord, the power of all things, the Father's will. For all you who are images (*eikones*) yet not all true likenesses (*emphereis*), my wish is to bring you to your right form, to the archetype, so that you too may become like me.[78]

The Logos is the primary image of God, who then 'seals the gnostic with perfect contemplation, after his own image':[79] the mature Christian, inheritor of stable and secure knowledge, is now an image

on earth of the 'second cause' in heaven, 'life itself'.[80] In the likeness
of the Logos, we attain a 'full and secure contemplative vision'
(*kataleptikē theoria*) of God,[81] that solid nourishment of the flesh and
blood of the Word which is a 'comprehending (*katalēpsis*) of the
divine *dunamis* and *ousia* . . . *gnōsis* of the divine substance'.[82] As with
Philo, so for Clement there is a distinction between knowing or
seeing the Logos and knowing God: the Logos is the realm of
intelligibilia (among other things),[83] he is 'one as being all things'
(that is, not simply a unity in and for himself),[84] a circle in which
the diverse spiritual *dunameis* are gathered into one[85] (as radii gathered into the centre? or as pieces of clay rolled into a ball? more
probably, I think, the former).[86] Thus he is knowable and nameable,
in some sense, definable.[87] As plurality-in-unity, the Logos is
monas,[88] and Clement follows Philo in affirming the Father's transcendence of this level of unity,[89] though the doctrine of the Logos
as *eikōn* reminds us that this transcendence is not absolute discontinuity, and we can find strong statements of the unity between God
and Logos.[90] But the Father is still, it seems, to be grasped as an
achanēs, an 'immensity', beyond the *monas* that can be reached by
abstracting extension and location from contingent things.[91]

Thus far, there is almost nothing in Clement that could not have
been said by Philo, though the habitual language of Father and
Son is distinctively Christian and the range of Scripture available
for quotation is wider. But, while it has rightly been said[92] that the
Philonic Logos does not as such 'descend' into the world of sense
experience but draws us to rise out of it, Clement is not afraid to
say that 'the Lord descended, humanity ascended'.[93] God is actively
in search of his alienated children,[94] exhibiting his *philanthrōpia* by
showing mercy to spirits who (in their present state) have no claim
of kinship upon him;[95] and he elects to communicate with us in
human words, veiling great mysteries in the beauty and simplicity
of revealed teaching. The uncertain note, muffled in moral contradictions, that is given out by Greek liteeerature and philosophy must
give way to the clarity of Scripture;[96] and the final and decisive
teaching is that of the Word made flesh. His human life shows us
how to 'live well',[97] 'so that you may learn from a human being
how a human being may become God'.[98] Although we are, *de facto*,
alienated from God, we are still in origin his children: only the
manifestation of a completely new mode of human living can bring

us back to what we truly are, however, and for this the fleshly life of the Christ is indispensable.[99]

As we have already noted,[100] a Christian writer can hardly avoid that problem which does not arise for Philo, the problem of sorting out the relation between Logos as the knowable aspect of God and Logos as, in some sense, an agent in itself, capable of becoming identified with a specific material individual. The second-century Apologists largely followed the vague hint in Philo's *de opificio*, discussed above, postulating that the Logos emerged as a distinct subsistent at the time of, and for the purpose of creation, or else just prior to the incarnation.[101] Clement ignores the difficulty more or less completely in his major works;[102] but the difficult and fragmentary notebook *excerpta ex Theodoto*, consisting of extracts from and comments on Valentinian gnostic writings, suggests that he had some sympathy with the solution advanced by the Apologists. The famous and much-disputed section 19 of this notebook speaks of the saviour as a 'child of the Logos that is identical with God'[103] – as if there were a real duality between the eternal 'immanent' Logos and a personalized subject which comes into existence *en archē(i)*:

'And the Word became flesh' – not only when he became a human being in his *parousia* [on earth], but also 'in the beginning', when the Word identical with God (*ho en tautotēti logos*) became a Son, not in substance by by limitation [or: circumscription, *kata perigraphēn*]. Again he 'became flesh' when he had acted through the prophets;[104] and the saviour is called a child of the Word that is identical with God . . . Paul says, 'Put on the new man, the one created according to God ['s purpose]', as if he should say, 'Believe in the one created by God, according to God's purpose (*kata theon*), in the Word that is in God [or, more probably: according to God's purpose, that is, according to the Word that is in God]' . . . Still more clearly and distinctly, he says elsewhere: ' . . . who is the image of the invisible God', and goes on, 'firstborn of all creation'. For this 'image of the invisible God' is the son of the Word that is identical with God, yet also 'the firstborn of all creation'.[105]

Some scholars[106] have taken this together with a fragment of Clement's *Hypotyposes* preserved by Photius,[107] and with a curious quotation surviving in Latin which describes the Son and Spirit as 'primordial powers, first created, unchangeable, existing in their own right (*secundum substantiam*)',[108] and concluded that Clement did indeed teach what Photius charges him with, a doctrine of two *logoi*, one immanent, one subsisting independently as a result of the action of God by means of the other – a very clear foreshadowing of what Athanasius reports of Arius' teaching.[109] But this is a serious misreading of Clement – certainly of the *excerpta* passage, though we cannot know exactly what stood in the original text of the *Hypotyposes*. As Lorenz recognizes,[110] the crucial phrase in the passage quoted is 'not in substance, but by limitation'. Throughout these notes, Clement is attempting to come to terms with a system which *does* emphasize, very sharply, the formal distinction between the various grades of divine self-manifestation. The Valentinians see the intelligible world as a realm of separable forms and definitions: the heavenly powers, numerically separate from each other (*arithmō(i) diaphoroi*), can be spoken of as 'bodies' of a sort, each with its own (intelligible and immaterial) structure and sphere of action. They are 'formless' by comparison with the gross physical forms of earth, and the Son is 'formless' by comparison with the lower spiritual powers; but even he is determinate, circumscribed, compared with the Father.[111]

Clement is well aware that the Valentinians do not believe in a crude and anthropomorphic multiplicity of heavenly beings, or in a real distinction between the Son as he subsists in heaven and as he relates to the creation;[112] but he seems to be aware also of the risks of this kind of imagery.[113] The Logos *en tautotēti*, Clement insists, is entirely continuous with God, 'one God' with the Father.[114] The light which is seen in the incarnate Christ at his transfiguration is not a transient and created phenomenon, not a reduction or copy of his eternal glory, but the same reality, the light of the Father's eternal *dunamis* which is the eternal Son.[115] Hence the expression in 19: the Father's 'identical' Logos must take on form and definition, must be, as it were, 'incarnate' from the very beginning, to fulfil its role of manifesting the unknown *kolpos*, the 'bosom of the Father'; but this form and definition – as realm of ideas, and then as human agent and interlocutor – does not and cannot affect the essence of *what* is acting, God in his saving power and love. The person of the saviour can be called a 'child' of the eternal Word only in the loosest possible sense: God as Logos generates – even 'creates'[116] – the shapes in which he reveals himself, but does not become another *subject*. The forms and shapes are dictated by the context of manifestation:[117] God can meet what is determinate only by appearing in determinate form: 'Structure (*schēma*) is perceived by structure, face is seen by face, recognizable characteristics are grasped by beings with structure and substantial definition'.[118]

But Clement has to maintain a rather precarious balance of views. He is uneasy with the Valentinian tendency to carve up the heavenly world into distinct subsistents, as if the divine life could be partitioned: like later writers,[119] he may have been disposed to see in this an impossibly materialist view of divine substance, and so insists that God's life undergoes no change or diminution in the process of 'embodiment', the taking of determinate form, in which revelation consists. But there is a further problem in that the Valentinian technique confuses the fundamental difference between God and the world: the flow of reality from the Father down to human beings is sectioned off in various ways; but this means that the distinction between God and Logos can come to be seen as no different in kind from that between Logos and rational soul. Clement's Valentinian source says that the 'spiritual seed' in us is an emanation (*aporroia*) from the angelic seed;[120] and the angelic seeds come forth from 'the Male' (the highest principle after God, the Only-Begotten, Mind and Truth)[121] 'not as a creation, but as children'.[122] They are related to the Son in much the same way as Clement believes the incarnate saviour to be related to the eternal Logos. Thus Clement has to insist on a stronger *unity* between Son and Father than the Valentinians appear to allow, and on a deeper *discontinuity* between the Son and creation. The imagery of the 'seed' is scriptural enough; but Clement cannot grant that the potential for redeemed life is simply a natural capacity waiting to be activated in the elect.[123] We have seen already that he does not believe saving faith to be a natural endowment, but the product of free choice; and if we can rely on another Latin fragment,[124] the Word as *monas* is the work of God, but the 'dyad', the present multiplicity of the actual universe, is the result not of a cosmic catastrophe but of voluntary disobedience to the Law of God – and is presumably, therefore, to be overcome by voluntary penitence.

Clement leaves us with a good many difficulties unresolved. In his terms, it makes very little sense to ask whether the Logos is a subsistent eternally distinct from God: we *can only* conceive the Logos as having form and determination. It is God's capacity to present himself to us in intelligible shape, and so we cannot fail to see the Logos as distinct from God-as-such. Yet all the forms in which the Logos appears to us are manifestations accidental to the 'real' life of the Logos, which is in God, identical with God. When we come to be 'in' the Logos, we have attained a grasp, a *katalēpsis*, of whatever of God can be conceived and understood, and so have also come to the frontier of conceptual knowledge, to a position whence we can see into the depth beyond. Despite the ambiguity of much of his language, I do not think Clement believed that we could ever form a definition of God in himself. But here is the difficulty: how can the essence of God be partly knowable (as Logos) and partly unknowable? A Logos which (like Philo's) is an aspect of the divine *ousia* can still come dangerously close to the Valentinian projection of division and plurality into the divine life. It is worth noting that Arius (who explicitly rules out any *katalēpsis* of the divine substance)[125] in his confession of faith[126] and Alexander[127] both associate Valentinus and Sabellius: divine emanation makes the divine *ousia* a unity-in-plurality, and so less than perfectly simple and self-subsistent. Clement's rebuttal of Valentinianism and his ingenious theory of a 'Protean' Logos, generating the created forms of its manifestation, of which the supreme and most complete is Jesus Christ, threatens to erode the distinction between first and second principles, which we have already seen as a problem in the margins of Philo. Here again, the stage is set for the characteristic Arian agenda to emerge.

However, this is not to deny that Clement also passes on a positive legacy to Arius and his generation. We have seen that Clement's system allowed ample scope for free will – on the divine side as well as the human: God is not obliged to reveal or save, yet he does so. But, perhaps more interestingly, there are the numerous parallels in vocabulary between Arius' *Thalia* and the language of Clement.[128] In the introductory lines, *sunetoi*, 'those with discernment', is a word Clement likes to use for the spiritually mature;[129] *orthotomoi*, 'those who impart truth', echoes 'the apostolic and ecclesiastical *orthotomia* of [Christian] teachings';[130] *theodidaktos* we have seen used by Clement for the wisdom of the believer, bestowed by the Logos;[131] and the idea of receiving *sophia* and *gnōsis* from God is ubiquitous in Clement, as in Philo. As for the rest of the *Thalia* as it appears in *de synodis*, we may note that *arrētos* for God is found in Clement;[132] and that the 'good things' laid up for the believer in heaven, those things which constitute the beatific vision of God's *prosōpon*, are described by him as *arrēta* and *alekta;*[133] and that *aoratos* appears several times in a passage like Strom. V.11.[134] God as *didaskalos* is so frequent in Clement as to defy comprehensive listing here.[135] *Suniēmi* (as in Arius' *sunes hoti*), like *sunetos*, often refers to spiritual penetration in Clement.[136] We have noted Clement's habit of calling the Logos a *dunamis* of God; and he can speak of the divine power inspiring us to virtue through human *epinoiai*.[137] Clement is a major exponent of what I have called 'Academic' Christianity, the gnostic circle around its teacher; and, as Lorenz suggests, it is probably through the medium of teachers like Clement that Arius' roots go back ultimately to 'Judaeo-Hellenistic wisdom': 'Evidence for this is provided by the role of the Wisdom Literature (Prov. 8:22, and Wisdom 7:25) in the Logos doctrine of Origen, as also by the harmony of *pistis* and *sophia*, so reminiscent of Clement, in the prologue of the *Thalia*.'[138] Once again, it is less a question of a direct influence on Arius than of a common ethos – within which, as we have seen, there can be vigorous disagreement. Arius begins from the apophatic tradition shared by Philo, Clement and heterodox gnosticism, the descriptions of God as *aoratos, alektos*, and so on, which are so important a feature of the vocabulary of esoteric circles; but his importance lies in his refusal to qualify these descriptions by the admission *into the divine substance* of a second principle, with its implications of a continuous *scala naturae* from the world to God. In this respect, he can be said to have pursued more rigorously than Clement that master's insight into the centrality of freedom, divine and human, in any properly theological account of God's dealings with the world.

3 ORIGEN

The relation of Origen to Arianism continues to generate much dispute among scholars.[139] From very early on, there were those who saw Origen as the ultimate source of Arius' heresy: and it is noteworthy that perhaps the earliest such accusation comes from Marcellus of Ancyra,[140] complaining that Origen taught that the Logos was a distinct *hupothesis*. Indeed, one of the features of

Origen's theology that puts him decisively and pretty consistently over against Clement is that insistence on the fact that the Word or Son is an *hupothesis*,[141] *hupostasis* or *hupokeimenon*. In *contra Celsum* I.23,[142] Origen challenges Celsus to show that the Greek deities have *hupostasis* and *ousia*, rather than being pure inventions that only seem to be 'embodied' concretely. *Hupostasis* and *ousia* are obviously more or less synonymous here, and mean 'real individual subsistence', as opposed to existence as a mental construct only: in the background is the familiar philosophical distinction between what exists *kath' hupostasin* and what exists only *kat' epinoian*, 'conceptually'.[143] So, in *contra Celsum* VIII.12,[144] Origen states very plainly that he rejects the views of those who deny that there are two *hupostaseis* in God: Father and Son are 'two things (*pragmata*) in subsistence (*hupostasis*), but are one in likemindedness, harmony (*sumphōnia*)[145] and identity of will'. Elsewhere again,[146] he deplores those heretics who confuse the 'concepts' (*ennoiai*) of Father and Son and make them out to be one in *hupostasis*, as if the distinction between Father and Son were only a matter of *epinoia* and of names, a purely mental distinction which we make in reflecting on the single *hupokeimenon* of God. And in the *de oratione* 15.1,[147] Origen mentions that he has 'proved elsewhere' that Son and Father are distinct in *ousia* and *hupokeimenon*. That the Catholic Christian faith involves belief in three *hupostaseis* is stated firmly in the Commentary on John, II.10:[148] and this concludes an argument that the Holy Spirit has its own 'proper *ousia*',[149] being distinct from the Son as the Son is from the Father. Further on in the Commentary,[150] similar language recurs when Origen objects to the distortion of biblical language about the resurrection (the Father raising the Son) perpetrated by those who do not 'numerically' distinguish Father and Son and who say that they are one 'not only in *ousia* but also in *hupokeimenon*, distinct only *kata tinas epinoias* not *kata hupostasin*'.

In the light of all this, it is almost certainly right to conclude that Origen could not have spoken of the Son as *homoousios* with the Father.[151] The passage just quoted should not be taken as implying an endorsement of unity in *ousia;* as elsewhere, the word's meaning almost certainly overlaps, even if it does not wholly coincide, with that of *hupostasis*. There is one celebrated fragment, however, where Origen appears to sanction the use of *homoousios*, preserved in Rufinus' Latin version of Pamphilus' *Defence of Origen*.[152] But in its present form, this seems too closely bound to the specific interests of the post-Nicene period (for example, in insisting that the Son is 'alien from creaturely substance') to come directly from Pamphilus, let alone Origen. It is probable that Pamphilus did utilize Origen's lost commentary on Hebrews in Chapters III and V of the *Defence*, as our version records; what is uncertain is whether he used it to make the same points Rufinus wishes to make. The text needs to be looked at in some detail.

In Chapter V, we have a list of nine charges levelled against Origen,[153] to which Pamphilus undertakes to give a reply. The first three turn on the status of the Son: Origen is accused by some of calling the Son *innatus*,[154] by others of turning him into a Valentinian *prolatio*, an emanation, and by others (contrariwise to the first two groups) of reducing the Son to a mere human being, so that he cannot be called 'God'. To each of these, as to the remaining six, Pamphilus responds with a catena of texts from Origen, adding a few brief interpretative comments. We should expect the first of these catenae to concentrate on the Son's distinction from the Father.

In fact, it does not consistently do so. The first three quotations, from the Romans and John Commentaries, amount to little more than evidence that Origen called the Son *unigenitus* and *natus*. The next three, the quotations purporting to come from the Hebrews Commentary, raise different issues, and seem, puzzlingly, to focus on the Son's continuity in all things with the Father. We are referred first to Origen's observations on Hebrews 1:2–4, where the Son is said to have received 'the inheritance of all things', and to have 'inherited' a name 'more excellent' than those of the angels: mere human nature, runs the commentary, is not capable of receiving the inheritance of all rule and power;[155] the one who is 'more excellent' (*praestantior*, rendering the epistle's *diaphorōteron*) must surely be he who inherits 'in genus and species and substance and subsistence or nature, and all such things' from the Father. *Substantia et subsistentia vel natura* probably translate *ousia* and *hupostasis*. So far, there is admittedly nothing that could not have come from Origen: all that is said is that the Son receives his entire being and character from the Father, that the Father bestows on the Son some sort of generic likeness to himself. The Son's distinct reality (his *ousia* and *hupostasis*) derives directly from the Father; perhaps the Aristotelean dictum that 'inheritance is by nature, not a gift' is in the background[156] – so that Origen in his commentary would be, as the general context suggests, insisting on the Son's *kinship* with the

Father, as against those who deny the title *theos* to the Son,[157] and who interpret texts such as the one in question as referring to a human being exalted by grace.

The next quotation in the text is evidently Origen's comment on Hebrews 1:3: Origen associates the epistle's phrase, 'the effulgence (*apaugasma*) of his glory and the imprinted image of his subsistence (*hupostasis*)' with the language of Wisdom 7:26, where Wisdom is described as the *apaugasma* of the eternal light and (in the preceding verse) 'a breath of the power of God, the most pure emanation (*aporrhoea*, the usual Latin transliteration of *aporroia*) of the glory of the Almighty'. And in the next section cited, we have an explanation of how Scripture regularly works by using metaphors drawn from material reality to indicate truth to the mind: 'breath', *vapor*, proceeds from a bodily substance, Christ in like manner originates from the power (*virtus*) of God. Difficulties arise in the lines that immediately follow, however. 'So too', the quotation continues:

> Wisdom, proceeding from him, is generated by that selfsame substance of God. No less is the case with the likeness of a bodily *aporrhoea*, by which Wisdom is said to be a kind of pure and authentic *aporrhoea* of the Almighty. Both these metaphors quite clearly show that there is a communion of substance between Father and Son. For it would seem that an *aporrhoea* is *homoousios*, i.e. of one substance, with the body of which it is an *aporrhoea* or breath.[158]

The problem is not only that Origen in the *Commentary on John*, XX.18,[159] sharply repudiates the idea that the Son is generated out of the Father's *ousia*, as this implies that Father and Son are material realities; more strikingly still, in XIII.25 of the same commentary, we find[160] a rejection of Heracleon's view that those created spirits destined for salvation are *homoousios* with God, and[161] an exegesis of the same text from the Wisdom of Solomon that directly contradicts the fragment on Hebrews. Having said that the Father transcends the Son and the Spirit *more* than they transcend the creaturely world, Origen points out that Wisdom is called an *apaugasma* not of God but of his glory and light, and a 'breath' not of the Father but of his power. Judging from other passages,[162] as well as from the criticism of Heracleon in XIII.25, Origen understood *homoousios* to designate co-ordinate members of a single class, beings sharing the same properties. Since his gnostic opponents taught that holy souls were of one substance with God, they implied, Origen claimed, that God was as capable of change and corruption as any created spirit. Obviously this unacceptable corollary would not apply if the Son were spoken of as *homoousios;* but it would be impossible for Origen to regard the Son as another member of a class including the Father, and so it is difficult to imagine him using the term of the Son.

Essentially, he has a single set of notions in mind as his polemical target in these and other passages of the Commentary. Valentinian gnostics such as Heracleon give the impression of teaching that spirits destined for salvation are 'portions' of the divine substance: such spirits are the same *kind* of thing as God because they come forth from him (compare what we noted above about the doctrine of Clement's Valentinian opponents – the 'spiritual seed' as an *aporroia* from a higher level). Origen objects to the implication that the divine substance is divisible (and so material),[163] and, in XIII.25, appears to be objecting also to the way Valentinians use *homoousios* to describe this relation of derivation: 'they do not see that what is *homoousios* is a subject of the same predicates (*tōn autōn dektikon*)'[164] – that is, a co-ordinate reality. Thus the 'derivation' sense of *homoousios* and expressions like 'out of the Father's substance' equally reflect the materialist implications of gnostic teaching in Origen's eyes.

Rius-Camps[165] suggests that, while Origen objected to the Son being said to be '*generated* out of the Father's substance' (as in XX.18 of the John Commentary), he would not necessarily have denied that the Son could be described simply as 'from' the Father's substance. This does not help us with the Hebrews fragment, though, where Wisdom *ex ipsa substantia Dei generatur;*[166] and there is no clear evidence that Origen worked with a distinction of this sort. The problem of reconciling the passages quoted in the present text of the *Defence* with the opinions of Origen elsewhere expressed remains unsolved – especially as we are not dealing with a marginal point in his thinking. The polemic against gnosticism is a central concern.

If Pamphilus' text has been, as we must conclude, doctored by Rufinus, is it possible to see how this has been done? I believe it is.[167] The three extracts from the Hebrews Commentary bear no relation at all to the first charge in Pamphilus' catalogue (which there is no obvious reason for suspecting); but they *do* have some relevance to the second and third. The first quotation plainly makes the point that the Son is indeed to be called God, because human nature alone cannot receive the inheritance bestowed by the Father – as we noted earlier. This seems to be related to the *third* of the charges,[168] which evidently arose from some misunderstanding of Origen's Christology by a generation suspicious of anyone teaching the existence of a human soul in Christ, combined with a misunderstanding of his unwillingness to call the Son *ho theos*, 'God' in a simple or absolute sense.[169] The Commentary quotation answers both points in the charge, stressing that Christ is not solely human, and repudiating the theology of those who will not call the Son 'God'. Likewise the second and third quotations appear to be more at home with the second of the charges, that Origen thought of the Son as an emanation from the Godhead – perhaps based on Origen's fondness for the metaphor of will's relation to mind in speaking of the Son's relation to the Father? The second text merely connects what is said in Hebrews with the parent passage in Wisdom, where the words *vapor* and *aporrhoea* are employed; the third, as we have seen, reminds us that this is only an image drawn from material things. If these originally stood with the response to the second accusation, Pamphilus would be making the point that, although Origen might use the imagery of emanation at times, he was well aware that it denoted no corporeality in God himself – as the existing *responsio* to the second accusation makes clear.

It is quite likely, then, that Rufinus has taken quotations from the later *responsiones* to fill out the first. He has taken Pamphilus' original heading for the first catena – 'That the Son is born from the Father' – as an occasion for arguing that Origen believed in an unbroken continuity between Son and Father; thus he adds to the heading the words: 'and is of one substance with the Father, alien from creaturely substance'; he either ignores or fails to see Pamphilus' need here to establish a proper *distinction* between Father and Son. After all, the heresy of teaching 'two unbegottens' no longer has its old force by Rufinus' day, having been used so regularly by anti-Nicenes as a stick to beat their opponents with. Pamphilus' original series of *catenae* offers Rufinus a usefully comprehensive collection of extracts, and he is able to construct a catena on continuity without going beyond what already stands before him, or doing serious violence to the structure of Pamphilus' presentation. It has clearly escaped his notice that he has performed the considerable *tour de force* of making Pamphilus' first *responsio* say the exact opposite of what its compiler intended.

But if Rufinus is out to preclude any Arian use or orthodox abuse of Origen, it is not surprising that he adds his own brief gloss to the third extract from the Hebrews Commentary.[170] I suspect that *Sapientia . . . ex ipsa substantia Dei generatur* is Rufinus' rendering of a Greek original that read something like *sophia hupo* (or perhaps *para*) *tēs tou theou ousias genēta* or *ginetai*. And the words following 'Both these metaphors . . .' are an explanatory gloss by Rufinus: it is obvious that a *vapor* is of one substance with its source, so there should be no doubt that Origen, to all intents and purposes, taught the consubstantiality of Father and Son, since he was perfectly happy to use such imagery.

As has often been remarked,[171] we should not seek to enforce upon Origen a consistency he himself seldom seems to have worried about. Yet, although it is still just possible that the conclusion of the Hebrews fragment is authentic, even if deliberately misplaced, it is unusual to find so flat a contradiction on so significant a matter. Allowance may be made for the early date and polemical tendency of the John Commentary;[172] but we have noted that for Origen, as for Clement, the refutation of the implicit materialism of Valentinian cosmology is of first importance, and he would be most unlikely to use an expression that might give any countenance at all to it. The transcendence of the Father depends upon his having no 'coordinates' (if he is a member of a class, he must be distinguished from other members; if so, he has particular defining characteristics, and so is not infinite)[173] and on his being immaterial and indivisible. 'Participating' in God is not having a share of some material stuff, but doing what God does,[174] having one *praxis* with the Son in contemplating the Father.[175] To use the language of later Greek theology, we share in, perceive and are conformed to, the operation, *energeia*, not the essence of God.

Origen's Logos is thus (like Philo's and Clement's) that of God which is accessible to us and capable of being shared by us. But because Origen has so much clearer a doctrine of the Word's distinctive existence from all eternity, he has to deal rather more extensively than his predecessors in Alexandria with the question of how the Word is related to the Father. As is well-known to students of Christian doctrine, Origen believed that the Son was eternally, timelessly, generated by the Father.[176] If anyone is so foolish as to suggest that there was a time when the Logos did not exist,[177] they will have to explain why God did not bring him into being sooner; and, pressing the implications of the *reductio ad absurdum*, we come finally to see that, for God, there is no gap between possibility and effective willing, and so no impediment to his always 'having what he wants', so to speak. The only 'beginning' the Word has is God, 'from whom he is, of whom he is born' – a characteristic play on the many senses of *archē:* the Word does not have an *archē*, a point of origin, in time, only an *archē*, an origin and 'rationale' of existence in the being of God.[178] Origen adds an argument of some freshness and importance to this: God as father must have a son in order to be what he is.[179] If we take for granted the divine changelessness, as Origen and his interpreters did, what is said of God must be timelessly true: if part of what is said of God is that he is one term of a relation, the other term must also be eternal. Origen goes on to apply this to God's omnipotence, arguing for a kind of necessity in the eternal existence of creatures *over* whom God is omnipotent. This 'necessity' for creation depends on the prior fact of God's defining himself as Father: he creates 'in' the Word and Wisdom he has begotten.[180] This last point may be an attempt to avoid any suggestion of an 'automatic' creation: God creates because he first (logically not temporally, of course) *wills* to be the progenitor of Wisdom. This is none too clear, though, and Origen's posthumous reputation was to suffer on account of these speculations; the logic of the argument is more complex than Origen realized, and he seems to confuse the fact that (on his premises) statements about God must be timelessly true with the mistaken deduction that anything appearing as one term of a relation of which the other term is God must exist eternally. There is a muddle about the logic of relations here, as well as a confusion of endless/beginningless duration with timelessness or rather tenselessness. However, an improved form of the argument was to appear, to good effect, in anti-Arian writings of the fourth century.[181]

This discussion reveals a significant tension in Origen's thought. Much of the second chapter of his first book *On First Principles* (from which these arguments come) uses very freely the imagery of the Son or Word as *aporroia* and *vapor* commenting on the opening verses of Hebrews and their counterpart in Wisdom 7. Gnostic materialism is repudiated,[182] and the Word is said to come forth from the Father 'as the will does from the mind'.[183] Origen's profound concern for the simplicity, immateriality and indivisibility of the divine nature[184] naturally leads him to emphasize the analogy between God and the human mind; so it is not suprising that what 'proceeds' from God, his Word or Wisdom, should be conceived on the analogy of a mental operation. Wisdom is the *energeia* of a divine *virtus* of *dunamis*,[185] the actualization of a divine capacity. Origen exploits the technical sense possessed by the words used in Septuagintal or New Testament imagery; Wisdom is called a mirror of God's *energeia* or *dunamis* in Wisdom 7.26, and Origen tidies this up as 'a mirror of the *energeia* of the *dunamis* of God,' observing the Aristotelean order of potency and act. But of course this leaves him with the difficulty that a divine act is not a subsistent reality in itself; and he is equally eager to affirm the Word's subsistent reality, as we have seen. The Word of God is not only a cosmological convenience, but the paradigm for our knowing and loving the Father,[186] and so must have a 'hypostatic' existence comparable to ours: he must be a *subject* of knowledge and love. The Logos of Philo may be a paradigm for knowledge of God, but is so only *formally*, as that which contains those truths to which our minds must be conformed. Origen's Logos is also *Son*, glorifying and being glorified by the Father,[187] enjoying a relation with God which is far more clearly of a personal nature: hence the appeal to the logic of relation (if a father, then a son too) serves, in the *Commentary on John*,[188] to underline the real plurality and mutuality of the divine life. The Son is clearly seen as more than an instrument for connecting God with the world: he is the sharer of God's glory, irrespective of his role *vis-á-vis* the creation. Origen hints at a fundamental datum of later trinitarian thought, that the Father-Son relation is simply part of the *definition* of the word God, and so does not exist for the sake of anything other than itself.

Yet he also inherits and accepts the Alexandrian tradition of emphasizing the absolute transcendence and unknowability of the 'first God', the source of all,[189] and identifying the Logos with the world of divine ideas.[190] This involves thinking of the Father as 'simple' and the Son as 'multiple',[191] and stressing the Father's distance from the Son[192] (though some passages from works later than the *Commentary on John*[193] play down this element rather). Origen was certainly accused[194] of teaching that the Son did not know the Father perfectly, but on the basis of some very obvious misunderstandings of certain remarks in *On First Principles*.[195] However, this is a complex and intriguing question, and here too Origen shows a somewhat divided mind. It is essential for him to affirm that the Son knows the Father if the Son is to be the medium of *our* relation to the Father;[196] but what the Father is to and for himself does not *depend* on the Son. And, in at least one tantalizing section of the *Commentary on John*,[197] Origen suggests that, although the Father's joy in himself is in some sense shared and known and capable of being expressed by the Son, his contemplation of his own being is prior to and independent of, and perhaps beyond the capacity of, the Son.[198] The point is really less to do with the Son's knowledge of God than with defending the Father's self-sufficiency.

Origen is in fact far less inclined than Clement to emphasize the Father's utter incomprehensibility; but he does say that God transcends *nous* and *ousia*[199] – that is, the order of intelligible definition, *ousia* here having its quite common Platonic sense of 'structure' or 'form'. He is happier, it seems, to work with the *analogy* between God and *nous*, which allows him to speak freely of God as subject of knowing and willing; but because the Son is identical with the realm of ideas, and so represents that level of being where intellect is supremely dominant, the Father must, logically, be beyond intellect. As we shall see later on,[200] this is perhaps best understood against the background of the philosophical developments of Origen's age. It is a particularly clear instance of the rather uneasy relationship between the two controlling factors in Origen's thought: the given constraints of scriptural metaphor and the assumptions of Platonic cosmology. On the one hand, scriptural language about the Son's subordination and passages that seem clearly to envisage Father and Son as distant subsistents go reasonably well with a system emphasizing the gulf between an ultimate oneness beyond all relations and all understanding and the ensemble of intelligible forms within a cosmic 'mind'. On the other, it is hard to deny mind to the willing, purposive God of Scripture; and language about the perfect communion and mutuality of Father and Son, combined with Origen's own argument about the eternity or even 'necessity' of relations in which God is involved, militates against the idea that the Father can be seen simply as a self-sufficient absolute.

Hence Origen's ambiguities over whether or not the Son exists at the Father's *will*.[201] We have noted already that, within the same chapter[202] of *First Principles*, Origen can use the analogy of the relation between mind and will to illustrate how the Logos comes forth from the Father, and can also speak[203] as if the begetting of the Logos were the result of a choice (admittedly a 'timeless' choice) by the Father. Again, a passage in the *Commentary on John*,[204] discussing John 4:34 ('My food is to do the will of him who sent me'), clearly distinguishes the will of the Father from the will of the Son, while at the same time stressing that the latter is in all respects the perfect image of the former, 'so that there are no longer two wills but one'.[205] The Son 'holds' or 'defines' the Father's will[206] – and so, presumably, reveals it as perfectly as can be; just as he is the revealing *eikōn* of God's goodness, and his divinity the *eikōn* of the Father's divinity.[207] It is through this 'food' of perfectly imaging the Father's will that the Son is what he is.[208] Thus Origen, in spite of the metaphors of *First Principles*, veers away from Clement's apparent readiness to call the Son the *thelēma* of the Father;[209] yet there is relatively little to suggest any simple doctrine that the Father wills the Son into being in anything like the same sense as that in which he wills the world into being.

Origen almost certainly called the Son *ktisma* in the original text of *First Principles*[210] (as he called him a *dēmiourgēma* in *Contra Celsum*),[211] and was duly abused for it by his later critics;[212] but it is almost impossible to sort out exactly what he meant by it. It has been noted,[213] for instance, that he seems to make a distinction in various texts[214] between the *kosmos*, which is the world of our fallen state, and the *ktisis*, the primordial 'heaven-and-earth' of Genesis 1:1, the realm of rational spirits. As Origen explains in *First Principles*,[215] in a passage attacking gnostic predestinarianism, the first creation, of rational beings, is caused simply and exclusively by God's will, and therefore is a realm of absolute equality: the world we know, with its irrational variety, results from the variable wills of creatures. God limits this variety in so far as he sees to it that these diversities add up to a viable whole, a *consonantia;*[216] but they cannot be regarded as expressing his will. It could be said, though rather awkwardly, that the world we inhabit as material beings is not 'created' by God: it is made, or at least conditioned, by the choices of his creatures,[217] and regulated by his providence. 'Creation', *ktisis*, is strictly only the unimpeded expression of God's rational will.

It is not clear that the terminological distinction is consistently maintained, or that it really resolves the theological problem about the Logos. It does, however, remind us that Origen saw creation as primarily divine self-expression: there is nothing arbitrary about it. And since the generation of the Logos is the *archē* of all rational beings, the first 'expression' of God's will and the most perfect, there is no particular reason why Origen should not speak of him as 'created'. Yet he most probably repudiated the idea that the Son was created out of nothing. Rufinus' version of *First Principles* IV.4.1 may be heavily doctored, but the lines[218] in which Origen is represented as denying both that 'a part of God's substance is turned into the Son' and that 'the Son is generated by the Father from things that are not (*ex nullis substantibus*), that is, from what is outside the Father's own substance' make an intelligible antithesis – the Son is neither from 'inside' nor from 'outside' God's substance, because this is not how God's life should be conceived. It is plausible enough for Origen, and it is quite explicitly taught by followers of his.[219] That the Father alone is the *archē* of the Logos, as the Logos is the *archē* of all else,[220] means that the being of the Father provides the intelligible form of the Logos; and since the Logos' whole *identity* is to be the Father's image, it would be improper and misleading for Origen to speak to him as 'out of nothing' or 'out of the nonexistent'. It is a moot point whether he would have readily described the rational creation as a whole as *ex ouk ontōn* (though the sensible world clearly is)[221] – for the same reason, that it expresses the mind of God. But whatever may be the truth of this, the Logos is without doubt formed by the Father, directly and uniquely, in a way that sets him apart at least from what later orthodoxy understood as 'creation'.

These considerations may throw some light on another apparent contradiction in Origen. The *Commentary on John* states fairly clearly[222] that the Son is divine in virtue of his participation in the Father's being; and there is a passage in *First Principles*[223] which could be read in the same sense. Yet there are two exegetical fragments which teach precisely the opposite. The *selecta in Psalmos* preserve a comment on Psalm 134 in which Origen refers to Paul's 'gods many and lords many' (I Cor. 8:5) and then continues: 'but those apart from the Trinity who are called "gods" are so by participation (*metousia*) in the Godhead; while the Saviour is God not by participation but in substance (*ou kata metousian, alla kat' ousian*)'.[224] Similarly, a fragment on the Apocalypse[225] calls the Son 'He Who Is, in his very substance' (*ho ōn ousia(i)*)), applying to the Christ in Revelation 1:18 the divine self-designation of Exodus 3:13

as rendered in the Septuagint; what the Son is, he is not by *metousia* only.[226] Possibly, as Lorenz suggests,[227] the statment in *First Principles*[228] that the Son has 'substantial goodness' in himself also reflects something similar.

This raises several quite complex questions, to do with the definition of 'participation' itself, and the sense in which Origen, in his later years, might have wanted to emphasize the Father's transcendence of 'being' (so that he would be *beyond ho ōn*) – questions we shall return to in the third section of this book. For now, though, it can be said that what matters for Origen is that the Son does not *first* come into being and *then* receive additional qualities from God: his definition (*ousia* in the sense of 'form', 'ideal structure') is to manifest the Father, and he has no reality apart from this. If he is by nature or essence God's image, there is nothing in him that is not the Father's life revealing itself. Yet, since he comes from the Father, and is what he is by derivation from the Father, it would make some sense to say that he is 'made God by participation in the Godhead',[229] in order to guard against any suggestion of two first principles. If (as is probable) the exegetical fragments are later than the *Commentary on John*, Origen himself recognized that the language of participation in this connection could be misleading; and this would certainly accord with a tendency in his later works to minimize the gulf between Father and Son.[230]

Thus far, Origen presents us with so varied and nuanced a picture that it is easy to see why his relation to Arianism has been the subject of so much dispute. A few points, however, should be clear. First of all, Arius stands in the tradition of Origen in so far as he holds to the transcendence of the Father, the impossibility of believing in two co-ordinate *agen(n)ēta*, self-sufficient first principles,[231] and the substantive and distinct reality of three divine *hupostaseis* or *ousiai;* and he probably has Origen on his side in repudiating the *homoousios* and the idea that the Son is 'out of' the Father's substance. Both are passionately concerned to give no quarter to materialism, and to the materialist implications of calling the Son a *probolē*, both see Sabellianism and Valentinianism as the great enemies of orthodoxy.[232] But secondly, it is just as plain that Arius and Origen are fundamentally at odds over the eternity of the Son and the quasi-necessity of the Son to the Father. Origen, as we have noted, anticipates developed fourth-century orthodoxy in this at least, that he comes close to saying that the Father-Son relationship is intrinsic to the divine life as such – and also in that he has some notion of this relation as existing for its own sake, not as a means for connecting the One and the Many. Arius, on the other hand, remained firmly within the tradition which saw the distinct subsistence of the Second Hypostasis as connected to God's purpose as creator – a tradition with reputable ancestry in the Apologists,[233] and probably, as suggested above, in Clement. On other matters – the Son's knowledge of the Father and participation in the Father, and the dependence of his existence upon the divine will – Origen is ambivalent where Arius is clear: Origenian phrases, or even whole passages, that have an 'Arian' flavour on first reading are far more carefully qualified when seen in their context.

One or two other differences are worth remarking. Arius in the *Thalia* sees the Son as praising the Father in heaven; Origen generally avoids language suggesting that the Son *worships* the Father as God (there is one passage[234] which *might* be read in such a sense). Yet – paradoxically – while Origen notoriously discouraged prayer to the Son (Christian prayer should be made *in* the Son *to* the Father),[235] Arius and his followers apparently allowed it, thus giving Athanasius one of his most effective controversial openings[236] (the wording of the *Thalia* at S31 may reflect some early form of the *Trisagion* addressed to the Son).[237] Origen, for all his stress on the Son as an independent *ousia*, does not for a moment allow that the Son might be an 'object' to us in isolation from his relation to the Father; and since his relation to the Father is the eternal form and ground of *all* rational and spiritual relation to the Father, he can no more be an object to us than can our own spiritual growth. He is the soil on which we grow, the eyes with which we see. But this also implies that he cannot 'pray' to the Father in any sense resembling that in which *we* pray, as all our praise and worship is in and through him. Arius' insistence on the Son as an individual existing at God's will and receiving grace ironically makes it easier for him to treat the Son as both object and subject of worship.

Lorenz[238] has recently proposed that we should look for the antecedents of Arius' doctrine not in Origen's trinitarian theology but in his account of the incarnation. For here we have a created rational spirit who perfectly fulfils the vocation of all rational creatures, transcending its inherent liability to change and decay by freely and eternally cleaving to the Word and Wisdom of God, 'inseparably and indissolubly',[239] receiving all the glory that it possibly can and becoming 'one spirit' with the Logos.[240] In virtue of this, the soul of Jesus can rightly be called by names proper to the eternal Son ('Son of God', 'power of God', 'Christ',[241] 'Wisdom of God'), and the Son can be called 'Jesus Christ' and 'Son of man'[242] – the first attempt to work out a theory of *communicatio idiomatum* in the history of Christian theology. The soul of Jesus retains its contingency and its freewill in the incarnate state, and is properly called 'Christ' in relation to its consistent and meritorious virtue in this condition: the psalmist, after all, says that the divine anointing occurs because 'you have loved righteousness and hated iniquity'.[243] But before and during its earthly existence, its free will is so unswervingly directed to the good that its choices become 'natural' to it, and it is nonsensical to think that there is any possibility of its falling away.[244] It is thoroughly permeated and transformed, like iron in a fire.[245] God is the ground of all it does and all it knows, 'and so it cannot be said to be convertible or changeable'.[246]

This notion of a *de facto* immutability possessed by a creature in virtue of a consistent exercise of its freedom is indeed quite close to what Arius says about the Logos; and the use of that significant Arian proof-text from the forty-fifth psalm, in *Contra Celsum*[247] and in the *Commentary on John*,[248] as well as in *First Principles*[249] reinforces the parallel. The 'kenotic' hymn of Philippians 2 is also applied by Origen not to the Logos as such but to the soul of Jesus.[250] As with Arius himself, these texts about 'anointing' and 'exaltation' are carefully interpreted so as not to give countenance to any hint of adoptionism in the usual sense – that is, they are *not* taken to be referring to a promotion on the grounds of virtue attained in an earthly existence. It is, rather, a matter of a status of glory and dignity eternally possessed and never lost, sustained by the exercise of freedom in the face of temptation (so that it has value for us as an example):[251] this triumphantly preserved dignity is made manifest in the *declaration* of Jesus as chosen and anointed, the fact that, in the providence of God, he 'becomes' for us the one who exercises the royal power of the Logos.[252] But Origen does not suggest any temporal progression here: the royal anointing of Jesus is a gift, he does not possess the powers of the Logos by nature, yet the eternally existing soul of Jesus is never for a moment anything but the recipient of the grace of the divine Son in all its fulness. Throughout the first book of the *Commentary on John*, the *epinoiai* of the Logos, the multiple forms of his manifestation, are ascribed to 'Christ' or 'the Word' indifferently; just as, for Arius,[253] it is the created Son who can be said to have many *epinoiai* by which we can conceive him, so for Origen the created soul of Jesus is, to all intents and purposes, the subject of all that can be said about the Logos, at least as far as concerns our *apprehension* of the Logos. We can and must, in Origen, distinguish Logos and Jesus,[254] and yet they are not separable in the economy of revelation. Even if we move beyond the incarnate condition of Christ in our spiritual apprehension, the soul of Jesus is still a paradigm for the relation of rational beings to the Logos, as the Logos himself is the paradigm of relation to the Father. We are to become *christoi* through the anointed soul of Jesus,[255] as we become *logikos* and *theos* in the Logos.

The closeness of the two schemes is evident. Of course, the crucial difference remains that Arius' God requires a created individual for his self-revelation, while Origen's God is eternally and *almost* 'necessarily' one who manifests himself in his Word simply to respond to and glorify and rejoice in his own being, before and beyond creation. But Lorenz is surely right to underline the parallels, and to connect them[256] with Origen's interest in the 'incarnational' mythology of Alexandrian Judaism – angelic spirits descending to occupy mortal bodies – a mythology he refers to in discussing the idea that John the Baptist may have been an angelic pre-existent spirit (that is, not one who was *obliged* to descend into the material world).[257] Arius may very well have known the kind of Jewish or Jewish-Christian work which freely used the imagery of ascending and descending heavenly beings: we have seen that the *Ascension of Isaiah* was being read in Alexandria at the beginning of the fourth century, and there is plenty of material there about the incarnation of the Son as the descent of a celestial/angelic individual – and, incidentally, about the 'liturgical' role of Son and Spirit in heaven; we may recall Arius' stress on the Son as paradigm *worshipper*.[258] Origen, like Philo, is inclined to reduce the more obviously anthropomorphic elements of this tradition, though defending, of course, the real subsistence of the Logos: Arius seems to 'remythologize'. Hieracas had apparently woven together themes from both Clement and Origen in his reading of the *Ascension of Isaiah*, reducing the Son in himself to a barely personal emanation from God, yet maintaining an incarnational mythology in which heavenly individuals, identified *de facto*, though not in essence, with the innate and non-personalized powers of God, played crucial roles. Arius' firm denunciation of Hieracas[259] is tantamount to a claim that the imagery of Jewish-Christian apocalyptic – the heavenly liturgy, the archangelic high priest, the descent of the highest celestial power through the ranks of angels down to earth[260] – is not to be rationalized and allegorized away.

Origen's Logos is too closely bound to the divine life *in se* to 'carry' much of the venerable Alexandrian imagery of angelic liturgy; but the pre-existent soul of Jesus can take over at least some of it. How precisely, then, does it come to be transferred by Arius *back* to the Logos? The answer to this question will emerge more fully in II.D of our study: without anticipating too much of this, we can simply note for now that a great deal depends, in Origen's account, on his wider theory about the pre-existence of souls. Without this doctrine, the awkward question has to be faced of what can be done with the hallowed (and scriptural) imagery of a supremely endowed heavenly individual, 'more honourable than the cherubim and incomparably more glorious than the Seraphim'.[261] The Marian allusion is deliberate: Newman, in a famous passage of the *Essay on Development*,[262] wrote that, after the Nicene ascription of consubstantial divinity to the Son, 'there was "a wonder in heaven": a throne was seen, far above all created powers, mediatorial, intercessory; a title archetypal; a crown bright as the morning star; a glory issuing from the Eternal Throne; and a sceptre over all; and who was the predestined heir of that Majesty?' Whatever may be thought of Newman's ingenious and eloquent attempt to found the cultus of Mary as supreme intercessor (and the habit of applying the sophianic imagery of the Old Testament to her and not to Christ) upon Nicene Christology,[263] he articulates exactly the question which a repudiation of Origen's doctrine of creation and fall implied for third-century theology.

However, it would be a mistake to conclude that Arius is indebted to Origen's view of the incarnation in any direct way. The parallels noted add up simply to this, that a set of conventions used in one way by Origen reappears in a rather more archaic form in Arius. Arius inherits from his Alexandrian milieu not only the tradition of apophatic theology which we have already discussed at some length, but also the language of the *Thronwelt*, the realm of angelic worship and intercession before the throne and altar of God, the realm presided over by one to whom God gives a unique share in his properties, in whom he makes his Name to dwell.[264] And, of course,

147

from pre-Philonic times onward, these two themes are connected: the notion of a God beyond all name and form implies that the names and forms of a revealed God are something less than the divine life itself.

It might be more accurate to see Origen's legacy to Arius in relation to exegetical method. As the first Christian to comment *in extenso* and by *continuous* exposition, upon the Scriptures, Origen allows exegesis to take note of and to resolve apparent contradictions: exegesis can, and indeed must, be a problem-solving exercise. To take one important instance that we have already discussed, Psalm 45:7–8 can be seen as problematic in so far as it speaks of Christ apparently acquiring what he did not have before. Earlier theologians[265] had used the text without raising any detailed questions about it, because it serves a purely illustrative and 'occasional' function in their work. Origen is committed to working out a rational interpretation in terms of his *systematic* reading of the biblical text overall as providing a trinitarian and cosmological scheme; and by means of such interpretation he aims to defend Scripture's claim to be divinely inspired against accusations of inconsistency and contradiction from pagan or gnostic. Celsus and Heracleon alike must be shown to have misread a text whose continuity and unity lie at a subtle level accessible only to prayerful Catholic reading. But once the element of problem-solving is admitted, and the need for tight theological consistency in exegesis is recognized, exegesis becomes more and more the primary field of doctrinal conflict, in a way it is not in the earlier second century: debate with gnosticism turns not on the reading of specific texts so much as on the nature and extent of the canon itself; detailed exegetical dispute requires authoritative common ground.[266] If, as was proposed earlier, Arius is quintessentially an exponent of 'learned', rationally coherent, catechesis, he is in the succession of Origen; and, as with Clement, it is possible to see his vocabulary echoing that of the earlier master[267] and reflecting the ideology of the charismatic teacher and his circle of initiates. But in other respects, the confident ancient and modern judgment that Arius represents a development within an 'Origenist' theological school cannot be sustained in any but a radically qualified sense.

4 ALEXANDRIA AFTER ORIGEN

Part of the trouble is the very word 'Origenist'. Standard histories of doctrine have rather tended to assume that the majority of Egyptian, Syrian and Asian writers of the late third and early fourth centuries could be seen as 'Origenists' of one sort and another, and that theology in Alexandria in particular was dominated by Origen. Harnack[268] believed that Origen's successors in the catechetical school made no substantial modifications in his system; Loofs[269] proposed a distinction between Origenists of the 'left' and the 'right' (the former being more inclined to subordinationism in their trinitarian theology) – a distinction that has left a considerable mark upon subsequent accounts of this period. But what makes a theologian an 'Origenist' in the first place? 'Subordinationism'? allegorical exegesis? the doctrine of the pre-existence of souls?[270] The fact is that the 'Origenism' that caused such controversy around the year 400, and the views condemned under Justinian in the sixth century simply do not appear as a *system* in any earlier writer (it remains a moot point whether they should be treated as a system derived from Origen's own writings in any strict sense). In his admirable study of Dionysius of Alexandria, Wolfgang Bienert rightly says[271] that 'no "Origenist" theologian [of the third or fourth century] took over and unreservedly argued for Origen's system in its entirety'.

Likewise, Bienert suggests,[272] it would be wrong to look for a consistent tradition of 'anti-Origenism' in this period. Particular doctrines are criticized; and, as we have seen, there is evidence (from Pamphilus' *Apology*)[273] of the drawing up of catalogues of suspect propositions. Yet Athanasius can speak of Origen with respect,[274] and there is no suggestion before 399/400 of wholesale *official* repudiation by episcopal authority in Alexandria or elsewhere – however harshly individual bishops as theologians[275] might have criticized Origen. Even Bienert's own contention that there was a fairly consistent and deliberate policy of episcopal coolness towards Origen in Alexandria[276] may be overstating the case a little: Bienert himself proposes that, after a period of something like real hostility to Origen under Demetrius' successor Heraclas,[277] the reign of Dionysius (247/8–264/5) saw a relaxation of official attitudes – not unconnected with Dionysius' wish for closer relations with the Palestinian churches in which Origen's reputation stood so high[278] –

which survived until Peter renewed the attack in the early years of the fourth century.

Dionysius the Great is a figure of particular interest and importance in the background of the Arian controversy since there existed, by the forties of the next century, a small dossier of extracts purporting to be from his works which the Arians were using in support of their position. According to Athanasius,[279] the expressions in question come from a letter to Euphranor and Ammonius, dealing with the outbreak of Sabellianism that was afflicting the churches of the Libyan Pentapolis in the 250s. If the letter is identical with the one to 'Euphranor, Ammon and Euporus' mentioned by Eusebius,[280] its recipients were bishops in Libya, presumably supporters of the anti-Sabellian line (Euphranor was the dedicatee of another opusculum of Dionysius)[281] in need of additional theological armaments for controversy. Dionysius insisted[282] that the Son was a *poiēma* and a *genēton*, a thing made and generated, not 'proper' (*idion*) to the nature of God, but 'alien in substance' (*xenos kat' ousian*), as the vinedresser is different from the vine and the shipwright from the boat: 'and being a *poiēma*, he did not exist before he was generated'.

Zealous colleagues forwarded this text to Bishop Dionysius of Rome, who replied[283] in a long and strongly-worded letter, denouncing those (unnamed) teachers who in their eagerness to avoid Sabellianism spoke of three *dunameis* or separate *hupostaseis* or 'divinities' (that is, divine lives or natures, *theotētes*),[284] and repudiating as blasphemous all talk of the Son as a *cheiropoiēton*, a work of God's hands,[285] or a *poiēma*,[286] and of a 'generation' of the Son and a time when he was not.[287] The Son can be, and in Scripture is, said to be 'created' by God the Father, but not 'made': *ektise* in Proverbs 8:22 is not *epoiēse*.[288] And he is 'begotten' (*gegennēsthai*) but not 'generated' in the sense of 'deliberately produced' by the Father (*gegonenai*).[289] The attack on a doctrine of three distinct *hupostaseis* foreshadows Marcellus' criticism of Origen's language, and suggests that Dionysius of Rome, like Marcellus, considered 'two [or three] substances, subjects, or independent existents' as equivalent to 'two [or three] self-sufficient first principles (*archai*)' – a doctrine which the Roman pontiff associates with Marcionite dualism.[290] It is worth noting in passing, that, if the *bête noir* of Alexandria was Valentinianism, Rome's worry was Marcionism: a difference that helps a little in understanding the diverse emphases in their trinitarian schemes. Origen and Arius want to stress that the Son is no mere manifestation of the 'Protean', essentially remote yet infinitely divisible, divine life; while Roman writers work to avoid any suggestion of a gulf between creator and redeemer. As to the proposed distinction between 'making' and 'creating', we have seen a hint of this in Origen, but it seems to have no very clear ancestry: it is probably an exegetical convention in Dionysius' Rome – not a very subtle one, but at least a recognition, once again, of the demands of rational expository teaching in a Church obliged to defend the coherence of its foundational texts.

Dionysius of Alexandria's reply, says Athanasius, was to compose a pair of treatises, the 'interrogation' (*elenchos*) and 'defence' – possibly two of the four letters of his to Dionysius of Rome mentioned by Eusebius.[291] Doubt has recently been cast on the authenticity of Athanasius' citations,[292] partly, it seems, because they appear to make Dionysius too orthodox a fourth-century Nicene; but there are reasons for maintaining their genuineness. The foremost of these is simply that the passages quoted do not say what Athanasius tries to make them say. In sections 10 and 11 of Athanasius' pamphlet on Dionysius' opinions, for instance, he defends his predecessor's use of the vine and vinedresser analogy because it is based upon what Christ *as man* said of himself:[293] and the text of Proverbs 8:22, 'The Lord created me', justifies the statement that the Son is created because it is again to be read as spoken by Wisdom incarnate.[294] But Athanasius admits that Dionysius only *implies* all this, since he is reduced in section 12[295] to imagining what Dionysius might say to the Arians; and since the exegetical device of ascribing such embarrassing dicta solely to the human Jesus is so very characteristic of Athanasius[296] and so conspicuously lacking in earlier theology, Dionysius evidently did not defend himself along these lines. When Athanasius turns to quoting from Dionysius' own defence, he can adduce nothing corresponding to what he himself has just outlined. On the contrary, Dionysius is represented[297] as vigorously maintaining the propriety of calling the Son *ktisma* or *poiēma* since a human being can be said to be the creator of his or her utterance (*logos*) or a doer (*poiētēs*) of an inward quality or disposition. Even while quoting this, Athanasius still blithely asserts that Dionysius held God to be the creator of the Logos only *dia tēn sarka*, on account of his incarnate state[298] – apparently not noticing that Dionysius has no need to make such a move, given his main argument.

The appeal to a flexibility in secular usage for *ktizō* and *poieō* is unusual in the fourth century, especially in Athanasius.[299] Once the notion of the Son as *ktisma* had become the distinctive doctrine of Arius and his followers, it was almost impossible for a Nicene writer to develop such a point; consequently it is most unlikely that the material here ascribed to Dionysius is of post-Nicene origin. Indeed, as the treatise proceeds, the themes from Dionysius' apologia become increasingly close to Origen. Radiance is simultaneous with the source of light: the Son is *apaugasma* of the eternal light (Wisdom 7:25 is quoted).[300] To speak of a parent is necessarily also to speak of a child: 'the name [Father] is what provides the ground for the union [of Father and Son]'.[301] If *homoousios* means only *homogenēs*, as a human parent belongs to the same genus as his or her child, it is admissible:[302] Dionysius claims that he used this analogy as well as that of shipwright and boat. The *logos* of human beings is the *aporroia* of mind, proceeding forth and taking on distinct subsistence as it is uttered, but not diminishing the internal *logos* 'in the heart':[303] mind is never without its active manifestation in utterance, utterance is nothing without the mind that makes (*poiei*) it.[304] The Word is wisdom and truth, proceeding from the God who is beyond wisdom and truth[305] – so that, says Athanasius, Dionysius would not agree with the Arian idea of Logos in God generating Logos outside God, because God is not identical with wisdom, truth, or *logos*.

In fact, Dionysius obviously comes very close to the distinction of immanent and uttered *logos* so popular with the Apologists (Bienert and Orbe[306] are right to note the affinities here). But the *apaugasma* and *aporroia* language, the analogy of mental action (mind and will, for Origen, mind and speech for Dionysius), and, above all, the argument from the correlativity of the designations 'Father' and 'Son', an argument which Athanasius develops enthusiastically,[307] all adds up to a picture of a Dionysius standing very close to Origen in his trinitarian thought. It is still baffling that he is alleged to have said that the Son 'did not exist before he was generated': no response to this charge is recorded, and it is in very stark contrast to the Origenian views of Dionysius' defence overall.[308] I can only suppose that it was originally a corollary deduced by the bishop's opponents and listed with his authentic words in the letter of delation to Rome (that is, that it bears the same relation to Dionysius' actual thought as Athanasius' version of the *Thalia* does to the original); but I recognize that this is a rather desperate resort. This loose end apart, Athanasius seems to have been right in seeing Dionysius as a precursor. He does not read him very intelligently at times, but neither, it seems, did the Arians: the Origenian model of (a) eternal correlativity and (b) 'emanation' conceived very carefully on the analogy of the concrete act of mind subsisting over against undifferentiated and continuous mental life or substance, clearly prevails in Dionysius' theology. Like Origen, he both repudiates the Sabellian idea of a single divine individual undergoing diverse experiences, and also qualifies what might turn into unbalanced and equally mythological pluralism by the use of metaphors from human interiority, and the idea of subsistents whose *identity* is in defining and being defined by each other.

Dionysius was certainly critical of Origen's teaching on the pre-existence of souls[309] and all that went with it (thus he insists that the paradise in which Adam and Eve were placed at their creation was an *earthly* place):[310] and in this he was followed by Bishop Peter, at the beginning of the century following. Peter's lost treatise *On the Soul* (mentioned by Procopius of Gaza)[311] criticized Origen's allegorical reading of the 'garments of skins' with which the fallen Adam and Eve were clothed as being material and mortal bodies;[312] and, if the fragments published by Bienert in 1973 are also from this work, it also argued that human beings as images of God could not be the result of a *sunodos* of previously existing substances, and that we could have no authority for speaking of a premundane sin.[313] The indivisibility of body and soul is a theme that also underlies the quite numerous fragments of another work by Peter, *On the Resurrection*,[314] in which he maintains that resurrection must be the restoration of the identity we actually possess as humans, the transformation, not the total and unrecognizable mutation, of our mortal selves – a change, in fact, whose analogues we see in Jesus transfigured and Jesus risen.[315]

This does not add up, in Dionysius or Peter, to a repudiation of Origen – even of Origen's exegesis. Peter's criticism is not of allegorization as a technique, but of one particular and misleading instance of it, and Dionysius' battle against literalist views of the Apocalypse does not suggest a man opposed to Origenian exegesis.[316] Given that Methodius of Olympus' criticisms of Origen (to which we shall turn shortly) cover some of the same ground, it

153

seems that the most widely expressed dissatisfaction about Origen's teaching had to do with a particular area of his teaching: cosmology and anthropology. Even when we turn to the catalogue of complaints about Origen preserved in Pamphilus' *Defence*,[317] three turn directly or indirectly on the nature and destiny of the soul.[318] The three that concern the relation of Father and Son do not attack the foundations of Origen's understanding, but half-grasped features of it that are 'offensive to pious ears' (we should not pray to the Son, the Son is not strictly and in his own right 'good', and the Son does not fully know the Father). As we have seen already, Pamphilus is more concerned to defend Origen from the charge of crypto-Valentinian emanationism than to clear him from unduly subordinating the Son to the Father.

Later centuries had problems with the other Alexandrians of the third century precisely because their trinitarian ideas shared Origen's own ambiguities. Theognostus (probably Dionysius' successor as head of the *didaskaleion*) apparently called the Son a *ktisma*,[319] but also used the 'argument from correlativity', presumably to defend the Son's eternity as necessary to God's being Father.[320] He also spoke of the Son as *apaugasma* and *aporroia*, coming 'out of the Father's substance',[321] echoing Origen's discussion of Wisdom 7 and Hebrews 1, while being perhaps less wary than Origen of the possible materialism of language about derivation from the *ousia* of God (he goes on at once to deny that he intends any such implication); and a further fragment recalls Dionysius' view of the Son as the utterance of the divine mind.[322] The Son is also spoken of as image or 'imitation' (*mimēma*) of the Father, having complete likeness (*homoiotēs*) with him.[323] Of Theognostus' successor Pierius we know even less. Photius describes him as teaching the existence of two substances or natures (*ousiai* or *phuseis*) in God, just as Origen had done,[324] and also mentions a discussion of the cherubim flanking the ark and of 'the pillar of Jacob';[325] despite Radford's hesitations,[326] I think we can reasonably see here another bit of angelological speculation, based on Philo, probably identifying the cherubim with Son and Spirit, and perhaps picking up Philo's identification of Jacob/Israel with the Logos,[327] or using (as did Origen)[328] the *Prayer of Joseph*, or both. Little or nothing in what we have of the work of these two obscure teachers indicates a great gulf dividing them from either Origen or Dionysius.

It seems, then, that it is not wrong to think of an 'Origenian' consensus in Alexandria among both bishops and teachers, on the doctrine of the Trinity – not precisely an 'Origenist tradition', since it could co-exist with sharp criticisms of other features of Origen's thought, but a general contentment with certain images and arguments, and an agreement about the exegesis of Wisdom 7 in connection with Hebrews 1. Without this background, it would be impossible to make sense of Alexander of Alexandria's theology, as expressed in the lengthy letter to his namesake in Byzantium. He is careful to insist that there is only one who is *agennētos*, without origin, and that is the Father;[329] yet he denies that there is any 'interval' (*diastēma*) between Father and Son.[330] The Father is always Father, 'the Son being eternally with him'.[331] Hebrews 1[332] is quoted on the Son as 'heir of all things' and as *apaugasma* and image,[333] recalling once again Origen's exegesis of this passage; no explicit allusion is made to Wisdom 7, but the designation of the Son as *eikōn*, following immediately on the mention of *apaugasma* may be a conscious echo of the language of the Wisdom text. In any case, Hebrews itself is so marked by the vocabulary of the older work that it is impossible to allude to the one without the other. Alexander follows Origen in calling Father and Son two *pragmata*[334] and, like Pierius, uses 'two *phuseis*' as a synonym[335] – though he foreshadows later Christological confusions by using *phusis* also as equivalent to 'essence'.[336] The Son as image is a 'mediating being' (*mesiteuousa phusis*),[337] in some sense less than the Father, but contains all that is capable of being revealed and reflected in the Father's life;[338] as *agennētos*, the Father remains transcendent and inexpressible, greater than the Son.[339] But Alexander does not, it seems, hold that the Father alone is unknowable: the Son's mode of origin and his *hupostasis* are also beyond the grasp of created minds.[340] Both the self-subsistence of the First God *and* the nature of the one who derives directly from him (*ex autou tou ontos Patros*, 'from the truly existing Father himself')[341] are equally beyond conceptualization. Alexander here follows through the logic of Origen's insistence of eternal correlativity: if the begetting of the Son is an eternal and 'necessary' aspect of the divine life, part of the proper account of 'what it is to be God', the Father cannot be more unknowable than the Son; what is incomprehensible is not the person of the Father but the pattern of the divine *nature* – another significant 'Origenian' anticipation of full post-Nicene orthodoxy.

Alexander is no more wholly consistent than Origen, but he

provides a fairly thorough and systematic account of (at least) one important 'reading' of the Alexandrian tradition of trinitarian language. The apophatic concern – given a slightly novel twist – is much in evidence; so is the often rather awkward balancing of metaphors drawn from 'sapiential' texts in Scripture, which tend to stress continuity, identity, 'emanation', with the repudiation of any doctrine of one God in a multiplicity of shapes, one God composed, as it were, of disparate manifestations, and therefore divisible and quasi-material. Alexander predictably rejects the views of 'Sabellius and Valentinus' on emanations (*aporroiai*).[342] Also present, co-existing a little uneasily with the heavy emphasis on the co-eternity of Father and Son, is a residual notion of the Father's transcendence and of the Son's function as mediator between the absolutely self-subsistent and the wholly contingent. All in all, it is a bold but very precarious scheme: the conflicts we noted as embryonically present in Philo, especially a Philo conscripted into Christian service, are very close to the surface in Alexander. He is writing against a theologian who has already taken one of the possible drastic steps towards resolving these conflicts for good and all, by denying any *natural* continuity at all between Father and Son. Yet he himself does not quite take the final steps towards the opposite resolution, which is to abandon the identification of the Father with the first, transcendent and unknowable God, and to redefine primordial divine unity as a life subsisting in and constituted by a pattern of internal relations. Such a redefinition comes only after decades of complex reflection: it is hardly surprising that Alexander should not singlehandedly reconstruct Christian theology. But his significance as a mediator to Athanasius of certain classical Alexandrian themes, and his own boldness in handling them should not be minimized.

Arius is an unmistakable Alexandrian in his apophaticism, his interest in the mechanics of mediation between the eternal and the contingent, even his echoes of Judaic angelology; and he is the heir of a narrower Alexandrian tradition in his use of the vocabulary of esoteric illumination, inspired *gnōsis* and charismatic teaching authority. We have no real justification even for regarding him as a rebel in the matter of exegesis. He is not wrong or self-deceived in depicting himself as a traditionalist. Why, then, does he resolve the 'Alexandrian problematic' of the relation between the hidden God and the creative mediator as he does? The answer to this has itself some important roots in Alexandria, but appears with greater clarity when we look at it from a different perspective, that of reactions to and alternatives to the Origenian scheme in the theological world beyond Alexandria.

C

Theology Outside Egypt

1 ANTIOCH

The stark distinctions once drawn between Antiochene and Alexandrian exegesis or theology have come increasingly to look exaggerated.[1] Newman could write[2] as if the disputes characteristic of the fifth century were already foreordained well in advance of Nicaea; but in fact the pre-Nicene period is a great deal less polarized. Nor can we speak of a 'school' succession at Antioch comparable to that at Alexandria. Whether there is anything like an Antiochene 'tradition' in the first three Christian centuries is doubtful: Ignatius, Theophilus and Paul of Samosata are too startlingly different to justify supposing any clear theological style in the Antiochene church. All that can be said is that, from Paul of Samosata onwards, at any rate, certain questions recur with fair regularity in the life of that church. Newman's assumption that biblical literalism, subordinationism, and Aristotelean metaphysics or logic characterized Antioch, so that Arius can be seen as most naturally at home in such a context, rests on several errors or misinterpretations of the evidence. We have already observed that 'Arian literalism' is by no means as clearly-defined a phenomenon as is sometimes supposed; but even if it were, 'Antiochene literalism' has perhaps been exaggerated. Theophilus is a resolute biblicist and not given to extensive allegorization: but his *ad Autolycum* has perfectly plain elements of allegory in its treatment of the days of creation.[3] Paul of Samosata's exegesis probably included at least some elements of conventional typology.[4] Eustathius is eloquently hostile to Origen, yet cannot be said to have rejected allegory.[5] What seems to have happened is that the undoubtedly extreme literalism of Theodore of Mopsuestia has been projected on to his predecessors. Antiochene exegesis was obviously less given to extravagant allegorization of detail than

Origen had been;[6] but it cannot really be said that Athanasius, for instance, is resolutely Origenian in his reading of Scripture.[7] This whole area is one where over-schematic oppositions between 'traditions' of exegesis or theology associated with the churches of Antioch and Alexandria still do great damage to serious study.

Some suggestions of dogmatic continuity in Antioch, however, may be discernible. Theophilus, although speaking of a divine *trias*,[8] also teaches a primordial unity of God and Logos, the Logos being 'in God's heart' at first, and then 'generated' and made external (*prophorikos*) when God decides to create.[9] Paul of Samosata, almost a century later, was certainly believed to have taught that the Word was internal to the being of God and not a subsistent in its own right: Hilary of Poitiers[10] and Athanasius[11] record a tradition that Paul had used the word *homoousios* to describe the unity of Father and Son, which he regarded as something constituting them *solitarium atque unicum*.[12] Without entering into the very vexed question[13] of whether the bishops who condemned Paul in 268 repudiated the use of *homoousios* overall (which would have led them into difficulties with Dionysius of Rome, to whom their synodal letter was sent),[14] or merely rejected *Paul's* interpretation of it, we can conclude from this tradition that Paul's earlier opponents thought that he believed the Word to be without distinct subsistence. Yet there are fragments[15] implying that Paul could speak of the Word 'subsisting' (*huphistēmi* is the relevant verb) and being 'begotten from God'. It may be that he did follow writers like Theophilus in imagining a primitive undifferentiated unity, *solitarium atque unicum*, from which the Word emerged at some point as a quasi-personal subject to assist in creation;[16] but we have no firm evidence, and, as de Riedmatten observes,[17] Paul seems to have been prepared to use orthodox language fairly extensively, and may not have wished to become embroiled unduly in trinitarian as well as Christological issues – whatever his views on the *hupostasis* of the Word.[18]

What is perfectly clear in Paul is the distinction between the eternal Word (whether 'hypostatically' conceived or not) and the human Jesus: the Word is not born of Mary, but of God; Jesus of Nazareth is begotten by the Spirit in Mary's womb, and, apart from his (moral?) superiority to us in all things because of his miraculous generation, he is 'equal to us'.[19] Wisdom dwells in Jesus 'as in a temple': the prophets and Moses and 'many lords' (kings?) were indwelt by Wisdom, but Jesus has the fullest degree of participation in it.[20] The Logos is 'from above', *anōthen* – though this can mean simply 'celestial' perhaps implying that he *remains* 'above'.[21] But one of the most interesting reports of Paul's teaching turns on the meaning of the title 'anointed' as applied to the redeemer. Paul used the phrase *ho ek Dauid christheis*, 'the anointed one who descends from David', to refer to the human Jesus; and this is, it seems, related to the denial that the Word can be anointed: 'it is a human being who is anointed, the Word is not anointed. The one from Nazareth, our Lord, he is anointed.'[22] It sounds as if Paul's distinction between Logos and Jesus was supported by appeal to those scriptural passages where the saviour is spoken of as being 'anointed': the discussion in these terms of a word such as this is characteristic of exegetical argument, that is, argument presupposing the *givenness* of a certain word, phrase or title, in the sacred text. Since we know that Origen had discussed the question of who or what is being anointed in Psalm 45,[23] it seems very likely that Paul has the same text in mind: few other 'prophetic' passages raise the issue so directly for early Christian exegetes.[24]

Origen answered the question of the identity of *ho christheis* with the help of his theory of the pre-existent soul of Jesus. Paul's reported opinion may reflect the problems of a theology unwilling to accept this theory, yet assuming – as did Origen – that the Logos cannot receive 'anointing', being immutable and eternal. Paul believed Jesus to be fully human (that is, he did not believe the Logos to be present as a substitute soul in Jesus' body), and so had no alternative but to assume that *Jesus as a human individual* is the recipient of the anointing of God's grace (presumably the perfect indwelling of Wisdom). It is possible that he also used the Christological hymn of Philippians 2 in speaking of the grace given to the human Jesus: one fragment preserved by Peter the Deacon[25] implies a debate between Paul and his theological opponent Malchion over the nature of the *kenōsis* (*exinanitio*) described in the epistle; another[26] speaks of Jesus receiving the 'name above every name' as a consequence of his preserving intact his will to persevere and progress in virtue. Neither of these texts is by any means beyond suspicion,[27] yet they fit very well the theological concerns suggested in other reports. Given a widespread and decisive move away from Origen's scheme in the second half of the third century, it would be surprising if there were no discussion of the adoption or exaltation imagery of Scripture. It is certainly possible to see Paul as endeavouring to provide a believable alternative reading of such scriptural language for those uneasy with Origenian cosmology and worried about a possible degradation of the Logos if this language were to be applied to him.

If this is an accurate interpretation of Paul, there are some interesting consequences for our view of the early Arian enterprise. We have already seen that Alexandrian theology in the later third century was critical of Origen's ideas about the pre-existence of souls; this would have made the Origenian Christology in its full form unacceptable in Alexandria, and may well have at least weakened the possibility of speaking about a human soul in Jesus. After Paul's condemnation, the idea of Jesus' human soul would be *doubly* tainted: either it would suggest Origenian speculation or it would imply the radical disjunction of Logos and man for which Paul was anathematized. The only option left would be the identification of Logos and soul in Jesus; in which case, the possibility would have to be aired of the exaltation passages of Scripture referring to the Logos – with the necessary corollary of the Logos' inferiority to the immutable God. If, as Athanasius claims,[28] Arius and his supporters made use of Psalm 45 and Philippians 2, they were joining in an exegetical debate whose roots extend a good way back into the preceding century. And, as suggested earlier, Arius' highly complex idea of a supra-temporal, more or less simultaneous, creation, election and exaltation-in-reward-for-virtue of the Logos sounds like an attempt to avoid the crude notion of a Logos slowly advancing or gradually acquiring the merit that would justify a divine reward. Arius' Logos needs all his glory at the beginning of time, for his work in creation and revelation.

The ghost of a belief in Paul of Samosata's direct influence on Arius is an unquiet one, badly in need of final exorcism. Simonetti[29] is surely right to say that if 'adoptionism' means the kind of doctrine associated with Paul, Arius is emphatically not an adoptionist. In his concern for the unequivocally distinct subsistence of the Son, he ranges himself with those who most strongly opposed Paul (whatever exactly Paul himself taught). When Bishop Alexander accuses Arius of reviving the heresy of Ebion, Artemas, Paul and Lucian, we may suspect not merely prejudice and carelessness, but perhaps a touch of what Stead has dubbed *reductio retorta*[30] – accusing your opponent of implicitly pointing to the very position he believes he is attacking. Arius may be eager to avoid crude adoptionism; but, in Alexander's eyes, a mutable Logos can only be a creature acquiring merit and developing towards perfection exactly as we do. Whether the mutable saviour is a mere man (as for Paul) or a heavenly being (as for Arius), he is equally distant from the supposedly 'real' Logos in God himself.[31]

The mention of 'Lucian' by Alexander raised the much-disputed question of whether this is the same man as the martyr Lucian of Antioch, Arius' supposed teacher. Alexander describes Lucian as 'in succession from' (*diadexamenos*) Paul, and under sentence of excommunication during the reigns of three bishops of Antioch.[32] Loofs argued[33] that this 'succession' must be *episcopal* succession, and that the Lucian mentioned here is the leader of a schismatic Paulinian congregation. However, as Bardy notes,[34] and as we have observed in Part I of this book,[35] *diadochē* does not invariably have the sense of succession in office, and Alexander may mean no more than that Lucian was a disciple of Paul. Bardy himself assumed in 1923[36] that Alexander *did* intend to refer to Lucian the martyr, but was mistaken as to the cause of his excommunication – which might have been for his 'fidélité à l'origénisme';[37] but by 1936 he had considerably modified his views. Bardy's considered opinion in his *magnum opus* on Lucian and his followers was that the Lucian of Alexander's letter was an otherwise unknown Paulinian and that the martyr had never been out of communion with the church of Antioch.[38] He agrees with Loofs' point[39] that those to whom Alexander was writing knew Lucian as a hero of the faith; it would be unthinkable that they should suppose the heretic mentioned by the bishop of Alexandria to be the same person.

Bardy's conclusion remains overwhelmingly probable, and Loofs' suggestion should not be too summarily dismissed: the Paulinians certainly survived into the fourth century, and must have had a hierarchy.[40] But, whatever the truth of this, the Lucian of Alexander's letter is a red herring from the point of view of the study of Arian origins. As far as we can reasonably guess anything about the teachings of Lucian the martyr, it seems to have been of a 'pluralist' character, taking for granted the distinct subsistence of the Son, and perhaps also denying the presence of a human soul in Jesus;[41] it has little in common with the characteristic emphases of Paul. And the theory[42] that Lucian began as a Paulinian and later converted to Origenian pluralism is a quite unnecessary complication, with no evidence in its favour at all.

Our witnesses to Lucian's theology are fragmentary and uncertain in the extreme. Jerome[43] mentions a number of *libelli* and short letters in addition to Lucian's major work as an editor and commentator of the sacred text, but none has survived. According to Sozomen,[44] the second creed of the Dedication Council on Antioch in 341 was said to be a confession of faith stemming from Lucian; Rufinus[45] reports an apologetic oration delivered by Lucian before his judges; and the theology of Lucian's better-known pupils provides a few hints as to their teacher's thought. Overall, the picture is far from distinct; but a general impression can be gained. Even if the creed and the apology are not actually from Lucian, they were obviously thought to be congruent with what was known of him through his pupils.

The creed exhibits clear parallels[46] with the confession put out by the earlier Antiochene synod of 324,[47] with the creed submitted by Arius and Euzoius to Constantine,[48] with the fragments of Asterius,[49] and with the intriguing confession of faith ascribed to Gregory Thaumaturgus;[50] and it has some points of contact with the creed of Eusebius of Caesarea.[51] The Son is 'begotten before the ages out of the Father, God from God, whole from whole, the only one from the only one, the perfect from the perfect, the royal one from the royal, the Lord from the Lord';[52] he is the 'identical image' (*aparallaktos eikōn*) of 'the divinity, the substance (*ousia*), the will, the power and the glory of the Father'.[53] Lists of scriptural phrases and metaphors are used in characterizing the Son, in a way rather reminiscent of the list of *epinoiai* in the *Thalia*;[54] and the Spirit is spoken of in connection with the Matthean injunction to baptize, as in the creed of Arius and Euzoius.[55] The emphatic statement that the Son and the Spirit exist *alēthōs*, so that there is a triad of real hypostases, is again common to most of this family of texts.[56] The Son's immutability is firmly stated,[57] as in Arius' letter to Alexander;[58] and, although the scriptural 'first born of every creature' is quoted, the Son's distinction from the created order is quite clear. It is not suggested that the Son exists only at the Father's will.

As Bardy showed,[59] this creed was to be an important text for the 'homoiousian' party in the mid-fourth century, affirming as it did the Son's perfect likeness to the *ousia* of the Father; and, naturally enough, its theology was regarded with suspicion by the 'neo-Arians' who insisted on the Son's substantial *unlikeness* to the

Father. Philostorgius[60] reproached Asterius with *distorting* Lucian's teaching by using the words *aparallaktos eikōn tēs tou patros ousias*. Evidently (judging from Philostorgius) the later 'anomoeans' or 'neo-Arians' took great pride in claiming to represent authentic Lucianic tradition,[61] and any phrase allowing even a slight accommodation with Nicene views would be bound to be rejected as not authentically Lucian's. However, since the phrase occurs in the writing of one who was certainly Lucian's pupil and in a creed purporting to be Lucian's, it may well be his – which suggests that a good deal of the second article of the creed, in which *eikōn* is a pivotal notion, may indeed go back to a creed used by Lucian. Whatever was made of the offending phrase by the homoiousians, its original sense was probably no more than 'image of the Father's "reality" ' – reflecting the respectable pre-Nicene usage of *ousia* for primary (individual) substance.[62] Only when *ousia* has acquired a more restrictively generic sense ('*kind* of existence') does the expression lend itself to homoiousian interpretation, and create problems for the neo-Arians. It does not necessarily show that Asterius differed fundamentally from his colleagues – only that they or their immediate successors were readier to drop an unhelpfully archaic idiom. Arius himself, judging from the creed submitted to Constantine, was quite prepared to jettison the language of the Son as *eikōn*.

The 'apology',[63] redolent of the language of Arnobius and Lactantius and earlier apologists, has comparatively little that is really distinctive in its thought. It echoes what the two great Latin apologists of the age were saying about God's absolute transcendence of human knowledge,[64] describes the sending of divine *sapientia* into the world, 'clothed in flesh', to teach us the way to God,[65] and stresses – rather unusually – that the places where Christ's death and resurrection occurred are there for all to see.[66] This last point sounds like a later addition; but there is nothing in the earlier sections that could not have come from the beginning of the fourth century. Indeed, it is hard to imagine a later writer easily producing so resolutely pre-Nicene a text. Whether it comes from Lucian himself or not is another matter, of course: Rufinus himself (in Bardy's words)[67] 'introduit l'apologie . . . par un prudent *dicitur*'. The text may be originally one of the *libelli de fide* mentioned by Jerome,[68] and the certainly contemporary reference to the *Acta Pilati* circulated as pagan propaganda under Maximin[69] suggests a pamphlet or open letter responding to these new attacks on the faith. All that can be said is that Lucian's authorship cannot be ruled out in this case, any more than with the core of the Antiochene creed. But just as the creed has almost nothing to distinguish it from a number of comparable confessions,[70] so the apology too is mostly standard stuff. If Lucian actually composed these texts, he did little more than make a collage of existing theological common-places, perhaps adding, in the creed, some specific metaphors and biblical allusions.

The interest shown by the apology in God's inaccessibility to created understanding finds at least a faint echo in Philostorgius. As we have seen,[71] Philostorgius knew of a tradition that Arius and the Lucianists disagreed about the Son's knowledge of the Father, with Arius maintaining (as in the *Thalia*) that God was incomprehensible 'not only to human beings . . . but also to the only-begotten Son of God'.[72] The Lucianists presumably held (or were remembered to have held) that God was fully known by the Son, who was thus able fully to reveal him – which fits well both with the creed's *eikōn* theology and with the language of the apology. But even here, we do not have to do with a highly distinctive system peculiar to Lucian and his pupils: Eusebius of Caesarea says much the same.[73] What emerges is the distinctiveness of *Arius* in this period, and, as a corollary, the somewhat precarious nature of the alliance that bound him to the Lucianists. If he had indeed been a pupil of Lucian, this is unlikely to have been a determining factor in his intellectual development. All that the study of Lucian offers is some possible further insight into the *lingua franca* of confessional state-ments around the year 300; and this is not a negligible contribution, since it explains a great deal about the mixed feelings of sympathy and suspicion with which Arius was received in many parts of Syria and Asia. Arius himself could use this idiom to good effect (as in his profession of faith to Constantine), but if the *Thalia* is anything to go by, it was not his native tongue. He can mention the Son's status as *eikōn* in passing,[74] but it is very far from central to his thought; and his obstinate, consistent and radical agnosticism as to the nature of the supreme God, even in respect of the Son's knowl-edge of him, remains unique.

This is perhaps the point to repeat that Arius' role in 'Arianism' was not that of the founder of a sect. It was not his individual teaching that dominated the mid-century eastern Church.

'Arianism', throughout most of the fourth century, was in fact a loose and uneasy coalition of those hostile to Nicaea in general and the *homoousios* in particular; the pace was set for this coalition by those who looked to Lucian as their inspiration in theology, and the network of alliances only broke up when the descendants of the first Lucianists developed a theology more unacceptable in the eyes of the majority of the eastern bishops than the doctrines of Nicaea. Arius, idiosyncratic in his ideas, his death surrounded by discreditable stories, was not an obvious hero for the enemies of Nicaea; nor, as the Antiochene synod of 341 declared,[75] was a mere presbyter to be regarded as head of a party of bishops. The anti-Nicene coalition did not see themselves as constituting a single 'Arian' body: it is the aim of works like Athanasius' *de synodis* to persuade them that this is effectively what they are, all tarred with the same brush.[76] If any comprehensive name could be given to at least the leaders of resistance to Nicaea, and perhaps also to the vague consensus on which they relied, 'Lucianist' and 'Lucianism' are not bad designations; but, since Lucian's own teachings seem in turn to have been little more than a crystallization of the non-Paulinian consensus in Asia and Syria, the terms say very little. Historically, they seem to have referred to not much more than a network of personal links. Later divisions among the non-Nicenes represent the inability of Nicaea's opponents to hold together two key elements in this earlier consensus – belief in the Son's eternal hypostatic distinctness and dependence on the Father (leading to anomoeanism) and belief in the Son's perfect resemblance to the Father (pointing to homoiousianism). Athanasius' triumph was to persuade so many waverers that Nicaea alone could do full justice to the second of these elements (ultimately more important from the soteriological point of view), though at the cost of some necessary modification, even 'demythologizing', of the first. And, in the skilful hands of the Cappadocians, even this price came to seem less alarming than it might have been to the eastern episcopate.

'Lucianism', then, is little more than a convenient label for the kind of pluralist '*eikōn* theology' for which the language of Nicaea appeared dangerously eccentric. If Arius called himself a Lucianist and was able on occasion to present his views in conventional Lucianic terms, this does not mean that he saw himself as a member of a clearly-defined school, but that he rapidly learned to tap the rich resources of anti-'monist', anti-Paulinian feeling in Asia and

Syria – resources whose main guardians and spokesmen included the able and active group of bishops and teachers who had once been students of the martyr Lucian. Lucian does not 'explain' Arius, but he undoubtedly helps to explain Arianism – the phenomenon of long-lasting hostility to or unease with Nicaea among those who would have found the *Thalia* puzzling and none too congenial. Whether Lucian's exegesis had any influence on Arius is an unanswerable question: we know that his disciples had no rooted aversion to allegory,[77] and so we cannot ascribe Arius' views to the malign influence of Lucianist 'literalism'; but there is no serious evidence for saying anything further. Lucian himself remains largely an enigma, and it is difficult to avoid the conclusion that his individual significance in the background of the crisis in Alexandria has been very much exaggerated.

2 METHODIUS AND EUSEBIUS

We have seen that Bardy could, at one point, describe Lucian as an 'Origenist', and this assumption reappears in Lorenz and other more recent studies. The problem for students of this period is, in part, the lack of a convenient designation for a theology which takes for granted some sort of hierarchical pluralism in its talk of God. Origen is indubitably the most systematic and original expositor of such a scheme, and it would be surprising indeed if the theologians of Egypt, Syria and Asia in the next generation showed no trace of being influenced by his imagery and terminology – Christ as *eikōn*, as the multiple reflection of the riches of the Father's simplicity, as a distinct *hupostasis*, *hupokeimenon* and *ousia*. But none of these things, as should be clear by now, makes a writer an Origenist in anything like the later sense of the word; and the use of what I have inelegantly been calling 'Origenian' idiom is not even a mark of some sort of distinctively Alexandrian influence. There is thus no inconsistency at all in Lucian – or anyone else – echoing Origen on the Trinity, while repudiating other doctrines of his: the same considerations apply here as in the case of Origen's successors in Alexandria. And, if we bear in mind that the latter part of Origen's lengthy teaching career was spent chiefly in Palestine, we should be cautious about assuming that Origenian vocabulary reflects an alien element within Syrian or Asian theology.

167

So it is that Methodius of Olympus, who is the most vocal critic of Origen in the pre-Arian period, can be in many ways strikingly close to his great adversary, both exegetically[78] and theologically.[79] Once again, it is Origen's cosmology that is directly under attack: Methodius seems to assume that Origen's doctrine of the eternity of creation implies the eternity of matter as a rival self-subsistent reality alongside God.[80] This is, of course, *reductio retorta* once again, rather than pure misunderstanding – though the latter is clearly in evidence as well. The disciple of Origen obviously will not want to say (so Methodius argues) that God *begins* to impose form on matter, since Origen's case rests on the eternity and unchangeability of the divine creative act;[81] but this means that God must be eternally imposing form on matter, so that there is an eternal non-divine principle upon which God acts. The corollary is what Methodius sees as a gnostic world-view, in which evil is attributable not to free will but to an eternal 'resistance' to God's order;[82] and this radical dualism Methodius apparently ascribes to the influence of philosophy on Origen.[83] This dualism is not only subversive of Christian belief in the soul's freedom: it is also incapable of being logically articulated. Methodius advances[84] a version of the classical 'third man' argument to show that the concept of two *agenēta* is self-contradictory.

This polemic is closely linked to Methodius' critique of Origen's anthropology. If the soul's slavery results from free will – as Origen would agree – its liberation means the transforming of the will, not the discarding of the body.[85] Origen with his doctrine of pre-existent *noes* is taken to be once more implying that matter is the cause or the source of evil, or, at the very least, the dominant factor in the soul's empirical unfreedom. Methodius, who can use ideas and language very reminiscent of Origen at times, often seems to be implicitly accusing Origen of undermining his own best insights out of a misplaced reverence for pagan philosophical conventions.

Methodius is in fact determined to establish once and for all that belief in creation *ex nihilo* demands belief in a temporal (that is, punctiliar) beginning. As we shall see in Part III,[86] he is here joining a complex and venerable philosophical debate; what should be noted now is that his criticisms of Origen's cosmology and anthropology turn upon the inability of Origen's scheme to provide a consistent account of the Christian belief that God is wholly sufficient to himself, and thus creates out of his freedom and his gratuitous love. Origen's theology assumes throughout a disjunction of rational form and irrational matter, so that the creation of this world is God's uniting of what is essentially distinct; but if this is an eternal act, there must be that which is eternally passive to God's formative rationality, and which therefore exists independently of God's reasoning will. This is how Methodius sees the *logic* of Origen's world-view, ignoring the latter's explicit account of how the material universe is brought into being in response to the fall of the rational spirits; but he has some grounds for dissatisfaction with this account in the light of Origen's general assumptions about spirit and matter and about the nature of God's activity. And this 'logic' in Origen's system – irrespective of his none too coherent speculations about the beginnings of the material universe – militates against any adequate statement of the authentic Christian doctrine of creation.

Methodius' importance to our present enquiry is substantial. We have noted that Origen's views on the pre-existence of souls and the resurrection were unpopular in Alexandria; but in Methodius we see how disagreement on these points could be grounded in a far more fundamental critique, both philosophical and theological. Patterson suggests[87] that Methodius' stress on the creation of the world at a quasi-temporal point, so that there might be said to be an 'interval' between God's eternity and the time of the cosmos, looks forward to the Arian *ēn hote pote ouk ēn*. Methodius himself has little distinctive to say on the subject of the Word's generation: he describes the Word as existing *pro aiōnōn*,[88] as being eternally (not adoptively) Son,[89] and remaining for ever the same;[90] the Word is the *archē* of all things, yet distinct from the *anarchos archē*, the Father,[91] who is greater than he.[92] This seems very close to Origen; but Patterson observes that Methodius' language may mean only that the Word comes into being long before the visible creation, rather than that the Word is co-eternal in a strict sense.[93] It is true that *achronōs* is not always to be taken as 'timelessly',[94] and that Methodius assumes that origination implies temporal beginning. However, we do not have to find proto-Arianism in Methodius' own words to establish some connection. Characteristically, Arius tidies up the loose ends left by his precursors; and, in the case of Methodius, the next step is unusually clearly indicated. The Word exists in distinction from the Father, the idea of two *agenēta* is incoherent, and so the Father alone is *agenētos;* but the Father produces the *genēta* by his own free will out of nothing; and the world of *genēta* must have a temporal point of origin or else it would share God's *agenēsia*. Methodius still stands too close to Origen to see the question so clearly; or, perhaps more accurately, his polemical attention is too closely focused on the dangers of supposing the empirical universe to be eternal for him to be worried about the exact status of the Word.

Arius, however, is faced with a different threat. Episcopal teaching in Alexandria has increasingly canonized a number of formulae[95] emphasizing the continuity and correlativity of Father and Son, and Alexander is using the Origenian slogan *aei theos, aei huios*.[96] For anyone committed to a certain sort of view of the independent substantiality of the Word, this language compromises the divine freedom in much the same way as does the doctrine of eternal creation: it implies two 'first principles' – not, admittedly, two principles in opposition, like God and matter, but none the less an eternal reality not *willed* by God. Origen and Methodius do not have this problem partly because, for them, the direct derivation of the Word from the life of the Father leaves no room for a view of the Word's generation as a 'groundless' act of God's free choice. But, as we shall see in Part III, Arius' philosophical antecedents may well have disposed him to reject the possibility of this kind of continuity or participation: the Word does not proceed or emanate, for this compromises the immateriality of God and the simplicity of his substance – it is a 'Valentinian' view; so the Word must be another *kind* of reality.

This conclusion is further reinforced by Methodius' attack on Origen's anthropology. The unacceptable doctrine of the world's eternity is rightly seen as carrying with it the doctrine of the eternity of rational souls, and their separability from their material husks, a corollary which underlines again, for Methodius, the gnostic character of the whole cosmology. But, as we have already stressed, the abandonment of Origen's teaching on the soul at once raises a Christological problem. *What* is incarnate, if not a pre-existent spirit? The Word itself, obviously. And, after the condemnation of Paul of Samosata, it is hard to see this incarnation in any terms other than the Word's 'ensouling' of a body. The bodily life of the saviour is characterized by all the limitations of bodiliness, so the subject of these experiences must be vulnerable to change and limitation; and thus the Word is not *theos alēthinos*. Once again, it is overwhelmingly likely that Methodius himself drew no such conclusion; but he certainly provides the conceptual raw material for Arius' argument from 'all those passages referring to the economy of salvation and the low estate Christ took on himself for our sake'.[97] Arius would be familiar with objections in Alexandria to Origen's anthropology, and probably shared the common view that the Word acted as a soul in Jesus; Methodius shows us that this *could* be linked with a critique of Origen's doctrine of creation and of the 'correlativity' argument. If Arius is philosophically inclined to make a sharp distinction between Father and Word, theologically inclined to reject Origen's view of the soul, and thus exegetically inclined to read scriptural imagery about the 'creation' of Wisdom in a temporal sense and to ascribe the sufferings of Jesus directly to the Word, his conclusion as to the Word's nature and status is pretty well inevitable. His theology is clearly the result of a very large number of theological views converging towards a crisis at the end of the third century; but Methodius' special interest is that he witnesses to the existence at this juncture of just such a broadly based and wide-ranging attack upon Origen's cosmology as would make sense of Arius' own many-sided critique of the Alexandrian consensus of his day.

A word must finally be added about one further influential writer of the ante-Nicene period, Eusebius of Caesarea. There has been much dispute over whether he can rightly be called an Arian in the years immediately before and after Nicaea;[98] but, as Colm Luibheid admits, in his very sympathetic essay on Eusebius,[99] the question may be *mal posée*. As has been several times emphasized in these pages, we are not to think of Arius as dominating and directing a single school of thought to which all his allies belonged. In the light of what can be known about Arius' relations with his episcopal supporters in general, Eusebius of Caesarea is no more and no less correctly called an 'Arian' than is his namesake of Nicomedia. He is not a 'Lucianist'; yet nearly everything he has to say about the Father's relationship with the Son is paralleled in the various fragments and documents associated with Lucian and his pupils. Eusebius' theology is, from first to last, quite heavily marked by the *eikōn* theme:[100] the Son is *theos* because he is image, because the Father has given to him an unparalleled share in his own godhead.[101] What clearly distinguishes Eusebius' version of this theology from Origen's is the reiterated stress on the Father's *gift* of divine honour to the Son.[102] The Son enjoys the most perfect participation imaginable in the life of the Father, and so too the fullest degree of access to the unknowable Father,[103] but this results from the Father's decision. Eusebius – like Arius, though less radically – expresses some dissatisfaction with the venerable imagery of light and ray to describe Father and Son: the ray has no *hupostasis* of its own, it is intrinsic to the existence of the light-source and so does not come forth from it because of any choice, and it is simultaneous with the shining of the light. None of this can apply to the Father and the Son; and although this does not mean that we cannot use this metaphor (Scripture employs it, after all), we must recognize its inadequate and potentially misleading character.[104]

In his letter to Euphration,[105] Eusebius vehemently denies that Father and Son 'co-exist' eternally. He is as eager as Methodius and Eusebius of Nicomedia to repudiate any hint of two *agen(n)ēta;* and here again we can see how far the bishop of Caesarea is from being in total theological thrall to Origen. Like Methodius, he seems to take it for granted that co-eternity means the simultaneity of independent realities. Yet, as Luibhéid points out,[106] there is at least one place[107] where Eusebius, while still emphasizing the role of the Father's will in the Son's generation, appears to assert eternal co-existence. This passage is indeed puzzling; but what it might mean is simply that there is no point *within the history of the universe* at which the Son does not exist alongside the Father. The point here is to drive home the Son's absolute priority to creation, of which he is agent and ideal exemplar.[108] Faced with the notion that there was no 'interval' between Father and Son, Eusebius is not necessarily being inconsistent in stressing the Father's pre-existence. From our point of view, in the world's time, Father and Son co-exist; from the Father's point of view, so to speak, they do not and cannot. Here Eusebius is caught in the same toils as Arius in trying to make intelligible statements about supramundane or premundane temporality: the Origenian (and Thomist)[109] concept of timeless dependence eludes them.

As for Arius' assertion that the Son is *ex nihilo*, this seems to be contradicted by Eusebius pretty explicitly:[110] indeed, the fragment of a supposed letter of his to Alexander of Alexandria,[111] preserved in the acts of the second Council of Nicaea, seems to suggest that Eusebius believed Arius' party to be *falsely* accused of teaching this doctrine. It may be that, on this point, Eusebius was misinformed; but, more probably, he was eager to deny that Arius' supporters as a body held that the Son was *ex ouk ontōn* in precisely the sense other creatures were. This, after all, is how he puts the issue even in an earlier, non-polemical remark: it is wrong to say that the Son comes into being *ex ouk ontōn*, 'as is the case with other *genēta*'.[112] But the letter to Alexander suggests also a measure of perplexity: *ex ouk ontōn* sounds unsatisfactory, and must not be taken as a lowering of the Son's status to that of one creature among others; yet how is one to avoid the phrase, as there cannot be two self-subsisting realities?[113] The Father is eternally; the Son cannot be on the same level, and so must be made from nothing. Eusebius' unease comes perhaps from his strong sense of the Son's participation in the life of the Father, the way in which the Son's reality is constituted by the Father's gift to him of his own glory. Here indeed Arius stands apart; this aspect of *eikōn* theology is alien to his metaphysic, and Eusebius is enough of an Origenian to hold on to a model of participation for which there was no room in Arius' scheme.

Eusebius evidently shares Methodius' desire to preserve intact the Christian doctrine of God's freedom in creation, and his involvement with Arius illustrates how someone committed to the absolute gratuity of God's creative and revealing activity might have thought the theology of Alexander a greater menace than that of Arius. Did Eusebius also share Methodius' disagreement with Origen's anthropology? It is noteworthy that the *Defence of Origen* composed by Pamphilus and Eusebius appears to have evaded some of the questions raised about the master's doctrine of the soul in general, and the soul of Jesus in particular.[114] Certainly Eusebius shows no sign of having ever entertained a doctrine of the soul's pre-existence; and in his later work he makes it quite clear that he believes the Word to have animated a 'soulless' body.[115] The Word's individual subsistence is established by the fact that he can act as a soul in a human body,[116] so that this belief becomes a crucial element in Eusebius' polemic against Marcellus of Ancyra, a Paul of Samosata *redivivus* in Eusebius' eyes. It is unlikely that Eusebius changed his mind on this important issue; but some confusion has been caused by his fairly free use of language about Christ's *psuchē* in his Psalm Commentaries. Stead has proposed[117] that we should date those commentaries in the pre-Nicene period, before the question of

Christ's soul was of major dogmatic importance, as it is clear that references to the *psuchē* of the Lord in these works are theologically neutral. This is very plausible; but it may be possible to clarify the matter further. The *Defence* briefly claims legitimacy for Origen's language about the soul of Christ on the grounds of scriptural usage:[118] nothing is made of the fact that it is structurally central to his Christology. It may be that Eusebius chose to ignore what Origen said about the pre-existent *nous* of Jesus, while allowing that Jesus possesses *psuchē*, considered simply as the 'mechanics' of the inner life: he has that which enables him to feel human passions, fear or joy or grief, a link between the ultimate subject, the Logos, and the flesh.[119] In other words, Eusebius, at this earlier stage, may still assume that Origen's terminological distinction between *nous* and *psuchē* can be salvaged and exploited so as to defend the language of *psuchē* in Jesus, even when the 'core' of this psychic life is not a created *nous* but the Logos itself. Later, however, in a climate in which this distinction is not generally observed, he is readier to jettison this residue of Origenian idiom and to speak of the Logos taking flesh that is *apsuchon . . . kai alogon*, 'soulless and non-rational',[120] apparently using these terms in fairly close parallelism. This is highly speculative, but at least makes some sense of a real obscurity in Eusebius' theology. At all events, though, he is ultimately at one with Arius in considering the Logos as *constituting* the mind or spirit of Jesus.

Eusebius cannot be considered as a major influence on Arius, so far as we know, but he provides a further valuable witness to the wide diffusion of those theological priorites and anxieties that could make Arius' protest against Alexander a rallying-point for so much of the eastern Church: a concern – over against residual traces of gnosticism – for God's freedom in creation, the assumption that the Word is 'produced' by the unknowable Father (voluntarily) to mirror and manifest his glory, and the belief that the Word, as the subject of the event of incarnation, must be a distinct spiritual individual, sufficiently like a human soul to act as such in the body of Jesus of Nazareth. In defending such doctrines, Arius can claim to be speaking for what many, perhaps most, bishops of the hierarchies of Syria and Asia thought of as the essence of the faith to be safeguarded against the deadly errors of Valentinus, Sabellius and Paul of Samosata.

D

Conclusion

Arius was a committed theological conservative; more specifically, a conservative *Alexandrian*. He inherited a strongly accented doctrine of God's unknowability, and, in common with his Jewish and Christian predecessors, believed that God alone could overcome the distance that necessarily separated the divine life from the contingent order – just as God first 'transcended his own transcendence' to create the world. For God to relate, either as creator or as redeemer, to what is not God must be the result of God's own will. He is constrained by nothing: he does not have to accommodate his will to independent, co-eternal matter, nor is there any internal necessity generating a hierarchy of emanations from the primal purity of the divine life itself. Earlier Alexandrians, however, from Philo onwards, had been concerned also that God's will should in some way reflect his nature: hence the Philonic doctrine of the Logos, the intrinsic divine capacity to be creator of a rationally-ordered world. These two concerns, for God's unfathomable liberty and for his rationality, are constantly in tension in Alexandrian theology; and in so far as the divine rationality is assumed to imply the presence of pre-existent ideal forms within God, there is something of a problem over the divine unknowability. Knowing the forms is knowing God; yet the forms are 'contained' in a unity which is, as such, incapable of being conceptualized. Are we then to divide the divine substance into knowable and unknowable portions or levels, so that the Logos represents the world-oriented 'aspect' of God, as in Philo and (probably) Clement? But this seriously jeopardizes the divine simplicity. Yet it is jeopardized even further if the distinction between God and Logos is not preserved; in such a case, the divine freedom too is under threat, as the forms of the created order are made in some degree *constitutive* of God's *ousia* – as if he cannot be what he is without creative 'emanations'.

175

In Part III we shall see how some of these issues were being raised by philosophers of the period: they are not uniquely Christian or Jewish problems, though they are much intensified by the Judaeo-Christian assumption of creation *ex nihilo*. The point is that Arius inherits a dual concern that is very typically Alexandrian. Origen had taken the bold step of proposing that the Logos exists eternally alongside God, as a distinct subsistent: thus the Logos (and in him the ideal world) is not *part* of the *ousia* of the Father of all, which remains unknowable; but the Logos is none the less the fruit of the eternal fact that the *ousia* of the Father is active. For God to exist actively and concretely involves him in uttering or generating his Word: this *is* his eternal act of willing. And *what* he wills, in and through his Word, is the eternal world of reasonable spirits. This is a complex and delicately balanced theory, sketched rather than worked out in detail; it does not deny that God is free in creating, yet it also avoids suggesting that God could *concretely* exist without communicating his life to and in his Son. God does not arbitrarily decide to have a Son; but it is *as* the God whose nature it is to utter his Word that he wills or decides anything at all. The Word is God *in actu* – and God is never idle, nor ever only potentially what he is.[1]

This account is a striking advance on most earlier Christian speculation, in that it entirely dispenses with the pervasive idea of *logos* as a dimension or even 'territory' within the divine being, which somehow turns into a distinct reality when God decides to create the world. But it proved almost impossibly difficult for third-century theology, and its more speculative and ambiguous features (especially the theory of pre-existent *noes*) evidently vitiated it in the eyes of many. And with the abandonment of Origen's scheme as a whole, a new set of problems appears on the horizon. It is no longer possible to think of a pre-existent spirit comparable to our own spirits taking flesh in Jesus of Nazareth; and the notion of an ordinary created soul in Jesus has come, by the end of the third century, to be almost irretrievably associated with the theology of Paul of Samosata. Belief in the complete humanity of Jesus was seen as excluding belief in a real incarnation, and so as implicitly undermining the individuality of the heavenly Word.

With Arius' arrival on the scene, several strands of theological argument intertwine. The Word who is subject in the experiences of Jesus of Nazareth is a passible being, and therefore distinct from

God. As a distinct individual, *hupostasis* or *ousia*, he is not part of God, and could never have been 'within' the life of God; he is dependent and subordinate. And if God is free in respect of every contingent, mutable and passible reality, the Word exists because God *chooses* that he should. Of course God is not without his own *logos* and *sophia* – we cannot suppose him to be *less* than *logikos* or *sophos* – but there is nothing in this immanent rationality that compels him to create. There is no unequivocally necessary connection between his *logos* and the existence of an ordered world; thus we cannot say what 'being wise' or 'being *logikos*' means for God. He elects to create and so to manifest his glory; so as the first step he creates that which is closest to him, a creature, yet one endowed with all the gifts that can be given. This creature, Word, Son, indeed 'God' as far as the rest of creation is concerned, not only initiates the creative process, but also, in so doing, 'enables' the whole of the created order to unfold; and further, he represents to creation a knowable likeness of God. Yet because he exists solely at God's will, he also represents the unfathomable mystery of the divine free will: his glorious, but contingent and mutable existence – however much it is *de facto* godlike, immortal and unchanging – witnesses to the unbridgable gulf between God and all else. He is in some sense an 'image' of the divine life, but this does not stand first among his titles,[2] and does not of itself signify real continuity with the life of the Father. He is perfect wisdom and goodness in contingent and graspable form: what wisdom and goodness are in themselves, neither he nor any other creature can know.

As we have already seen, this is the theology of the *Thalia* – a remarkable and drastic reworking of a number of profoundly traditional themes. It is conservative in the sense that there is almost nothing in it that could not be found in earlier writers; it is radical and individual in the way it combines and reorganizes traditional ideas and presses them to their logical conclusions – God is free, the world need not exist, the Word is other than God, the Word is part of the world, so the Word is freely formed *ex nihilo*. Furthermore, earlier theologians had been selective and doubtfully consistent in exegesis; language about the Word's creation had had to be qualified by the parallel scriptural language about generation or begetting. In order to justify a hermeneutical priority for the former, Arius and his associates had to demonstrate the loose and flexible nature of the latter – hence their interest in cognate texts in which the language of 'begetting' is used of beings other than the Logos.[3] Exegesis is a major concern for Arius, but it would be wrong to see him as *starting* from a narrowly exegetical problem (let alone from any one text). His theological inheritance raises questions to which a more refined exegetical method will help to provide answers.

He is not a theologian of consensus, but a notably individual intellect. Yet because his concerns are shared with a large number of bishops and teachers outside Egypt, he can, albeit briefly, be the figurehead for a consensus of sorts. For many of his contemporaries, Arius' conception of orthodoxy at least ruled out what they wished to see ruled out; but relatively few would have endorsed, or perhaps even grasped, the theology of the *Thalia* in its full distinctiveness.

It is *not* true to say that Arius' synthesis could have been predicted by anyone who had understood the implications of rejecting both Origen's cosmology and Paul of Samosata's Christology (any such judgment of any radically novel moment in history is superficial). But it might be said that there were tensions and loose ends enough in third-century theology to make it predictable that the fourth would produce some sort of doctrinal crisis. Why it should come when and where it did, by the agency of Arius rather than anyone else, is not the sort of question to which we can expect a satisfying answer. Others, in and out of Egypt, shared a similar agenda, but did not come up with the *Thalia*. However, it is perhaps possible to isolate one area in which Arius seems to have had special skills and interests not shared by all his contemporaries. In Part III of this book we shall be examining his relation to the philosophy of his age; it may be that it was this which provided him with some of the impulse, and some of the tools, to weld his complex theological heritage into a new and more systematic unity.

Part III

Arius and Philosophy

A

Creation and Beginning

Plato's *Timaeus* served as the central text upon which discussions of the world's origins focused, not only in late antiquity, but right up to the revival of Christian Aristotelianism in the thirteenth century. It is, however, a notoriously complex text, and one which is hard to read as a single consistent argument: '[Plato's] influence was . . . due to his very unclarity and suggestiveness, which left room for so many subsequent interpretations.'[1] By the third century of the Christian era, there was vigorous disagreement among Platonists themselves, as well as between Platonists and some of the critics of their master. What Christian theologians of this period and after found to say about God, creation and the beginning of time must be seen against the background of such debates. On the whole, it is impossible to say whether or to what extent any particular theologian knew the work of any particular philosopher; but there can be no doubt that for many of the most influential writers of the age, from Origen to Eusebius Pamphilus,[2] the contemporary discussion of time and the universe shaped their conceptions of what could intelligibly be said of creation.

Plato begins his investigation by distinguishing (27D–28A) between what exists always and never comes into being, and what is always in process of coming to be and never exists simply and stably. With the former, it is implied, the question of causal origin is nonsensical; with the latter, such a question is central. The universe as we perceive it is evidently a world of 'coming to be': we encounter it in sense perception and it is the object of uncertain opinion, so it cannot be eternal and stable (28BC). *Gegonen*, says Plato firmly (28B), 'it has come to be', and it begins from some *archē*. What then is its cause? The cosmos may be a place of transience, but it is also beautiful; it must therefore be modelled upon what is higher and better. The craftsman who made it must have had before his eyes the eternal world that is known by *logos* (28C–29A).

The creating deity, then, creates in the desire to make something like himself (29E) – something capable of reflecting order and beauty. But here the complications begin to arise: he does not make the cosmos out of nothing, but 'takes over' (*paralabōn*, 30A) a disorderly world of visible or tangible realities which he brings from discord to order. Thus he first produces a 'living being', the rational system of heavenly bodies, which reflects as fully as possible that higher 'living being' that is the world of ideas (30B-D).[3] So that the created 'living being' may more fully reflect the rationality of the higher *zōon*, God regulates its movements by creating time – 'a sort of moving image of eternity' (37D). Only at this point, then, does it come to be appropriate to speak of divisions or intervals of time, and to use 'was' or 'will be'. 'Time came into being (*gegonen*) along with the heavens' (38B): the particular heavenly bodies are made in order to measure and regulate time. All that remains 'now that time has come to be' (*mechri chronou geneseōs*) is for God to create the particular kinds of life that will reflect the various potentialities contained in the ideal world, the absolute *zōon* (31E).

Aristotle[4] assumed Plato to be asserting that the (rational) universe had a punctiliar beginning, and criticized him for combining this belief with the view that the universe would nevertheless, by God's providence,[5] last for ever: if it is capable of unending existence, Aristotle argued, there is no reason for ascribing a beginning to it – indeed, it is *contradictory* to do so. If the world has a beginning, it is capable of not-existing: there is a time at which the cosmos can not-be. *Genētos* means 'capable of earlier not-existing';[6] but if the world exists endlessly, there is no time at which it is true that it might earlier not have existed: for every time at which the cosmos exists, there is therefore an earlier time at which it exists. For *specific realities in time*, individual subsistents, it makes sense to say that they possess contradictory potentialites – that is, they can exemplify different predicates at different times. But the cosmos as such is not a comparable case, not a particular thing existing within a circumstantially limited time-scale. The capacities of the cosmos taken as a whole are capacities relating to infinite time (or perhaps better, *indefinite* time, a time-span not determined by specific contingent factors); thus if the cosmos-as-a-whole can not-exist, this capacity for not-existing relates to no specific time.

If it is capable of not-existing, it is capable of not-existing in 'infinite time', that is, at any and every moment. But if we know that the cosmos *will* always exist, then it *can* exist at any and every moment; and because the cosmos is a unique case (not a timebound individual), it should be clear that it cannot simultaneously be capable of everlasting non-existence and of everlasting existence. If it now exists and will go on existing, it is patently not capable of everlasting non-existence; therefore it cannot be 'capable of earlier not-existing', and must be *agenētos*.[7]

This complex (and probably flawed)[8] argument is Aristotle's chief contribution to the question of time and creation, though there are a few other pertinent discussions among his works,[9] especially his attack on the idea of time beginning at a 'temporal' point in Met. 12.6.1071–8. The force of Aristotle's case is that he appears to demonstrate the *logical* impossibility of God's creating a world that has a beginning but no end, and this demonstration was generally assumed to be valid by the majority of later philosophers in antiquity. Already, by the time Aristotle was writing the *de caelo*,[10] there were those who defended Plato's account by claiming that the *Timaeus* account of creation was a pedagogic myth, in which the temporal categories were no more to be taken literally than might be the idiom of a geometer who describes in sequential terms the structure of a particular figure (a triangle is 'given', lines are then 'produced', and so on). The figure is not, of course, something constructed by a process; it exists timelessly. Aristotle was unimpressed, but such arguments survived and flourished. Those Platonists – relatively few – who assumed that Plato meant more or less what he said, and defended the idea of a beginning for the cosmos, came under heavy fire from the Neoplatonists of the third to fifth Christian centuries.[11]

As already indicated, what exactly *is* the 'literal' meaning of the *Timaeus* is by no means clear. Despite the statement that it is only with the beginning of time (that is, the creation of the heavenly bodies) that it becomes possible to employ tensed expressions like 'was' and 'will be', Plato very freely uses such expressions in describing pre-cosmic reality. Although – as the wording of my last sentence shows – it is practically impossible not to fall into this trap in discussing cosmic beginnings, it is clear that Plato does envisage something that can only be called a *process* leading up to the beginning of time. Guthrie[12] usefully points out that *chronos* in the Greek of Plato and Aristotle refers not to simple duration but to regulated cyclical time – precisely, in fact, the time measured by the rotation of the heavenly bodies. Before the *genesis* of the cosmos, therefore, there is duration but no means of measuring it – disorderly time, in which the 'disorderly motion' of formless matter occurs.[13] Whether or not this is exactly what Plato meant, it was what he was taken to mean by that minority of Platonists who argued that the universe was *genētos* – particularly by Plutarch and Atticus in the first and second Christian centuries. These writers distinguish between the disorderly motion which is *agenētos*,[14] and the rational universe which is *genētos apo chronou;*[15] in effect, therefore, they distinguish two kinds of time.[16] Problematic as this is, it does at least make some sense of the *Timaeus;* and it is paralleled in, and doubtless influenced by, the primitive Pythagorean view as presented by Numenius,[17] that the 'dyad', the world of material multiplicity, is co-eternal with God (*aequaevum Deo*), and can only be called *genita* when it comes to be 'adorned' or ordered by God.

Up to about AD 200, then, the consensus among philosophers was that God and matter were co-eternal (that is, matter was *agenētos*). God is not responsible for the existence of the eternal pre-cosmic chaos, but only for its organization into a rational world; the question under debate is whether this organization is also eternal. Aristotle probably did not think at all in terms of a divine *act* of organization: his 'first mover' eternally *causes* the regular and harmonious movement of the heavens,[18] but it is not clear whether it is the cause of their being there at all; and its causal agency is in no sense a deliberate, conscious, discrete act.[19] This notion of a changeless or timeless causal operation was what became normal and normative for most Platonists in the early Christian era;[20] and Neoplatonism established it as part of its own orthodoxy. Plotinus and his successors, of course, firmly repudiate the idea of eternal matter 'over against' God:[21] not only the rational world, but matter itself is in some sense a stage in the universe's eternal flowing forth from the One.[22] If 'form' is eternally active, there must be that which is passive to it,[23] that which is formed; this disjunction timelessly holds true in the intellectual realm, but both active form and passive matter, though eternal, are *genētos*, in the sense of being derived.[24] In contrast to Plutarch and Atticus, Plotinus insists on the priority (logically, not temporally) of form:[25] Porphyry was to make explicit[26] the implied rejection of Atticus' idea that irrational matter can exist

184

before the ordered, formed material cosmos. Matter is by nature what lacks and receives form: indeed, its most general definition is the *indeterminate* element in any reality, not only realities perceived by sense. It cannot but be passive to and participating in the intelligible actuality of the good: it cannot simply exist on its own, independent of form.[27] And form itself, the realm of active ideas, is eternally in the primal *nous*, which generates the ideas out of its own being, not taking them from elsewhere[28] – except in the sense that *nous* is what it is in and through contemplation of the One.[29]

Philosophers who believed in the eternal generation of matter evidently found difficulties in expressions like 'made out of nothing'. Aristotle advances his account of the first mover partly, he tells us,[30] to avoid an explanation of the rational harmony of the cosmos that has recourse to supposing the world to be *ek mē ontos;* but this seems to mean only that he repudiates any suggestion of a 'chaotic' matter preceding the ordered universe. However, he has enough arguments elsewhere[31] to make it plain that he would not be able to countenance the idea that a total void precedes the existence of the world or of matter:[32] at any moment at which a particular reality comes into being, the event of its generation presupposes the coming together of already existing realities. There is no pure matter 'lying around' waiting for some new form to unite with it, and no period therefore when matter exists in anything but orderly motion, a world of rationally structured particulars: form succeeds form in the changes of matter without interruption. There is thus never anything new in the world that is not 'made out of something', the issue of a process in which form *informs* matter. Matter as such, then, cannot ever be a new thing; by definition, unformed matter (matter in the abstract, so to speak) cannot be the issue of a process in time. And formed, orderly matter *is* by definition the issue of such a process. Rational, harmonious motion in the universe cannot but be eternal; and so time is incapable of starting or stopping – being, as it is, the measure of relation and distance in the continuum of orderly movement.[33] There cannot, then, be an absolute beginning, a point preceded by nothing; and this is evidently how Aristotle understood the idea of a making out of nothing,[34] as a process that is logically incapable of being *described* as a process – a kidnapping of temporal language to do an impossible job.

Philo's view[35] that God caused matter and its rational structure to come into being at a point is apparently unique in philosophical antiquity; and this highlights the difficulty which Jews and Christians had in assimilating practically any of the available idioms and philosophical reflection on the origins of the world. Plutarch certainly enjoyed popularity among Christians,[36] and Atticus is approvingly quoted by Eusebius;[37] but no Christian admirer grasps the nettle of their belief in the eternity and *independence* of formless matter. It is clear, though, from Methodius[38] that there were Christians who shared the Neoplatonic objection to multiple *archai* or *agen(n)ēta*. Methodius takes the Origenian assumption that God cannot 'begin' to be the creator of a world of ordered matter (as Plutarch and Atticus suggest), and turns it against Origen by pointing out that an eternally passive material principle cannot but be an *agenētos* substance in the strong sense of the adjective – a self-subsisting principle, an *archē*. In fact, of course, Origen appears to teach (as does Philo in some passages) that intelligible form temporally *precedes* the making of the present material world out of nothing;[39] first there is a world of immaterial individuals. But Methodius is perhaps not just being polemically bloody-minded or stupid. Throughout his attack on Origen he is challenging (as a good Aristotelian or a good Plotinian might) the idea that form and matter can exist as separate *things:* that there can be matter independently of what organizes it as *intelligible* matter and that there can be form which has nothing to 'inform' and act upon. In effect, he assumes the equivalence of Origen's pre-existing rational substances with the world of forms, at least as far as concerns the human constitution: the reasonable soul is the 'form' of the body, as in Aristotle.[40]

If form and matter imply each other, and if matter comes into existence at a punctiliar beginning, at God's will, then the corollary is that the world of forms also comes to be at God's will. This in turn means that the world of forms must not be understood as in any way internal to the *being* of God: God is what he is quite independently of his being the source of a rational creation, and the Philonic notion of a Logos who constitutes that 'dimension' of the divine life in which exist the potentialities of the rational creation becomes insupportable. Methodius' polemic makes it necessary to distinguish very sharply between the primal divine unity in itself and the 'one-as-many', the unifying structure of the cosmos, and to treat the latter as the issue of divine will. It is in this latter respect that we move away from the Philonic, Neopythagorean and Ploti-

186

nian distinction between first and second principles:[41] not even Philo, who has the clearest notion of divine will here, implies what Methodius does about the radical disjunction between God as he essentially is and God as creator.

But why should this disjunction be seen as temporal, as ruling out the chronological infinity of the created order? There are some hints in Methodius suggesting an answer. Otis[42] and Patterson[43] have both (originally in independence of each other) drawn attention to Methodius' account of the nature of time, in the *de resurrectione*[44] time is what advances in measurable intervals, *diastēmata* – a view with sound Stoic[45] and, indeed, Platonic,[46] ancestry. Time is the measure of motion; intervals of time mark the advance of processes of change. *Diastēmata* are therefore obviously not to be found in eternity. But how is one to express the distinction between time and eternity itself? In the *de autexusio*,[47] in the course of his celebrated anti-Valentinian demonstration of the impossibility of two first principles, Methodius observes that, if there *are* two *agen(n)ēta*, there must be a *diastasis* between them. 'Distance' or 'differentiation' is here a more natural translation than 'interval', but *diastasis* and *diastēma* have an almost identical range of meaning.[48] If there is such a *diastasis*, it must be brought about by something or exist in virtue of something – which means we must suppose a third 'first principle', distinct from the initial two, which causes the differentiation; the argument can be continued *ad infinitum*. The implication seems to be that differentiation is necessarily the result of *processes* with assignable causes. *Diastasis* is a matter of change, motion; and, if so, an eternal, beginningless *diastasis* is inconceivable. In however eccentric a sense, then, *diastasis* and perhaps *diastēma* would have to apply, on Methodius' showing, to the gap between creator and creature. There is no causeless separation; separation means change; change means time.

The strength of this argument (if I am right in supposing there to be a real *argument* buried in these texts) lies in the apparent simplicity of its fundamental premiss: if there is anything other than God, it exists as the result of a divine act which brings about a new or distinct state of affairs. This might be thought to imply change in God; but Methodius argues[49] that if we are prepared to say that, after creating the world, God is at rest, yet not changed by being no longer actively engaged in giving the universe its beginning, then we ought not to find any difficulty in saying that he is not changed by so acting in the first place. From the point of view of the universe, we might say, the fact that God is now no longer acting to constitute it or initiate it (temporally) represents a new or different state of affairs; but he has not ceased to be the creator, and so is essentially unchanged. Thus it makes sense to say that he is equally creator before the moment at which the world begins. His act of creating constitutes a 'difference' for creation (the difference between being and not-being), but not for him. However, to put the case in these terms at once shows the weakness of Methodius' reasoning. The universe's 'transition' from not-being to being is not a change in the universe, not a process producing a movement from one state of affairs to another. Nor can creation out of nothing represent a change in the relations between God and creation: 'creation' is itself the relation in which what-is-not-God stands to God. Methodius, in ruling out the idea of creation as the imposition of form on matter, or the clothing of intelligible reality with sensible, quite correctly excludes any possibility of talking about changing relations. The difference between God and creation is not a separation, a *process* of differentiation. Methodius is understandably concerned to affirm that the existence of God is not the same as the existence of God-with-his-creatures (otherwise creatures would partially define what it is to be God); but he lacks the philosophical equipment to distinguish this essentially *grammatical* point from a juxtaposition of two 'states of affairs', God alone, and God with his creatures. If the latter are indeed, as he seems to think, comparable situations within a single continuum, he is quite justified in asking how one state might yield to the other, since they cannot co-exist.

The resolution of all this depends upon making it clear that God's creative act is not in *any* sense, for him or for any reality, the bringing about of a new situation in an existing continuum. Hence Philoponus[50] denies that God's activity is movement; and Aquinas,[51] much later, sums up the arguments against thinking of creation as change or process. These refinements, however, lie well in the future. As far as the background to Arius is concerned, we have only to bear in mind the existence of Christian thinkers at the beginning of the fourth century who not only held to the notion of a punctiliar beginning for the world[52] (including the world of immaterial realities), but were also able to argue that this entailed a *diastēma* between God and creation that was in some sense comparable to time-intervals in the world. In fact, the earliest literature of the Arian controversy suggests that the temporal sense of *diastēma* and *diastasis* was common ground between Arius and Alexander, and that Arius is reluctant to use the words for this very reason. Alexander twice, in *hē philarchos*, insists that there is no *diastēma* between Father and Son: the concept cannot even be formulated by the mind[53] – presumably because it involves some sort of contradiction. And the nature of the contradiction is subsequently spelt out[54] when Alexander asks what the expression 'he was not' could possibly refer to except some *diastēma* in time, some distinct period, and then points out that 'every period, every time, and all *diastēmata*' came to be through the Son. For Alexander, clearly, there is no premundane time. Arius and his supporters are presented,[55] on the other hand, as asserting the existence of a *diastēma* in which the Son is not generated by the Father. However, Alexander's rhetoric implies overall a desire to *force* the Arians to admit that they must be talking of a time-gap, a *diastēma* in the normal sense, rather than a genuine use of the word by Arius.

In Arius' own letter to Eusebius of Nicomedia, the matter is more carefully put: Alexander is accused[56] of teaching that the Father does not 'have precedence' over the Son in any *epinoia* or *atomos* – does not have any conceptual priority or any element[57] not present in the Son's being. Alexander's denial of a *diastēma* is clearly taken by Arius to involve a denial of the process of generation by which the Son comes to be, a denial that the begetting of the Son makes a difference for God, and so the erection of a rival first principle. Yet Arius is wary of arguing against Alexander that *diastēma* is a word that ought to be used of the differentiation, and uses expressions that are carefully ambiguous: the Father's 'precedence' may be temporal or logical, the *atomos* of distinction may be an instant of time or an infinitesimal reality. He goes on[58] to emphasize the fact of the Son's generation 'before times and ages', yet adds[59] that he 'was not' prior to his being generated by God's will. Arius is obviously sensitive to using the same sort of language for the 'interval' between Father and Son as for that between creator and creature more generally; none the less he feels bound to assert that the Son has a beginning, and that his non-existence must therefore precede his existence. He faces a particularly acute version of the terminological dilemmas in the philosophical cosmology of his culture – particularly acute, because he has to allow not only for the eternity of God and the duration of the world but also for a pre-cosmic existence of the Logos – *pro chronōn kai pro aiōnōn*, a duration separate from the measurable time of the cosmos.

Whence does this necessity arise? It may be that, once again, Methodius can cast some light on the problem. We have seen that, in Methodius' understanding, the world of matter and the world of form come into existence simultaneously. In the *de creatis*,[60] he suggests that the Father alone creates *ex ouk ontōn*, 'by naked will', while the Son 'sets in order and variegates', the material world that is made out of nothing, by imitating the Father. This language of order through imitation is familiar both from the *Timaeus*[61] and from Philo:[62] the demiurge contemplates the perfect 'living being' which is the world of forms, so as to order formless matter in the likeness of the intelligible realm. But in the context of Methodius' system, the meaning must be radically different, for there is neither a pre-existent formless matter, nor an eternal realm of immaterial paradigms either in the mind of the creator or independent of it.[63] The action of Father and Logos must be, in effect, simultaneous: intelligible multiplicity appears *as* the material world appears. It is at this point only, it seems, that the Father's single and simple being becomes imitable in manifold form, its simplicity refracted through the prism of the Logos' contemplation.

The idea of the Father's simplicity being mediated as a 'world of ideas' through the Son's beholding of the Father is a standard Origenian view;[64] and it clearly establishes the priority of the Logos to the rest of the universe (as *archē tōn allōn*).[65] If our universe has a beginning, the Logos is 'before' it. However, the Logos' role is also, on this account, closely tied to the beginning of the universe: his contemplation of the Father is the means by which the plurality of the world of ideas comes into being so as to make a cosmos out of what the Father has produced out of nothing. It is no very great step from this to the conclusion that the Logos, qua mediator, principle of plurality, source of intelligible structures, exists primarily for the sake of creation, and has no discernible role prior to the Father's decision to create. Material world and intelligible world are equally dependent upon the divine will; in so far as the Logos is to be identified with the intelligible world – which, remember, on Methodius' principles, cannot exist eternally and independently 'in' God – the Logos must also be the issue of divine will. As the principle of ordered creaturely plurality, the Logos has a beginning like the universe itself – not identical with that beginning, not in the same time-continuum, but a punctiliar beginning none the less. The Logos as condition of plurality must exist in some sense 'between' God's eternity and the *chronos* of the universe.

This is not Methodius' explicit conclusion – nor, as we have noted, do we have to think of it as a conclusion that would have been congenial to him – but it is certainly a plausible deduction from his view of creation. Yet again, it seems, we are confronted with what happens to Origenian cosmology stripped of its assumptions about the co-eternity with God of rational subsistents. The Logos as the container of all *logikoi* is far more manifestly bound up with the *voluntary* act of God in creation when the necessary connection of intelligible and material reality is affirmed. The problem that is becoming more and more sharply defined is that of the status of the intellectual realm. In Arius' own writing, this is expressed in a particularly gnomic line of the *Thalia*:[66] 'You should understand that the Monad [always] was, but the Dyad was not before it came to be.' Arius' use of *duas* here has occasioned a good deal of puzzlement: Stead[67] believes the associations of the word to be 'uncomplimentary', though he notes that it appears in Philo[68] in connection with *logos*, and is paralleled in the *Chaldean Oracles*[69] and perhaps echoed in Numenius;[70] is it perhaps a metrically dictated equivalent for *deuteros* (*theos*)? I am not sure that we need to resort to this explanation. *Duas* certainly represents the level of being inferior to the One, but it is by no means invariably a term with straightforwardly negative associations. Numenius reports[71] a shift within the Pythagorean tradition on the question of how the 'dyad' should be defined: Pythagoras himself saw it as initially the unformed matter co-eternal with God, and, as such, *ingenita*, becoming *genita* only when 'embellished' by intelligible form; later Pythagoreans, however, insisted that the dyad is, from the first, generated by the monad. It is what comes into existence when the monad first differentiates itself from what is not, that is, from plurality. Since this more clearly puts the dyad within the sphere of some kind of divine action, it cannot be seen as implying that *duas* is a derogatory term: it is simply the first level of being beyond or below primordial unity.

It is indeed defined almost in so many words by Anatolius, Iamblichus' teacher, in his work *On the Decad*.[72] The dyad is the first stage of separation from the monad, and is related to the monad as matter is to form.[73] Mathematically speaking, it is wholly the opposite of the monad;[74] but it should be noted that the dyad is not simply *equated* with matter in the archaic Pythagorean style, let alone being seen as a co-eternal independent principle. The 'opposition' is a logical affair, and all that is being said is that the relation of dyad to monad is *comparable* to that between matter and form: the one is passive and diffuse, the other active and unitive. From the simplicity of the monad, there comes forth[75] a distinct order of being: the unitive potential of the monad is activated by its own creative property (*poiētikon kai ergatikon idiōma*)[76] in the production of a reality that is 'many-in-one'. The monad simultaneously establishes an indefinite plurality, sheer indeterminate potentiality, *and* an ordering, formative principle that actualizes this indeterminate possibility in harmonious and dynamic reality. The monad is shown to be not merely unity in-and-for-itself but a unity that actively *unites;* and for it to appear thus, it must generate an amorphous plurality on which it can work. The dyad, then, is not simply matter, but the fusion of passive, indeterminate potential with an active but derivative principle of ordered movement. Hence it is called 'motion, generation (*genesis*), transformation . . . synthesis, sharing (*koinōnia*), relation (*to pros ti*), form in analogy (*logos en analogia(i)*)'[77] – sameness in diversity.

The text is elliptical and deliberately aphoristic, but the general drift is clear. Anatolius, like Plotinus, represents the results of that steady drift away from the primitive 'two principles' cosmology ascribed by Aristotle to Plato[78] – the world as the product of the interaction between unity and formless plurality (the 'indefinite dyad', *aoristos duas*). By the third Christian century there is an influential philosophical constituency committed to the idea that plurality *derives* from unity. Instead of being the principle of rivalry and resistance to the One, the dyad is the first stage in the One's self-diffusion and self-manifestation: it is a *dyad*, it appears, in so far as it represents the polarity of form and formlessness. But this form is not the unadulterated presence of the One as such, it is rather that 'refracted' image of the primal unity that is capable of being the unitive principle in a world of manifold realities. It is in this sense, presumably, that the dyad as a whole can be understood by Anatolius as relating to the monad in the way matter relates to form: the form within the dyad depends upon, but is not identical with the pure activity of the monad, and, as dependent, is 'passive' in respect of that primary activity whose image it is – the 'sun' to which it is the 'moon'.[79]

There are obvious parallels to this in Plotinus, though there is no evidence that Anatolius knew the *Enneads*. We have already noted Plotinus' view[80] that 'matter' exists in the intelligible world as the substratum of receptivity upon which form eternally acts: it is the bare potential for the coming into existence of separate realities.[81] *Enneads* 2.4.4 explains that the realm of ideas is, *as ideal*, a unity; the forms are not in themselves separate and distinguishable, but exist as distinct only because of some element other than their pure formal and intelligible life. What else but matter (that is, lack and passivity) can cause this diversification? Plotinus goes on (2.4.5) to elucidate further by suggesting that what we are talking about is the first movement *from* the One, which, because it separates from the One, is in itself indeterminate and formless; but this movement at the same time absorbs the reality of the One and reflects it, but in differentiated shape. Thus (2.4.16) matter is not an active principle of differentiation (which would make it something intelligible), but the *fact* of distance from the One, lack of true or intrinsic actuality. The plurality of the intelligible world measures, so to say, the endless gradations of possible distance from true actuality.

This 'bare potential', this empty, indeterminate otherness or distance, is explicitly identified with the 'dyad' in 5.1.5 and 5.4.2: 'The "dyad" here', writes Armstrong,[82] 'is the indefinite life or sight which is the first moment in the timeless formation of Intellect by procession from and return upon the One.' The intelligible realm is in one sense wholly shaped by the One, so that it can rightly be called its image,[83] but in another sense it is conditioned by what takes place in its own life, the actualizing of a manifold potential. It is caused by the One yet not *willed* by the One, since the One can have no goal to which it moves.[84] The One naturally diffuses its radiance, as fire naturally produces heat, but it does not itself move or change:[85] movement is simply the *effect* of the pure energy of the One. The One is unaffected by the appearance of the dyad: it is not that the One has now become *one of* a pair of principles, or that its unity has ceased to exist and split into two. The unity of the One is not a *relative* unity, that is, a collective unity produced by the unifying and abstracting action of our minds; and so it cannot be seen as a unity that changes or disappears when duality arises.[86] The One acts upon and in the intelligible world, but not as an agent descending from one level to another; like Aristotle's first mover, it moves or affects what it is not simply by being what it is. As the unchanging, unifying principle which holds the intelligible world together as a coherent whole, it remains itself, present in the lower order of multiplicity *en analogia(i)*, to borrow Anatolius' expression, as the unity obliquely evidenced in a harmonious diversity. This, of course, for Plotinus as for Anatolius, is a general truth about the properties of numbers, based on the Pythagorean tradition: 'twoness' is not a matter of adding one unit to another (a *sustēma monadōn*, as Anatolius has it),[87] but is unity itself confronting what it is *not* – indefinite potential – so that there comes to be a 'secondary' unity engaged in relation with what is indeterminate and non-unified; that is, there comes into existence the process of generation or change, the realizing of potential in new actuality, the kind of reality that is measured in *time* (whereas simple unity can be spoken of only in terms of a 'now').[88] To speak of something as it *is* is to abstract from time, change and relation, to speak of *ousia;*[89] to speak of it as it enters into relation as an element in a process, as part of the network of potential producing a new state of affairs, is to move to the temporal and relative level of 'twoness', the dyad, sameness-and-otherness. This pattern holds for all reality; but its archetypal case and cause is the primordial monad generating the primordial dyad, the intelligible world.

Iamblichus, predictably, echoes both Plotinus and Anatolius. The dyad is what produces processions or emanations and differentiation (*proodōn kai diakriseōs chorēgon*);[90] it represents 'creative division' (*dēmiourgikēn . . . diairesin*) and emanation downwards from the creator.[91] But Iamblichus' characteristic tendency to multiply distinct levels of reality leads him to further refinements. Some comments made by Damascius[92] suggest that Iamblichus distinguished between a completely incomprehensible One and a secondary One, 'prior to the dyad', which is active and productive; this second One is capable (as the ultimate One is not) of entering into relation with indeterminate otherness, and so generates the dyad in which 'limit' (*peras*), which is the image of the generative One, and formlessness (*to apeiron*) combine and in turn produce *to hen on*, the monad of actual contingent being that contains both intelligible and sensible worlds. All this rather startling elaboration is in keeping with Iamblichus' central model: reality necessarily exists in three modes, first as immutably itself, as unrelated to

194

anything else, second as potentially related to other things beyond itself, thirdly as actually in relation. This is the triad of 'unpartici- pated, participated and participating', which dominates so much of Iamblichus' metaphysic. His postulation of three rather than two primordial levels, the absolute One, the generative One, and the dyad, results from his concern to tie up one of Plotinus' more conspicuous loose ends. Although Plotinus insists on the motionless- ness of the One, it is still the principle of the cosmic process, active in some sense; Iamblichus pushes the One in itself beyond all action – though, presumably, it still has somehow to give rise to the secondary One. The difficulties involved in trying to free the One- as-such from all contact with what it is not (even causal relation) are manifold: one can see the point of E. F. Osborn's pleasing characterization of Iamblichus' system as being in thrall to the 'bureaucratic fallacy'[93] – that greater definition and effectiveness can be achieved by the proliferation of mediating agencies or realities.

In short, the trend of Platonic philosophy in the period after 200 is consistently but cautiously towards the greater 'inflation' of the absolute first principle. Plotinus puts it beyond *nous*, but still gives it a generative potential;[94] Anatolius insists on the idea of the monad as timeless form, but calls it *nous*[95] and grants it a 'creative property'; the elusive Alexander of Lycopolis, who taught in Alexandria late in the third century, calls the first principle *nous*, but places it beyond *ousia:* like neo-Pythagoreans such as Eudorus and Anatolius, he argued for the derivation of matter from *nous*.[96] Iamblichus seems to be the most consistent thinker in this succession of Platonic or Neoplatonic and Neopythagorean figures, in not only stressing a sharp separation between monad and dyad but also postulating an intermediate monad or 'second One'. The philosophical climate of these circles was more than friendly to the apophatic impulse in regard to the first principle so characteristic of Alexandrian theology; the question we are left with is how far it might be plausible to think of Arius as directly familiar with or sympathetic to this world of thought.

No very firm answer can be given. But, even granted the generally rather slight impact of post-Plotinian philosophy on the Christian world before the later fourth century,[97] there are a few indications that Arius could have had some contact with this tradition. First and most obviously there is his use of *duas* itself as, apparently, a title for the Logos, a use which does not seem to be paralleled in

Christian literature; further, his sharp rejection of the 'correlativity' of Father and Son, his repudiation of *to pros ti* as a proper account of this, would fit well with something like Anatolius' association of *to pros ti* with the dyad and what comes from it, in opposition to the monad which is conditioned by no relations. Anatolius was a prominent Christian figure in Egypt and Syria, and a hero of Arius' ally Eusebius Pamphilus. Alexander of Lycopolis, another Alexandrian, shared the Christian hostility to Manichaeism, a hostility to which Arius witnesses. And it has also been suggested[98] that the Alexandrian school as a whole had a strong element in it of covert Neopythagoreanism. In the light of all this, it would – at the very least – be unsurprising if Arius knew something of Anatolius, and even of his great pupil Iamblichus, and perhaps a little of Plotinus or Porphyry. If we can take it that Arius shared and developed further the anti-Origenian views and arguments of Methodius, we may assume that he believed the world of intelligible multiplicity to be the product of divine will, coming into being as the first stage in the creation of the empirical universe. It comes into being at a point, though not a point *within* a worldly time-continuum: although Arius describes the Son as begotten *en chronois*, we should probably take this as meaning, more strictly, either 'together with time', or else 'after [endless] ages' – ages, that is, in which the Father existed alone. The world that exists in and because of the Logos does not subsist as a thing in itself, but as the ground and condition of the empirical world; hence it could be said by a hostile reader (like Athanasius) that the creation is the sole *raison d'être* of the Logos, who is therefore, in one sense, dependent on *it* – though this rather distorts the emphasis of Arius' own thought. Crucial to all this is the conviction that the world of ideas or forms is not intrinsic to the being of God: God is *God* independently of there being a creation, and thus independently of his being creator. A theologian with such presuppostions would undoubtedly find an exceptionally strong philosophical anchorage in the Neoplatonic and Neopythagorean isolation of the monad over against the dyad as ground of contingency and plurality. The opposition between the Father as 'simple' and the Son as 'multiple' goes back, as we have seen, to Origen at least, and provides clear precedent for seeing the distinction in such terms; but there is little hint in Origen of the more strictly mathematically conceived opposition between monad and dyad defined by Anatolius. The more a theologian wishes to do consistent justice to the utter unrelatedness and unconditionedness of God in himself, the more Origen's distinction is liable to be pressed with logical rigour – as is comparably the case in the development of metaphysics from Plotinus to Iamblichus.

Origen never consistently denied *nous* to the first principle;[99] no Christian committed to a belief in an active, free and loving God, could easily do so, and no Christian would be likely to defend the extreme view of transcendence argued by Iamblichus. We know that extravagant language about divine ineffability was liable to recall Basilidean gnosticism for some fourth-century Christians,[100] and Athanasius is critical of any proposal that implies stripping God of 'mental' attributes, however analogically these may be understood.[101] Arius – as we shall see later – has some hints of a doctrine of analogy, and does not argue for an Iamblichan degree of stasis and indescribability in the first principle – another indication, perhaps, that he remains an exegete using philosophical tools, rather than the reverse. Yet it seems that Athanasius would not be far wrong in accusing him of making a clear distinction between *logos* in God and 'the' Logos. If God can be spoken of as *nous* and as *logikos*, it cannot be in any sense that suggests that the content of the divine mind in God's eternal life is *identical* with the world of forms: the latter is, as a pupil of Plotinus or Anatolius would have put it, the fusion between pure, single, simple active reality and sheer indeterminacy. The *logos* of God is reproduced in absolute otherness, in fragmentation (though ordered fragmentation) – *logos en analogia(i)*. But, for Arius, God plainly retains *nous* in some very nuanced sense; otherwise what could be meant by saying that God *wills?* Here is the most clearly marked difference between Arius and the whole post-Plotinus tradition:[102] the nearest any philosophical writer comes to it is Anatolius' ascription of active creativity to the monad – perhaps, like his use of *nous* for the monad, a trace of Christian bias. Arius does not by any means turn his back completely on the Origenian (and perhaps Lucianist) picture of a continuity between prototype and image; in this respect, his distinctiveness lies in his refusal to countenance the idea that the prototype *necessarily* generates an image. There is a true natural capacity – Anatolius' *poiētikon kai ergatikon idiōma* – but it must be activated by a specific act of self-determination, a 'punctiliar' decision to create and reveal.[103]

For Arius, the notion of sovereign divine will resolves the problem of the monad's relation to all else which was part of Plotinus' legacy to his successors. The natural gulf between God and the world remains unqualified, and God is indeed beyond all natural relation: to this extent Arius stands with Iamblichus against the Plotinian model of a 'natural' movement from the One to *nous*. But because the monad possesses, in incomprehensible wise, something analogous to mind, purpose and self-determination, it may freely generate relation and multiplicity. The activity of the One is conceived less as eternal and unspecific energy, more on the pattern of the acts of created intelligence; hence, as Athanasius' paraphrase of the *Thalia* suggests, and as some Arians apparently said in so many words, there was some sense in which potency as well as actuality could be spoken of in regard to God – a problematic corollary, which we have no idea how Arius himself handled, if he handled it at all. What is noteworthy, though, is the fact that absolute transcendence for Arius is to be conceived as the freedom of self-determination rather than as the mere fact of unrelatedness.[104] Whatever the problems raised by this, it is a view that reflects a distinctively Christian perspective (even if it is not the only possible move to make in the light of this perspective), dominated by a belief in the creation as an act neither necessary to God, nor consummated through a struggle with recalcitrant matter, but flowing from a love both rational and gratuitous. Whatever philosophical props Arius employed, this is the vision they were called on to support.

B

Intellect and Beyond

In the *Timaeus*, the demiurge contemplates a world of rational structures outside his own being, and forms the empirical world accordingly. The Plato of the *Timaeus* does not hold himself answerable to
the requirements of an absolutely monist metaphysic; and in this
respect he leaves to his successors (yet again) the legacy of a formidable philosophical agenda. The demiurge is evidently a mind of
sorts, and the self-subsistent 'living creature', the *autozōon*, which
is the container of the rational forms, is an object for mind or
understanding: the demiurge is *nous*, and the forms are *noēta*. The
problem for later Platonists was that the existence of an eternal
subject and object together, an active mind working on passive
objects of thought, was an insupportable notion: as we have seen
in the preceding section, form, thanks to Aristotle, came to be seen
as in itself an active principle, not simply a structure but a *structuring*
force, more than the object of the demiurge's contemplation -- and
Plato had already hinted at this himself in ascribing 'life' to the
ideal realm; further, the growing tendency to interpret Plato in
more strictly Pythagorean terms, and to look to the *Parmenides* for a
comprehensive key to Plato's view of the universe, meant that *nous*
and *noēta* would, sooner or later, have to be arranged in some kind
of hierarchy and relation of dependency, so that primordial unity
could be safeguarded.

Thus, by about the beginning of the Christian era, certain
'eclectic' thinkers (those who sought to harmonize Plato's doctrines
with Aristotle's) seem to have proposed that the ideas exist in the
mind of the demiurge;[1] by the time of Albinus, in the second Christian century,[2] this was common teaching among Platonists. When
God forms the universe, that is, imposes rationality on chaotic
matter, he contemplates not a distinct 'realm of ideas' but his own
being. However, not all would-be Platonists were in agreement

about this, and there are signs, in the same period, of strong reaction against eclecticism. Atticus, whom we have already seen defending the idea of a punctiliar origin for the rational universe out of loyalty to the *ipsissima verba* of Plato, is by no means disposed to take for granted the identity of *nous* and *noēta*. Since it is clear to him that the demiurge, being perfect, cannot be contained within the *autozōon* as a member of the class of intelligible things, he sees the demiurge as separate from the *noēta*, and superior to them; he appears to have identified the demiurge with *tagathon*, 'the Good'.[3] Whether, and in what sense, he thought the demiurge might be responsible for the existence of the world of ideas we do not know; but in any case it is clear, as Proclus noted,[4] that he did not consider the creation as the result of divine self-contemplation. Atticus' creator, then, is intellect, yet beyond the realm of intelligible beings – the subject, but not the object, of noetic activity. This view was evidently rather eccentric in the world of second-century Platonism, and was regarded as equally eccentric (though for different reasons) by later Neoplatonists. But in fact Atticus represents a significant moment in the process we have been examining in the preceding section, the process of 'isolating' the first principle: in denying that the creator is an object of intellection, he looks back to the apophatic elements in Plato's own work,[5] and forward to the absolute Neoplatonic separation of the first principle from the *nous* that contains the objects of intellection within itself.[6]

Plotinus early in his philosophical career[7] still allowed the first principle to be *noētos*, and to enjoy some kind of intellectual self-awareness, different from the self-contemplation of the second principle, the *nous* in which are the forms and numbers; in his philosophical maturity, however, he consistently separates the One from any sort of intellection. The third treatise of the fifth Ennead represents Plotinus' most sophisticated reflection on the nature of *nous* and its relation to the One. Here he poses the question of whether self-understanding is necessarily something possible only for a complex reality – that is, one with a 'knowing' and a 'known' part. The logical difficulty is that this could be only *partial* self-knowledge;[8] it would mean that the knowing element would not, in fact, know itself at all. 'If [someone] knows themselves like this, they will grasp themselves as the object of contemplation, but not as the subject';[9] and this is knowledge of something *other* than oneself (since the self is actively contemplating). Thus, if there is such a thing as self-understanding – and how can *nous* be imagined as understanding everything except itself?[10] – we are driven to the conclusion that it is not the act of a complex or composite reality: in essence, *nous*, understanding, is the same as what it understands. Only this guarantees the possibility of truth, which is the possession not of appearance but of reality.[11] What *nous* sees in grasping rational structure (which is real, that is, immutable being) is itself: it sees rational, ordered, activity – which is simply what it is.[12] *Nous* does not understand by employing anything other than itself; it works by its own light,[13] and exists only for its own sake. It is not, in other words, to be defined in terms either of any cause or of any purpose beyond its own perfect activity.

Thus far, we might be dealing with a refinement of Aristotle's account of divine activity as self-contemplation in the *Metaphysics;*[14] but Plotinus presses on to the question of whether we need to posit something beyond *nous*,[15] and embarks on one of his most passionately imagined[16] and carefully wrought arguments about the One. Thinking and understanding, even the perfect understanding of simple *nous*, involves duplication and distancing. Understanding may not be 'complex' in the sense of actually consisting of distinct components, but it is inescapably multiple: it seeks itself in other-ness. And even though that 'otherness' is generated from *nous* itself, so that *nous* is nothing but the unceasing generation of understand-able images, the fact remains that *nous* is inherently a relative term, and one that signifies movement. It would be wrong to think of it as moving from possibility to actuality in the ordinary sense (Plotinus has made this plain in 5.3.5), yet there is in it a moment of formless desire, pure openness: *nous* is in motion because it seeks to satisfy this primordial need with graspable forms. The paradox of understanding is that, as pure need or openness, *nous* is truly in contact with the One; but in its seeking to realize itself actively *as* understanding, it produces the multiplicity of the world of ideas, which separates it from the One.[17] The One therefore eternally eludes *nous:*[18] only in those unattended moments when *nous* somehow looses its hold on images and forms and becomes no more than its own fundamental desire is there communion – fleeting communion – with the One. *Aphele panta*, Plotinus concludes, 'Take away everything!'[19]

The One cannot be known, nor can it know. 'Knowing' suggests that movement rising out of need which constitutes the activity of *nous;* and the One can have neither need nor motion. It must be complete and it must be still, otherwise there is no end to the regress of actuality and possibility. There must be that which is eternally and necessarily in act; and if it is so, it will have no movement because it can want nothing. It can have no *purpose*, for the same reason – so that *nous* comes from the One simply 'as light from the sun', not because of any decision or self-determination by the One.[20] Plotinus allows that it may sound very strange to deny that the One has any awareness of itself, but insists on the point that thinking means need or desire, and thus involves an inner distancing of self from self, a deficiency in the 'adequacy' of self to self. The pure self-sufficiency of *nous*, its existence for its own sake, is its unchanging presence to itself in the multiplicity of its operations; but this means that its self-harmony is *achieved* in its movement, as the immanent goal and term of movement. Beyond this is something quite other, in which is no 'achievement'; we cannot even say, 'it is present to itself'.[21] And *we* cannot possess it in thought, word or image ('We say what it is not; what it *is*, we do not say')[22] because not even to itself is it an object. There is nothing there to know; yet there is everything *there*.

Nous exists as it does because of its fundamental hunger for the One; and what it seeks in all its activities is the contemplation of the One. In so far as it knows the first principle, it knows itself (and, presumably, vice versa), knows that it is from the One, and so knows something of the One's self-diffusion: 'in this [process] it will know itself, being itself one of the things "given" [by the One], or rather, the entirety of what is "given" '. Yet, in another sense, of course it cannot see the One clearly, since that 'seeing' would be identical with what is seen; so it is always in the process of coming to know itself, rather than abiding in static self-knowledge, finished and perfect. Its *hēsuchia*, its stillness or repose, is the unceasing process of its own activity of self-seeking and self-finding.[23] Thus understanding can at one level be said to be perfect *self*-understanding, in that it sees nothing but itself, and lacks no object for it to perceive. Its perceiving is the same as its self-perceiving; its activity is its self-awareness. There is nothing other than itself that it needs to discover. Yet at another level, its perfect self-knowledge is a perpetual movement from not-knowing to knowing: as ceaseless motion, *nous* everlastingly generates new forms and images, and so *is* itself and *knows* itself in constantly new ways. If it enjoyed any other, higher kind of *hēsuchia*, it would not be *nous* but the One.

Enneads 5.3 is a highly characteristic Plotinian fusion of dense conceptual argumentation and visionary clarity. Although similar arguments may be found elsewhere in the fifth Ennead (notably in 1, 5 and 6), this is perhaps his most careful statement of what is involved in denying that the One thinks, and his most subtle analysis of the essentially dynamic nature of understanding. *Nous* is a perpetual self-quest which, because it seeks nothing *but* itself, is at the same time wholly self-sufficient; yet because it is at heart the effulgence of the One as reflected in indeterminate desire, its seeking of itself is also the seeking of the One. And since the One is never graspable by the understanding, the quest is endless, though without restlessness. Plotinus' picture finds striking echoes in those developments in later fourth-century Christian spirituality that emphasize the unending progress of the soul towards a God never fully to be grasped[24] – though there are even more radical discontinuities involved in this latter account because of the difference made by the doctrine of a gratuitous creation. Plotinus, however, does more than simply produce another variation on the venerable apophatic theme; his achievement is in making this theme integral to his exploration of the very nature of understanding. In this, as in many other ways, he takes us far beyond the agenda set by earlier debates about the *Timaeus*.

What, then, of the relation of this discussion of intellect and intelligibilia to the problems of the Judaeo-Christian tradition? As Henry Chadwick notes,[25] Philo is the first thinker we know for certain to have identified the realm of forms with thoughts in the mind of God. No Jewish or Christian thinker could happily settle with the notion of a dimension of reality not deriving from divine agency; and so the *autozōon* becomes the *logos*, God *qua* source of intelligible multiplicity. As we have seen,[26] Philo distinguishes between union with the *logos* and union with God in himself: God is certainly *nous* for him,[27] but the realm of the *logos*, it seems, is not completely coterminous with the divine mind in its unattainable primordial unity. God alone truly knows what he is, and contact with the *logos* does not deliver such knowledge to the created mind. Like Plotinus, though with less exactitude and conceptual refinement, Philo suggests[28] that the mind cannot possess an adequate concept of its own substance: its self-knowledge consists in an awareness of its nothingness apart from the creator – that is, it knows itself in a significant way only as related to God, not as a complete object in its own right. For Philo, then, the sense in which God is *nous* and the sense in which we are so is different. God is free and purposive and self-aware, as we are, so that, presumably, it is better to call him *nous* than not; but for us to realize fully our noetic nature, to become as fully *nous* as we can by union with the *logos* and contemplation of the noetic world, does not mean that we know what God knows. His 'intellectuality' is not defined by the noetic world, as ours is; his self-contemplation is a thing apart. Again, for Philo, the question of whether the second principle knows the first does not arise. The *logos*, as we have seen, is not truly a subject; although Philo notes[29] that it is in Scripture called 'Israel' because it 'beholds God', this must be taken as meaning simply that the *logos* is that in virtue of which any being can see God. Instead of an archaic Platonic picture of the creator contemplating a separate world of forms, we have something quite close to the ideas of Albinus and some of his contemporaries, though with two important differences: the derivation of everything (including matter) from God,[30] and the twofold self-contemplation of God, his inaccessible and indescribable awareness of himself as One and Being in-and-for-itself, and his awareness of himself as *logos*, as many-in-one.

The distinction between Father as *nous* and Son as *logos* appears in Clement[31] and in Origen,[32] and we have already noted[33] Origen's fondness for the metaphor of the Son's emergence from the Father as the generation of an act of will in the mind. Both the great Christian Alexandrians are disposed to differentiate between the simplicity and transcendence of the Father and the multiple and determinate nature of the Son,[34] and it seems that, in this context, *nous* more satisfactorily expresses primordial divine simplicity. Yet Origen is well aware of Plato's location of the first God 'beyond *nous* and *ousia*', and, in the *contra Celsum*,[35] describes God the Father both as *nous* and as 'creator and father of every *nous*'. Intelligent reality is the image of that primordial mind, but the mind of God is not to be numbered among intelligent beings as one among others. In the background is the analogical principle formulated by Albinus,[36] that certain things may rightly be predicated of God in so far as he is their source and cause: he is *nous* not because he can be numbered among other *noes*, but because intelligence is what he

204

brings into being, so that it must be (at least) compatible in some sense with what he is.

Origen's Logos contemplates the Father, and finds in that contemplation the whole world of rational beings coming into existence in its (his) own life. He comes forth from the Father as the Father's everlasting act and turns back to the *bathos*, the depth, from which he comes; he sees the Father's simplicity in the only way he can see it, as the wellspring of an infinite (or potentially infinite) variety, and so gives multiple and determinate reality to the limitless life flowing into him in his contemplation. In him all things come to be, in harmonious relation and rational unity, since he mediates to each its proper degree of sharing in the life that comes from the Father.[37] Thus, for Origen, the contemplative demiurge and the realm of ideas are fused together, just as in Origen's younger contemporary, Plotinus:[38] and the Logos looks to and cleaves to the unutterable unity which is its source, as does Plotinus' *nous*. The difference is the familiar Jewish-Christian insistence on ascribing will or purpose to God, so that he can still be assimilated to mind and ascribed a kind of self-understanding. Not that Origen or any other classical Christian thinker would disagree with Plotinus about God needing nothing (the eccentric notion that God requires the world to understand and realize himself had still to wait for some sixteen centuries); but that God's self-diffusion and generative power are rooted in something like conscious decision (and so can properly be seen as intelligent love) is a conviction that consistently challenges the Neoplatonist view of a wholly purposeless deity throughout later patristic theology. Plotinus can, in more metaphorically loaded passages,[39] speak of the One as gracious and well-disposed, but this has more to do with how we receive and apprehend it and its 'impersonal' generosity than with any specualtion about the One's subjectivity.

The question of how far Origen parallels Plotinus in supposing the second principle to know the first only imperfectly is difficult to resolve. Certainly Origen was accused[40] of teaching that the Son 'does not know the Father as the Father knows himself', chiefly on the basis of a rather inconclusive remark in *On First Principles*.[41] It is better to say that the Father 'comprehends' (*emperiechō*) the Son than that the Son 'comprehends' the Father; and John 14:28, 'The Father is greater than I', might be taken to suggest that the Father knows himself 'more perfectly' than he is known by the Son. The question is left open. A related discussion in the *Commentary on John*[42] suggests that Origen was not happy with the idea that the Father *knows more* than the Son. The Son is truth, and so must know the totality of all known or knowable things (*ginōskomena*) – unless there is some *ginōskomenon* beyond truth. What this might mean is clarified a little later in the commentary,[43] when Origen argues that the 'Father of truth' is beyond truth, just as, being 'Father of wisdom', he is beyond wisdom, and so on. Origen is obviously uncertain as to how best to characterize the Father's transcendence of the Son in respect of knowledge, and is anxious lest excessive enthusiasm in exalting the Father may do less than justice to the Son. Overall, it seems likely that he *does* want to say that the Father's self-contemplation is not identical with the Son's knowledge of the Father, but is hesitant in using any language which might suggest simply that the Son lacks some element of knowledge which the Father possesses. The Father – as we might put it – does not have extra *information;* but – presumably – he knows his own simplicity *as* simplicity, while the Son knows it as cause and source of the multiple world of rational forms.

Something of this appears in a later passage in the *Commentary on John*[44] in which Origen discusses the mutual glorifying of the Father and Son. The Son is glorified by the Father because of his 'perfect knowledge' of the Father; this knowledge is at the same time a knowledge of himself, so that we can also say that the Son is glorified '*in* himself' by the Father (John 13:31–32). The Father's work in glorifying the Son, however, is greater than the Son's in glorifying the Father: the Father first glorifies himself in his own intrinsic and ineffable self-contemplation, and on the radiance of this glory the Son depends for his knowledge of the Father. It is because of this light that, along with the Father, the Son, the Son alone and no creature, can 'properly' express or articulate the Father's glory.[45] In short, all that *can be known* of the Father's life is known by the Son, except that the Father's primary self-awareness remains primary and, in some very elusive sense, 'greater' than the capacity of the Son. What the Father brings to the relation with the Son is more than what the Son brings – which does seem to suggest an asymmetry in their mutual knowledge. Once again, Origen shows his awareness of the difficulty of speaking about what the Father knows of himself as simply a further bit of knowledge lacking in the Son. The whole discussion, in fact, trembles on the brink of the radical Plotinian solution: in such a case, why not drop the idea of 'knowing' entirely where the first principle is concerned, as its use is strained to the point of equivocation?

Origen's logic leads him in the direction of an unbridgable epistemological gulf between the simple Father and the multiple Logos; but he is also aware of the obvious impropriety of saying that the Son knows the Father imperfectly. The whole of the rhetoric of Johannine Christology militates against such a statement. And if the list of charges against Origen preserved by Photius does indeed, as Nautin argues,[46] go back beyond the sixth century (though this is very far from certain),[47] there were those who shared Origen's unease. And if so, it is not surprising that Arius' views on this subject were so rapidly seized upon by his opponents,[48] and were to provide an occasion of controversy even among his own followers. We have more than once[49] noted Philostorgius' report that Arius' teaching on the Son's knowledge of the Father was repudiated by the mainstream Lucianists; they probably shared some of Origen's uncertainties about this. Certainly the Lucianist doctrine of the Son as perfect image of the Father would produce the same sorts of difficulty as experienced by Origen (how can the Father have what the Son has not?). But the next generation of anti-Nicene controversialists, pupils and successors of the earlier Lucianists,[50] and mentors in turn of the 'neo-Arians' of the mid-century, transmitted this disagreement with Arius to their followers, so that Arius' uniquely rigorous apophaticism found echoes among later 'Arians'. Aetius himself, the chief theoretician of 'neo-Arianism', assumes that to know God as *agennētos* is to know his *ousia*.[51] He also assumes that the Son knows himself to be *gennētos* in essence; there is no hint that the Son is as ignorant of his own *ousia* as he is of the Father's.

There is evidence that the neo-Arians were not simply chilly logicians, utterly insensitive to the imperatives of authentic theological reticence; it may be that they spoke for those who were anxious at the gnostic resonances of a doctrine of God's essential incomprehensibility.[52] That God could be *truly* known was a presupposition of some soteriological importance, and Athanasius makes much of it.[53] Nicene and non-Nicene Christians were agreed at least on the need to avoid suggesting that God did not reveal himself as he really was. But while the neo-Arians solved the problem by supposing that God revealed the correct designation of his *ousia* to creatures, later Nicenes – Gregory Nazianzen[54] and Gregory of

Nyssa[55] above all – offered a more epistemologically nuanced account: the Father was known wholly and perfectly to the Son, because the Father's *ousia* was wholly communicated to the Son; the revealer, the incarnate Son, therefore possessed perfect knowledge of the Father, as no creature could; and so, for the creature, knowing God perfectly meant not grasping the concept of the divine *ousia* but living the life of the Son in faith and love. By this identification with the Son, we know truly but not exhaustively, since our discipleship is always developing and never reaches conclusion.[56] Knowledge of the ideal structure of the world is only a stage along the road to *theologia*, which is beyond forms and images.[57] In this context, the second divine hypostasis can be said to contain the ideal world,[58] but is not identified with it: to know the ideas is not to know what it is to be God, the life which Father, Son and Spirit equally share. Despite more obvious Neoplatonic parallels, Philo is more influential than Plotinus;[59] the difference is that Philo's transcendent God is re-conceived as a God whose very life is in relation and communion within itself. It is because God is first a God whose nature is in generating relationship, whose nature it is to beget a Son, that he can, through the Son, generate the ideal world and its material analogue.[60] The problem of 'what it is in God' that grounds the existence of rational multiplicity[61] is resolved without supposing God to be in any way determined by his creatures: his eternal, unchanging and simple essence is a process of gift and response. Cappadocian and later orthodoxy is characterized by a vehemently apophatic concern, yet it parts company with a Plotinian definition of the primal unity as being no less incapable of *self*-relatedness than of relatedness to a contingent world. We have seen how the fact that Plotinus' One is still in some sense generative or self-diffusing led to the multiplication of 'Ones' in Iamblichus, in the effort to isolate a *perfectly* unrelated and qualityless first principle. Christian theology, legitimately or not, sidestepped the whole issue by envisaging the primal unity as concretely consisting in a pattern of relations – not a real multiplicity in God, however, since the trinitarian subsistents are not diverse and 'parallel' images of a higher unity, not *reducible* to anything beyond themselves.[62]

This is to move rather far ahead; but it should remind us of the fact that the question of the Son's knowledge of the Father was no peripheral matter in fourth-century theology. It had to do with fundamental questions of the nature of theological truth on the one hand – the possibility of speaking rightly about God – and the relation between theology and active Christian life and prayer on the other. Arius' opponents rightly treated his views in this area as crucial. It should be fairly clear by now that these views were unusual in the Church of his day, if not completely without precedent of some sort in Origen. Kannengiesser suggests[63] that we should look directly to the fifth Ennead for the background to Arius' ideas, and for an explanation of the heresiarch's 'break with Origen and his peculiarity with respect to all the masters of Middle-Platonism with whom he has been compared'.[64] For Kannengiesser, it is clear that Origen's fundamental sympathies are with Arius' critics on the question of the Son's knowing of the Father[65] (he concentrates on various texts from *On First Principles*, and allows perhaps insufficient weight to the evidence of uncertainty in the *Commentary on John*); only the radical disjunction between first and second principles for which Plotinus argues can fully account for Arius' novel teaching in this area. 'Arius' entire effort consisted precisely in acclimatizing Plotinic logic within biblical creationism.'[66]

At first sight, this may seem an overstatement; as noted above, the doctrine of divine *will* is lacking in the Plotinian metaphysic, and this ought to set Arius quite decisively apart from the great pagan. Kannengiesser's words, however, are carefully chosen: given that Arius takes wholly for granted the scriptural perspective of voluntary creation, might it not be that the *logic* of Plotinus' scheme can be deployed to safeguard precisely this – the total, unconditioned liberty of the transcendent God? I think this is perfectly possible, though it must be regarded as far from proven; Rist's strictures[67] on too readily assuming Plotinian or other Neoplatonist influences in Christian thought before the later fourth century must be borne in mind. Nevertheless the transcendence of the first principle in respect of the second, conceived as the intelligible world, is a sufficiently distinctive point in Arius' theology to lend some seriousness to the conjecture of Neoplatonic influence in this matter; and it is hard to see anywhere other than the fifth Ennead from which Arius might have derived the dual assertion of the Son's ignorance of the Father *and of himself.* It has long been a puzzle to scholars of the period why the Son's ignorance of his own *ousia* should figure in the catalogue of Arius' heresies. If it is not simply related to Philo's general point about the unknowability of the mind's *ousia*, it is surely best associated with Plotinus, who at least provides a structure of thought in which *nous'* falling short of the simplicity of the One is *necessarily* connected with the dynamic, always questing and always finding, character of *nous'* own self-apprehension. If something of this sort lies behind Arius' formulations, we are once again cautioned against the fantasy of an Arius who sets out gratuitously and consistently to diminish the dignity of the Logos. The baffling doctrine of the Son's lack of knowledge of his own *ousia* becomes an intelligible feature of a complex and sophisticated cosmology; and, in the preceding section, we saw some reason to suppose that Arius was accustomed to think of the Father and Son in the appropriate terms of simplicity over against multiplicity, or stillness over against movement and change.

There is a further point in the *Thalia* which may be illuminated by a comparison with the fifth Ennead. Arius announces that he will 'say in plain words how the Invisible is seen by the Son', and continues:

> It is in [or 'by'] the power by which God himself can see, [but] in his own degree,
> That the Son endures the vision of the Father, as far as is lawful.[68]

Athanasius gives a loose paraphrase in the contra Arianos: 'what he knows and what he sees he knows and sees in proportion to (*analogōs*) the measure of his own capacities'.[69] The 'in his own degree' of the metrical text and 'the measure of his own capacities' in the paraphrase represent the same Greek words (*idiois metrois*). Stead[70] noted the oddity of the wording, wondering whether, in the first metrical line, 'God', *ho theos*, could have a generalized meaning ('Using the power by which divinity can see' is Stead's suggestion); but, as he admits, this is unlikely. However, if we compare this with a passage in the fifth Ennead, a passage once again from the treatise 'On the Knowing Hypostases', and one which we have already discussed as possibly significant for Arius, an interpretation suggests itself. Plotinus is discussing how *nous* contemplates the One, and how it sees and knows itself in the light of the One:

> For it will know all those things which it has from him[71] [the One], and the things he has given, and the things he is capable

of (*ha dunatai*). Learning and knowing these things, then, it will in this [process] know itself, being itself one of the things 'given' [by the One], or, rather, the entirety of what is 'given'. So: if it knows That One, learning according to his powers (*kata tas dunameis autou*), it will know itself too, as it is brought into being from that source and has received from it what it is capable of (*ha dunatai*). But if it is not able to see him plainly – because such a 'seeing' is equal to what is seen – then in this respect particularly it would still have the task left of seeing and knowing itself, if indeed this 'seeing' *is* the same thing as what is seen.[72]

A perfect seeing or knowing of God (and Plotinus, like Arius, uses the terms more or less interchangeably)[73] is identical with the being of God, and hence, for Plotinus, not strictly a 'knowing' at all; thus the perfect vision of the One is not possible for *nous*, nor can *nous* perfectly complete its knowledge of itself. Yet *nous* learns of the One according to the *dunameis* of the One (in spite of the slight grammatical ambiguity, this must be the sense, rather than 'according to its own, *nous*', powers'). Although Armstrong[74] takes this as a reference to the very familiar doctrine that God is known through his 'powers', not in his essence, such a reading perhaps does less than complete justice to Plotinus' painstaking terminology. *Nous* knows that it is from the One, and so knows what the One is 'capable of'. What it *receives* from the One is what the One is capable of (I take both occurrences of *ha dunatai* to apply to the capacities of the One; the second could refer to *nous*, but I am not sure that Plotinus would use the same expression twice in such a brief space with different meanings). Thus the activity of *nous*, its knowing of itself and of the One, depends on the One's capacity; it is 'according to the One's *dunameis*'. A little more light is thrown on this by a couple of other passages in the same treatise: 5.4 and 5.8 both attempt to define the role of *nous* within the human *psyche*, character-izing the closer approximation to *nous* as a closer approximation to self-sufficiency. Our own understanding is, properly, an identifi-cation with 'the knowing power'; as we truly know, we *become nous* and see ourselves *as nous*.[75] We thus participate in the self-sustaining action of *nous*, the light which shines from itself upon itself.[76] The whole argument of the treatise assumes that the closer *nous* gets to the perfect grasp of itself, the closer it gets to the One: in other words, the self-sufficiency of *nous*, the (qualified) identity of subject and object, is its likeness to the One or the Good;[77] and this self-sufficient character results from the 'presence' of the One in the life of *nous*.[78] The *nous'* intellective activity, then, exists as a kind of reflection of and participation in the unimaginable being of the One: it understands in virtue of the One being what it is, a reality both self-sufficient and self-diffusing.

The lines quoted from the *Thalia* make tolerably good sense against a background of ideas such as these. The Son sees the Father according to the *dunamis* of the Father's own self-perception;[79] his intellective activity is a multiple and determinate image of the Father's simple vision. As we have seen, it is very unlikely indeed that Arius should have followed Plotinus in denying understanding to the Father, and his statement in the *Thalia* is accordingly more straightforward than the subtleties of *Enneads* 5.3, in which *nous* is both the image and the opposite of the being of the One. Arius' point seems to be that, although the Father is in essence incomprehensible to all being outside his own, the power of his own self-contemplation generates the possibility of a partial or analogical knowledge of him. He is, in a very carefully-qualified sense, knowable because he first knows. As in Plotinus, the second principle knows the first *solely* because of what the first is, by the 'power' of the first principle's life flowing forth to generate a different level of reality and so becoming present in another reality than itself, in limited and fragmented form. The difference lies in the nature of the continuity envisaged between the activity of Father and Son: in Arius' scheme, it makes more sense to speak of a real analogy between the Father's knowing and the Son's, while Plotinus' system represents the total repudiation of anything that could rightly be called analogical knowledge of the One. To use a rather Plotinian phrase, we know *that* the second hypostasis is animated by the first and participates in the first, but we cannot know *how*. If we were to say that the activity of *nous* is 'like' the activity of the One, we should be speaking so misleadingly that it would be better to say nothing; for *nous'* 'likeness' to the One lies only in its striving after its own dissolution as a distinct hypostasis.

If the argument of this and III.A is at all plausible, we must, then, envisage Arius as following Origen in identifying the Son or Logos with the world of intelligible realities, but also as pursuing Origen's vague and uneasy speculations about the consequences of this identification to a distinctly un-Origenian conclusion. Arius is, it seems, more sensitive to the radical nature of the disjunction between absolute unity and multiplicity-in-unity than are most of his predecessors – perhaps because of an acquaintance with some variety of the 'Pythagoreanized' Platonism of Anatolius (or even Iamblichus?), with its particular interpretations of the *monas-duas* polarity. He appears, at any rate, more at home in this context than in that of unadulterated Middle Platonism. His concern for the disjunction between first and second principles would have disposed him to respond sympathetically to certain elements in Plotinus, despite some very basic disagreements. And here he would also have found an argument to persuade him that if the second hypostasis did not perfectly know the first, it could equally have no perfect understanding of its own substance. At the same time, the Plotinian scheme would have made it plain that the second hypostasis' noetic activity, though an eternally incomplete process, in contrast to the One's everlasting repose, existed only in dependence upon the pure act of the One. Supposing Arius to have taken for granted the anti-Origenian 'backlash' of the second half of the third century, supposing him to have sought for a logically tighter version of Methodius' assertion of the 'distance' between God and the intelligible world so as to underline the doctrine of a free creation and the essential indescribability of the creator, the philosophical environment we have been examining would offer many of the tools he needed. We should not expect to find him reproducing precisely the arguments of Plotinus or any other particular philosopher, and we cannot determine exactly what texts he read; he remains, as Kannengiesser insists,[80] a theological exegete with no particular interest in metaphysics or epistemology in their own right. But if we ask the question posed at the end of Part II, the question of how it was that Arius came to express his theology in such idiosyncratic, novel and 'sharp-edged' terms, we cannot wholly ignore those philosophers of his age with whose distinctive positions he exhibits so many apparent parallels.

It remains to consider more closely the way in which Arius is likely to have understood the limited 'analogical' continuity he affirmed as existing between Father and Son. As we have already indicated, large and general questions are in the background here, to do with the truth of theological utterance and the nature of revelation. In looking at these matters, we may indeed come as close as we are likely to do to the core of what was distinctive in Arius' teaching.

C

Analogy and Participation

The words *methexis, metousia* and *metochē* – all normally rendered as 'participation' – play a crucial role in classical philosophy, a role still in need of full documentation and analysis.[1] The discussions in which they figure all turn on one of the central questions of classical metaphysics and philosophy of mind and language: how is it that the same name or word attaches to a diversity of things? This may be a question about 'universals', about the assigning of objects to a class; or it may be to do with the way in which a single term is linked to diverse objects in quite different senses. Plato's language about 'forms' and 'ideas'[2] is designed to show how diverse realities in the world are unified in virtue of their having a share in (participating in) a transcendent reality, an ideal structure which is both a paradigm for other things which manifest its characteristic nature in diminished or fragmented ways, and the cause and source of these lower and less satisfactory realities. In the *Republic*, Plato is content to describe the relation between the participated ideal and the particular worldly reality as that between prototype and image: when I say that Socrates is wise and that Gandhi is wise, I must mean that Socrates and Gandhi both have a certain share in the non-worldly 'ideal' substance of wisdom, and that therefore they each *resemble* this non-worldly substance in differing degrees. The ideal form of wisdom is, so to speak, 'as wise as could be', and the wisdom of other things is measured and assessed by reference to it.

Later, in the *Parmenides*,[3] Plato himself expressed his dissatisfaction with this way of putting it (and indeed his awareness of numerous other problems connected with the theory); but he did not abandon the language of 'forms' itself. Allen, among other scholars,[4] has shown that the central elements in Plato's account of forms need not involve the fallacious notion that the ideal structure and the particular (worldly) substance belong to the same category of realities, and the consequent fallacy of 'self-predication' ('wisdom is wise', 'largeness is large', and so on). The participation of the particular in the ideal cannot be treated as 'a mere description of a relation between two sorts of already existing things':[5] precisely because the ideal *causes* the particular instantiation, it is obvious that idea and particular do not exist in the same way or on the same level. The form of wisdom is what makes Socrates wise; if it were only a bigger and better version of Socrates, this would make very little sense. Socrates cannot have a share in another particular, another *thing*, as that would mean taking 'participation' in the sense of splitting something up and sharing it round,[6] which makes nonsense of the unifying role of the ideal form. The form is whatever it is 'in' a particular reality that gives that particular reality a structural correspondence to or unity with other particulars in this or that respect; and Plato's contention is that there would be no such unity or correspondence *between* particulars of a certain kind if they were not first united to some reality *independent* of all particulars of that kind. The wisdom of Socrates and the wisdom of Gandhi are not to be regarded as the same simply on the grounds of a resemblance between a characteristic c_1 in person a and a characteristic c_2 in person b; we should still be left with the question of how we could justify calling c_1 and c_2 by one name, not two. But if c_1 and c_2 are both *first* related to the ideal c, then of course they are one. In this scheme, c is not something which has a (maximally) higher content of c-quality than c_1, c_2, ... c_n; it is simply that which makes c_1 what it is. The 'participation' of c_1 in c is a *real* relation, one which is constitutive of c_1, one which enters into the definition, the essence, of c_1; and c itself does not 'participate' in c, for it can hardly be what it is in virtue of being related to itself. Yet we call it c, and we – metaphorically – speak of c_1 and c_2 as being 'like' c, or 'images' of c. This is, as Plato knew, an awkward and misleading habit, but it is hard to see how we could avoid it. Allen illuminatingly discusses this issue[7] with reference to reflections in a mirror: the scarf is red, and its mirror image is red, but in the latter case, 'you cannot mean the *same* thing you mean when you call its original red'.[8] The image does not stand alongside the original exemplifying the same characteristics: what it is is entirely defined by its being a reproduction of the original. This does not stop us saying that both scarf and image are red, but we should acknowledge the difference between this and saying that a scarf and a flag are both red.

This helps in clarifying the continuity and the discontinuity between form and particular, though it leaves open the vexing question of precisely *how* the redness of scarf and image are one: is there not a rather formidable problem in suggesting that 'red' means something *quite* different when applied to each in turn?[9] It may be that, as Bigger suggests,[10] the later Plato, in the *Theaetetus* and the *Sophist*, is moving away from the idea of participation as essentially the relation of particular to form and beginning to conceive it in terms of relations between particulars; participation would then mean simply the relation between a and b whereby a realizes in b an ideal form which is independent of a, yet not itself a substantive reality acting upon a in the way a acts on b. This is a bold reading of the later Plato, which, as Bigger fully admits, brings him closer to Whitehead than to any ancient philosopher; but whether or not it is correct, Platonic participation was none the less understood universally in antiquity in the terms outlined by the earlier Plato – as primarily the relation between particular and form. And it was criticized accordingly, from Aristotle onwards. In the *Metaphysics*, Aristotle asserts that it is 'empty talk' to call the relation between idea and thing one of 'participation';[11] and the great third-century commentators on his work, Alexander of Aphrodisias and Porphyry, elaborated his critique with great energy. The notion of separable forms is rejected,[12] so that there is no *prior* reality of which the particular can have a share. Similar things can be said to be so by 'sharing' a common form, but this is metaphor;[13] *metochē*, 'participation', is simply the exact comparability or equality of essential qualities in two or more particular things,[14] it is *koinōnia kat'ousian*, common essence or definition.[15]

When two or more things in this way 'participate' in a common definition, they are spoken of in terms of 'synonymy' (or, as we should more readily say, 'univocity'):[16] designations applied to such things are true of each of them in the same sense. This, of course, reinforces Plato's own point in the *Parmenides* that form and particular cannot bear the same name in the same sense. It also means that, strictly speaking, anything other than 'synonymous' or univocal naming cannot be treated as an aspect of participation. 'Homonymy', equivocity, is the linguistic relation between the designations of *non*-participating substances, those which, as Aristotle puts it,[17] have a different *logos tēs ousias*. The same identifying expression spoken of two or more subjects that do not have *koinōnia kat'ousian* is bound to have different senses. Porphyry offers[18] a classification of the types of equivocity that was to be influential in later interpretations of Aristotle's treatment of the subject in the *Categories*. Apart from purely 'accidental' or 'chance' homonyms, there are four kinds of intentional, conscious homonyms. One thing may have the same name as another because of *likeness* – sharing some of its attributes, but not its fundamental definition. Or it may have the same name because of *analogy* – it stands in the same relation to something else as does the other reality (the roof of a mouth, the roof of a house; or the eye as the 'window' of the soul; and so forth).[19] Or the equivocity may depend on a single *prosēgoria* in different things – the same purposive function or activity is going on in separate subjects, as a book, a diet, or a dose may all be called 'medicinal'. Or, finally, diverse things may be called the same because they are all directed to a single *telos:* a meal, a climate, a room, a rule of life may all be called 'healthy' because they all produce or preserve or show health in a person (this is what Aristotle called[20] *pros hen* predication, and it was regularly treated in later philosophy as a variety of analogy; but for Porphyry, analogy is more strictly tied to the idea of proportion). This last Porphyry, like Aristotle,[21] is reluctant to call equivocation, as there is a central controlling sense for the expression in question, specified by one usage (a *person* is healthy in the primary and proper sense); the other uses are intelligible only in relation to this, and can thus be said to be dependent on this definitive case. Other sorts of equivocation do not necessarily involve dependence of this kind.[22]

The significance of all this for our talk about God becomes clearer once we recall that for Plato, in at least some of his works, the realm of ideas was itself ultimately structured and unified by a single form generative of all others. In the *Republic*,[23] the 'Form of the Good' is the ultimate, transcendent, active principle; it is to the world of ideas what the sun is to the order of material things, both an illuminating and a generative reality.[24] In the *Parmenides*, the One is that from which all numbers are generated, and in which they all participate.[25] Both the Good in the *Republic* and the One in the *Parmenides* are said to be 'beyond being'[26] – that is, they are not structured by anything beyond themselves, they do not belong in any class, they are self-sufficient and are to be understood only in terms of themselves. However, this ultimate principle or reality, however characterized, is not strictly infinite or wholly transcendent,[27] since it remains a reality defined by its own intelligible structure. 'The Good beyond finite beings may for Plato have been limited by itself, in the sense of a limit beyond other limits',[28] and the One also appears to be a 'limit of limits';[29] neither wholly escapes 'limit' itself. In the terms in which the problem has several times presented itself in this study, Plato's first principle is always more like the harmonizing power that unifies the diversity of the intelligible world than like the utterly self-sufficing one-in-itself;[30] his scheme seems to require that the ultimate monad is the *active* beginning of the world of relations rather than a wholly absolute and independent unity.

Thus Plato's first principle is accessible to the mind as it ascends to and through the intelligible world. As the celebrated simile of the Divided Line and its dialectical elaborations in the *Republic* show,[31] it is possible to perceive and know the intelligible world through the proportional similarity between two or more relations: as belief or firm opinion stands to knowledge, or as acquaintance with the outer shape of things stands to rational understanding of them, so the world of particulars stands to the world of forms, 'becoming' (*genesis*) to 'being' (*ousia*). The advance of the mind to greater security and generality and unity of perception mirrors the hierarchy of reality itself, at the summit of which is the supremely stable and unifying level of existence, the Form of the Good. The implication is that the way in which the Form of the Good functions can be known analogically when considered in relation to the function of whatever unifying, clarifying or stabilizing reality there may be at the level of 'acquaintance with the outer shape of things'; hence the earlier and related simile of the Sun, and the later dramatic allegory of the Cave. As the man who escapes from the cave gradually acclimatizes his eyes to the objects visible in the sunlight and then to the sight of its source, the sun itself, so with the philosopher who gradually perceives not only the forms, but that in virtue of which they exist, the Form of the Good.

Analogy, in this scheme, can at least give us a grasp of how the supreme principle works upon the lower levels of intelligible reality; what it takes for granted is that the first principle, though very definitely a *special* case, is none the less a *case* of intelligible reality. 'God is among the *noēta*', as Plutarch was to put it.[32] He can be understood in some real fashion in virtue of his relation to other things; he is 'participated' by the ideal forms (or ideal numbers or ratios, in a more Pythagorean idiom) in a way comparable to that whereby forms themselves are 'participated' by particulars. This is not Plato's language, but it is common by the 'Middle Platonist' era,[33] in a context in which the intelligible world has come to be seen as an image or imitation of the first principle. *This* is why the third and fourth Christian centuries are such a significant and turbulent period in the development of religious epistemology. If Numenius and Plutarch represent a sort of conservative consensus, based upon elaboration of the language of participation in superior realities by inferior, it proved to be very far from secure. Revolutionary reconstruction was impending. As we have already seen, the great Aristotelean commentator, Alexander of Aphrodisias, revived his master's criticisms of Plato on forms at the beginning of the third century, and was followed later in the century by Porphyry – at least in the rejection of the 'vertical' sense of participation, the sharing of lower beings in higher. Neoplatonism, of course, in Plotinus, Porphyry and all who come after, most certainly does not reject the notion of an intelligible order of real subsistents;[34] but the metaphor of participation is either abandoned in favour of, or revised with reference to, that of 'procession'.[35] The lower reality is constituted or formed in this or that respect by the active life of the higher, but *does not reproduce the 'essence' of the higher;* there is no question of univocity between form and particular, or of the form perfectly exemplifying what the particular imperfectly exemplifies. The relation is a version of *pros hen* equivocity, the fourth kind of equivocity recognized by Porphyry: a can be called f because some aspect of its existence can be understood by reference to a central or normative fact of something being f; but a's f-ness is not itself a *case* of f that can stand alongside the normative f. Thus the agency of form goes out from its own reality not to produce imitations of itself but to cause certain related and purposive activities in a lower reality. There is not and cannot be any question of participation between form and particular in the sense of their simply exhibiting a common structure in different degrees. Plato's own misgivings about an over-simple 'imitation' doctrine in respect of forms and particulars are here pressed to a radical conclusion.

As to the possibility of speech about God, this is obviously affected by such a reading (and revision) of the Platonic system. The first principle is not participated by the forms any more than they are by particulars; it cannot be a supreme paradigm among the forms, attainable by analogical ascent, because the possibility of analogy, at least in the style suggested by the *Republic*, depends upon a version of the forms doctrine heavily dominated by the model of original and image, a version which Neoplatonism treats with the greatest reserve and surrounds with qualifications. The forms are not simply that of which particulars are imitations; nor are the forms themselves imitations of the Form of the Good or the nature of Good. In Plotinus, as we have seen, *nous* can be thought of as an 'image' of the One in the sense that it enjoys a kind of self-sufficiency; but it is a somewhat paradoxical 'imitation', in two respects. First, the very existence of *nous* as dyad is in opposition to the One, it is *essentially* what the One is not; second, the more *nous* approximates to the One's self-sufficiency, the more it approaches a condition of which, by definition, nothing can be said. The analogical ladder is effectively dismantled.

A negative theology, affirming God to be *arrhētos*, 'inexpressible',[36] is certainly represented in Middle Platonism, not least in the idea of finding God by *aphairēsis* – thinking away specific material predicates until you come to the most formal and empty ones (such as location), then thinking away that also.[37] But the point of this is simply to deny that any *fully* adequate concept of the first principle can be formed by the finite mind, or that it can be thought of in terms of lower levels of being. It is not to deny the idea that the forms reflect the life of the first principle; or that the first principle stands at the summit of the world of forms, or that it is legitimate to make predications to the first principle in the light of what it effects.[38] Plotinus' picture is far more austere. Alexander (as far as his views can be pieced together) believed that God directly united form and matter in the formation of the cosmos, rather than setting up a chain of activity from higher to lower – though the medium of his action is the motion of the heavenly bodies under his guidance.[39] He thus breaks with the idea of any sort of 'natural' continuity between God and the forms in the sense of their being *agents* mediating the divine agency. But Plotinus goes further, in denying deliberate agency to the One; a rather odd kind of natural continuity is thus restored, in that *nous* 'emerges' from the One by some kind of overflow, but it emerges (as we have seen) as the image of the One in total otherness. Porphyry and later Neoplatonists qualify this slightly – Porphyry by (it seems) blurring the sharpness of the distinctions between the three primary hypostases and between *nous* and the One,[40] Iamblichus by refining the concept of participation so that, at every level of reality, we find three terms, an 'unpartici-pated' (*amethektos*), a 'participated' (*methektos*) and a 'participating' (*metechōn*).[41] The substance of each subject remains incommunicable; but it exists not only *in* itself but also as acting to produce relation *to* itself; and so it exists finally in another subject as sharing in that subject's life or contributing to its definition. No *ousia* (in the intellectual realm, which is what is under discussion here) can be *part* of another *ousia;* but a lower level substance can be made to be what it is by the agency of a higher, and so may be said to 'contain' the higher, though in a very extended sense.[42]

The upshot of all this, however precisely it is expressed, is that the substance of God cannot be participated, cannot enter into the definition of any other substance or admit any qualification by any other substance. As we have already seen,[43] Iamblichus is sufficiently anxious on this score to erect a hierarchy of 'Ones', ascending towards a more and more total ineffability, inaction and imparticipability. If we turn from this world to that of the early Arian controversy, the parallels are clear. Arius, like Iamblichus, condemns the idea of a fusion of substances into a 'consubstantial' compound: the Son is not a *homoousios* 'portion' of the Father – or, if we take an alternative reading, he is not a portion of a *homoousios* mixture.[44] In the *Thalia*, we read that the substances of Father and Son are *anepimiktoi*, incapable of mixing with one another,[45] and Athanasius accuses Arius of teaching that Father, Son and Spirit are substantially *ametochoi*, without participation[46] – probably a paraphrase of the *Thalia* line. It is Eusebius of Nicomedia who says in plain terms[47] that the Son's nature 'is something entirely without participation in the nature of the unbegotten one'. Whatever is communicated from Father to Son, then, is not *ousia* or *phusis*. It is equally clear that the Aristotelean sense of *metochē* or *methexis* or *metousia* is ruled out: God and the Son cannot be joint 'participants' in a common form of Godhead. One of the most consistent complaints of Arius and his supporters was that Bishop Alexander's position implied the existence of two *agen(n)ēta* – the view which Methodius had so effectively rebutted in his treatise *On Free Will*.[48] *Metochē* as defined by Porphyry (equality of *propria*) cannot be the relation of Son to Father, for the Son 'possesses nothing proper to

God, in the real sense of propriety,/ For he is not equal to God, nor yet is he of the same substance'.[49]

It seems quite probable that Bishop Alexander and his circle had been using some sort of language about 'substantial' unity between Father and Son, or perhaps – as Numenius had done[50] and as Eusebius of Caesarea continued to do[51] – had spoken of the Son enjoying *metousia* or *metochē* of the Father's life, in a still fairly untroubled Middle Platonic fashion. It is possible too that the word *homoousios* itself was current in Alexandria, in the wake of the controversy between the two Dionysii half a century before, meaning little more than did related expressions about participation in God's *ousia*. As Rist has shown,[52] the general philosophical climate in Alexandria at this time was little if at all touched by Neoplatonic radicalism; the spirit of Numenius still animated it, and there seems still to have been a considerable influence from the pagan Origen, fellow-pupil with Plotinus of the elusive Ammonius Saccas. With this general background, in which the first principle was still thought of as intelligent and active, the language of participation in or imitation of the divine *ousia* continued to be usable. If this is a fair picture of the intellectual atmosphere of the Alexandrian church, and if Arius was indeed a man with some sort of dialectical training, it does indeed look as though his own formation depended on sources rather outside the mainstream currents in his environment. It is not only that he uses strong words to deny the continuity between God and the Son, but also that, in the *Thalia*, he takes up the (Plotinian) paradox that the first principle is known for what it is through its opposite: 'We call him unbegotten on account of the one who by nature is begotten;/ We sing his praises as without beginning because of the one who has a beginning'.[53] And a good deal of Arius' polemic, in the *Thalia* and in his letters, hangs together very consistently if it is read as a refutation of *all* the available senses of substantial identity or participation applied to God and the Son, the whole range of possible meanings covered by *homoousios, ek tēs tou patros ousias, idios tēs tou patros ousias*, and so forth. God and the Son are not one subject – *homoousios* in what was probably Paul of Samosata's sense; the Son is not a 'property' of the Father, not *idios* to the definition of God. *To idion*, for a Porphyrian or Aristotelian logician,[54] means the substantial quality or condition of something, not a thing in itself; but the Son, existing *alēthōs*, with his own distinct properties and none of the Father's defining properties,

223

is a subject in his own right. Nor can Father and Son combine to form a *homoousios* compound; there are no such things outside the material world (following Iamblichus). Nor are they co-ordinates, members of a 'class' of unbegotten beings – *homoousios* in a well-attested generic sense.[55] Nor are they *homoousios* in the Valentinian sense of a higher *ousia* separating itself out into higher and lower by emanation;[56] the immaterial essence of God does not move or change or divide itself.

In short, when we look at Arius' attack on Alexander's theology, we see, at the very least, a close parallel to the Neoplatonist dismantling of earlier Platonic models of God's relation to the world. Consciously or not, Arius is a 'post-Plotinian'; yet, like Porphyry, he is not willing to be perfectly consistent in denying all predicates to the first principle. We have seen in the preceding sections how important it is for Arius to retain the language of will and mind in speaking of God, precisely because, in contrast to the Neoplatonists, he holds to the centrality of specific acts of revelation.[57] He is thus particularly vulnerable to the question which seems to have been pressed on him by his opponents: if the Son reveals God in his 'oppositeness' to God, and if he cannot have any part in what it is to be God, in what conceivable sense do the divine predicates ('spirit, power, wisdom, glory, truth . . . radiance, light', as Arius himself enumerates them) attach to him? Alexander[58] and Athanasius[59] both claim that Arius held the Son to possess the divine attributes only by *metochē*, in the weakest sense of the word: the Son has his wisdom, goodness, and so on, *by sharing in God's grace*. He thus can be said to have these qualities in a transferred or 'improper' sense (since God alone fully and properly possesses them). If he has them only *katachrēstikōs*,[60] this amounts to saying he has them only 'notionally' (*kat'epinoian*)[61] or 'nominally' (*onomati*);[62] it is a *metaphor* to call the Son 'wise', for instance, and a metaphor in antiquity was regarded as the transfer of a name from one subject to another which already had a name of its own.[63] Such language can tell us nothing about the essence of that to which it is applied.

It seems most unlikely that Arius himself used this kind of vocabulary[64] – though his Origenian use of *epinoiai* to describe the various aspects of the Son's life[65] gave an obvious opening to hostile critics. At first sight, Athanasius' implicit point is very weak. To say, 'Either the Son possesses divine qualities in exactly the same sense as the Father or he possesses them in a purely metaphorical sense', is to ignore the quite detailed discussion, which we have already touched upon, that deals with the different kinds of homonymy or equivocity. However, the argument does have some force in this particular instance. Taking Porphyry's four varieties of equivocation, we should have to conclude that the statement 'God is wise and the Son is wise' was incapable of fitting any of them very comfortably. There is no natural resemblance between creator and creature; no question of identity of proportion, since God is *necessarily* what he is, and the Son, as creature, cannot be; no sense in which God and the Son function identically in some other subject (God as such does not enter into 'participate in', another subject); no sense in which the Son's wisdom is something oriented to the paradigmatic exercise of wisdom in God, while being predicated of the Son in a wholly difference sense (there is no comparison with the relation between 'Socrates is wise' and 'your decision is a wise one'). Athanasius is no philospher, but he *has* succeeded in identifying a dilemma which for Arius is more grave than it would have been for a pagan Neoplatonist. In so far as the work of Christ is to reveal to us a saving knowledge of the Father, to create in us a transforming *gnōsis*,[66] it is of real importance that his being should truly show what the Father is like. For a strict Plotinian, even for Porphyry and Iamblichus, the human goal is to become fully *nous*, and (it may be) touch some higher level of being in moments of pure intellectual receptivity; *nous*, however, though it reflects something of what is higher, cannot be said to transmit or 'enact' the life of the One, let alone to perform the will of the One. There is no graspable content to enact, no will to perform, only an everlasting pure agency, sufficient to itself and exclusive of all relation. The Neoplatonist does not and cannot look for a divine initiative to bridge the gulf between absolute and contingent, nor for a mediator expressing and articulating that initiative and establishing it as rooted in the divine essence.

As we have several times observed, Arius is entirely committed to the idea that God is free and active; and he is therefore bound to have some doctrine of the Son's manifesting the Father. The 'glories' of Son and Father are incalculably different and unequal,[67] yet there is some sense in which the Son is rightly called *doxa theou*, and even *eikōn*[68] – a term which Arius very noticeably avoids in his credal professions. Arius cannot have believed that *logos* and wisdom were ascribed to the Son only by some kind of distortion of language. In so far as God is identical with his own reason and wisdom, he *is logos* and *sophia* by definition, and the Son is so only as a matter of fact; but because the Son is what he is solely and directly by God's will,[69] this 'matter of fact' has nothing to do with the contingencies and vulnerabilities of the created order. All that the Son is is what the Father wills and does, and in this sense he is rightly called *eikōn*. If we read lines 23–25 of the *Thalia* as Athanasius seems to have remembered them in the *contra Arianos*,[70] Arius is saying that the one *we call* 'Wisdom' came to be 'Wisdom' because the (truly) wise God so willed it; and accordingly (*goun*) this is the way in which all the various 'epinoetic' names of the Son come to be given him – that is, he is 'spirit' and 'power', for instance, because of the will of the God who is spirit and power 'in truth', necessarily. *Eikōn* fits rather awkwardly in the list of names when it is read in this sense; but perhaps it need not be understood in quite so precise a way, and Arius is merely emphasizing that it is only by God's will, not by any natural or automatic resemblance, that the Son is God's image. It is in this sense alone, then, that (as the next line goes on to say) the Son is 'radiance' and 'light' – a clear rejection of anything like the Plotinian use of the light metaphor to explain how *nous* comes from the One without any decision on the One's part.

Arius' insistence that the substances of Father and Son have no natural communion or participation thus functions as part of an argument that tends in a quite different direction from post-Plotinian Neoplatonism. There is no communion of *ousia* between Father and Son, *yet* the Son appears as divine redeemer and revealer, and we receive saving knowledge from him. Like any Christian theologian, Arius cannot but start from the fact of renewed or reconstructed experience of God, arising not from human endeavour but from the event of Jesus Christ. The Son, then, is not, cannot be, by nature a part of the life of God, or even a natural reflection of God, a reflection according to some neutral cosmogonic process. God as *monas* is by definition beyond division or comparison, and cannot be the first term in a process of descending emanation. How then is there knowledge of him at all? Only by his own choice. He brings into being a mediator between himself and all else, whom he endows with all the glory a creature can bear; a mediator in whom his divine activity meets no obstacle and totally fulfils its purpose. Because of the intimacy so created, the mediator is more than a 'product' of the divine will, he is also called 'Son' – the 'perfect creation of God, but not like one among other creatures', the one who possesses 'the inheritance of all things'.[71] He knows the Father because his own supreme creaturely wisdom is a (willed) likeness, necessarily imperfect and always seeking, of the Father's self-identical self-perception: 'Mighty God as he is, he sings the praises of the Higher One with only partial adequacy'.[72] And because this glorious god appears to us turned towards one still greater, 'We sing his [the Father's] praises as without beginning because of the one who has a beginning.'[73]

That there is a glorious and everlastingly wise, good, rational and powerful mediator shows us that wisdom, goodness and so on can truly exist in the order of contingency; that this mediator points beyond himself shows us that there is an unimaginable higher principle who is yet graciously disposed because he has chosen that there should *be* a mediator.[74] Further, as God is necessarily what he is, he cannot choose something contradictory to his nature. Thus a *sort* of analogy is established by this choice, in so far as the source of the mediator's glory cannot be qualitatively utterly unlike the mediator – even though, as Arius delights to repeat, they are wholly opposite from the strictly logical or mathematical point of view. Arius is attempting a bold and delicate task, simultaneously stressing the total disjunction between monad and dyad, in strongly Neoplatonist and Neopythagorean style, and asserting real knowledge of the monad as a gracious will. He is walking exactly the same tightrope as the Cappadocians later in the century.[75] Theological analogy is indeed distinct from the varieties of equivocity identified by Porphyry; if God and his Son (for Arius) or God and the general order of creation (for the Cappadocians, Pseudo-Dionysius and Aquinas) can be said to have some *homoiōsis* that enables the same terms to be predicated of both, this is not because both belong at the same ontological level.[76] All likeness of this kind depends on God – not in the sense of being part of a process of which God is the first term, but because of God's free self-determination.

In III.A we noted the way in which Arius uses belief in the divine will to resolve the problems over the monad's relationship to the world of multiplicity. Here again, the will of God acts almost as a *deus ex machina* to explain how theological predicates fully and necessarily proper to God alone can be eternally but contingently ascribed to the Son. It is the notion of divine will that stops the gap which so disturbed Athanasius and led him to accuse Arius of teaching that the divine predicates were true of the Son only 'in a manner of speaking'. Arius certainly intends to say more than that; but, for him, the sole guarantor of continuity between creator and cosmos is, and cannot but be, God's will. He inherits the legacy of third-century philosophy, in the sense that he seems to take for granted the dismantling of the Middle Platonist consensus about God, the intelligible world and the empirical world as a chain of participating life. However, the paradoxes and aporiai of Plotinus' apophaticism are dissolved in the bald affirmation that continuities which are naturally inconceivable, *true* reflections of the divine in the contingent, can be established by the naked will of God. A Plotinian style of negative theology is being quite skilfully deployed in defence of some very un-Plotinian conclusions. For Arius, the unutterable mystery of the being of God is stressed so as to secure the absolute liberty of the divine action in creating, revealing and redeeming.

This of course still leaves unsettled the question of the sense in which God's free decision enacts or reveals his essence – a question on which Athanasius focuses very effectively in the third treatise *contra Arianos*.[77] Athanasius is responding to the dilemma posed by his opponents, 'does the Father beget the Son by will or by necessity?' and his counter-challenge is to accuse the Arians of failing to understand the necessary 'grammar' of speaking about God's nature and action. The anthropomorphic model of 'deliberation' is, in respect of God, profoundly unhelpful. What sense does it make to say that God 'decides' to be what he is? Yet it is part of the definition of God that no other reality *makes* him what he is, no necessity is imposed on him. The human antitheses between purposeless and purposive (deliberative) action and between my choice and what is imposed on me from outside cannot apply to God. He does not *decide* to be good; yet he is consciously and purposively good, and no external force compels him to be so.[78] God does not act by activating an innate habit or disposition (*hexis*) at different moments of time, in the temporal succession of understanding, deliberating and willing.[79] To speak like this is to revive the errors of Valentinus and his disciple Ptolemy, for whom God must first generate the principle of 'thought' before he can actually will.[80] But since Scripture makes it clear that the Word *is* the understanding and purpose of the Father,[81] then to claim that the

Son exists by an act of will is absurd: he *is* the Father's conscious, purposive act. Deny this, and you end up with the gnostic picture of an indeterminate divine void, which might turn out to be anything, at the source of being; unless you say that the Father's *expressed* thought or will exists in virtue of an *innate* thought and will that must be in some way different from it (Athanasius refers[82] to the *Thalia* line about 'Wisdom' coming into being through Wisdom) – which negates the essential scriptural idea of the Son as simply and directly the reasoning act of the Father.

Athanasius identifies what is undoubtedly a weak point in Arius' account. If not even the continuity Plotinus sees between One and *nous* is admitted, and if everything is made to depend on the Father's totally undetermined will, does that will express the divine nature or not? If it does, the first step to a Nicene account is taken; if it does not, an *arbitrary* deity is suggested, equally offensive to pagan and Christian, and – as we have seen – evidently worrying to Arius' allies. For Athanasius, the Father is naturally 'generative':[83] what he does in producing the Son is the enactment of what he is; and as his acts are not temporal and episodic, he always and necessarily 'does' what he is – by the necessity of his own being, not by any intrusive compulsion. In the last analysis, the God of Arius, beyond all analogy and participation, can only be an empty abstraction, galvanized into concrete life and activity by the upsurge of causeless will from the void within it; or so Athanasius would have us believe. The problems set up by the extreme apophatic consequences of the third-century shift in philosophical thinking cannot be sidestepped by the appeal to will without a fundamental irrationality being introduced into the Godhead itself.

D

Conclusion

All that has been said about Arius' relation with the philosophical developments of the third Christian century is inevitably speculative, and no extravagant claims about influence or dependence can be made. What this final part of our examination has attempted to suggest is simply that, in so far as we can catch a glimpse of Arius' metaphysics and cosmology, it is of a markedly different kind from the philosophical assumptions of Eusebius of Caesarea or, for that matter, Athanasius himself in his apologetic works.[1] Arius' cosmos is not that of 'Middle Platonism'; ascent to the first principle by a graded sequence of images, knowledge of God through the created works which show his wisdom and through the primary *eikōn*, the Son, are not at the heart of Arius' understanding. And in his insistence on the utter independence and separateness of the source of all, he unquestionably stands close to Plotinus and his successors. As I remarked much earlier,[2] it is tempting to think that Anatolius of Laodicaea is the 'missing link' connecting Arius with the Neoplatonic world; but this must remain at best a rather distant possibility. We can at least say that in logic and ontology, in his views on participation and the incommunicability of substantial predicates between separate hypostases, and in his general account of the relation between first and second principles – specially in regard to the latter's knowledge of itself and of the former – he belongs firmly in a post-Plotinian and post-Porphyrian world.

Yet he is not a philosopher, and it would be a mistake to accuse him of distorting theology to serve the ends of philosophical tidiness. On the contrary: the strictly philosophical issues are of small concern to Arius and his understanding of the completely undetermined character of God's will allows him to bypass the issue of how it is *conceivable* that plurality should come out of unity. He risks, in fact, what all extreme forms of voluntarism risk, the inability to say anything about the subject of willing beyond the mere assertion that it wills – an inability that, as Athanasius seems to have noticed, suggests a very bizarre idea of what it is to *act* at all. The price of an uncompromising stress on the divine freedom is to weaken rather than strengthen the vision of a God whose being is essentially and eternally active, by seeming to postulate a God in whose depths is a void of bare potentiality, the pure indeterminacy which for a Platonist was equivalent to non-being. Athanasius has some justification in invoking the spectre of a gnostic divine 'abyss', which can in some abstruse sense be said to be 'there' prior to and independently of its actualizing of itself in intelligence and intelligent action.[3]

Arius is seeking, so it appears, for a way of making it clear that the doctrine of creation allows no aspect of the created order to enter into the definition of God; he thus requires a metaphysic both monist (in the sense of deriving the being of everything from primal unity) and absolutist (placing the essence of this primal unity beyond all relation). If the analysis in the foregoing pages is accurate, what finally sets him apart as a theologian is the attempt to incorporate such a metaphysic within an account of God's creating and revealing work drawn largely from Scripture and retaining a strong personalist element in its view of God. Post-Plotinian cosmology and logic are what make Arius an 'heresiarch'. As we have seen, the notion of a hierarchy of distinct hypostases, the criticism of Origen's doctrine of an eternal intelligible realm independent of the cosmos we now know, even the uncertainty over the Son's knowledge of the Father are none of them themes unique to Arius; they take on a distinctive colouring because of his attempt to state them with new rigour, employing the methods and conclusions of what was still in his day a radical minority group among philosophers. In relation to the three areas examined in this part of our study, Arius' argumentation could perhaps be expressed in three syllogisms:

(i) The Logos of God is the ground and condition, the rational or intelligible structure, of the world;
But that structure has no existence independent of the world which it structures;
Therefore the Logos does not exist prior to the divine decision to make the world: *ēn hote pote ouk ēn.*

231

This can be filled out by appeal to the scriptural doctrine of a punctiliar creation; and, as noted in III.A, Arius is not insensitive to the problems caused by temporal language used of God.

(ii) God the Father is absolute unity, God the Son (as the realm of intelligence and intelligibles) is multiplicity;

But absolute unity cannot be conceptualized by any knowing subject without its being distorted into multiplicity (as something existing *over against* a subject);

Therefore the Son can have no concept of the Father's essence, no *katalēpsis*.

This can be elaborated along Plotinian lines to show how the Logos can have no *katelēpsis*, no final grasp, of his own essence either, because of the dynamic and restless nature of intelligence itself.

(iii) The Logos truly exists as a subject distinct from the Father;

But the defining qualities, the *essential* life, of one subject cannot as such be shared with another;

Therefore the divine attributes traditionally and scripturally applied to the Son must be true of him in a sense quite different from that in which they are true of the Father.

For Arius, this is elucidated by appeal to the Father's unconditioned will being able to form what it pleases in the life of a creature.

In each of these cases, the first term would have been relatively uncontroversial, certainly for an Alexandrian; and in each case the second term depends on an implicit critique of conservative 'Platonic consensus' doctrines, and a far stricter differentiation, even opposition, between monad and dyad. In Part II we were able to see the extent to which Arius could rightly be seen – and see himself – as a theological conservative; what Part III proposes is that he became the centre of a controversy because of his fusion of these conservative themes with a very un-conservative ontology, which isolated him not only from Alexander and Athanasius but also from his Lucianist allies and their successors.

Postscript (Theological)

'Isolation' is a word that recurs in discussing Arius, both in his career and in his thinking; and we constantly find a paradoxical mixture of the reactionary and the radical in this. In Alexandria he represented not only a conservative theology, but also a conservative understanding of his presbyteral role *vis-à-vis* the bishop, and a traditional Alexandrian confidence in the authority of the inspired contemplative and ascetic teacher. In philosophy, he is ahead of his time: he recognizes the mythological and materialist elements in a loosely Middle Platonist account of God's relation to the world and the world's participation in God, and presses the logic of God's transcendence and ineffability to a consistent conclusion – that 'what it is to be God' is incapable of conceptual formulation, and of imitation or reproduction by any natural process of diffusion. In many ways – and here is a still stranger paradox – his apophaticism foreshadows the concerns of *Nicene* theology later in the fourth century, the insights of the Cappadocians, or even Augustine. If he had his problems with the Lucianists, he would have found the 'neo-Arians' of later decades still less sympathetic.

This serves as a necessary reminder of the point made at the conclusion of Part I: there was no such thing in the fourth century as a single, coherent 'Arian' party. Those who suspected or openly repudiated the decisions of Nicaea had little in common but this hostility – certainly not a loyalty to the teaching of Arius as an individual theologian. The protestation made at Antioch in 341 ('We are not followers of Arius') was no doubt perfectly sincere: bishops are not going to be marshalled as a faction by a presbyter, even if that presbyter's teaching is generally acceptable. Arius evidently made converts to his views, many Libyans, the Illyrian clerics Ursacius and Valens, perhaps others; but he left no school of disciples. The way in which Athanasius in *de synodis* introduces the *Thalia* and other fragments suggests that they were not well-known in the 350s, certainly not treasured by the anti-Nicenes; the bishop relies on such texts being a positive embarrassment to most of his opponents. Actual quotations from Arius in polemical works (as opposed to histories) are seldom found outside the writings of Athanasius (Victorinus has a Latin version of U.1 and 8).[1] Philostorgius knows that Arius wrote popular songs,[2] but is not recorded as quoting any texts; his hero is Eusebius 'the Great' of Nicomedia, not Arius, of whose theology he, as a 'neo-Arian', is critical. The textbook picture of an Arian system, defended by self-conscious doctrinal dissidents, inspired by the teachings of the Alexandrian presbyter is the invention of Athanasius' polemic; most non-Nicenes would probably have been as little likely to call themselves Arians as Nicenes were to call themselves Athanasians.[3]

This book has attempted to view Arius without the distorting glass of Athanasian polemic intervening and determining our picture of the heresiarch. Although such an enterprise can probably never be entirely successful, it is, I think, worthwhile; if Athanasius' account *does* shape our understanding, we risk misconceiving the nature of the fourth-century crisis. It is very far from being a struggle by 'the Church' against a 'heresy' formulated and propagated by a single dominated teacher; rather it is, in large part, a debate about the kinds of continuity possible and necessary in the Church's language. Both Arius himself and the later critics of Nicaea insist on the catholic and scriptural nature of their language, and see themselves as guardians of centrally important formulae – God is the sole *anarchos*, he begets the Son 'not in appearance but in truth', there is a triad of distinct *hupostaseis*, and so forth. But Arius was suspect in the eyes of the Lucianists and their neo-Arian successors because of his logical development of the traditional language in a direction that threatened the reality and integrity of God's revelation in the Son;[4] hence the attempts in the credal statements of conservative synods in the 350s[5] to bracket the whole Nicene discussion by refusing to allow *ousia*-terms of any kind into professions of faith.

This rather desperate obscurantism proved to be itself in need of philosophical elaboration, and, notoriously, opened the door to the eccentricities of Eunomianism and a doctrine of the knowledge of God that threatened to deliver too much rather than too little. It was, in fact, impossible by the middle of the century to pretend that the lost innocence of pre-Nicene trinitarian language could be restored. By the 360s – as Athanasius had seen – it had become necessary to choose what *kind* of innovation would best serve the integrity of the faith handed down: to reject all innovation was simply not a real option; and thus the rejection of *homoousios* purely and simply as unscriptural or untraditional could no longer be sustained. Very slowly, the bishops of the Christian East had come to agree, implicitly at least, that the continuity of Christian belief was a more complex matter than the plain conversation of formulae. In the debate on the *homoousios* and, perhaps even more, in the controversies over the role of the Spirit, it became necessary to say new things and explore new arguments, even while still professing to make no changes in the deposit of tradition.

Arius had perceived the necessity of new argument, of a critical and logical defence of tradition in the face of increasingly dangerous theological ambiguities in the teaching of his day; and the consequence of this was the remarkable fusion of the traditional and the radical that we find in the *Thalia*. As we have seen (in II.A of the present study), Arius was accused by Athanasius of producing an essentially individualistic and subversive scheme, in that the new arguments and formulations he offers present as much of a threat to certain aspects of the Church's faith and practice as any loosely-phrased utterances of Bishop Alexander or others. But Athanasius and the consistent Nicenes actually accept Arius' challenge, and agree with the need for conceptual innovation: for them the issue is whether new formulations can be found which do justice not only to the requirements of intellectual clarity but to the wholeness of the worshipping and reflecting experience of the Church. The doctrinal debate of the fourth century is thus in considerable measure about how the Church is to become intellectually self-aware and to move from a 'theology of repetition'[6] to something more exploratory and constructive. Athanasius' task is to show how the break in continuity generally felt to be involved in the credal *homoousios* is a necessary moment in the deeper understanding and securing of tradition; more yet, it is to persuade Christians that strict adherence to archaic and 'neutral' terms alone is in fact a potential betrayal of the historic faith. The Church's theology begins in the language of worship, which rightly conserves metaphors and titles that are both ancient and ambiguous; but it does not stop there. The openness, the 'impropriety', the *play* of liturgical imagery is anchored to a specific set of commitments as to the limits and defining conditions within which the believing life is lived, and the metaphorical or narrative beginnings of theological reflection necessarily generate new attempts to characterize those defining conditions.

There is a sense in which Nicaea and its aftermath represent a recognition by the Church at large that *theology* is not only legitimate but necessary. The loyal and uncritical repetition of formulae is seen to be inadequate as a means of securing continuity at anything more than a formal level; Scripture and tradition require to be read in a way that brings out their strangeness, their non-obvious and non-contemporary qualities, in order that they may be read both freshly and truthfully from one generation to another. They need to be made more *difficult* before we can accurately grasp their simplicities. Otherwise, we read with eyes not our own and think them through with minds not our own; the 'deposit of faith' does not really come into contact with *ourselves*. And this 'making difficult', this confession that what the gospel says in Scripture and tradition does not instantly and effortlessly make sense, is perhaps one of the most fundamental tasks for theology.

It is a particularly thankless task in any period when the Church faces an apparently unmanageable and menacing array of changes. Part of the anger and bitterness of the Nicene crisis may have something to do with the fact that – as Part I of this book emphasized – the first half of the fourth century witnessed some deep and complex shifts in the self-images of the Church. The conservative anti-Nicene response is intelligible at one level as the fruit of deep-rooted uncertainties as to what exactly was happening to the Church. Eusebius Pamphilus had produced a convincing and encouraging version of the Christian story as coming to its climax and resolution in the reign of Constantine: unified, faithful, self-consistent and continuous, the Church had emerged from the era of martyrdom to be at last embraced by the empire. Nicaea – an uneasy memory at best for Eusebius – was an awkward reminder of the extent to which the Church had not fully decided what it was saying. The euphoria of the Constantinian triumph had briefly seemed to promise an almost magical solution to the Church's unfinished business: the Church was the baptized *oikoumenē* under the emperor, who was under the *logos*. What the Church discovered in the painful years after Nicaea was that its own inner tensions could not after all be solved by a *deus ex machina* on the imperial throne; and that its relationship with the empire intensified rather than solved the question of its own distinctive identity and mission. It was unable to avoid reflection on its defining conditions, unable to avoid a conscious and critical reworking of its heritage, unable, in short, to avoid theology. Although the radical words of Nicaea became in turn a new set of formulae to be defended (intelligently or unintelligently), the actual history of the Church in the succeeding centuries shows that some kind of doctrinal hermeneutics had come to stay; continuity was something that had to be re-imagined and recreated at each point of crisis.

Newman's essay on Arianism demonstrates how fatally easy it is to settle on misleading contemporary parallels for the fourth-century crisis; but the risk is still worth taking. If we seek to understand Nicaea from the perspective I have just outlined, I suggest that we might think of certain aspects of the 'German Church Struggle' in our own century. Here we have a church faced, in the aftermath of the First World War, with the challenges of 'modernity' – industrialization, economic crises, social unrest and political agitation, along with the moral and cultural ferment of Weimar Germany;[7] offered an integral place – on certain conditions – in the new Reich, it is pitiably eager to abandon theological self-questioning and to allow the political *deus ex machina* to brush aside the uncomfortable residue of inner conflict or self-doubt. The clichés of a complacent 'liberalism', for which the Church has become almost synonymous with national culture at its highest, have eroded the whole question of the distinctiveness of the Christian gospel; and the raising of fundamental theological issues by dissidents like Barth and Bonhoeffer, before and after the Barmen Synod of 1935, is met with a mixture of panic and incomprehension. Barmen demanded not a mindless confessional conservatism (though some caricatured its tone in just such terms), but a re-engagement with authentic theology: a 'making difficult' of a gospel buried under the familiarities of folk piety.

Of course the analogy cannot be pressed too far (with Arius as Emanuel Hirsch and Eusebius of Nicomedia as Reichsbischof Müller?); and it is an emotively loaded one, unfairly so. It seeks only to emphasize that the nature of the Nicene crisis is not something utterly remote: churches are still in our own age tempted to sidestep the question, 'What, in our own terms, is it that is distinctive in the Christian proclamation, and so in the Christian form of life?' and to allow such a question to be muffled by social and ideological accounts of what the Church is. They are still tempted to suppose that formulaic liturgical continuities are the most important guarantors of an abiding identity: there have been discussions of liturgical revision in the Church of England that have, astonishingly, appealed to the theological 'neutrality' and underdetermination of the Book of Common Prayer over against the self-conscious theologizing of newer rites. In short, it is still worth stressing that theological self-awareness is not a luxury for the Church. Proclaiming *now* the same gospel as before is a great deal less easy than it sounds.[8]

But one fortuitous aspect of the analogy between the Nicene problem and the 1930s is a certain irresistible parallel between Athanasius and Barth: difficult and ambivalent figures, both of them, but in one notable respect joint witnesses to something that is very closely bound up with the question of the distinctiveness of the gospel. Both insist that there is no gap conceivable between God as he acts towards us – as the Father of Jesus Christ – and that activity in and by which God is eternally what he is. Athanasius' refusal to separate the divine will from the divine nature in considering the generation of the Son is an implicit denial that God's nature can be an object of thought in itself, passive to the human mind. God is knowable solely because he is active; what can be said of him can be said because he 'utters' himself as Word or Son.[9] So too for Barth: theology has no power over that of which it speaks, because it is essentially response to the free address of God. Yet that address is not an arbitrary or momentary act, but expresses God's eternal 'self-determination' as trinity. To encounter God at all is to encounter him in his freedom; and when we grasp what that freedom means – that no created circumstance affects or determines God – we understand that what he *freely* does he *everlastingly* does. He is never without his saving Word, never a merely potential Father, Redeemer and Reconciler. If he acts, he acts eternally and he acts consistently; and since nothing beyond him can determine this action, what he does cannot be other than the 'enactment' of what he is. On the foundation of God's 'faithfulness to himself', the life of human faith is built. Its dependence on God alone gives it an identity and a *locus standi* in principle free from any political and intellectual totalitarianism in its environment.

When all the necessary qualifications have been made, it remains true that both Athanasius and Barth were able to sustain their confidence in a spiritual authority not answerable to secular rulers because they were confident of an authorization grounded in the nature of God, as eternally the Father of the one from whom and in whom the Church exists. This authority stands in opposition on the one hand to the 'natural' authorities of a fallen world, kings and governments, and on the other to the authority of a holiness or inspiration rooted in 'punctiliar' and discontinuous acts of God as he reveals himself afresh to the charismatic or gnostic individual apart from the historical community of believers and their worship and practice. What is revealed in the incarnation of the Word is the eternal nature of God, not a moment or aspect of his life, which might be supplemented or balanced from other sources or other alleged moments of revelation; and our access to the incarnate Word is in Scripture and the corporate life of the Church. Hence the quest for an 'ecclesiastical' reading of Scripture, one that accords with the confession, the prayer and the aspiration of the community in those moments of its life when it sets itself most clearly in the presence and under the judgment of the incarnate Word – baptism and Eucharist, with their public enactment of what is involved in saying that Jesus is Lord or God.

This being said, it has also to be recognized that the language of spiritual authority and fidelity to the sacramental community is capable of as much ideological distortion as its opposites. In the career of Athanasius himself, the faith that is at one level a resource for witness and resistance can also justify unscrupulous tactics in polemic and struggle, and – if the celebrated papyrus evidence[10] is to be trusted – brutality towards opponents. Theologically speaking, an appeal to the Church's charter of foundation in the saving act of God, rooted in the eternal act of God, can never be made without the deepest moral ambiguities, unless it involves an awareness of the *mode* of that saving act as intrinsic to its authoritative quality and as requiring its own kind of obedience. That is to say, the God who works in *disponibilité*, vulnerability and mortality is not to be 'obeyed' by the exercise *or* the acceptance of an ecclesial authority that pretends to overcome these limits. But this is a refinement not readily to be discerned in Athanasius: the notion of incarnation as triumphant epiphany is still perhaps too dominant for another note to be struck.

Returning to the matter immediately in hand, it is important not to forget that Arius claimed with no less fervour and sincerity to speak in conformity with Scripture and Catholic practice – which is why Athanasius' replies seldom stray far from exegesis, both of Old and New Testaments and of Christian liturgy, and turn, time and again, on what it is that the Church hopes for. Only God can 'deify', only the unequivocally divine saviour can decisively transform our lives, only the creator can re-create.[11] The distinctiveness of the Christian identity is bound up with the idea of 'new creation', of an event that makes a radical, decisive and unforeseeable difference in the human world: something is brought out of nothing, life from death.[12] Without this conception of its foundations, the Christian Church will inevitably 'shade off' into the religious or intellectual climate in which it finds itself; so that the struggle for a certain critical distance from the contemporary milieu, and the struggle to establish the *difference* of the redeemer, his creative and thus 'divine' status, may be expected to go hand in hand. In the eyes of Athanasius, Arius, for all his stress on the divine freedom, fails to see that freedom *directly* involved in redemption as well as in creation: Arius' God does not act without mediation to save us, and so the liberty of the redeemed lacks any share in the finality, the absoluteness, of divine liberty. How, asks Athanasius,[13] can the Son create in us what has to be created in him? If God can truly give a share in his freedom and his glory to a creature by pure causeless will, resting on nothing in his own being, why can he not give directly to us what he gives the Son? If, on the other hand, we do not receive a real share in the divine life through the Son because he, as a creature, is as far from God as we are, what is the point of his incarnate work? On either showing, the history of salvation becomes meaningless when God is held not to be directly at work in it. If he can bestow *theōsis* by mere *fiat*, there is nothing to be said for there being a *history* of salvation;[14] but if God has to work through the Son, and the Son cannot fully recreate us, how is it a history of *salvation?*

Faced with the choice between an arbitrary and an impotent God, Arius' supporters – according to Athanasius[15] – opted for the former. More accurately, they seem to have argued that the creaturely status of the Son did not affect the power of the divine word uttered through him: the *agent* of redemption remains God alone. Athanasius' retort is to ask why, in this case, there should be an incarnation at all: what matters theologically is not what God 'can' do in the abstract, but what is appropriate to the reality of the human condition. The only *decisive* redemption – as opposed to continual divine acts of grace or pardon – is the transfiguration of the human condition from within, the union of grace with the body, as Athanasius puts it.[16] The argument returns to the point of the absolute newness and difference of redeemed humanity; for this newness to make sense, we must suppose a critical rupture in the continuities of the world; and for this, God alone is adequate – yet God acting upon us not 'from outside', but in union with human flesh.

Arians claimed to take *theōsis* no less seriously than Nicenes;[17] but Athanasius makes a powerful case for denying that this can be done while still clinging to the idea of a mediatorial created redeemer. Such a redeemer must himself have a history of relation with God, must in some sense therefore be passive to God, and so cannot embody God's activity directly. Even the mediator stands at a distance from God and enjoys only an 'external' relation with him. The Athanasian picture, on the other hand, absolutely rules out a 'history' in God; there are no transactions in eternity, and Father and Son do not relate as active and passive principles.[18] The divine act of being is itself inseparably both an initiative and a response, generative love that is eternally generative *of* love.[19] And if this is the character of the divine life, the activity of God cannot be seen as a kind of pure 'linear' agency, flowing out from one subject to another, acting *on* creatures: it is, rather, something that intrinsically *includes* its own answering image, and so resists characterization in terms of an ultimate, indeterminate *Grund* of divine liberty that proceeds to define and articulate itself thus-rather-than-otherwise in the Son, and so to relate thus-rather-than-otherwise to creation. The trouble with this characterization, from the Athanasian point of view, is that God as he actually is remains at a distance – the distance conceptually expressed in the notion of the primal abyss of potentiality that stands 'above' or 'behind' the active life of God as trinity. Here, of course, there are some questions to be put against too simple an assimilation of Athanasius to Barth, in so far as Barth (especially in the earlier volumes of the *Church Dogmatics*) makes bold and extensive use of the language of 'self-determination' in discussing the trinitarian being of God; though it would be a mistake to charge Barth with what he emphatically did not believe, the idea that there could be an actually existing divine life *prior* to the

Trinity. For Barth, the *Urentscheidung*, the primal determination, of God in uttering his Word is co-extensive with his actuality. Yet this language undoubtedly introduces an ambiguity that Athanasius might well have challenged.

The Nicene faith as interpreted by its greatest defender thus alters the nature of our reflection on apophatic theology. The unknowability of God ceases to be simply the inaccessibility of a kind of divine 'hinterland', the mysteriousness of an indefinite source of divinity. The language of 'source' or 'cause' applied to the Father certainly continues to be used,[20] but not in such a way as to suggest an *actually* prior reality about which nothing can be said except that it determines itself as Father of a Son or Utterer of a Word. There is no overplus of 'unengaged' and inexpressible reality, nothing that is not realized in and as relationship, in God.[21] Thus post-Nicene Catholic theology turns away from the assumptions that so shaped Arius' thought. Arius' passionate concern to secure God against the claims of created understanding to mastery and possession had very naturally expressed itself as a theological transcription of the hierarchical and mathematically-influenced cosmology of Neoplatonism: God is pure singularity, and the purely single can only be known as the negation of duality; what it is apart from this negation is strictly beyond conceiving, yet it would be a mistake to *reduce* the One to being no more than a negative ideal limit. There is thus 'more' to unity than duality can show. Post-Nicene theology, on the other hand, opposes not first and second principles but creator and creation: the divine simplicity is seen as belonging to the divine *life*, rather than to a primal monad. To say that in God there is absolute identity of nature, will and action is indeed to say something that challenges the claims of understanding and impels us towards the apophatic moment in our theology: it means that the divine nature cannot be abstracted from God's active relationship with the world.[22] And since that relationship, in which the theologian as believer is caught up, is not susceptible of being distanced and exhaustively defined, neither is God's nature. His everlasting act is as little capable of being a determinate object to our minds as the wind in our faces and lungs can be held still and distant in front of our eyes.

This is the apophatic theology of the Cappadocians – as of Victorinus, Augustine, Pseudo-Dionysius, Maximus, and, for that matter, Aquinas and John of the Cross. It is no less serious in its negativity than Arius or Plotinus. The crucial difference, however, is that this energy of conceptual negation is bound up with a sense of intimate involvement in the life of God, rather than of absolute disjunction. The disjunction *is* there, in the fact that created sharing in the life of the divine is precisely a ceaseless growing into what is always and already greater and does not itself either grow or diminish: the fulness of the divine eludes us because it is further 'back' than our furthest and remotest origins, and beyond all imaginable futures. Yet this is a disjunction of a different kind from that envisaged by Plotinus, for instance, where, however fully we become *nous*, the One remains an inaccessible other, over against us, except in those fleeting moments of something like dissolution when we drop into its depths. Set this beside Gregory of Nyssa's or Augustine's account of a steady and endless enlarging of the heart through union in prayer and virtue with the Word, which is also a steady and endless growth in knowledge of the Father, and you can perhaps see the fundamental difference made by Nicaea.

The identity of nature and act in God is what is inaccessible to the mind; but that identity – that 'metaphysical' simplicity – is also the condition of God's *accessibility* to faith and charity. Because his activity and life are self-differentiating, a pattern of initiating gift, perfect response, and the distinct and 'new' energy that is the harmony of these two movements, created difference, otherness, multiplicity, may find place in God. If the life of God is eternally in response as well as in initiating, then created response is not necessarily 'external' to God but somehow capable of being attuned to and caught up in God's own movement in and to himself. Donald MacKinnon writes[23] of Jesus' involvement in the necessarily tragic limitations of history that:

> Jesus' acceptance of this part of his burden can arguably be interpreted as a painfully realized transcription into the conditions of our existence, of the receptivity, the defined, even if frontierless, receptivity that constitutes his person. It is indeed as that which makes such transcription possible that we must first see the divine relation to the temporal. It is a relation that we will misunderstand except we see the God so related as triune.

In other words, the God whose 'simple' nature is eternally real only in a pattern of interactive plurality is a God capable of relating to creatures in a way impossible for a primal monad: transforming union or indwelling can be conceived without the utter dissolution of the limits of creatureliness. The Nicene faith establishes a 'classical' shape for the aspirations of Christian spirituality; and it could be argued too, taking up what MacKinnon hints at, that Nicene Christianity also does something to secure a certain seriousness about the conditions of human history. Rather paradoxically, the denial of a 'history' of transactions in God focuses attention on the history of God with us in the world: God has no *story* but that of Jesus of Nazareth and the covenant of which he is the seal.[24] It is a matter of historical fact at least that the Nicene *verus Deus* was the stimulus to a clarification of the *verus homo* in the century and a half after the council: the Word as God is the condition of there being a human identity which is the ministering, crucified and risen saviour, Jesus Christ; but the existence of Jesus is not an episode in the biography of the Word. It remains obstinately – and crucially – a fact of our world and our world's limits.

These questions, however, take us further afield than is the scope of these concluding remarks. The purpose of these last pages has been simply to indicate that the foregoing study is not entirely an archaeological exercise. To trace the political and intellectual pre-history of the Nicene crisis and to attempt to understand the odd fact that Arius was at once a radical and a figurehead for conservatism is to gain some perspective on what might be called the paradigmatic stresses and temptations of Church and theology. 'The perils of modernizing Nicaea' are not to be minimized, and I hope to have avoided too much grossly anachronistic misreading; but we are dealing here with developments that determined the future course of Christian theology and that still haunt contemporary discussion.[25] Even those who believe, as I do not, that Nicaea represented a damaging or mistaken shift in the history of doctrine[26] are bound to consider how it has shaped and continues to shape Christian speech and prayer. As for those content to affirm the faith of Nicaea, they too have questions to answer as to the nature of doctrinal continuities, questions which the very *fact* of a doctrinal crisis in the fourth century presses upon us. This book is meant as an attempt to give focus to some of these questions, in the hope of assisting a little the enormous contemporary task of critically appropriating once again the heritage of doctrinal history – and, more remotely but more importantly, assisting that proclamation of the gospel which must be the goal of all doctrinal exploration and reappropriation.

Appendix 1:

Arius since 1987

Between 1975, when Manlio Simonetti published *La crisi ariana nel IV secolo*, and 1988, which saw the publication of R. P. C. Hanson's *The Search for the Christian Doctrine of God*,[1] studies of the doctrinal crisis of the fourth century proliferated.[2] By 1990, in the wake of several substantial monographs and a very large quantity of articles, some elements of a new scholarly consensus were slowly emerging, though debate in many areas remained vigorous. During the 1990s, research priorities moved away from questions about the origins of the crisis and the sources and character of Arius' teaching towards other matters – the development of non-Nicene theologies in the West and the relation of these, for example, to the thought of Augustine and Ambrose,[3] issues around asceticism[4] and liturgy,[5] studies of other doctrinal conflicts interwoven with the Nicene controversies[6] and so on. But certain features of the discussion that reached its peak in the eighties unmistakably helped to shape these studies.

Two points in particular can be noted in this respect. First, there is the growing sense that 'Arianism' is a very unhelpful term to use in relation to fourth-century controversy. There was no single 'Arian' agenda, no tradition of loyalty to a single authoritative teacher. Theologians who criticized the Creed of Nicaea had very diverse attitudes to Arius himself, and part of the continuing difficulty of identifying the main lines of Arius' theology arises from this fact. 'Arianism' is the polemical creation of Athanasius above all, who was determined to show that any proposed alternative to the Nicene formula collapsed back into some version of Arius' teaching, with all the incoherence and inadequacy that teaching displayed.[7] If that is the case, any quest for the essence of Arianism is doomed to failure. Second, there is a far sharper awareness that the doctrinal crisis was part of an enormous upheaval in how the Christian Church understood itself, exercised power, located the sacred and managed its worship. As patristic studies in general (but especially in the United States) moved away from a simple 'history of ideas' model into the bracing new climate of cultural, political and gender-oriented interpretation, it became harder to isolate issues of 'pure' intellectual influence and development.

The foregoing pages represent an attempt towards the end of the period I have been describing to crystallize some aspects of this new set of perspectives, though with very limited clarity: I was still, in 1987, prepared, even with reservations, to use the adjective 'Arian' in a way I should now find difficult, and my analyses in terms of social history were rudimentary. In this appendix, I do not intend to try and write another book, the book I should perhaps now wish to replace the existing text in the light of (I hope) a better understanding of these and other themes, but only to sketch in some of the contributions made in the last fourteen years – and also to respond to some of the comment and criticism that the book's first edition attracted, in the hope of indicating where the reader may need to use caution and where I believe there may still be material on which further research might be built.

1. PERCEPTIONS OF ARIUS AND THE 'ARIAN' CRISIS

The first section of the book surveys the history of interpretations of Arius since the seventeenth century; but this task has now been far more definitively performed by Maurice Wiles, in his 1996 monograph, *Archetypal Heresy. Arianism through the Centuries*. After giving an overview of the history of non-Nicene Christianity in the late patristic period and its revival in the far left-wing of the Reformation, he charts with great clarity and skill the way in which, in the post-Reformation period, 'Arianism' conceived strictly as a belief in a supernatural and personal but not divine mediator constantly slips into the metaphysically simpler Unitarianism, which does not require belief in supernatural individuals. 'Arianism' is a victim of the Enlightenment, the gradual depopulating of the invisible world where angels and demons are still taken seriously, Arius' teachings have some plausibility; as the eighteenth century proceeds, this is lost. Wiles relates these matters to the continuing struggle over subscription to the Thirty-Nine Articles of the Church of England, rightly noting that trinitarian belief and political conformism were closely allied in many Anglican minds,[8] and that some eighteenth-century Anglicans managed a surprising (if unpopular) degree of agnosticism as to the necessity of the Nicene formula (see pp. 129–32 on two episcopal sympathizers with non-Nicene faith, one of whom exhibits startling parallels with just the kind of Jewish-Christian angelology that may have influenced Arius himself). He discusses also the complex question of how far the subordination of the Son to the Father in the Trinity is compatible with full-blown Nicene orthodoxy – an issue still vexing for Newman when he came to write his *Arians* in the nineteenth century.

On Newman, Wiles is barbed but appreciative – appreciative, that is, of the intellectual boldness of the book, and of Newman's correct diagnosis of what was at issue between 'Arians' and 'orthodox': not a simple battle between literal and nonliteral ways of reading the Bible, but 'a question of which of them had the truer understanding of "the sense of Scripture" viewed as a whole'. As Wiles comments, 'that is a much more difficult issue to determine' (p. 171). I shall return to Wiles's brief but pointed criticism of this book's doctrinal conclusion; his own final statement emphasizes a view which he has fully articulated in many publications. The fourth-century doctrinal resolution, if Nicaea and Constantinople can be called that, assumes the right of the Church to declare certain interpretations of the Bible unacceptable; yet the entire history of the controversy, up to and beyond the eighteenth century, ought to show us that all the participants 'were seeking to answer questions for which the material, properly understood, does not provide the requisite resources' (p. 185). The case is well and attractively made, but this formulation encapsulates precisely the question which some would argue is being begged: what *is* the 'material'? In what sense does it include patterns of devotion, issues about consistency of language in respect of divine action, the pressure to keep open the *maximal* scope of what can be said about Jesus Christ?[9] Wiles is surely right to put question marks against the assumption of both parties in the controversy to claim that they alone grasped the 'real' meaning of biblical texts, in the sense of the original authorial intention; but the problem Wiles sees as raised by Newman is a real one. Is there a global scriptural context within which more and less adequate readings can be assessed?[10]

Newman's work has been studied by other authors, notably Stephen Thomas, whose *Newman and Heresy* (1991) has an informative and original chapter on the *Arians*, as well as numerous helpful observations in passing. He locates the book firmly in the context of Anglican anxieties in the early 1830s about the weakening of confessional requirements for public office. Signs of confusion or indifferentism about doctrinal formulae among fourth-century bishops (especially those Newman calls 'Semi-Arians', the group who identified neither with Nicaea nor with the Homoian party) are clearly read as fore-shadowing the delinquencies of the bishops of the 1820s; and, curiously, criticism of doctrinal formulae on the grounds that they are 'unbiblical' is seen as a mark of liberalism, a rejection of the *sensus communis* of the Church (pp. 36–7). Thomas also notes Newman's discussions of 'Eclectic' philosophy (what we should call Neoplatonism) as, if not a source, then a kind of parallel to Arianism as he construes it, a rationalist movement, hostile to mystery even while it canonizes certain kinds of uncertainty (pp. 40ff., 48–9). Newman assumes, with Keble, the priority of 'ethos' over intellect (pp. 25–6), and identifies orthodoxy with a specific kind of superior ethos, a spirit of humility and receptivity, which has political as well as theological repercussions (pp. 29–30, 45, 49). In another somewhat paradoxical move, Newman, even before the composition of the *Arians*, argues for an element of obedience, subordination, in the Trinity (as had Bishop Bull, though Newman did not read Bull until he began his work on the book) – an argument which provoked criticism from his teacher Whately. But it can be seen as making sense against the background both of Newman's general reverence for the ideal of obedience and (though Thomas does not explore this so fully) his sense that the pre-Nicene Church, in its reluctance to formulate doctrine and its confidence in its own powers of spiritual formation through prayer, discipline and liturgy, furnishes in some ways a healthier example of the Catholic Christian ethos than the Church of the Councils.

Something of the same point is developed in an essay on Newman's *Arians* by the present writer, published in 1990. Newman sees doctrinal definition more as tragic necessity than as the exercise of ecclesial power – a point that throws light on his later attitudes to the Vatican Council. But this essay also examines more of the background of Newman's historical typologies in the doctrinal histories of the preced-ing century. The great German Protestant historian Mosheim had seen the early development of doctrinal language as a process of the corrup-tion of biblical faith by alien philosophy, most notably by Middle Platonism and Neoplatonism (Newman's use of 'Eclecticism' for this follows Mosheim). The chief source of such corruption is Alexandria, the seat of metaphysical speculation – and in this Mosheim echoes Catholic historians of the preceding century such as Petavius and Maimbourg. In this light, Newman's almost obsessional concern to present Alexandria as a bastion of religious purity (spiritually mature, conversant with more than the literal sense of Scripture) as opposed to Antioch, corrupted by literal exegesis and this-worldly interests, becomes intelligible. It has the deplorable result also, as noted in the text above, pp. 3–5, of bringing out the virulent anti-Semitic prejudices which make some passages of Newman's book such unpleasant reading now: Antioch is the home of 'Judaizing' Christianity, represented above all by Paul of Samosata, and this means compromise and spiritual failure. The connections of all this with the politics of the 1830s is treated more extensively again – with much inspiration from Thomas and from Peter Nockles's 1994 study of the antecedents of the Oxford Movement – in the new edition of Newman's text prepared for the Millennium edition of Newman's works.[11]

The full history of the invention of 'Arianism' and its vagaries in modern scholarly discussion remains to be written, though Wiles has covered much of the ground. My 1987 text suggested that an *Ideologiekritik* of doctrinal history was a highly desirable prelude to any contemporary essay on the development of doctrinal language, and this is a commonplace of serious modern scholarship. In general, I think the analysis of the models offered over the centuries for understanding 'Arianism' will stand, although it needs a great deal of filling out. My own specific suggestions about reading Arius' material in social/ecclesial context have had a mixed reception, and my own ideological slant has not been neglected by reviewers! But the principle remains. One of the most fruitful areas, I believe, for future research will be the history of Church history itself.

2. CHRONOLOGICAL AND RELATED QUESTIONS

The reading proposed of the material associating Arius with the Melitian schism has generally found favour. Annik Martin (1989:2) argues very persuasively that the Arius material in the *passio* of Bishop Peter originates in an Alexandrian tradition whose purpose is to absolve the martyred Peter of the responsibility for ordaining the heresiarch Arius – a tradition facilitated by the coincidence of another Arius being involved in the beginnings of the Melitian schism; the excommunication of Arius the Melitian is a retrojection of the excommunication of Arius of the Baucalis, confirming Peter's spiritual discernment (pp. 407ff.), and the entire narrative illustrates a particular genre of polemical literature whose aim is to assimilate opponents of

251

very different kinds as 'objective allies' because of their common opposition to the truth (p. 413). I don't think that this necessarily conflicts with the suggestion in the text above (p. 39) that the identification of the two Arii may have originated with the anti-Nicene historian Sabinus, who hoped to make capital out of just the same fact of the shared hostility of Melitians and 'Arians' to the Alexandrian episcopate. Both sides in the controversy have some interest at some stage in such assimilation.

The arguments advanced for a redating of the early texts of the controversy have proved more controversial. In a brief paper of 1990, Uta Loose defended the traditional chronology advanced by Schwartz and Opitz against my reconstruction: she identifies a number of points at which the revised chronology rests on shaky foundations and, at the very least, offers no better a resolution to the problems of the material than the conventional dating. I have argued, she says, that it is difficult to imagine Colluthus protesting against leniency to Arius at a lateish stage in the controversy, when Arius had been formally condemned in Alexandria and forced out of the city; but, given Licinius' ban on synodal meetings, it is quite plausible that there should have been no major public synodal action in response to Arius' return to Alexandria and his establishment of separatist congregations. There would then have been no major synodal action against Arius in the period immediately before 324, the supposed date of *hē philarchos* (p. 90). The difficulty alleged against this date for *philarchos* (on the grounds that Alexander speaks of Arius as disturbing a period of peace for the Church, when in fact the immediately preceding months had been overshadowed by Licinius' harrassment of Christians) is also capable of resolution. This language is standard heresiological rhetoric: all heretics are 'disturbers of the peace' (ibid.). Colluthus' rehabilitation in 325, immediately prior to the composition and delivery of *henos sōmatos*, is regarded by Loose as a very unsatisfactory basis for explaining Colluthus' subscription to the encyclical on the assumption that it comes from late in the course of events before Nicaea; why does the encyclical not mention this diplomatic and disciplinary triumph, especially given Constantine's desire to see evidence of the will to restore unity in the Alexandrian Church? As for the failure of *philarchos* to mention Eusebius of Nicomedia and the odd phrase in *henos sōmatos* about Eusebius reviving his former evil ways, this can be explained by supposing (a) that *philarchos* deals only with recent events and so ignores Eusebius' early involvement in calling a synod supportive of Arius (and for the same reason does not mention the 'synod of a hundred bishops' referred to in *henos sōmatos*), and (b) that Alexander's ascribing of *kakonoia* to Eusebius intends to allude to the scandalous fact of Eusebius' transfer of diocese from Berytus to Nicomedia some years earlier (p. 91).

In short, the chronology of Opitz should stand, and we must take *henos sōmatos* as Alexander's earliest public declaration against Arius. These are all reasonable and plausible points in themselves, but I am unconvinced; and I believe there are other reasons for holding the revisionist chronology. Loose's account of Colluthus' activities presupposes that Arius *did* return to Alexandria and was allowed to function without public condemnation; but it is far from clear from the texts that we need to suppose such a return, and not very likely that it would have gone unchallenged especially since the supposedly prior *henos sōmatos* refers to so substantial an earlier condemnation by the hundred bishops. The reference to breaking the peace of the Church is indeed frequent in polemic; but in this context, and combined with Alexander's obvious unease about unfavourable reaction among unbelievers resulting from these upheavals, I think it sits oddly in a period which has seen real public assault on the Church. We do not know how widespread a matter of concern Colluthus' schism was, and so have no means of assessing whether it would have been something Alexander would have mentioned in an encyclical (rather than a missive directed to the local churches only); as I have suggested, the placing of Colluthus' name in a position of prominence among the subscriptions might tell its own story. The phrase about Eusebius' malice or evil-mindedness can be read as Loose proposes; but the more natural interpretation would be to take it as referring to previous hostility specifically between Alexander and Eusebius. And a letter written late in the controversy to the bishop of Byzantium would surely make some reference to the very considerable exertions of a leading prelate in a neighbouring province, even if nothing very recent or notorious had happened. Is it really credible that, by this date, Alexander would wish to mention only three episcopal supporters of Arius? My conclusion is that the general plausibility of the alternative narrative can be sustained.

But the extra factors have to do with the accounts of Arius' theology in the two Alexandrian letters. *Philarchos* gives a rather jumbled catalogue of errors, apparently relying on verbal report at several points; but by 324 Arius' *Thalia* must, on pretty well any chronology, have

253

been in circulation. The heresy is described with much emphasis on faulty scriptural interpretation and the assimilation of Christ's condition to that of other humans and to things made out of nothing – hence the attempt to associate him with Paul of Samosata. *Henos sōmatos*, on the other hand, offers a connected summary of teaching recognizably related to the propositions of the *Thalia* (though not without hearsay again), and avoids the more simplistic arguments of *philarchos*. The long-standing suspicion that it was written by Athanasius has been very fully discussed in an excellent article by Christopher Stead in 1988, where detailed examination of the vocabulary and style of the two letters establishes beyond reasonable doubt that they come from different hands – and that the second hand is likely to be that of Alexander's deacon, who had digested thoroughly the theology of the *Thalia*. As Loose grants (p. 90, n.14), this could strengthen the case for a later dating of *henos sōmatos* – though Stead himself disagrees, chiefly on the grounds of the Colluthus problem; he is not persuaded by my suggested solution to this (Stead p. 91, n.23). It is difficult to believe that Alexander would have written a lengthy rebuttal of Arius's ideas with no reference to Arius' manifesto, had this been available; equally difficult, I should argue, to read the account of Arius in *philarchos* as representing a later stage in the understanding of the points at issue than is found in the other letter. What is more, the fact that Athanasius could not have been more than 22 in 319, the date proposed by Opitz for *henos sōmatos*, should give us pause; although we cannot be absolutely sure about canonical ages for ordination at this date, it is a little hard to believe that a deacon only just ordained should have been entrusted with such a major task. And if *henos sōmatos* does show signs of a knowledge of the *Thalia*, there would have to be an awkward compression of events to squeeze in the composition of this work by Arius in the very earliest phase of the controversy.

These are, I grant, not fully conclusive points, but I believe they generally reinforce some unease over Opitz' dates. Hanson, it should be noted, finds no problem with the traditional chronology, and is willing to put the composition of the *Thalia* before Arius' flight from Alexandria, referring to Lorenz's view that the *Thalia* represents a less developed form of Arius' thinking than the letter to Alexander (p. 138); given the very different intentions and audiences of the two documents, though, I do not think too much can be made of their divergences in tracing a process of evolution. As I have said in the text above, not a very great deal hangs on these issues – though the

Athanasian authorship of *henos sōmatos* opens up significant lines of study. Equally with the chronology of the post-Nicaea period, no enormous issues are at stake; and here again, unresolved problems remain. Hanson (pp. 209–10) dismisses the detailed case made by Timothy Barnes,[12] following and correcting Henry Chadwick (1948) for dating the fall of Eustathius of Antioch to 327, and reaffirms the traditional date of 330 or 331; but he meets none of Barnes' points, and leaves us with the problem of fitting an uncomfortably large number of bishops of Antioch into a short timespan. A more radical set of questions is posed by another article of Annik Martin's (1989:1). Like most recent scholars of the period, she insists, rightly, that we should read the fifth-century Church historians like Socrates and Sozomen with care, even suspicion; as noted in the text above, they were often in much the same position as we are, faced with a dossier of documents whose relations to one another were unclear, obliged to draw conclusions from such internal evidence as the documents provide rather than reproducing a publicly confirmable chronology. On this basis, Martin lists the relevant documents and argues that one or two relatively small errors in their interpretation may give a false impression of an entire course of events.

Her boldest suggestion[13] is that the letter normally ascribed to Eusebius and Theognis (above, p. 72), apparently addressed to a synod that has recommended the rehabilitation of Arius and dated to 328 should be regarded as wrongly attributed – a mistake originating probably with Sabinus and reproduced by Socrates. Martin notes that we have no clear evidence that Eusebius and Theognis were actually condemned at Nicaea or at any other synod; their sentence was passed after the Council by the emperor. Yet here they appeal to a judgement apparently by the bishops they are addressing, and request that it be reversed (pp. 311–16). Martin proposes that the synod in question in this letter must be that held in Jerusalem in 335, the only one that can be shown unambiguously to have decided in Arius' favour, and that the real authors are probably the Libyan bishops Secundus and Theonas (pp. 316–19).

This is a coherent and attractive proposal, and may well be correct. However, I am not completely sure that we need to discount the possibility of the original ascription, for reasons connected with the arguments in the text. Martin seems to be assuming (as have a good many others) that we need a quasi-ecumenical synod somewhere between 325 and 335 to account for the apparent changes in policy around

255

327/8. I have suggested that we need only think of successive meetings of the local Bithynian synod to deal with disciplinary matters. If such a synod did indeed readmit Arius to communion in 327 (assured of imperial support), there is nothing against an appeal to the next session of the same synod by the local bishops who had been exiled. Since their deposition would have had to be confirmed by an earlier session (late 325), they would indeed be dealing with the synodical body competent to review their case. And if we hold to the Chadwick/Barnes dating for the fall of Eustathius, we have good reason to believe that the reversal of policy which allowed Eusebius and others to be reinstated was the culmination of a quite brief and intensive process in the two years after Nicaea. Martin's thesis has the appeal of economy; but would there really have been no attempts at all before 335 to secure some kind of formal rehabilitation for Arius, given the recovery of influence by his erstwhile allies?

3. ARIUS' THEOLOGY

There is some impressive new work on the text of the *Thalia* by Karin Metzler (1991), which builds upon the recognition by earlier scholars that some of the surviving fragments are clearly designed as an acrostic. If the whole composition was so envisaged, we have some solid ground both for concluding that the portions preserved in *contra Arianos* 1 and those in *de synodis* 15 do indeed come from the same source, and for raising some questions about the order of the surviving lines and the possible lacunae in what we have. This essay marks a substantial advance in the analysis of the fragments, and, while it does not as yet suggest any major revision in the theological interpretation of what we have, it helpfully reminds us that there may be solutions to problems in the text contained in missing passages.

Commentators on Arius' theology, and on the discussion of it in the text above, have quite rightly observed that it is difficult to reconstruct a system on the basis of such slender evidence.[14] My own account has been questioned on the grounds that I have underrated the importance of soteriology. Hanson (p. 91) says that 'Williams twice declares [in my 1983 article on 'The Logic of Arianism'] that Arianism is not a theology of salvation', and regards this as a significant defect; R. C. Gregg, reviewing the book in 1989, likewise identifies a failure to spell out how Arius' assumptions could have issued in a doctrine of redemption, and is critical of the idea that we could characterize Arius' ideas as coming from a 'school' environment.[15] From a slightly different perspective, Rebecca Lyman (1989) questions my conclusion that Arius' soteriology must have been fundamentally the same sort of thing as that of Athanasius – i.e. not particularly concerned about the question of Jesus as moral exemplar; there is in my analysis no exposition of a soteriology that would go along with what I believe to be Arius' doctrine of God.[16] She goes on to argue that the soteriological significance of Jesus as moral subject can be demonstrated from other texts from the fourth century in which anti-Manichaean polemic lays emphasis on the human liberty of Jesus.[17]

Hanson rather misinterprets what was said in the 1983 essay, where my point was simply to question whether Gregg and Groh were correct to see the particular Christological emphases which they ascribed to Arius as dictated by a soteriology in which Christ was the exemplar for our own 'promotion' to divine filiation. But Gregg himself makes a fair comment: my emphasis in the text above was certainly on cosmological rather than soteriological questions. However, the matter is more complex: to acquire divinely-originated wisdom about the cosmos is, for many in the early Church, an essential aspect of salvation, and this is how I would see Arius' project. To describe Arius as representing an 'Academic' approach to faith might be misleading if we were to take for granted the usual contemporary sense of the word, but the language is not at all meant to associate Arius with an esoteric minority. The point is that Arius represents a model of church life itself, a model closer to the philosophical school than to what we conventionally think of as a church; and that this was an intelligible and fairly popular model in Alexandrian Christianity, not the preserve of a learned minority. Hieracas, flourishing just a few years before the Arian crisis, evidently stands in this tradition, in which the inspired teacher is the focus of authority. There is not, I would argue, the kind of separation Gregg sees between all this and popular piety: it is a *form* of popular piety, however strange that may seem to modern eyes. Nor is there a contradiction between the ideal of a God-inspired teacher and reference to such a teacher's proficiency or learning: everything we know about Origen bears this out. It is absolutely true that Athanasius can use comparable language about Antony, as Gregg notes, but I would regard this as strengthening the general point being made. David Brakke's 1995 monograph on asceticism and authority uses the suggested contrast between 'Catholic' and 'Academic' to good effect in helping us understand how ecclesiastical authority developed in the post-Nicene period by the co-option of the residual Academic style into the episcopal office by way of appeal to ascetical authority or credibility, and discussing with great care the paradoxical results of this (the risks of elitism being replaced by what could be a mixture of authoritarianism and populism).

But the underlying problem is whether Arius can be credited specifically with a doctrine of salvation depending upon the notion of a creature promoted to divine honour because of virtue. My reluctance to accept this is not on the grounds that it conflicts with later orthodoxy, but rather because the theology suggested is not something that is clearly identifiable in any patristic writer, orthodox or otherwise. There are varieties of exaltation Christology, in which Jesus is advanced to some kind of status in heaven; there are doctrines of the heavenly Logos, personalized or not, entering or 'adopting' a human subject; there are accusations that this or that writer taught that Jesus was *purus homo*. Alexander's *hē philarchos* does indeed charge Arius with some such doctrine, and Athanasius' *contra Arianos* addresses some of the possible texts that might justify it. But Alexander explicitly depends on hearsay at this point, Athanasius' work deals with strictly exegetical issues and it is not clear what in Arius' own theology it responds to, and none of the unquestionably authentic texts from the early days of the controversy suggest that it was a major area of debate. The doctrine is not condemned in any formal synodical enactment, it is not anathematized at Nicaea, it is quite alien to what we know of the tenor of 'Lucianist' thinking, and it does not figure in, for example, the debates between Eusebius of Caesarea and Marcellus. If it was so central, novel and distinctive a feature of Arius' thought, it is odd that it figures only in passing in what has to be recognized as a somewhat unreliable report. Compared with strongly contested issues like the Son's eternity or mutability or knowledge of the Father, it is very elusive. And it has also to be added that, even if the adoption-on-the-basis-of-virtue model could be traced in Arius, we know for certain that Christ cannot be a model of *human* virtue or liberty, as he is first and foremost a 'discarnate' subject, a heavenly agent whose achieved moral or spiritual stability is hard to connect with the circumstances of his earthly life. Lyman, like Gregg and Groh, seems to move too rapidly to the distinctively modern assumption that what is of theological interest in all this must be a human biography.

Of course the exercise of Jesus' human freedom can be of immense devotional importance, as Lyman stresses. I would not dispute the significance of the theme in all kinds of writers. But this is emphatically not the same as claiming that Jesus' moral performance is the hinge of salvation, the prototype of an earned advance to heavenly status. Two aspects of the soteriological are being confused: that Christ's free and intelligent choices may frequently in patristic thought be appealed to as a model and inspiration for the leading of the 'saved' life can hardly be in dispute; that Christ's free and intelligent choices *constitute* his saving significance or determine his role and authority is a quite different proposition which I cannot discern in Arius or indeed in any early theologian in precisely those terms.

Lyman also queries the argument that, in the *Thalia*, the celebrated line traditionally rendered so as to refer to Christ's adoption should be read as referring simply to the Father's begetting of the Logos, appealing to uses of *teknopoieō* to mean 'adopt'. But there seem to be few or no instances of the verb in the *active* voice to mean this; in classical and patristic Greek, it can be used in the *middle* in this way, but in the active it seems regularly to mean 'beget'. The instance quoted by Lyman from Athanasius is in the passive, and does not help us much. If Arius had wanted to speak of adoption in the *Thalia*, he would have had a number of far clearer ways of doing so; why not *huiothēsas* or (from the rather rare *huiotheteō*) *huiothesis*? Even *teknopoiēsamenos* would have been better, though not unambiguous, as *teknopoieō* in the middle voice can still mean *either* 'adopt' *or* 'beget'. Why should Arius, when writing of what is argued to be a central tenet of his theology, use what is at best something of a solecism to express it, with a verb which could mean just what he supposedly does not want to say? But the ambiguity of the verb is in fact significant. It is actually rather difficult to distinguish absolutely clearly in Greek by lexical means alone between natural and adoptive parenthood. After all, *teknopoieō* simply means 'to make a child'. Just as *gennaō* can be used of the baptismal rebirth of believers, and *gennēma* of the Christian, so we cannot treat *teknopoieō*, active or middle, as a word that deliberately marks 'adoption' *as opposed to* 'begetting'. No weight can be placed on this line to support a straightforward exaltation/adoption Christology in Arius.

Finally, as to Lyman's discussion of anti-Manichaean material, a very interesting discussion in itself, I am not convinced that it really helps her case at all.[18] Certainly Alexander of Lycopolis is concerned with the model of Jesus as teacher by word and freely chosen example, over against what he sees as Manichaean determinism; but he is not interested (and we should not expect him to be) in Christology, as he is not a Christian theologian. I am sure Lyman is right to see anti-Manichaean concerns as widespread in Egypt and Syria at this time – and Arius shows proof of this, as does Pamphilus' *Apology for Origen*. But – to repeat the point – an enthusiasm for Jesus' exemplary free will is not the same as a belief that this is the crucial issue for Christology. The other text Lyman appeals to, the *Acta Archelai*, is a really intriguing document; but its theological world is emphatically post-Nicene, indeed Antiochene and anti-Arian. 'Manes' in this dialogue attempts to ridicule the arguments of the orthodox Christian Archelaus by saying that they imply a divinization of Jesus *per profectum*, 'by advance' or 'by degrees'. Archelaus does not wholly repudiate this, but the point is that what is being disputed is not to do with any change or advance in the heavenly Logos, nor with a transformation of Jesus' humanity into divinity, but with the nature of the Spirit's work in the human Jesus. Archelaus is defending the view that the heavenly Son dwells in Jesus as in a tabernacle, leaving his humanity integral and free – precisely the language of one of Arius' fiercest critics, Eustathius of Antioch (the verbal parallels are striking and have not been fully examined). 'Manes' is, on the contrary, defending a view in which Jesus is not in any recognizable sense a free human agent. Whatever this shows, it casts little light on what Arius might have thought. Rather, it may be of interest in showing how, in the Antiochene sphere of theological influence, anti-Arian and anti-Manichaean polemic might have stimulated each other. Antiochenes want to defend the human liberty of Jesus so as to avoid the imputation of mutability to the divine Word; such a defence of human liberty has obvious and helpful implications for debate with Manichees. So far from suggesting an 'Arian' substrate to the argument in the *Acta*, this section of the fictional dispute confirms, I believe, a strong pro-Nicene background for the text.

All this being said, I admit that my earlier discussions neglect some of the ways in which we need to connect Arius with something other than just speculative traditions, even in exegesis. In a paper of 1997, I proposed that one important source for Arius' thought might have been the Alexandrian liturgical tradition. If we can assume – and it is admittedly less than certain – that the extant earliest texts of the Liturgy of St Mark represent at least some pre-Nicene elements, we have a powerful liturgical rhetoric of participation in the heavenly worship that is led by the 'two most honourable living beings'. This must be an allusion to the kind of model found in the *Ascension of Isaiah*, where the Son and the Spirit lead the worship of the heavenly sanctuary. Lorenz noted in 1980 the liturgical 'feel' of some phrases in the *Thalia*;[19] and there is enough in the pre-Nicene Alexandrian thought world in general to encourage the belief that this mythology of the *Thronwelt*, with its archaic Jewish-Christian echoes, was a strong presence. It is perfectly possible that Arius could have appealed to the familiar eucharistic texts of his day in support of his theology: an obvious bridge between 'learned' exegesis and popular piety.

And on the wider background of Arius, it is worth mentioning the magisterial study of Eusebius of Caesarea's theology by Holger Strutwolf (1999), which traces in great detail the kind of Platonism Eusebius assumes into his trinitarian thinking – and, significantly (p. 31) concludes that Eusebius initially misunderstood Arius as saying something similar to himself, and then distanced himself more and more from the Alexandrian as he realized his error, while still opposing the theology of the correlativity of Father and Son advanced by Alexander, following Dionysius and Origen. Peter Widdicombe (1994) has explored some of the theological treatments of this latter theme, demonstrating clearly how much of a specific Alexandrian tradition could be invoked on the question. I have also, in a brief essay[20] attempted to expand my suggestions about what might have happened to the text of Pamphilus' *Apology* during the later fourth century: some of the Origen extracts there are misleadingly placed or relocated so as to answer the questions of the end, not the beginning, of the century, and we shall better understand Origen's relation to the controversies around Arius himself if we bear this in mind.

4. ARIUS AND NEOPLATONISM

Strutwolf[21] characterizes Eusebius' theology as standing 'between Numenius and Plotinus' – a description that brings neatly into focus one of the possible areas of tension between the theology of Eusebius and that of Arius as reconstructed in the foregoing pages. The thesis that Arius might represent a more post-Plotinian metaphysic has been variously received. Hanson[22] finds some plausibility in it, as does Barnes – though the latter also sounds a warning note, pointing out that, as Plotinus and Porphyry taught in Rome, we should not be too confident about how familiar they were to thinkers in the eastern Mediterranean at this point.[23] This is fair comment – though we know that a good deal of Porphyry was familiar, and that Iamblichus was active in the east. However, the suggestion that Anatolius, Iamblichus' teacher, is to be identified with the Christian bishop Anatolius of Laodicaea is one that I adopted over-enthusiastically; it is stated as fact (above, p. 196), when it is at best conjecture, and a conjecture regarded very sceptically indeed by several well-qualified judges. I still find it attractive, but must admit to more doubts than in 1987.

This is one of a number of very weighty criticisms made of the entire thesis of Neoplatonic influence on Arius by Christopher Stead in an article published in 1997. This challenges most of the cardinal points of my interpretation in a good deal of detail, and is not easily sum-marized. Essentially, though, Stead's charges concentrate mostly on the account given of alleged shifts in the idea of participation in Plotinian and post-Plotinian philosophy; there are also some rather more minor complaints about overconfidence in claiming analogies between Arius' phraseology and that of the Neoplatonists, and a severe criticism of the interpretation I proposed in 1983 of the significance of the phrase *idios tēs ousias [tou patros]* in the controversy. I had argued that this was a turn of phrase used by Alexander and his circle, repudiated by Arius on the grounds that calling the Son *idios* in relation to the Father would have reduced the Son to an impersonal property of the Father, and I referred to Porphyry's *Isagōgē* for an analysis of *to idion* which would rule out applying *idios* to a substance in its own right. Stead objects to 'careless formulation' (p. 42): obviously *idios* can be used of a substance in relation to another, as with the biblical 'his own Son' and many comparable examples. Porphyry is talking of *to idion*, the abstract notion of being 'proper' to a substance, not the use of the commonplace adjective *idios*. To deny that this could be used of a sub-stance commits us to a nonsensical conclusion prohibiting the ordinary expression by which we assert that something belongs to something else.

Let me attempt to respond to this before turning to the thorny question of participation. To the accusation of careless formulation I must, alas, plead guilty. I must also say that I am now not convinced that *idios tēs tou patros ousias* was a phrase current in the early days of the debate; its prominence comes in by way of Athanasius' discussions of it in *contra Arianos*, and I strongly suspect that it is a post-Nicene expres-sion. However, the point I was trying to make, clumsily, was that to assert something is proper to another *substance* is strictly to say that it is an aspect of the definition of another substance; as such, it cannot be a substance in its own right. Of course we can and do say that this or that belongs to someone or something without denying its substantive reality, but if we were to get a little more technical and say that it is a defining property of something else, we should be saying that it existed only in virtue of that something else being what it is, not as an independent subject. Greek, like other languages, uses the same words for the non-technical relation (ownership) as for the strict or technical (propriety): in Welsh, *perthyn* means to belong as in ownership, to be related by kinship, and to be definitionally proper. I agree that I failed to make clear that I had in mind the last-named of these only; I agree also that when Arius in his own (proper) undoubtedly authentic writings speaks of *idion* or *idiotēs*, he is making a quite different point about how the Son does not possess by nature any of the defining properties of the Father's substance. Whether he also rejected, as I originally suggested, a view that appeared to reduce the Son to a property of the Father (making him, in effect, a metaphorical personification of the Father's wisdom or whatever) must be more doubtful, though I do not think it alien to Arius' theological agenda. And finally, on this, I am now also inclined to agree that we do not have to appeal to Porphyry as a source for a doctrine that Arius could have found, as Stead suggests, (p. 43) in Clement.

I had also suggested that Arius' documentable hostility (before Nicaea) to the use of *homoousios*, on the grounds of its materialistic resonance might owe something to the fact that Iamblichus uses the word very specifically to refer to a compound of different substances, which could in principle be broken down into 'consubstantial portions'. Although, as Stead notes, Iamblichus does not use *meros*, 'portion', himself, it is a natural word in the context (Stead quite rightly says that of course a *meros* in a compound is *homoousion*). Since even the best-informed Christian writers of the period otherwise show no knowledge of Iamblichus, there is a *prima facie* unlikelihood of any influence. I grant the relative unlikelihood; I merely note a usage which may throw light on precisely why Arius disliked *homoousios* so intensely. The specific sense given by Iamblichus is just sufficiently distinctive, I would argue, to suggest a slightly different slant on the term and its possible readings to provide added fuel for someone to deny its appropriateness in regard to God. But whether anything like direct contact with Iamblichus is imaginable I am agnostic, more so than in 1983 or 1987.

Stead's objections to my discussion of participation are the most serious in his article. I proposed that Arius represented a theological equivalent of that movement in late antique philosophy which came to stress the incommunicability of substance – so that any talk of substantial participation or the bestowal of a share in the substance of a higher reality upon a lower would have to be ruled out. Hence my language about 'vertical' and 'lateral' participation. If the term does not mean the share of a lower reality in a higher, its focus is the relation of co-ordinate substances sharing common definition. My point in respect of Arius was that, in contrast to earlier theologies, his scheme assumes that God cannot communicate *what* he is to another, and that the only sharing of substance that makes sense is the co-ordinate model – which rules out any community of substance between Father and Son, since God is never a member of a class of beings.

Stead is particularly severe on this hypothesis. There is no such shift in ancient philosophy as I suggest; it is not true that Alexander of Aphrodisias and Porphyry introduce a doctrine of 'lateral' participation. The use of *metochē* and cognate terms to describe what Stead prefers to call a 'symmetrical' relation (i.e. one between individuals on the same ontological level) goes back beyond Plato and is a commonplace. What Alexander of Aphrodisias has to say about this is just possibly relevant, but my reference to Porphyry to support the idea of a new sense being given to *metochē* is a straightforward misreading. In any case, the logical work of Alexander and Porphyry is most unlikely to have been known to any Christian writer; those who show some awareness of these authors never refer to the kind of material I adduce. As to the broader point of Arius' apparent critique of a doctrine implying that Father and Son were two members of a class of *agennēta*, this is weakened by the fact that no-one ever seems to call the Father *homoousios* with the Son, as would surely be the case if the term indicated a 'symmetrical' relation of particulars sharing a substantial definition. Finally, where the language of *metochē* is used by fourth-century writers, it seems to be primarily in respect of the sharing of attributes rather than any issues about substance (pp. 47–50).

There are several matters of detail which would need more argument than I can offer here to contest effectively; but I shall mention some of the larger issues. First, an examination of the 1983 article's claims will show that I am not supposing that Alexander and Porphyry introduce an unheard-of novelty into Greek vocabulary. Of course *metochē* means a symmetrical relation in ordinary usage before the third century CE. My point was rather that the use of such language for the relation of an individual to a higher form was dismissed by Aristotle and by that generation of philosophers who first seriously sought to combine Aristotelean logic with Platonic metaphysics. 'Substantial participation' cannot mean the transfer of substantial content from a higher or paradigmatic 'possessor' of the substance in question to a lower. Hence the reference to Porphyry's phraseology, from the *Isagōgē* 22 (and elsewhere): 'participation in form is equal, participation in accidents is a matter of more or less'. My mistake in the 1983 article was a very evident confusion as to when I was referring specifically to substantial or formal participation rather than to participation in general, and I do not dispute that my reference to these Porphyrian texts gives a misleading impression. But if this trend in third-century thought is accurately identified, the looser language about the second god or the world having *metochē* in God (and Stead, p. 52, quotes some pertinent examples) will not be useable. This is not a simple repudiation of Plato; it is an aspect of that strenuous reconfiguration of Plato's cosmology which produces the varied and immensely complex intellectual world of Neoplatonism.

I referred earlier to Strutwolf's characterization of Eusebius as 'between Numenius and Plotinus'; and precisely what I was attempting to identify was whether Arius represents a stage beyond this position (in which the participatory relation of the second god to the substance of the first could still be seen as a solution to the increasingly vexed question of the sense in which the Logos was divine), a stage in which affirming the substantial difference of the Logos from the Father was an intellectual necessity for theology. If a 'Numenian' solution was increasingly indefensible in the metaphysics of the third century outside the Christian world, should we imagine a comparable move within the Christian world, producing something like Arius' scheme? The point is well taken that an affirmative answer to this would require us to believe what we have no hard evidence for – that Arius or some unknown teacher of his had more direct acquaintance than almost any contemporary with early Neoplatonic writings (hence my probably over-bold identification of Anatolius as the link figure here). The solution may be rightly regarded as unproven, but I believe the question is a real one. And, despite Stead's denial that 'symmetrical' participation between Father and Son is not an issue in the fourth century, the repeated denunciations of 'teaching two *agennēta*' and Arius' repudiation of equality between Father and Son do strongly suggest that the problem of a lateral or symmetrical participation in divine substance implied in the Alexandrian stress on the eternal correlativity of Father and Son[24] was a real one to some theologians of the period, and may have been exacerbated for some by the awareness that the old formulations which implied a bestowal of divine substance from higher to lower were looking intellectually shopworn. More than this it would be rash to claim with any confidence.

CONCLUSION

In terms of the intellectual history of the controversy sparked by Arius, I was more concerned in 1987 to establish the fact that a theological crisis was brewing at this point than to construct, once and for all, an explanation of it. I allowed in the text that it was a matter of exegetical as well as philosophical tangles; but there are unmistakable issues about metaphysics around in all this, and I don't think we can reasonably suppose that they are entirely secondary or that they have absolutely no relation to the rest of the intellectual climate of the early fourth century. How much of the detail of my own reconstruction will survive, time will tell. But the theology of Arius does not come from nowhere; and part of my aim was to show how a theological tradition that is not responsive in some ways to wider intellectual currents can become stuck, its fruitful paradoxes turning into simple *aporiai*.

Thus the postscript to the original text of this book sets out to sketch some issues around the methodology of dealing with tradition – building a little on exactly what Newman does with this sort of question (subsequent work on Newman has only served to strengthen the intuitions here). My allusions to possible parallels with the German Church struggle of the 1930s provoked some pained protests: Maurice Wiles aptly says that I evidently think Arius' problem was that he had not read Barth (p. 178; cf. pp. 237–239 above). But there are questions about the interaction of theology and models of power that arise, questions which do not easily yield, I admit, answers unambiguously favourable to the 'orthodox' resolution to which I give my own theological loyalties.[25] The work of defending the plausibility of Nicene Christianity today cannot be done in terms simply of clarifying intellectual history as if it had an isolated life of its own.

Yet there are movements in intellectual history, the introduction of new paradigms and images which slowly and often unpredictably shift the possibilities of thinking. Wiles' own demonstration that Arius' theology of the semi-divine mediator does not survive very well in a cosmology where there are fewer or no intermediate levels of life between this world and God is, in fact, a very suggestive observation. One long-term effect of the Nicene settlement was that it eventually

..de it impossible for orthodox Christianity to conceive God as an individual. It was already beginning to effect what Wiles sees as the process of early modernity's clearing of the air: there are no dramas, no cosmogonic transactions to be imagined in which God determines what is needed to pursue the great labour of creation. Rather there is the divine life as a system of threefold relation set over against the history of the universe which wholly depends upon it. The story of the latter again and again provides the scaffolding for speaking of the former, but again and again requires stripping and demythologizing. The history of theology is a history of such fertile and suggestive mistakes (revealing mistakes, we might say). Nicaea and its later refinements set down the grammar of Christian speech about God, as has often been said, warning against canonizing in theology the tempting idioms of human personal interaction, requiring us to strain beyond these if we are to begin to hold to any sense of the radicality of divine gift. If God is not an individual, God does not compete with us for space;[26] if God is not an individual, God's will cannot be adequately understood in the terms of self-assertion or contest for control in which so much of our usual discourse of will is cast. The implications for theology, for ethics and for prayer and spirituality are enormous; and we are still discovering them.

267

Appendix 2:

Credal Documents

(a) The 'Creed of Lucian of Antioch'
(from de syn. 23, Opitz 249)

Following the evangelical and apostolic tradition, we believe in one
God, the ruler of all, the former (*dēmiourgon*) and maker and provider
of everything, from whom are all things; and in one Lord, Jesus
Christ, his Son, the only-begotten God, through whom are all
things,[1] begotten from the Father before all ages, God from God,
entire fulness from entire fulness (*holon ex holou*), the only one from
the only one, the perfect from the perfect, king from king, lord from
lord, the living Word, living Wisdom, true light, the way, the truth,
the resurrection, the shepherd, the door; immutable and unchanging, the exact image of the substance (*ousia*) and will and power
and glory of the Father's divinity, 'the firstborn of all creation',[2] the
one who is 'in the beginning with God',[3] God the Word, according
to what is said in the gospel: 'and the Word was God';[4] 'through
whom all things came to be',[5] and 'in whom all things cohere';[6]
who in the last days came down from above and was begotten of a
virgin, in accordance with the Scriptures, and became a human
being, 'a mediator between God and human beings'[7] the apostle of
our faith[8] and author (*archēgon*) of life,[9] as he says: 'I have come
down from heaven not to do my own will, but the will of him who
sent me':[10] who suffered on our behalf and rose on the third day
and ascended into the heavens, and took his seat on the Father's
right hand, and is coming again with glory and power to judge
living and dead; and in the Holy Spirit, given to believers for
encouragement (*paraklēsin*) and sanctification and perfection,[11] just
as our Lord Jesus Christ ordered his disciples: 'Go forth and teach
all nations, baptizing them in the name of the Father and of the
Son and of the Holy Spirit'[12] – that is, of a Father who is truly

269

Father, a Son who truly is Son, a Holy Spirit who truly is Holy
Spirit'[13] these names are not assigned casually or idly, but designate
quite precisely the particular subsistence (*hupostasis*), the rank and
the glory[14] of each of those named, so as to make them three in
respect of subsistence, but one in concord.[15]

[The conclusion with its list of anathemas is clearly dependent
on Nicaea.]

(This formula, discussed more fully on pp. 163–4 above, is notable
chiefly for its extensive use of biblical citation and its rich accumu-
lation of metaphorical titles for the Logos. It is most unlikely to
represent exactly any confession of Lucian's, but certainly contains
material that goes back to his original circle.)

(b)   The statement of faith of Arius and his Alexandrian supporters
      (from Opitz, U.6 = de syn.16, Epiphanius, haer. 69.7)

Our faith, which we have from our forefathers and which we have
also learned from you, holy father, is this: we acknowledge one God,
the only unbegotten (*agennētos*), the only eternal (*aïdios*), the only
one without cause or beginning (*anarchos*), the only true, the only
one possessed of immortality, the only wise, the only good, the only
sovereign, judge of all things, controller of all things, administrator
of all things, immutable and unchanging, righteous and good, the
God of the Law and the prophets and the New Covenant, the
begetter of his only Son before endless ages; through whom he made
both the ages and all that is; begetting him not in appearance but
in truth, giving him subsistence by his own will; [begetting him as]
immutable and unchanging, the perfect creation of God, but not
like one among other creatures, a begotten being (*gennēma*), but not
like one among other generated things (*tōn gegennēmenōn*); not the
Father's offspring in the sense of an emanation (*probolē*) as Valentinus taught; nor the Father's offspring in the sense of a consubstantial portion (*meros homoousion*) of the Father, as Manichaeus
explained it; nor, as Sabellius said, splitting up the [divine] monad,
a 'Son-Father' (*huiopatōr*); nor, as Hieracas [said], a lamp lit from
another lamp, or, as it were, a single light [divided] into two;
nor something existing beforehand and then later begotten or re-
established as a son – as you yourself, holy father, have many times

270

condemned those who put forward such accounts, in your public teaching in church and synod (*en sunedriō(i)*). But rather [it is] as we say, that he [the Son] was created by the will of God before all times and all ages, receiving from the Father his life and his existence, the Father making the Son's glories exist alongside himself.[1] For the Father in giving him the inheritance of all things[2] did not deprive himself of what he has self-sufficiently (*agennētōs*) in his own life; for he is the source of everything.

So there are three subsisting realities (*hupostaseis*); but God, being the cause of all things, is without beginning and supremely unique (*monōtatos*), while the Son, timelessly (*achronōs*) begotten by the Father, created and established before all ages, did not exist prior to his begetting, but was timelessly begotten before all things; he alone was given existence [directly] by the Father. For he is not eternal or co-eternal or equally self-sufficient (*sunagennētos*) with the Father, nor does he have his being alongside the Father, [in virtue] as some say, [of] his relation with him (*ta pros ti*), thus postulating two self-sufficient first principles. But it is God [only], as monad and first principle of all things, who exists in this way before all things. That is why he exists before the Son (*pro tou huiou*) – as we have learned from you, holy father, in your public preaching in church. Accordingly then, since he has his existence, his glories and his life from the Father, and all things are delivered to him,[3] it is in this sense that God is his principle and source (*archē*). He has authority over the Son as his God, and as the one who exists before him. But if the expressions 'from him'[4] (*ex autou*) and 'from the womb'[5] and 'I came out from the Father and have come here'[6] are understood by certain people in terms of a portion of something consubstantial[7] or in terms of an emanation, then, according to them, the Father is compound and divisible and changeable and material; as far as they are concerned, the God who is without a body is undergoing the experiences proper to a body.

(This is a carefully phrased text, insisting on its orthodox and traditional character, yet at the same time arguing clearly and pertinaciously for a distinctive and controversial interpretation of the faith received. Arius' skill as a dialectician is discernible in these lines, though they are less idiosyncratic than the *Thalia*. The various parallels with Bishop Alexander's own phraseology suggest that there are elements of an official Alexandrian creed in this formula;

271

the anti-heretical slogans are probably 'official' catechesis, for example. But the concluding section (the second paragraph above) is clearly individual exposition.)

(c)   The orthodox faith according to Alexander of Alexandria
      (from Opitz, U.14 = Theodoret, h.e. I.4)

About the Father and the Son, this is how we believe, as the apostolic Church declares: [We believe] in one unbegotten (*agennēton*) Father, who has no cause of his existence, immutable and unchanging, eternally possessing his nature thus, in the same way, incapable either of improvement or of diminution, the giver of the Law and the prophets and the gospels, the Lord of the patriarchs and the apostles and all the saints; and in one Lord Jesus Christ, the only-begotten Son of God, begotten not out of non-existence, but out of the Father, the truly existent one (*ouk ek tou mē ontos, all' ek tou ontos patros*), not in any bodily way – by splitting off, or by the emanation of distinct levels of reality, as Sabellius and Valentinus teach[1] – but in an unutterable and inexplicable fashion, as that writer whom we have already quoted says, 'Who shall declare his generation?';[2] since his subsistence (*hupostasis*) defies investigation by any entity that has come into being (*pasē(i) te(i) gennētē(i) phusei*) – just as the Father himself defies investigation – since the form of his divine generation is not to be grasped by the natural capacities of rational beings.

Those who are anointed by the Spirit of truth will have no need to learn these things from me: the voice of Christ has already begun to prompt us on all this, the voice that says in its teaching, 'No one knows who the Father is except the Son, and no one knows who the Son is except the Father.'[3] We have learned that the Son is immutable and unchanging, self-sufficient (*aprosdeē*) and perfect, just like the Father, except for the Father's quality of being 'unbegotten'. For he is the exact and precise image of the Father,[4] as it is plain that an image contains all those qualities in virtue of which the greater paradigm (*emphereia*) exists;[5] thus the Lord himself taught us, saying, 'My Father is greater than I'.[6]

Accordingly, we believe that the Son exists eternally in dependence on the Father (*ek tou patros*), 'for he is the effulgence of his glory and the imprinted image of the Father's subsistence'.[7] But no

272

one should take 'eternally' to imply 'unbegotten', as some people, whose mental faculties are blinded, think. To say, 'He existed', and 'existed eternally', and 'existed before the ages' is not the same thing as to say 'unbegotten'; in no way could human understanding contrive to work out a name expressing what it is to be unbegotten. You too, I think, would approach the matter in this way; I have complete confidence that all of you[8] hold the correct view, [which is] that none of these expressions means 'unbegotten' in any way at all. All of them seem to relate to some kind of temporal duration, and are incapable of expressing properly the divinity and – so to speak – the 'primordiality' (*archaiotēta*) of the Only-begotten; they are the words of holy men struggling as best they each of them could to make the mystery clear, and at the same time asking pardon from their audience with the quite legitimate defence that they had said, '[This is true] only as far as we have managed to grasp it.' But if those people who claim that what is 'known in part' has been 'done away with' as far as they are concerned expect more than human lips can utter, then obviously 'existed' and 'eternally', and 'before the ages' leave much to be desired; such expressions, whatever they amount to, are not the same as [a definition of] 'unbegotten'.

So the unbegotten Father's dignity is safeguarded for him; no one can be said to be the cause of his existence. And the appropriate degree of honour is accorded to the Son as well, in ascribing to him an eternal (*anarchon*)[9] generation from the Father. As we have said, we give him the worship that is his due when we use of him the expressions 'existed' and 'eternally' and 'before the ages' in the sense consistent with true religion and reverence. In doing so, we do not deny his divinity; we ascribe to him, as the image and imprint of the Father, an exact and complete likeness [to the Father]. But we still hold that to be unbegotten is solely the property of the Father – which is what the Saviour himself says: 'My Father is greater than I.'

As well as this properly reverent view concerning Father and Son, we also confess belief in one Holy Spirit, just as the holy scriptures teach, the Spirit who motivated[10] both the holy men of the old covenant and the godlike (*theious*) teachers of what we know as the new covenant; and in one and one only catholic Church, the apostolic Church, which can never be defeated, even though the whole world should conspire to attack it, victorious over all the

273

irreverent rebellions of heretics. We are confirmed in this belief by the words of the master of the household of the Church: 'Be of good cheer; I have overcome the world.'[11] And over and above this, we acknowledge the resurrection from among the dead, the resurrection of which our Lord Jesus Christ has become the firstfruits:[12] he took on a body, in truth, not in appearance, from Mary the Mother of God (*theotokou*);[13] when he had come to dwell among the human race at the end of the ages, for the taking away of sins, he was crucified, he died, and yet in all this did not undergo any lessening of his divinity. And when he had risen from the dead, he was taken up into heaven and took his seat on the right hand of majesty.[14]

In this letter, I have set out these things only in part, thinking that it would be tedious to write in full detail on each point, as I have said, since your godly keenness will hardly have avoided becoming aware of them! These things we teach, these things we preach, these things are the apostolic tenets of the Church.

(As with Arius' statement, certain elements of an Alexandrian credal form are discernible in this text – the list of divine predicates, the phrases describing the Father as God of Old and New Covenants alike, the repudiation of Sabellius and Valentinus, the use of *hupostasis* for the divine entities, the use of Hebrews 1. Alexander alone has the article on Spirit and Church; but, since this has some affinities with Arius' later confession ((g) below), we may consider it likely that this too reflects a common credal form in the Alexandrian background. Alexander's exposition is awkwardly ordered, as he only rather belatedly returns to the statements about the Word's incarnate life that we should expect earlier. But this has the interesting effect of making the conventional anti-docetic affirmations of this portion of the creed a gloss on the hope of bodily resurrection: the incipient 'two nature' rhetoric (true flesh, undiluted Godhead) looks forward to later Alexandrian Christology in associating Christological balance with the possibility of giving full weight to the promise of concrete transformation for the believer, bodily glorification, in the age to come.

Alexander's defensiveness about the expressions 'existed eternally' and so on strongly suggests that some such phrases had been introduced into the formal catechesis, or the creed itself, at his insistence – perhaps to counter some sort of gnostic teaching that the Son is a 'development' of the divine being in its complex relation with the cosmos, perhaps to combat Sabellianism (exactly what Arius wanted to do). Arius' letter to Eusebius of Nicomedia makes it clear that Alexander was in the habit of coining new theological slogans in his teaching.

The most distinctive feature of this text, however, is probably its markedly apophatic character. The tension between the *eikōn* theology of some passages and the insistence elsewhere on God's abiding inaccessibility to reason is no less pronounced for being very typically Alexandrian.)

(d)   The creed of the Synod of Antioch, 325.
      (from Opitz, U.18; the translation is from Schwartz' Greek version of the Syriac original, checked against the Syriac at various unclear points.)

This, then, is the faith that was set forth by spiritual men,[1] whom it is not right to think of as living or understanding according to the flesh at any time, but as always formed and trained in the spirit by means of the holy writings of the inspired books. It is: to believe in one God, the Father, the ruler of all, incomprehensible, immutable and unchanging, the providential overseer and governor of all things, righteous and good, maker of heaven and earth and all that is in them, Lord of the Law and the prophets and the New Covenant; and in one Lord Jesus Christ, the only-begotten Son, begotten not out of non-existence, but out of the Father, not as a thing made (*poiēton*) but as a begotten being (*gennēma*) in the strict sense (*kuriōs*), generated in an unutterable and indescribable fashion, since only the Father who begat and the Son who was begotten know [its mode] – 'No one knows the Father except the Son, or the Son except the Father.'[2] He always exists and did not earlier on not exist. For we have learned from the holy scriptures that he is the sole image [of the Father],[3] and is not unbegotten, since it is clear that he is, so to speak, 'from' the Father.[4] The scriptures call him a begotten son, in the strict and proper sense (*kuriōs kai alethōs*) – not just by convention (*thesei*),[5] for it would be irreverent and blasphemous to say this. Just so do we believe that he is immutable and unchanging, not begotten or brought into being by will or [only] conventionally speaking, [or?] in such a way that he would seem to be [generated] out of non-existence, but begotten in the way appropriate for him, not in the likeness or the nature of anything that has come to be through him, or mixed with them at all – which it is not lawful to imagine. Rather do we confess, then, because he transcends all conception or understanding or thought, that he was begotten out of the unbegotten Father, God the Word, the true light, righteousness, Jesus Christ, the Lord and Saviour of all. For he is the image not of the will or anything else, but of the actual *hupostasis* of the Father.[6] This Son, God the Word, having also been born and made flesh out of Mary the Mother of God (*theotokos*), and suffered, and died, rose from the dead and, when he had been taken into heaven, took his seat on the right hand of the power of the Most High,[7] and is coming to judge living and dead.

Further, as the holy scriptures teach us to put our faith in our Saviour, so too they teach us to put our faith in the one Spirit, the one catholic Church, the resurrection of the dead, and a judgment in which everyone will be repaid for what they have done in the flesh, whether good things or bad; and we anathematize those who say or think or preach that the Son of God is a creature or something brought into being or made and is not truly a begotten being, or that there was when he was not. For we believe that he was [always] and that he is [? . . .] and that he is [the true?] light.[8] We further anathematize those who propose that he is immutable by his own free will, and those who introduce the notion that his generation is out of non-existence and that he is not by nature immutable in the way the Father is. For as our Saviour is proclaimed to be the image of the Father in every respect, he is so especially in this particular.

(The sources of this confession are not easy to disentangle; its links with (c) are obvious, and parallels with the *ekthesis* ascribed to Gregory Thaumaturgus have been noted (Abramowski (1975)). Its pre-Nicene character appears in its innocence of the *homoousios* and of the language of the Son's derivation from the Father's *ousia*. The anathemas closely foreshadow those of Nicea, but are rather less clearly focused. It may be that the text shows the dominating influence of Alexandrian interests at the Synod, leading to a statement heavily dependent upon Alexandrian models; but the similarity to Gregory's confession might suggest that there existed an Origenian formula known in the Antiochene sphere of influence, which possessed one or two features lacking in the Alexandrian creed of the early fourth century. It may, but need not necessarily, rest on some more primitive Alexandrian model transmitted by Origen. There are surprisingly few points of real contact with 'Lucian'. The ascription of a 'natural' immutability to the Son in virtue of his being the Father's image is distinctive, and reflects Alexander's interpretation of Arius as some sort of adoptionist because of his insistence on the Son's free will and deliberate virtue.)

(e)   The creed of Eusebius of Caesarea[1]
      (from Opitz, U.22 = de decr. 33. 4–6., Socrates, h.e. I.8, Theodoret, h.e.I.12)

We believe in one God, the Father, the ruler of all, the maker of all things visible and invisible, and in one Lord Jesus Christ, the Word of God, God from God, light from light,[2] life from life, the only-begotten Son, the firstborn of all creation, begotten of the Father before all ages, through whom all things came to be; who for our salvation was made flesh and dwelt among human beings and suffered and rose on the third day and ascended to the Father and is coming again in glory to judge living and dead. We believe also in one Holy Spirit, believing[3] that each one of these exists and subsists,[4] the Father truly [existing as] Father, the Son truly as Son and the Holy Spirit truly as Holy Spirit, just as our Lord said when sending out his disciples to preach: 'Go forth and teach all nations, baptizing them in the name of the Father and of the Son and of the Holy Spirit.'[5]

(This was Eusebius' attempt at a compromise formula for Nicaea, and no doubt represents pretty exactly the baptismal creed of Caesarea. It is appropriately rather neutral in flavour, somewhat surprisingly makes no use of *eikōn* language, and contributes nothing specific to the Nicene debate. Despite Eusebius' claims, and despite the role he is likely to have played at the council, it met with little support; but it did provide, in style, structure and vocabulary, a starting point for the drafting of a final formula.)

(f)   The creed of Nicaea
      (from Opitz, U.24 = de decr. 33.8)

We believe in one God, the Father, the ruler of all, the maker of
all things visible and invisible; and in one Lord, Jesus Christ the
Son of God, begotten as the only Son out of the Father,[1] that is,
out of the substance of the Father, God from God, light from light,
true God from true God,[2] begotten, not made, *homoousios* with the
Father, the one through whom all things came to be, things in
heaven and things in earth; who, for the sake of us human beings
and our salvation, descended and became flesh, became human,
suffered, and rose on the third day, ascended into the heavens and
is coming to judge living and dead; and in the Holy Spirit.[3]

As for those who say, 'there was when he was not', or 'he did
not exist before he was begotten', or 'he came into being out of non-
existence', or who fantasize that the Son of God is [made] from
some other *hupostasis* or *ousia*, or that he is created or mutable or
changeable, such people the catholic and apostolic Church
anathematizes.

(A strikingly brief confession, blending the uncontroversial terms of
Eusebius' creed, and perhaps other Syro-Palestinian models, with
aggressively novel expressions, designed to rule out any possibility
of a doctrine of the Son's creation. In spite of its oddity, it was
never to be seriously challenged as the final statement of the catholic
position in the fourth century. Although the creed of 'Lucian'
enjoyed some popularity among 'homoiousians' in the middle of the
century, the non-Nicenes had no comparably economical and
official statement – a fact that the polemic of Athanasius exploits
to the full.)

(g)   The confession of Arius and Euzoius[1]
      (from Opitz, U.30 = Socrates, h.e. I.26.8, and Sozomen, h.e.
      II.27)

We believe in one God, the Father, the ruler of all; and in the Lord
Jesus Christ, his only Son, the one who was begotten[2] from him[3]
before all ages, God the Word, through whom all things came to
be, things in the heavens and things on earth; the one who

descended and took flesh and suffered and rose and ascended into the heavens and is coming again to judge living and dead. And in the Holy Spirit, and in the resurrection of the flesh and in the life of the age to come and in the Kingdom of the heavens and in [the] one catholic Church of God [extending] from one end of the earth to the other.

We have received this faith from the holy gospels, where the Lord says to his disciples, 'Go forth and teach all nations, baptizing them in the name of the Father and of the Son and of the Holy Spirit.'[4] If we do not so believe these things, and if we do not truly accept Father and Son and Holy Spirit[5] just as the whole catholic Church teaches, and as the Scriptures (which we rely on in all things) teach, God is our judge, now and on the day that is coming. So we entreat you in your devoutness, most God-beloved emperor, that we, who are clerics holding the faith and sentiments of the Church and the holy Scriptures, may be united to our mother the Church through your peacemaking and reverent devoutness, with all questions put aside, and all the word-spinning arising from these questions, so that both we and the Church, being at peace with each other, may all make together the proper and accustomed prayers for your peaceful and devout rule, and for all your family.

(As befits a plea for amnesty, this is a studiedly uncontroversial composition. The opening reads like a severely abbreviated version of (f), omitting all the novel phrases of the original, but retaining a pale semblance of some of its vocabulary. The order of items in 'third article', however, is distinctive, following none of the other eastern creeds of the period, and, as noted above (p. 97), may reflect some formula current in Arius' place of exile. The Alexandrian creed evidently included reference to Spirit and church, but the resurrection-life-kingdom sequence is not paralleled.)

Notes

PART I ARIUS AND THE NICENE CRISIS

A ARIUS BEFORE ARIANISM

1 haer. 69.1, 152.19.
2 They appear (improbably) as signatories of Arius' letter to Alexander of Alexandria (Opitz, U.6, 13.23) at an early stage of the controversy, and are also named in the encyclical *henos sōmatos* of Alexander (Opitz, U.4b, 7.16–17). Philostorgius (h.e. I.8, 9.13–14, I.9, 10.1–2, I.10, 11.4–8) makes it clear that they were loyal to Arius at Nicaea. Secundus in particular is often mentioned by Athanasius (e.g. in ad ep. Aeg. 7, PG 25, 553A, and hist. Ar. 65, Opitz 219.2ff., and 71, Opitz 222.13–20) as a persistent thorn in the flesh.
3 E.g. Athanasius hist. Ar. 65, loc. cit.
4 On the history and topography of Libya in antiquity, see Pauly-Wissowa 25.1, 146ff. on Libya in general, 28.1, 1881–1883 on Marmarica, and 37.1, 509–10 on the Pentapolis.
5 Ptolemais was the chief city of Libya Pentapolis; the largely desert area of Marmarica had few candidates for an episcopal seat. The coastal town of Antipyrgos appears later as the name of a see (Pauly-Wissowa 1, 2534), but some lists of Nicene fathers include a bishop of Antipyrgos who is clearly not the same as Theonas, whose see remains a mystery.
6 h.e. I.8, 9.12–21.
7 See the excellent discussion in Chadwick (1960), especially pp. 176–9, 190–2.
8 Opitz, U.34, 69–75; cf. below, I.B.3.
9 Opitz, U.29, 63.5–6.
10 According to the 'Festal Index', the chronological table attached to Athanasius' Festal Letters, IV, PG 26, 1352BC (*Hoc anno visitavit Pentapolim et Ammoniacam*).
11 haer. 69.3, 154.12.

12 Opitz, U.34, 73.33ff.

13 Boularand (1972), p. 10, alludes to this consensus among 'les patrologues', but brings forward no solid reasons for adopting the suggested date.

14 Sozomen, h.e. I.15, 33.1; Rufinus, h.e. I.1, PL 21, 467A, implies that Arius was a presbyter before the accession of Alexander to the bishopric; the *acta sincera sancti Petri*, PG 18, 466AB, describe Arius' ordination to the presbyterate after the death of Bishop Peter in 311.

15 Newman (1833), Section I, passim.

16 Despite the warnings entered by Gwatkin (1900), pp. 17–20. Further discussion of Arius' supposed connections with Antioch will be found in II.C.1, infra.

17 Athanasius, syn. 23, Opitz 249.11ff. The attribution to Lucian is found in Sozomen, he.e. III.5, 106.30–107.3, who probably derived this tradition from his Arian source, Sabinus of Heraclea (cf. n.74, below).

18 And was martyred in January 312 (Eusebius, h.e. IX.6.3, 812.10–15). On his presence there in 303, see Bardy (1936), p. 84.

19 Wallace-Hadrill (1982), p. 83.

20 Philostorgius, h.e. II.3, 14.7–8, II.14, 25.10–14.

21 Ibid. II.3, 14.1–9.

22 This useful term has been popularized by Kopecek (1979) to distinguish the Aetians and Eunomians of the mid-century from the first generation of anti-Nicenes.

23 Socrates, h.e. I.5, PG 67, 41A, Sozomen h.e. I.15, 33.2–3.

24 Williams (1983).

25 Barnes (1978), p. 105, gives firm evidence for locating Iamblichus between c.290 and c.300.

26 h.e. VII.32.6–13 (718.13–722.12), 20–1 (726.6–14).

27 haer. 69.3, 154.12–16.

28 Or possibly, 'advanced in years'.

29 Or 'with a stooping figure'.

30 vit. cont. 38.

31 haer. 69.3.154.17ff.

32 Supra, n.14.

33 haer. 69.1.152.20–1, 69.2, 153.26.

34 h.e. I.15, 32.20–33.2.

35 As Barnes (1981), p. 11, notes, other pieces of legislation (in economic affairs) were never promulgated in the West.

36 There was a brief remission in the spring of 311, when Galerius was dying (Eusebius h.e. VIII.17.1–10, 790.12–794.22, with a Greek translation of the emperor's monition – not, strictly speaking, an

edict; the Latin is in Lactantius, de mort. pe 34). Maximin had resumed persecution by November of that year.

37 According to the Coptic *passio* of Colluthus, Reymond and Barns (1973), p. 147; the date is given by the text as 304. See also Barns and Chadwick (1973) for Peter of Alexandria's – possibly authentic – letter to Apollonius.

38 So the letters and historical fragments on the Melitian schism from Codex Verona LX suggest (critical text in Kettler (1936), pp. 159–63): we read (PG 10, 1566B and Kettler, (1936), p. 160, 11–14) of those left in the churches who are authorized to 'visit', and it seems (1568A and Kettler, ibid., p. 162, 5) that they are presbyters; though the appended letter of Peter (PG 18, 509–10 and Kettler, ibid., p. 162, 18–19) is less clear and could be read as implying a distinction between the presbyters and those charged with the care of the *egentes*.

39 Schwartz (1905:1), pp. 103–4, esp. n.1 on p. 104, doubts whether they were presbyters and emends the Verona text (PG 10, 1568A, Kettler, p. 162, 5) accordingly (*presbyteros* et *quibus dederat*, corresponding to the phraseology of Peter's letter); he alludes to a possible parallel case in Eusebius, de mart. Pal. 11.22, 932.28–31, where we seem to have an instance of a layman formally charged with responsibility for charitable work. This is inconclusive: it is difficult to generalize from the Palestinian case reported by Eusebius (which anyway does not purport to deal with powers delegated directly by a bishop in emergency); Alexandrian presbyters (cf. infra, I.A.3) enjoyed considerable powers in any case, and seem to have preached regularly in their own assemblies; and the Verona text is simply unclear. Telfer's conclusion (1955, p. 228) that preaching and liturgy ceased in Alexandria in Bishop Peter's absence from the city is over-confident.

40 Apollonius remained in office after his apostasy; 'his people were most understanding', according to Arrianus, governor of the Thebaid, who presumably witnessed the bishop's sacrifice (Reymond and Barns, p. 147). Melitius must have been elected to the see after the martyrdom of Colluthus in May 304, and before the end of 305 (the imprisoned bishops were executed probably in February 306; infra, n.43). It may be that this helps to explain the otherwise puzzling fact that a bishop from the Thebaid should interfere in the affairs of the Delta churches. As far as we know, the bishop of Alexandria continued to consecrate all members of the Egyptian hierarchy (see the references below, n.100): did Melitius originally come to Alexandria for his episcopal ordination in 305, shortly before Peter went into hiding, and then decide not to return to Lycopolis in view of the critical situation in the Delta?

41 PG 10, 1566C, Kettler, p. 161, 6–7; *pater*, here as elsewhere in the letter must represent *papa* in the Greek, a venerable title for the Alexandrian bishop.

42 As represented by the *passio* tradition; see Telfer (1949), p. 125, who believes that this tradition is reliable. For the list of hiding places in the Greek passion, see Devos (1965), p. 167, for the Latin, PG 18, 458C.

43 February is the date given by the martyrologies, and the year has normally been assumed to be 306; thus Halkin (1963), p. 5, n.1, following Vandersleyen (1961). Phileas was executed during the prefecture in Egypt of Culcianus, who is attested as prefect up to May 306; Vandersleyen argues that Sossianus Hierocles succeeded Culcianus late in 306 or early in 307, so that the probabilities point to Culcianus having vacated the office by February 307. However, the date of Hierocles' prefecture is far from certain, and Barnes (1976) argues – along with several other recent scholars – for a later date. In this case, 307 would be possible for Phileas' death, and so Barnes concludes (1981 and 1982). I am still inclined to favour the earlier dating, none the less, since most of our indications as to the chronology of the Melitian schism point to 305/306 as the time of its origins; see Athanasius, apol. sec.59, and cf. Williams (1986), p. 41, n.26, on a possible piece of evidence from a mistake in Theophanes' Chronographia.

44 *doctoris desiderium habens* is difficult; Schwartz (1905:1) and Kettler (1936) assume that the Latin translator read *didaskalou* for *didaskaleiou*, so that the two Alexandrians were eager to have a *didaskaleion*, a school or party, of their own – or, possibly, to have a position in the catechetical school. Telfer (1955), p. 228, however, suggests a quite different interpretation: Isidore and Arius are eager to see preaching and teaching restored in Alexandria (cf. n.39, supra). This seems a little strained.

45 *commendans eis occasionem* again raises problems: 'urging the suitability of the time for action' is Telfer's suggestion (1955, p. 228). The defaulting presbyters are summoned to make amends and resume their proper work (so also Kettler, p. 162, n.8). But *occasio* in the Latin of the Dark Ages can mean *casus*, in the sense of 'occasion for complaint or condemnation', and such a reading would fit well with the phrase that follows.

46 *separavit eos:* again the identity of the *ei* is not clear. It *could* mean (so Telfer) that Melitius effectively 'separated' the presbyters from Peter's jurisdiction, but would more naturally suggest separation from the Church, i.e. excommunication; see Kettler, p. 169, on the translation problem.

47 Following Schmidt (1901) against the consensus view that Melitius ordained these persons during either his or their captivity. See Williams (1986), p. 37, on this question.

48 *ex mea auctoritate presbyteros et quibus permissum erat agentes visitare* (PG 18, 509–10, Kettler, p. 162, 18–19) is taken as a unit by Kettler, so as to mean 'presbyters [etc.] belonging to my authority' or even perhaps 'holding my authority'; but *ex mea auctoritate* could also go with the verb here, *conaretur separare* – Melitius has dared to 'separate' clergy from their canonical obedience. Cf. n.46, above; in this case, the latter interpretation seems preferable.

49 The first wave of persecution had affected the clergy primarily; the further edict of 308 was more generally directed. Thus the needs of laity in prison would not have been to the fore prior to this date. The problem arises between the clerical martyrdoms of 306, and the mass deportations of c.308.

50 haer. 68, 140.19–143.30 for the beginnings of the schism; Achelis (PRE), 560.6–19, suggested a document composed by a Melitian convert to Catholic obedience.

51 PG 18, 168–508.

52 Epiphanius, haer. 68, 143.22.

53 If Melitius was elected by a majority at Lycopolis, we should have to suppose either that Arrianus' assessment (supra, n.40) of the Laodicean qualities of this church was over-optimistic, or, following Barns and Chadwick (1973), p. 449, that a revulsion of feeling followed Apollonius' death.

54 Bell (1924), p. 39, has to suppose that Melitius was sent to the mines some time after 306 and released in 311 (for which we have no firm evidence), but does not argue for an *Egyptian* imprisonment. If Epiphanius is right in dating Melitius' time in the mines *after* 311 (haer. 68.3, 143.11ff), Bell's hypothesis is a little awkward. Further discussion in Williams (1986), pp. 36–7.

55 apol. sec. 59, Opitz 139.5–6.

56 h.e. I.15, 32.20ff.

57 PG 18, 453–66.

58 Devos (1965), pp. 162–77.

59 Ibid. p. 164.

60 Telfer (1949), pp. 122–3 summarizes the translator's remarks on this, which do not appear in the ms from which the PG text is printed.

61 Telfer (1949); for a fuller discussion of Telfer's case, see Williams (1986).

62 Thus Telfer, art. cit. p. 123, alluding to Gregory the Great's letter to Eulogius of Alexandria, PL 77, 892–5.

63 Even Telfer admits (art. cit. p. 126) that 'we cannot pretend to

recover actual words or phrases of the Jubilee Book' in the work of the Latin versionist. Certainly there are no plausible verbal parallels between the Verona narrative fragment and the Latin *passio*, even in passages supposedly covering the same ground.

64 The reference to *apices* and *litterae*, PG 18, 455BC (*ubique dirigens apices*, and *Petrus . . . Meletianos ab ecclesia per litteras segregavit*), could be so taken; only one letter from Peter survives in the Verona Codex. Cf. the references to exhortatory letters to confessors, written from exile, PG 18, 459A.

65 Opitz, U.14, 19.11ff.

66 E.g. ad ep. Aeg. 22, 23, PG 25. 589A–592D, apol. sec. 59, Opitz 139.18ff.

67 haer. 68.6, 145.27–146.21.

68 haer. 68.4, 144.1–5.

69 Boularand (1972), p. 25, and Frend (1974), p. 29.

70 Canon 19, Mansi 2, 675–7.

71 Eusebius, h.e. VII.7–9, 642.12–648.13.

72 Batiffol (1898), p. 269.

73 Canons 8 (Mansi 672) and 19 (677); Socrates h.e. I.9, PG 67, 77Dff. If the Egyptian elements in the Verona collection were originally sent from Alexandria to North Africa, as Telfer (1943) convincingly argues, we should *not* expect it to include any hint that Alexandria had ever wavered on the question of schismatic baptism. A Donatist would have been delighted to discover an ally in Peter of Alexandria.

74 Compiler of a collection of synodical decrees that probably appeared in the 370s. See Batiffol (1898) on Sozomen's relation to Sabinus.

75 E.g. h.e. I.8, PG 67, 65B–68A, II.17, 220B–221A, criticizing his manifest bias against the Nicene party, and his failure to record the violent behaviour of the Arians.

76 Batiffol (1901) supposes the 'Athanasian' collection to be a riposte to Sabinus. But if the core of this collection does indeed belong in Athanasius' lifetime, the relationship with Sabinus (if any) must run the other way, as suggested in the text.

77 A cleric would normally be identified as such in any official document: the Verona text has only *Arius quidam*.

78 Cf. n.64, supra on the possibility of further letters of Peter in the original collection.

79 Opitz, U.4, 7.15 (*heteros Areios*); 6, 13.22; 14, 29.25. The name is a common Egyptian one: Reymond and Barns (1973), p. 7, suggest that the *praeses* Arrianus was originally Areios, but had 'improved' his name in accordance with his rise in social standing.

80 Theophanes, chronographia, PG 108, 77B; Cassiodorus, historia tripartita, I.12, PL 69, 902A.

81 Supra, n.64 on Peter's letters to those in prison in Egypt. He is described as writing to them throughout the period of his absence, which suggests that there may have been letters to the four bishops.

82 Mönnich (1950), Boularand (1972), Frend (1974), Simonetti (1975) and Kopecek (1982), in addition to Telfer, assume the truth of Sozomen's story, and Mönnich and Kopecek build further hypotheses upon the assumption. Marrou (1973), p. 537, n.8 and Barnes (1981), pp. 202 and 374, n.117, are sceptical.

83 Supra, n.14; Boularand (1972), p. 17, takes Achillas to be the former head of the catechetical school, whose praises are sung by Eusebius (h.e. VII.32.30, 730.3–7), and, to explain Achillas' leniency towards one who (Boularand believes) already had a schismatic record, he adds the somewhat sinister remark that 'les intellectuels ont entre eux de secrètes affinités'!

84 h.e. I.2, 6.14–18.

85 h.e. I.3, 6.8–10.

86 adversus Valentinianos 4, CSEL 47, 180.25–6.

87 Epiphanius, haer. 67, 132.12–140.16; this lays heavy emphasis on Hieracas' debt to Origen.

88 Ibid. 67.3, 135.9–136.6, 67.7, 139.3–30.

89 Opitz, U.6, 13.1.

90 haer. 67.1, 133.1–9, 67.3, 136.9–11.

91 Frend (1974), pp. 22 and 28–30, rather overstates the gulf between Peter's 'Alexandrian orthodoxy' and Melitius' Coptic rigorism and biblicism. Hernández (1984), pp. 156–7, goes far beyond the evidence.

92 Lewis (1983) has some useful material on knowledge of Greek among the lower classes (p. 82) and intermarriage between urban Greek speakers and their Coptic neighbours (p. 62), though he also notes (p. 191) the need for interpreters in the law courts.

93 haer. 67.3, 135.23–136.6.

94 As Hieracas evidently was: haer. 67.1, passim, for his stress on asceticism. Cf. infra, I.C.

95 PG 10, 1566C, Kettler, p. 161, 6–7; the *papa* may give permission to a bishop to officiate in another diocese during an interregnum; but Melitius has neither assured himself that the bishops in question are dead, nor consulted Peter.

96 Telfer (1952, 1955).

97 Eusebius, h.e. VII.7.4, 644.7.

98 Above, n.41.

99 Eusebius, h.e. VII.11.3, 654.12, 8.20, 674.14–15 (*tois kat Alexandreian sumpresbuterois*). The term survived as a formal address in episcopal

letters to clergy, but was felt to need elucidation by the end of the fourth century; see the PGL entry for *sumpresbuteros*, 1290A.

100 Telfer (1952); Kemp (1955) qualifies Telfer's speculative conclusions considerably, but agrees that presbyteral succession prevailed up to the early fourth century.

101 h.e. II.16.1, 140.21 (*ekklēsias*), V.9, 450.9 (. . . *tōn kat'Alexandreian ekklēsiōn*), V.22, 486.22–3 (. . . *tōn kat'Alexandreian paroikiōn*), VI.35, 590.11–12 (*ekklēsiōn*), and perhaps VII.32.32, 730.12–13 (*ekklēsiōn;* cf. *tōn ep'Alexandreias*, 730.8–9, which could refer to people or to churches).

102 Philo, Fl. 55: 'five quarters named after the first letters of the alphabet'.

103 The city was quartered by two intersecting colonnaded roads; the fifth district may have been the Pharos island. See Schubart (RAC) 271–2, as well as Leclercq (DACL), Hardy (1952), pp. 3–10, and Pearson in Pearson and Goehring (1986), pp. 145–8, 157–9.

104 haer. 68.4, 144.6–9, 69.2, 153.14–26. See Leclercq (DACL) 1107–18, for a fuller, though in some respects questionable, treatment of the Alexandrian churches.

105 Formerly the temple of Augustus (cf. Athanasius, hist. Ar. 74, Opitz 224. 6–8), its conversion was apparently begun under the Arian bishop Gregory (with imperial subsidies, apol. ad Const. 18, PG 617D–620A); see Epiphanius, haer. 6.9.2, 153.16–23.

106 PG 18, 461 CD. Leclercq (DACL), 1111–1112 and 1117–1118, appears to distinguish the church from the *memoria* of Mark's martyrdom, but this must be simply an ambiguity in presentation. De Zogheb's map, reproduced by Leclercq (1099–1100), compounds confusion by locating an 'Église de S. Marc' near the centre of the city: whatever this is, it is not the ancient shrine.

107 haer. 68.4, 144.5, 69.1, 152.21, 69.2, 153.26. The name 'Baucalis' is unusual (the Greek word can mean a wine-cooler): Philostorgius (h.e. I.4, 6.11–17), in what seems to be a very garbled passage, implies that the name of the church derives from the nickname of a presbyter, Alexander, 'second in rank' to Arius, who denounced him to the bishop. This sounds improbable; but the church might have got its name originally in some such way. It is far more likely, though, to have been a vintner's warehouse turned over to Christian use. Its identity with the church in the 'Boukolia' is not certain; but this latter name is only attested later, and it is an intelligible corruption from 'Baucalis' (*ekklēsia tēs Baukaleōs* to *ekklēsia tēs Boukolias*) – a more familiar word replacing an odd one. Pearson in Pearson and Goehring (1986), p. 153, however, argues for 'Boukolos' or 'Boukolia' as earlier,

on the evidence of the (originally early fifth-century?) *Acts of Mark.* See also Calderini (1935), p. 105.

108 PG 18, 464B.

109 hist. Ar. 10, Opitz 188.24.

110 By the late medieval Arab historian, al-Maqrizi, *Historia Coptorum Christianorum in Aegypto Arabica,* tr. Wetzer (1828), pp. 40/41.

111 Festal Index XLII, PG 26, 1359C; the Mendidion church was, as this passage indicates, known by the name of 'Athanasius' after his death.

112 Implied by apol. ad Const. 14–15, PG 25, 612B–613A.

113 Athanasius, apol. ad Const. 15, PG 25, 613B.

114 historia acephala, IV, PG 26, 1443D, Festal Index X (PG 26, 1353D), XXVIII (PG 26, 1356D).

115 Leclercq (DACL), 1111.

116 Cf. PG 18, 462C: *Petrus initium apostolorum, Petrus finis martyrum episcoporum Alexandriae.*

117 Thus the *passio* of Peter, PG 18, 461CD and 462C.

118 Meinardus (1970), pp. 351–4, summarizes later Coptic traditions, but is agnostic as to precise historical origins. If Eusebius' account of Mark in Alexandria (h.e. II.16.1, 140.20–2) derives, as the context might imply, from Clement, the tradition is at least as old as the second century; cf. Morton Smith (1973), pp. 83, 2279–81.

119 h.e. II.24, 174.18–20.

120 Possibly the Serapion mentioned by Philip of Side as a head of the catechetical school; Philip's list of Alexandrian scholarchs survives only in a somewhat inaccessible fragment; see Radford (1908), pp. 1–2, n.1, for details.

121 Eusebius, h.e. VII.32.30, 730.4; and Philip of Side, in the fragment referred to in n.120.

122 Barns and Chadwick (1973), p. 446.

123 BS X, 574–7, gives details of this; cf. AS Nov. II.1, pp. 254–64.

124 Barns and Chadwick, art. cit. p. 446, n.2.

125 We have noted Hieracas' use of the *Ascension of Isaiah.* If Morton Smith's Mar Saba ms of Clement is authentic (Morton Smith, 1973), we have further evidence of the use of extracanonical works. On gnosticism in Alexandria in general, see Bauer (1972), pp. 44–53 – with caution – as well as Morton Smith, and Pearson, Klijn and van den Broek in Pearson and Goehring (1986).

126 Bauer, op. cit. pp. 53ff; cf. Trigg (1983), pp. 130–1.

127 As does the ordination of bishops for the churches outside Alexandria; see Telfer (1952), pp. 1–3, Bauer (1972), pp. 53–4.

128 h.e. I.5, PG 67, 41A.

129 Opitz, U.17, 33.1–5.

130 Opitz, U.14, 20.2–5.

131 Carponas and Sarmatas: Epiphanius, haer. 69.2, 154.1, Opitz, U.4b, 7.14–15, U.6, 13.22, U.14, 29.25.

132 Opitz, U.4b, 7.14, U.6, 13.21, U.14, 19.11, 25.15, 28.25, 29.24.

133 h.e. VII.32.30, 730.2–7. This identification is maintained by Radford (1908), p. 1, n.1 and Barnes (1981), p. 202, who rightly points out that if Eusebius' Achillas was the Achillas who briefly succeeded Peter as bishop, we should expect Eusebius to record the fact.

134 Opitz, U.4b, 10–11; there are eighteen presbyteral signatures from Alexandria.

135 Opitz, U.14, 19.11–20.2.

136 haer. 69.2, 154.4–10.

137 apol. sec. 74, Opitz 153.34ff, 76, 156.6ff.

138 See Telfer (1958), p. 232. Colluthus' seniority is suggested by the place of his name at the head of the list of signatories to Opitz, U.4b. Seeck (1896), p. 323, argued that Colluthus must have been consecrated as a bishop by Melitius; but Athanasius' account in apol. sec. rather suggests that he never underwent any kind of episcopal ordination. And if Melitius *had* consecrated Colluthus, we might expect some explicit record of this from Athanasius. The Melitians were quite happy, as apol. sec. makes clear, to take up the cause of any stray 'Colluthians' they might find, but no historian or controversialist of the period suggests a real link.

Seeck also (pp. 329–30) proposed that Colluthus had been a Melitian rival to Arius and Alexander in the election of 312 or 313, thus explaining the later hostility of Colluthus to Arius. Once again, solid evidence is entirely lacking. Feidas (1973) – the only extended study of Colluthus and his party yet published – follows Seeck in envisaging a Melitian Colluthus, but repudiates the idea of a purely personal (rather than theological) cause for Colluthus' opposition to Arius: he argues that Colluthus must be the real inspiration behind Alexander's theological polemic against the heresiarch. Alexander, initially sympathetic to Arius, is finally persuaded by Colluthus' arguments – although, by the time this has happened, Colluthus is already in schism (pp. 49–89). This is ingenious but not very plausible: Arius does, after all (as in U.1), plainly assert that he objects to the *bishop's* theology, and does not attribute this theology to any particular malign influence.

139 Telfer (1955), p. 232, n.29: 'Colluthus may have seized Alexandrian Church funds for the support of his men.'

140 Infra, I.B.1.
141 Athanasius, apol. sec. 76, Opitz 156.6–8.
142 These take us from the beginning of the controversy to about 333.

B THE NICENE CRISIS: DOCUMENTS AND DATING

1 Opitz (1934); his conclusions are defended by Schneemelcher (1954) against the attacks of Telfer (1946).
2 de syn. 17, Opitz 244–5.
3 Much unnecessary confusion has arisen over this: Schwartz (1905:2), pp. 131–2, notes the absence of a fully formal address as to a colleague (*sulleitourgos*), and argues that the addressee is a presbyter. Opitz in his edition accepts that Alexander was not yet a bishop, but assumes that the letter must have been sent to a diocesan, and proposes Alexander of Thessalonica. But there is no need for this: forms of ecclesiastical address need not have been so uniform at this date; and all our evidence points to Alexander becoming bishop of Byzantium well before 320 (see e.g. DHGE 2.184ff).
4 There are several plural forms in the letter (e.g. *agapētoi* at 21.7, etc.), and it was probably designed as a circular for a number of potentially sympathetic bishops, perhaps in the province of Thessaly, and in some parts of Asia. Cf. n.57, below.
5 Opitz U.17, 32–5.
6 VC 2.63, 73.17–25. On Ossius' travels, see de Clercq (1954), pp. 201ff.
7 Barnes (1981), p. 212, summarizes the probable reasons for this royal progress, and notes (p. 378, n.24) that evidence from coinage at Antioch suggests that Constantine got at least this far. The journey is unlikely to have taken less than three weeks, and was probably a good deal slower. The emperor will not have reached Antioch much before the winter solstice.
8 VC 2.72, 78.21–4 (= Opitz U.17, 35.22–5).
9 See Barnes (1981), p. 212, referring to Cod. Theod. 1.15.1 as establishing Constantine's presence in Nicomedia in February.
10 VC 1.51, 42.6–14.
11 Cod. Theod. 16.2.5 is a Constantinian enactment presupposing Licinius' attempts to compel soldiers and civil servants to sacrifice. It has commonly been dated (following the mss) in May 323, but Barnes (1981), pp. 718, 321–3 (n.87), gives sound reasons for putting it in December.

12 See Honigmann (1953), pp. 15 and 20ff, on the execution of the bishop of Amasea, possibly on the grounds of treasonable (pro-Constantinian) intrigue with Armenia. It is likely that Licinius' main batch of anti-Christian enactments was prompted by Constantine's violation of his borders in spring/summer 323. It is at this point that assemblies of Christians – potential or actual fifth columnists – become a *concrete* political threat (Boularand (1972) p. 24). Note that Barnes (1981), p. 376, n.154, suggests that the ban on episcopal meetings may be as early as 320. This is possible, but I see more pressing reasons for such a ban at the later date proposed. And the suggestion of Calderone (1962) that the ban was *lifted* in 323 lacks any solid support.

13 See above, L.A.3.

14 Opitz, U.14, 19.11–20.5.

15 Opitz, U.10, 18.4–5.

16 Opitz, U.14, 19.11–20.1.

17 Ibid. 20.1–5.

18 Opitz (1934), p. 149; Barnes (1981), p. 205 agrees. Simonetti (1975), p. 35, n.16, does not.

19 Opitz, U.4b, 8.13.

20 Opitz, U.14, 25.15–17.

21 Opitz, U.4b, 11–13.

22 The parallels are first itemized by Newman (1842, vol. 2), p. 5, in the course of his admirable note on the probably Athanasian authorship of the *henos sōmatos*. See also Bardy (1926), pp. 528–9.

23 Especially con. Ar. I.5, PG 26, 21A–C, de decr. 6, Opitz, 5.23–30, ad ep. Aeg. 12, PG 25, 564B–565C.

24 Thus Bardy (1926), pp. 530–1, who is in no doubt that *henos sōmatos* should be dated later than *hē philarchos*.

25 The use of the Thalia in de syn. 15 is evidently meant to embarrass non-Nicenes, who would not necessarily wish to be identifed with the extreme views of Arius himself. See Williams in Gregg (1985), pp. 12–16, and cf. below, pp. 63–5.

26 Telfer (1936), p. 63

27 Opitz, U.6, 13.21–3. Athanasius' text of the letter in de syn. 16 lacks this list.

28 Cf. Opitz, U.4a, 6.9. He is evidently the leader of Arius' supporters in the Mareotis, but does not appear in the lists of excommunicates in U.4b and U.14.

29 Note that the introductory greeting in U.6 (12.1–2) mentions only 'presbyters and deacons' as sending the letter, which further puts into question the authenticity of the episcopal signatures.

30 See Athanasius, apol. sec. 24 (Opitz 105.5–25).

31 As Constantine's letter (Opitz, U.17, 33.2–5) might suggest.
32 Opitz, U.14, 20.17–19, 29.24–6.
33 Ibid. 20.20.
34 Ibid. 20.3–4, 17–18.
35 Ibid. 25.16.
36 Opitz, U.1, 2.4–5.
37 Opitz, U.14, 20.20–5.
38 h.e. I.15, 34.22–35.2.
39 See above, I.A, n.133.
40 h.e. VII.32, 30, 730.3–7.
41 To do with the impossibility of fitting the whole sequence of events leading up to Nicaea within a mere seven months or so.
42 Opitz, U.1, 2.5.
43 The bishops whom Arius lists as condemned by Alexander include some from Cilicia; Alexander, in writing *hē philarchos*, was no doubt aware that the Syro-Palestinians he denounces had allies further north.
44 Opitz, U.2, is probably a fragment of his reply.
45 de syn. 18, Opitz 245.21ff.
46 Philostorgius, h.e. II.14, 25.15.
47 h.e. I.15, 34.20–2. Athanasius does not mention this synod, but Sozomen, throughout I.15, relies on the Arian Sabinus' collection of synodical documents.
48 Opitz, U.4b, 7.5.
49 Ibid. 7.13.
50 The case of Ischyras, in the Mareotis, was to become celebrated; see Athanasius, apol. sec. 76, Opitz 156.4ff.
51 Ibid. 156.6–8.
52 Supra, pp. 45–7, 50–5; how far did the 'outbreak of heresy' result from pressure applied by the bishop, provoking an extreme reaction?
53 Cf. Athanasius' remarks in ad ep. Aeg. 22, PG 25, 589B.
54 Possibly, but not all that probably; there is no hard evidence that Arius sought outside help before leaving Alexandria, and Alexander's condemnation of the foreign bishops need not have been a synodical decree.
55 As listed in Opitz U.4b, 6, and 14. Two names are lacking in 14; Loeschke (1910) discusses the problems surrounding the relation between the list in 6b and that in 14, and offers a plausible solution, though his overall argument for the prior date of U.6 is inconclusive.
56 See Boularand (1972), p. 31, for a rather stronger statement of the likelihood of collaboration between bishop and civil authority.
57 h.e. I.4.25.10–11; cf. n.4 above on the probability of *hē philarchos* being a circular.

58 The precedent of Christian appeal to the secular authorities had been set in the case of Paul of Samosata; see Eusebius, h.e. VII.30.19, 714.3ff.

59 Athanasius of Nazarba may well have seen a copy of *hē philarchos* before writing, Opitz, U.11; see below, p. 59.

60 Opitz, U.4b, 8.13.

61 29.31.

62 Possibly – as Athanasius hints in de syn. 18 (Opitz 245.29–31) – the propaganda campaign being waged by Asterius had proved somewhat counter-productive.

63 So Opitz, U.8, 15.2–5, suggests.

64 Barnes (1981), p. 214, draws attention to the importance of Licinius' execution in late 324 or early 325. Constantine may well have wished to be back in Nicomedia as soon as possible in the political unsettlement surrounding this event. See also below, p. 67.

65 Above, p. 46.

66 Chadwick (1958) authoritatively argues the case for Ossius' presidency.

67 Opitz, U.18, 37.1–12 (Syr.), 2–14 (Gr.).

68 Opitz, U.18 (36–41), with Schwartz' retroversion into Greek.

69 Opitz, 40.6–7 (Syr.), 5–6 (Gr.).

70 Ancyra is mentioned in U.18.18 (Syr.), 17 (Gr.); a further Syriac fragment (U.20, 41–2) purports to be Constantine's notification of the change of plan. See further below, p. 67.

71 23.29–30.

72 E.g. 24.4–5.

73 4.4–10, cf. 5.9–10, 6.1–2.

74 An immediate response to Arius' initial request for ecclesiastical hospitality and support, for instance. But, since the text mentions neither Arius nor Alexander, it is impossible to locate with any precision – though, on balance, it is overwhelmingly likely to be pre-Nicene. It is certainly more strongly (or indiscreetly) worded than Eusebius' letter to the church at Caesarea.

75 22.9, cf. 21.10.

76 U.11, 18.7–8.

77 23.29ff.

78 U.12, 19.3–5.

79 14.5 and 7.19f, 14.14f and 7.23, 15.3 and 7.20 (though note also a parallel with *hē philarchos*, 21.8–9). *Henos sōmatos* insists that Arius teaches that the Son is *heis . . . tōn poiēmatōn;* Eusebius' letter (14.10–15.2) vehemently insists that Arius explicitly denies this, despite what 'your [Alexander's] letter' claims.

80 4a invites the subscriptions of the local clergy to a letter addressed

to Alexander's *sulleitourgoi;* this can hardly be other than *henos sōmatos*, with its long list of signatures from the city and the Mareotic district.

81 27.5.

82 In a letter to Constantius, CSEL 65, 91.24–92.2.

83 Or the *ante ordinationem Athanasii* could be taken as qualifying what follows (the excommunication of the Arians) rather than dating the letter or letters.

84 The minimum age of thirty for presbyteral ordination is attested by Canon XI of Neocaesarea (Mansi 2, 542D). Canon XIV of the Quinisext Council of 692 provides that a deacon should be twenty-five at ordination, but there is no canonical evidence for earlier practice. On the whole question, see Patsavos (1973), pp. 225–6.

85 Stead (1973) and Barnes (1981) both argue strongly for Eusebius' fundamental accord with Arius; Luibheíd (1978) makes a spirited case on the other side, but is not finally persuasive in the light of Eusebius' extensive practical involvement in the pre-Nicene phase of the controversy, and the incontrovertible fact that he continues to be associated with the Lucianists in post-Nicene intrigues.

86 Mansi 2, 673D–676B.

87 Such persons should not be *dektoi* (676B); the word is of vague application, but can imply official recognition.

88 Beryllus by Origen (h.e. VI.33, 588.4–24), Paul of Samosata by Malchion (h.e. VII.29, 704.10–18).

89 E.g. h.e. VII.20, 674.15 (Dionysius of Alexandria writes to his *sumpresbuteroi* in the city); cf. VII.11, 654.12, and perhaps VII.7, 642.19, both quotations from Dionysius. As PGL testifies, the word *sumpresbuteros* survives in the post-Nicene period as an address from bishops to clergy, influenced, no doubt, by 1 Pet. 5:1, but is evidently a rather rare archaism.

90 Cf. n.62 above.

91 It must remain uncertain whether Arius himself so entitled the work; Athanasius' wording in de syn. 15, saying that Arius wrote *hōs en Thalia(i)*, 'as if in a "song for a dinner party"', might lead us to think that the title is Athanasius' invention; Socrates, h.e. I.9 (PG 67, 84B) assumes that the title is from Arius, but he is unlikely to have had sources for this other than the text of Athanasius.

92 Recent discussions include Stead (1978), Kannengiesser (1982), (1984) and in Gregg (1985), Williams in Gregg (1985) and Hall in Gregg (1985).

93 de syn. 15, Opitz 242.1–7.

94 Going back to Newman (1842), and reproduced by Robertson (1892).

95 Telfer (1936).

96 Kannengiesser (1971).

97 It involves an awkward disjunction between the two participles, one referring back to the 'casting out' referred to in the preceding sentence, one going with the phrase *para tōn peri Eusebion*.

98 See Müller's *Lexicon Athanasianum*, 1084; and cf. Telfer (1936) and Kannengiesser (1971), p. 347, on the sense of *para*.

99 See, for example, the opening of Athanasius' *in illud omnia*, PG 25, 209A, for an abrupt introduction of 'Eusebius', with no further identification – though it is pretty certain that this is the bishop of Nicomedia.

100 See Müller's *Lexicon*, 1169–70.

101 Philostorgius, h.e. II.14, 25.10–15. Those named are Eusebius, Maris, Theognis, Leontius (later bishop of Antioch), Antony of Tarsus, Menophantus (of Ephesus), Numenius, Eudoxius, Alexander and Asterius. Of Numenius, Eudoxius and Alexander, nothing further is known.

102 Lorenz (1978), p. 52, does not, but gives little firm argumentation for this.

103 II.3, 14.1–9.

104 Leontius and Antony, who are listed among Lucian's pupils, were also teachers and patrons of Aetius, according to Philostorgius, h.e. III.15, 46.1–12; 16, 47.25–48.1.

105 con. Ar. I.6, PG 26, 24B.

106 de syn. 15, Opitz 242.11ff; see below, II.A, pp. 101–3 for a full translation of the text as quoted here.

107 Ibid. 19, and 243.6–8.

108 Ibid. 242.21–3.

109 If this is the provenance of U.15, as suggested above, we have only a very incomplete account of what Arius is being condemned for.

110 Opitz, U.8, 16.6–7: the Son's generation is incomprehensible not only to human but to superhuman understanding.

111 Ibid. 16.6.

112 Ibid. 16.9–10.

113 A theme prominent in the creed ascribed to Lucian of Antioch (de syn. 23, Opitz 249, 11ff) and in Asterius (as quoted, for instance, in Philostorgius, h.e. II.15, 25.26–7).

114 ad ep. Aeg. 7, PG 25, 553A; written about 356.

115 Ibid. 5, 548C.

116 Kannengiesser (1982), (1984), and in Gregg (1985).

117 (1982), p. 16, (1984), pp. 149–50, (1985), pp. 70–5.

118 (1982), p. 16, (1984), p. 151; (1985), p. 74 withdraws this suggestion. For detailed criticism of this whole case, see Kopecek (1982), pp. 53–7 and Williams in Gregg (1985), pp. 2–9.

119 (1982), p. 16, (1985), p. 74.

120 It can hardly have been written in Alexandria, given that *hē philarchos* both appears ignorant of it, and strongly suggests that Arius has by now left the city.

121 Cf. above, p. 58.

122 Barnes (1981), p. 214.

123 Theodoret, h.e. I.7, 32.3ff seems to imply this; Lorenz in TRE 10, p. 544, considers this no more than a local Antiochene tradition, but it cannot be ruled out as intrinsically implausible. Cf. Spanneut (DHGE) 14–15, who gives a more positive evaluation of the tradition.

124 E.g. de decr. 3, Opitz 3.2–3, de syn. 43, Opitz 268.25.

125 ep ad Afros 2, PG 26, 1032B.

126 See especially Honigmann (1939), pp. 65–76.

127 Even with the minimum figure allowed by Honigmann, we can allow at least some of those listed by Philostorgius as sympathetic to Arius. See n.129 below.

128 Vita Const. III.8, 85.12–14; though Cf. Honigmann (1939), pp. 67–8. I am unconvinced by the argument here advanced: although Socrates knows a text of Eusebius' *Vita* mentioning 'more than 300', this seems more likely to be an attempt to bring Eusebius into line with Athanasius than to be an original reading.

129 h.e. I.8, 9.10–21.

130 Basil of Amasea; see Honigmann (1953) and cf. n.12 above. A pro-Nicene Basil from Armenia or Pontus is mentioned by Athanasius, ad ep. Aeg. 8, PG 25, 557A.

131 Philostorgius' Amphion of 'Sidon' is almost certainly the Amphion of Opitz, U.18, 36.4 (Syr.), 4 (Gr.); and this is probably Amphion of Epiphania in Cilicia – an opponent of Arianism (Athanasius, ad ep. Aeg. 8, PG 25, 557A). 'Tarkondimatus of Aegae' appears in the same list of subscriptions to the Antiochene synod (Opitz, U.18, 36.10 (Syr.), 36.9 (Gr.)).

132 Of the three Cappadocian bishops, Leontius, Longianus and Eulalius, Listed without their sees, the first two were in later years firm supporters of Nicaea: Leontius of Cappadocian Caesarea and Longianus, apparently bishop of Neocaesarea in Pontus, are both mentioned as allies by Athanasius in ad ep. Aeg. (see reference in preceding note), as is yet another of Philostorgius' names, Meletius of Sebastopolis in Pontus. Eulalius cannot be identified with complete certainty, though some of the Nicene lists have one or more bishops of this name from Asia Minor. Gwatkin (1900), p. 34, n.4, observes with commendable tact that 'there must be some mistake, deliberate or otherwise' in Philostorgius.

133 Menophantus of Ephesus and Theodotus of Laodicea are two obvious cases in point. Menophantus, another Lucianist (Philostorgius, h.e.

II.14, 25.14) is several times mentioned by Athanasius and Hilary as an uncompromising anti-Nicene.

134   I.20, 41.15–16.

135   See Luibheíd (1982) for a helpful survey, esp. pp. 67–88.

136   Theodoret, h.e. I.8, 34.4–11.

137   Cf. de decr. 3, Opitz 3.1–6, for an account of the Eusebians' defence, and its repudiation. Stead (1973) argues for Eusebius of Caesarea as the party concerned, but it is difficult to square this with the general assumption by later historians (not overly sympathetic to Eusebius Pamphilus) that the bishop of Nicomedia was the prime mover on Arius' behalf before, during, and after the council.

138   h.e. I.7, 33.5–10. This may be a recollection of the same event described by Eustathius, but it sounds like a last-ditch Eusebian attempt to find a compromise.

139   h.e. I.8, PG 67, 68C–69A.

140   Arius (Opitz, U.6, 12.11, 13.18) makes it plain that his objection to the term rests partly on its possible materialist resonances: a *homoousios* substance could be one in which two distinct substances combined to constitute a third. See below III.c, and Williams (1983), pp. 64–5.

141   See preceding n. for references.

142   Opitz, 244.17.

143   de fide III.15.125, CSEL 78, 151.15–21.

144   p. 42.

145   5–6, PG 26, 1036D–1040C.

146   See Wiles (1967), p. 36, for a blunt statement of Arius' 'responsibility' for the presence of the *homoousios* in the creed.

147   Socrates, h.e. I.9 (PG 67, 77D = Opitz, U.23, 48.9) implicitly corrects I.8, PG 67, 68C, where the Libyans and the Bithynians are lumped together.

148   h.e. I.7, 8.1–9.2.

149   III.6–15, 83.18–89.10.

150   Opitz, U.22, 42–7.

151   Ibid. 43.9–25.

152   ep. ad. Afr. 5, PG 26, 1037BC, de decr. 19–20, Opitz 15–17.

153   Belief that the Son truly 'exists' and 'subsists' (*einai kai huparchein*, Opitz, U.22, 43.15–16) falls short of belief in the Son's necessary divine existence; cf. the ambiguities of 46.18–21.

154   Their identity is unknown; but Ossius and Eustathius are likely to have had some hand in this task. If Eustathius had been involved, this would certainly explain the venomous feelings towards him of the dissidents in the years following the council.

155   Opitz, U.22, 44.1–7.

156   Ibid. 45.21–5.

157 Opitz, U.23, 47–51.
158 Ibid. 48.8–9.
159 Not explicitly mentioned in the synodical letter; but he writes later alongside Arius, as if sharing his exile.
160 I.9, 10.35–11.16.
161 h.e. I.8, PG 67, 69A.
162 h.e. I.21, 42.15–18 – a piece of Arian face-saving tradition from Sabinus?
163 h.e. I.8, 37.19–38.1.
164 Ibid. I.19, 65.22–66.18; the implied chronology is not possible.
165 h.e. I.9, 10.5–6.
166 Ibid. II.1, 12.22–7; there is some uncertainty as to whether the exile was to Gaul or Galatia, according to Nicetas' epitome (ibid. 26), but Galatia seems improbably close to home for the bishops.
167 Athanasius can still use *homoia ousia* in con. Ar. I.21 (PG 26, 56A); it has not become a party slogan by this date.
168 apol. sec. 7, Opitz 93, 16–18.
169 Opitz, U.27, 58–62.
170 Ibid. 62.5.
171 Ibid. 61.11–13.
172 Ibid. 62.1–7; Constantine seems to imply that these are heretics, but Barnes (1981), p. 226, assumes that they are schismatics.
173 *Hupedexanto* is an ambiguous word, which may mean no more than 'welcomed them'; but sacramental communion is suggested by the seriousness with which the bishops' actions were taken.
174 Opitz, U.31, 65–6.
175 Perhaps, as with the bishops suspended at Antioch early in 325, there was some provision for a review of their sentence at a future synod – in this case probably a local one (Bithynia, or Bithynia with a neighbouring province; cf. n.243, below).
176 Vita Const. III.23, 94.10–17.
177 The *Egyptian* episcopate overall seems to have been solidly Nicene. If 'Egyptian' is taken strictly here, Barnes' suggestion should be accepted.
178 Mansi, 2, 669CD.
179 Ibid. 669BC.
180 Opitz, U.27, 60.11–13.
181 h.e. II.1, 12.15, 23ff.
182 A notable exception is Hernandez (1984), pp. 166–7.
183 Opitz, U.31, 65.15–16.
184 U.31, 65–66. Gelasius' version is rather fuller than the others.
185 Ibid. 65.8–9.
186 Barnes (1981), p. 229, interprets the letter as meaning that they

accept Nicaea; but in fact, the text is studiedly unclear on just this point.

187 An idea first proposed by Seeck (1896), accepted by Schwartz (1911) and Opitz (cf. his (1934) heading for U.31). Lorenz (1979) reviews the debate, cautiously accepting the likelihood of some synodical action in 327 leading to a petition for Arius' recall from exile, but involving no repudiation of the creed of Nicaea and no conciliar judgment on Arius' orthodoxy.

188 Barnes (1978 and 1981) argues for a 'Council of Nicomedia', along the lines indicated by Philostorgius, h.e. II.7, 18.21–19.10.

189 h.e. I.14, PG 67, 109B–112A.

190 h.e. II.16, 70.20–6.

191 Socrates, h.e. I.23, PG 67, 144A, Sozomen, h.e. II, 18–19, 74.19.

192 Chadwick (1948), Barnes (1978).

193 Asclepius of Gaza (Chadwick, 1948, pp. 31–2), and perhaps Euphration of Balanaeae, Cyrus of Beroea and others at the same time (Barnes (1981), p. 228).

194 Opitz, U.29.

195 h.e. I.11, PL 21, 482C–184C (= X.12, 976.23–977.19).

196 See above, p. 54 on Eusebius of Nicomedia's imperial links. Constantia died in imperial favour, as seems to be indicated by Constantine's renaming of Gaza as Constantia in her memory (Vita Const. IV.38, 135.2–5); this event is hard to date with certainty, but Eusebius implies that it was shortly before the Council of Tyre. We have no other evidence that would help in dating Constantia's death, so that Rufinus' story does not help in dating Arius' recall.

197 Opitz, U.32, 66. Constantine seems to have thought that Arius and Euzoius had actually accepted Nicaea.

198 h.e. II.7, 18.21–19.1. Lorenz (1979), p. 31, n.66, considers this an error by the epitomist.

199 Socrates h.e. I.33, PG 67, 165A; this may have been Opitz' U.30, the creed submitted to Constantine some years earlier.

200 Above, n.128; the parallel is unlikely to be coincidence (Honigmann, (1939), p. 68, proposes that the current reading of *Eusebius*' text is contaminated from the source used by Philostorgius) especially since few if any of the great synods of the fourth century had so large an attendance. Cf. Athanasius' remarks on the numbers attending synods, in de syn. 43, Opitz 268.22ff.

201 This would then be the second regular canonical synod of the Bithynian province for that year.

202 Following the Festal Index, PG 26, 1351B.

203 Sozomen, h.e. II.17, 72.17–25 (again probably from Sabinus); Philostorgius, h.e. II.11, 22.9–23.10, 23.32–9. Allowing as usual for Philo-

storgius' bias and lack of critical judgment, there is certainly some truth in the tradition of a vocal resistance to Athanasius' election. For Athanasius' own version, see apol. sec. 6, Opitz 92.17–29.

204 Socrates, h.e. I.27, PG 67, 152B; Sozomen, h.e. II.18, 74.9–14.

205 Sozomen, h.e. II.22, 79.5–15: Melitians as well as Arius' supporters are envisaged in the emperor's letter.

206 Athanasius, apol. sec. 59, Opitz 139.15ff; this is a most difficult passage to interpret. As it stands, it reads as though Alexander died within five months of Nicaea, and thus has been used as evidence for the 'second session' of Nicaea (see e.g., Lorenz (1979), pp. 27–8); but since Athanasius makes it plain that the council in question both condemned the Arians and 'received' the Melitians, it can hardly be the council that *recalled* Arius and his allies. Telfer (1955), p. 234, assumes that the allusion is not to the death of Alexander but to his completion of the reconciliation of the Melitians. The simplest solution would be to translate so as to give the sense 'hardly five months separated Alexander's death from the renewal of Melitian activity'; but it must be admitted that this severely strains the Greek.

207 Sozomen, h.e. II.21, 77.6ff.

208 Ibid. II.22, 79.19–22; and cf. Epiphanius, haer. 68.6, 145.27–146.21.

209 Opitz, U.63, 29.5–6.

210 He was certainly there in the early 30s, by the sound of U.34. Socrates, h.e. I.27, PG 67, 152B, describes an unsuccessful visit to Alexandria which could be placed shortly after the rehabilitation of Arius by the synod of 328.

211 Athanasius, ad ep. Aeg. 19, PG 25, 584B.

212 Festal Index, PG 26, 1352B.

213 He was in the Thebaid, Melitius' home territory, in 329 or 330 (PG 26, 1352A); the dates given in Migne's published text are obviously confused, and are rightly amended in Robertson's translation.

214 Barnes (1981), p. 232.

215 Opitz, U.34, 70.18–19.

216 Opitz, U.70.30–71.6; and cf. 73.6ff.

217 Ibid. 70.31. He is clearly seeking to avoid the charge that his system deprives God of *logos;* implicit here is his characteristic distinction between God's 'proper' *logos* and the being who is *called logos.* Cf. below II.A, III.C, and Williams (1983), pp. 73–80.

218 Ibid. 72.2.

219 Ibid. 74.16ff.

220 He refers to Paterius as prefect of Egypt (ibid. 75.6); the only other reference to Paterius is in the heading for Athanasius' Festal Letter for 333 (PG 26, 1379C), where the name is written 'Paternus'.

221 Ibid. 69.26.

222 III.323ff; the quotation seems to derive from a Latin version older than the one we are familiar with.

223 Ibid. 71.23–8.

224 Ibid. 71.4–6 seems to presuppose Nicaea: Constantine rejects Arius' belief that the Son is an 'alien hypostasis' from the Father and insists on the unity of *ousia* between Father and Son. No reference is made to any other creed or conciliar enactment; which constitutes a weighty argument against the hypothesis of a single major post-Nicene synod which reversed Nicaea's decisions.

225 Ibid. 73.34–74.4.

226 Ibid. 74.16ff.

227 Ibid. 69.21–2.

228 Opitz, U.33.

229 h.e. I.28, PG 67, 160A; numbers were dramatically swelled by Athanasius' bringing forty-eight Egyptian bishops with him to support his defence (apol. sec. 78, Opitz 159.1–24). These do not seem to have been members of the council, strictly speaking.

230 Socrates, h.e. I.35, PG 67, 169C, Sozomen, h.e. II.25.87.2–7.

231 Socrates, h.e. I.33, PG 67, 164C–165A.

232 h.e. II.27.90.16ff.

233 de syn. 21, Opitz 247.22–248.17; apol. sec. 84 (Opitz 162.28–163.10), probably implies that the imperial letter or letters were forwarded.

234 Socrates, h.e. I.31–32, PG 67, 164AB, Sozomen, h.e. II.28, 91.3–4, Theodoret, h.e. I.30, 87.9ff, apol. sec. 86, Opitz 164.12, 165.5–9.

235 h.e. I.37, PG 67, 173BC.

236 Sozomen, h.e. II.29, 93.14–16; cf. Socrates h.e. I.37, PG 67, 173BC.

237 Socrates, h.e. I.37, PG 67, 173C.

238 Sozomen, h.e. II.33, 98.22–7.

239 Socrates, h.e. I.36, PG 67, 172C–173B.

240 Sozomen, h.e. II.33, 98.12–99.2.

241 Socrates, h.e. I.34, PG 67, 168B.

242 Socrates, h.e. I.36, PG 67, 173A, assumes that it was a continuation of the Tyre-Jerusalem synod, but this is most unlikely.

243 Canon XIV of Antioch, Mansi 2, 1309D (either the 'Dedication Council' of 341, or, as has been proposed, the pre-Nicene synod of 325) rules on the case of an accused bishop whose confrères in his own province cannot agree on a sentence. The metropolitan is empowered to call on bishops from the neighbouring province to help in reaching a decision.

244 Sozomen, h.e. II.29, 93.14–23.

245 Socrates, h.e. I.36, PG 67, 172C, Sozomen, h.e. II.33, 99.5–7.

246 Socrates, ibid. I.38, PG 67, 176C.

247 ad ep. Aeg. 18, PG 25, 580B–581A.

248 Socrates, loc. cit.

249 ad ep. Aeg. 19, PG 25, 581B, ad Serap. 2, Opitz 179.14.

250 Athanasius, ad ep. Aeg. 19, PG 25, 581BC, ad Serap. 3, ibid., 15–28, Socrates, h.e. I.38, PG 67, 177A. Rufinus, h.e. I.13–14, Pl 21, 485C–486A (= IX.13–14, 979.10–19), improves the story further by claiming that this took place as Arius was actually on his way to the church.

251 Kannengiesser (1983), pp. 375–397, gives sound reasons for preferring this date to the later one commonly assigned by previous scholars. This makes it substantially less likely that the whole story is fiction.

252 h.e. II.29, 94.13–17.

253 ad Serap. 4, ibid. 29–30.

254 And the remarks of the bishops at Antioch in 341 (de syn. 22, Opitz 248.29ff), while somewhat cool towards Arius, do not suggest any dramatic scandal attaching to his memory.

C CONCLUSION

1 Just as 'Lucianist' was an acceptable term; cf. Epiphanius on party names in Alexandria, haer. 69.2, 154.4–8, where it is implied that the faithful of different 'parishes' might use the name of their presbyter in this way. Athanasius, con. Ar. I.3, PG 26, 17AB, might suggest that the Arians were not uniformly reluctant to be called so in Alexandria in the early days of the crisis, but not even Athanasius can claim outright that this is how they style *themselves.*

2 con, Ar. 2, PG 26, 16B, with its reference to non-Nicenes 'calling Christians [i.e. Nicenes] after their teachers', indicates that Nicenes were probably called 'Athanasians' (and perhaps 'Eustathians' or 'Marcellans'?) by their opponents.

3 Athanasius, de syn. 22, Opitz 248.29–30.

4 See Williams in Gregg (1985), pp. 12–16.

5 Kannengiesser (1984), ch. 2, passim, especially pp. 119–120, 122–7, 181–6.

6 I Clement 42–4 is the earliest document to speak unequivocally of the present ministry as established by the apostles; the linking of this succession with specific single presidents ('monarchical' bishops) becomes standard only in the mid to late second century, when succession-lists are first produced. See von Campenhausen (1951) and (1969), pp. 156–77, and Molland (1954/1970). Irenaeus, adv. haer. III.2.2–4.3 (Harvey, vol. II, pp. 8–18) and IV.40.2–42.1 (ibid., pp. 236–8), offers a classical statement of the theology of succession; it is essential to note that continuity here is continuity in *teaching*, not

of office in a formal sense. *Successio* represents the important Greek term *diadochē* (see Nautin (1961), pp. 65–73, Javierre (1963), Abramowski (1976:2), Glucker (1978), pp. 121–58), already used for the succession of masters in a philosophical school. Gnostic thinkers may well have built on the idea in the later Platonic Academy of an esoteric succession of teachers parallel to but independent of institutional continuities (see Glucker (1978), pp. 296–315): the task of 'Catholic' apologetic is precisely to hold together institutional continuity with the personal transmission of charismatically inspired 'saving truth' – hence the difficulties discussed below.

7   He is committed to the idea of a visible church with tangible criteria of continuity (de princ. I. praef. 2, 8.20–8), and stresses the teaching responsibilities of the church's leaders (Hom. Lev. 6.6, 367.21–370.11, Hom. Num. 12.2, 99.29–101.9); see von Campenhausen (1969), pp. 250–1.

8   1, 9.22–10.14.

9   *Doctor* here may well refer to the office of presbyter; cf. e.g. Hom. Lev. 6.6 (n.7 above). On the teaching authority of the presbyter in Alexandria, see Marrou (1973), pp. 535–8, Hornschuh (1960), pp. 198–205, and cf. von Campenhausen (1969), pp. 249–50, on Origen's unwillingness to separate *principes* or *presbyteri* or *sacerdotes* from *doctores*. For a rather different view of the Alexandrian *didaskalos* as representing a continuous survival of the primitive ministry of the evangelist, as distinct from that of the ordained presbyter or bishop, see Tuilier (1982) – a very speculative case; it is far from clear that we can speak of a *diadochē* of teachers in the 'Alexandrian school' in any very strict or formal sense before the time of Origen – or even later. On this question, see Bardy (1937). Eusebius wishes to stress the interweaving lines of episcopal and 'school' succession at Alexandria in his history (Grant (1980), pp. 51–3), and thus assimilates the latter to the former more tidily than strict historical veracity would warrant.

10   (1969), pp. 251–64.

11   Ibid. p. 256.

12   Ignatius of Antioch's famous designation of himself as *theophoros* in the introductions to his letters is a reminder of this early fusion of personal charism and public office; see von Campenhausen (1969), pp. 104–5, and Flesseman-van Leer (1954), pp. 119–21.

13   See, e.g. Hanson (1962), ch. 4, esp. pp. 157–76, and Zizioulas (1985), ch. 5.

14   E.g. de unit. 5 (213–214), ep. 56.3 (650); von Campenhausen (1969), pp. 276–7.

15   See Theodoret, h.e. I.2, 6.14–15, on Arius' 'licensing' as an expositor of Scripture and cf. n.9, above.

16   Above, I.A, p. 42 and n.100.

17   This introduction (as it presumably is) to the *Thalia* is preserved by Athanasius, con. Ar. I.5, PG 26, 20C–21A. The first four words are a quotation from Titus 1.1.

18   See Williams in Gregg (1985), pp. 4–7, on some elements in the vocabulary of these lines. For discussion of the language of 'wisdom' in this context, see also Gregg and Groh (1981), pp. 163–4, and Schoedel (1975) for some suggestions about continuities in Alexandria between Jewish and Christian wisdom-traditions.

19   h.e. II.2, 13.6–10, 24–9.

20   See, e.g., Eusebius, h.e. VI.27, 570.10–13, VI.27, 580.16ff, etc.

21   At a synod of Egyptian bishops, according to Photius, bibl. cod. 118; the passage is reproduced in Nautin (1977), p. 103, n.12, and discussed, pp. 103–5. Photius implies that Demetrius' decision to refuse recognition to Origen as a presbyter was not supported by a majority.

22   A period during which, it should be remembered, communication between churches could be slow and irregular, and the overriding priority was still, for the most part, the preservation of a common front against residual gnosticism.

23   The debates about baptism in the middle of the century are a case in point; despite the differences between Rome, Africa, Egypt and Asia (Eusebius, h.e. VII.2–9, 636.18–648.19, gives some of the details), many of the churches involved do not seem to have broken communion, or not for any length of time – though not all shared the remarkable tolerance of Dionysius of Alexandria.

24   Eusebius, h.e. VII.30.19, 714.3ff, on the emperor's action in this matter, in response to an episcopal petition.

25   Arius, in the introduction to the *Thalia*, claims both.

26   Chs. 4 and 5 of Zizioulas (1985) are of great importance for understanding this theme, though his sharp separation of episcopal from teaching succession (p. 198, n.97) rests on a somewhat one-sided reading of the evidence.

27   On succession in the Platonic Academy, cf. the references in n.6 above. Peter Brown (1980) offers a similar typology of the different roles philosophers were expected to play in the late antique period, as either 'experts' or 'heroes'. 'The "expert" achieves a recognized excellence in performing at specific times and places a function that is regarded as useful or necessary for a group, while the "hero" stands permanently for the untarnished values of a group at its best, shorn of incoherence and compromise' (p. 32). Brown discerns a shift towards

'heroic' expectations in late antiquity. The Church, in contrast, would seem to show a move *from* the 'heroic' (ascetic, confessor) to the 'expert' (bishop) in its perceptions of what was necessary in its leadership. See also the admirable study by Cox (1983), especially ch. 2, on models of the inspired sage-thaumaturge.

28 Telfer (1962), chs. 7 and 9, gives a clear picture of these developments; see also Chadwick (1979).

29 h.e. VII.27–30, 702.1–714.27.

30 See especially the language used in the Laus Const. 5, 203.20–206.3; and NB 204.21ff – 'This emperor is truly a philosopher, solely a philosopher [or: the only real philosopher], as he knows himself'. Cf. ibid. 10, 222.22–4.

31 Ibid. 222.14–15. *Diatribē* for 'school' is a good Origenian expression: cf. con. Cels. I.3 (57.28), I.64 (116.22), VII.47 (199.3), etc. On the development of the term in philosophical circles, see the excellent discussion in Glucker (1978), pp. 162–6.

32 Vita Const. IV.24, 128.19–24.

33 Laus Const. 2–5, passim, esp. 204.18–20, 26–205.9.

34 Opitz, U.34, is full of the rhetoric of intense master-disciple relationships: Constantine repeatedly asserts what he *knows* to be doctrinal truth, and ends by inviting Arius to come to his presence for the emperor to discern his true spiritual state and restore him to the true path.

35 Opitz, U.29, 63, and, more dramatically, U.31, 74.30–75.4, where Arius is summoned to appear before the 'man of God', who has miraculous insight into the secrets of human hearts. Compare the emphasis in the Vita Const. on Constantine's eagerness to settle matters in his own presence and to take a personal part in restoring harmony to the Church; see, e.g., I.44, 38.25–39.8, III.12, 87.16–88.2, III.23, 94.12–18, III.63–6, II7.7–119.31.

36 Extravagant language about Nicaea and its statement of faith goes well back beyond Athanasius' de decr. and kindred works to Constantine himself (see Opitz, U.32, 66.15–16) and Eusebius (Vita Const. III.6, 84.3: 'what had been done [in calling the council] was seen to be the work of God').

37 E.g. Basil, ep. 186, PG 32, 661D, serm. ascet. 2.1, PG 31, 881B; Gregory of Nyssa, de anima et resurrectione 3, PG 46, 677D. Cf. Steidle (1956), pp. 181–2.

38 See the classical description of Origen's circle in the tribute ascribed to Gregory Thaumaturgus, PG 10, 1052A–1104A, esp. ch. 6, 1068D–1073B; 1072AB speaks of the master's teaching leading to the ultimate *didaskalos*, the Word of God. Nautin (1977), pp. 183–97, discusses the work at length, but treats the ascription to Gregory as

an error; the question must be regarded as still open. Cox (1983), ch. 4, offers a most suggestive analysis of Origen as philosopher and teacher, distinguishing between the youthful Alexandrian intellectual and the mature spiritual father in Caesarea – a distinction deliberately elided by Eusebius.

39 Though he was certainly recalled as a saint, and as one in whom God's presence was manifest; see the remarkable story, preserved in Philostorgius, h.e. II.13, 25.1–9, and in the Codex Angelicus Vita Constantini, ibid., 195.19–196.19, of how his disciples celebrated the Eucharist with him in prison, using Lucian's own breast as an altar. The martyr with his pupils around him on every side together constitute a 'holy shrine'.

40 Epiphanius, haer. 69.3, 154.15–19, mentioning a community of nuns under Arius' charge.

41 'Someone never out of the Alexandrian bishop's earshot'; Gregg and Groh (1981), p. 131. On the question of authorshop, see Heussi (1936); but von Hertling (1956), p. 15, considers the Athanasian authorship of the work to be more or less settled. Recent researches on the Syrian textual tradition have suggested that this judgment may be over-optimistic: for a thorough recent account, see Barnes (1986).

42 Vita Antonii 69, PG 26, 941A.

43 Ibid. 74–80, PG 26, 945B–956A.

44 Gregg (1980), p. 5, sums up the various suggestions; p. 132, n.9, for bibliographical information. Steidle (1956), pp. 159–83, effectively disposes of the view that classical paradigms are uppermost in the author's mind by documenting the purely biblical and Christian models and motifs in the work – prophet, apostle, martyr, angel.

45 See Gregg and Groh (1981), ch. 4, on the possibility that the Vita Ant. is a deliberate attempt to claim Antony decisively for Nicene Christianity in the face of possible counter-claims by Arians. That the Vita is polemical is clear; whether it is so in precisely the sense proposed by Gregg and Groh is less so. Their reconstruction depends heavily on seeing the Arian position as moralist and voluntarist – so that exemplary asceticism is of great importance, needing to be balanced, from the Catholic side, by repeated assertions of the primacy of grace, as found in the Vita.

46 The hostility between Arian bishops and ascetics in Egypt can be seen as a local matter, explicable partly by Athanasius' personal popularity in monastic circles. But the enactments of the moderate non-Nicene synod at Gangra in 340 also show a pronounced – and largely justified! – suspicion of ascetic groups in Asia at this period.

47 Rousseau (1978) is a particularly valuable study.

48 E.g. Pagels (1978) and (1980), Schoedel (1980), Vallée (1980).

49 See Robert L. Wilken's (1971) book of this title for a helpful analysis of the phenomenon. On the modern suspicion of history written by the winners, and its rather ambiguous effect on patristic studies, see Henry (1982).

PART II ARIUS AND THEOLOGY

A THE THEOLOGY OF ARIUS

1 Kannengiesser (1983), pp. 457–60, esp. p. 457.

2 Text in Opitz, U.18, 38.9 (Syr.), 12 (Gr.). Abramowski (1975) is a very important discussion of the parallels between these documents.

3 Opitz, U.6, 12.4–7, U.18, 38.11–13 (Syr.), 14–17 (Gr.).

4 Opitz, U.6, 12.8 (*ou dokēsei all' alētheia(i)*), U.18, 39.3 (Syr.), 3 (Gr.). *Alēthōs* normally underlines the fact that the Son is a subsistent in his own right, not a mere 'aspect' of the divine life; cf. the other uses of the word in non-Nicene confessions of faith (see e.g. below, n.11, and Appendix (a)). Antioch says something slightly different: the Son is so called *kuriōs kai alēthōs (maranayit w'sharirayit)* – i.e. this is his *proper* designation, not a metaphor. *Kuriōs* is the opposite of *katachrēstikōs*, 'metaphorically', or 'in a transferred sense'; see Williams (1983), pp. 76–7.

5 Opitz, U.6, 12.6, 12.9, 13.11; U.18, 38.11–12 (Syr.), 15 (Gr.), 39.1–2 (Syr.), 2 (Gr.), 39.4 (Syr.), 4 (Gr.).

6 Opitz, U.6, 12.3.

7 On the problems surrounding the authenticity of Gregory's confession, see Abramowski (1976:1) These parallels need not, however, lead us to conclude (with Abramowski (1975), p. 7) that all these texts belong in an *Alexandrian* nexus: there are some significant contrasts with Alexander's *hē philarchos*, and features in common between this and Arius' U.6, not shared by U.18 or Gregory's *ekthesis*.

8 Opitz, U.30, 64.7. Valesius has *gegenēmenon* in his edition of Socrates and Sozomen; Opitz follows a less reliable ms tradition in supplying the extra n. *Gegenēmenon*, 'brought into being', would in any case be a slightly odd variant of *genētos*, and likely to be more controversial at the time. *Gegennēmenon* is orthodox, and so more likely to have dropped out in the transmission of a text by a condemned heretic.

9 Opitz, U.30, 64.20–1.

10 Below, II.C.1.

11 Opitz, U.30, 64.15.

12 Opitz, U.1, 2.1.

13 Ibid. 2.6.

14 Ibid. 2.6–3.1 ('self-subsistent' = *agennētos*).

15 *Analloiōtos;* ibid. 3.1–3.

16 Ibid. 3.4: 'We are condemned [just] because we say "the Son has an *archē* but God is *anarchos*" '.

17 Ibid. 2.10–3.1, 3.5–6. The argument is perfectly clear, and there seems to me to be no need for Nautin's doubts about the authenticity of *ex ouk ontōn* here (Nautin (1949)). The Greek is balanced with a neat chiasmus: 'We are condemned because we say (*diōkometha hoti eipomen*): "the Son has an *archē*, but God is *anarchos*. For this too we are condemned, because we say (*diōkometha kai hoti eipomen*): "he is from nothing". And so we *do* say (*eipomen*), in so far as he is not a portion of God, nor from some [other] substance; for *this* we are condemned (*diōkometha*)!' Arius does not claim the phrase *ex ouk ontōn* as his own, but admits that in a certain sense, it is a necessary corollary of what he is saying. For a full discussion, see Simonetti (1965).

18 Above, I.A, pp. 30–1.

19 See Abramowski (1975), p. 66, for a list of usages in relevant literature.

20 Opitz, U.6, 13.18–20; U.1, 2.7–8, U.6, 12.10–11, 13.17–18.

21 E.g. Opitz, U.1, 3.3 (*horisthē(i)* probably suggests deliberation).

22 Opitz, U.1, 3.2.

23 Opitz, U.6, 13.8–9.

24 Opitz, U.1, 2.1–3, U.6, 13.10–14.

25 Opitz, U.1, 3.3, U.6, 12.9.

26 Opitz, U.6, 13.5–7, 15–16. On *sunupostēsantos*, see the n. to the tr. in the Appendix.

27 Opitz, U.6, 13.7; cf. U.30, 64.12–17, for the usual scriptural foundation for this.

28 Opitz, U.6, 13.12–13.

29 Ibid. 12.6–7.

30 Ibid. 13.6; cf. U.1.3.1–2, if Opitz' emendation is accepted (reading not *plērēs theos*, 'fully God', but *plērēs charitos kai alētheias, theos*, 'full of grace and truth, [a] god'.

31 On the metre of the *Thalia*, see Stead (1978) and West (1982). The latter convincingly shows that the de syn. extract is composed in ionic tetrameters, 'very similar to the sotadean and with the same protean variety of form' (p. 100).

32 de syn. 18 Opitz 246.1–21, de decr., Opitz 16.36–17.5, con. Ar. II.37, PG 26, 225B–228A.

33 West (1982), pp. 101–2, proposes a number of small additions to the introductory lines in con. Ar. which would improve their metrical regularity and their accord with the de syn. extract.

34 Kannengiesser (1982), pp. 15–16; though the conclusions he draws from stylistic considerations about the dating of this text are not, I believe, defensible (see Williams in Gregg (1985) and pp. 65–6 above).

35 Opitz 242.7; in con. Ar. I, Athanasius introduces his allusions to the *Thalia* by saying that they contain 'this sort of thing' (*toiauta*), and concludes by saying that the reported propositions are 'parts' of the work only.

36 Stead (1978), pp. 24–38; even Kannengiesser (1982), who is disposed to think that A is a superior source, admits (p. 14) that we do not have here 'the *ipsissima verba* of Arius'. Lorenz (1983) considers Stead too sceptical, but does not argue the case in any depth.

37 Above, I.B.2, pp. 63–5.

38 = de syn. 15, Opitz 243.5 (5.23 below) – reading *sophia sophia(i) hupērxe* in the de syn. text as well as in con. Ar., rather than *sophia sophia hupērxe*, ' "Wisdom" came to be Wisdom'. The context in con. Ar. makes the former very slightly more plausible and intelligible than the latter, though both readings are quite possible. See also below, III.C, p. 222–9.

39 The translation follows the Greek line by line, except in the last two lines, where the Greek word order makes it impossible.

40 This has normally been taken – as by Gregg and Groh (1981) – to be a straightforward adoptionist statement. Hall (1982), reviewing Gregg and Groh, rightly challenges this assumption. As translated here, the force of the line is perhaps 'God both formed the idea of such a creature and actually produced him as a real *hypostasis*'.

41 Opitz' punctuation (242.22) unhelpfully breaks up this line: there is obviously a continuity of thought from 13 to 15, perhaps from 11 to 15.

42 *Hekaterōn allotrios houtos.* Who or what is meant by *houtos*? There may have been a line or lines following, dealing with the Spirit.

43 See above, n.38.

44 Opitz, U.6, 12.9–10.

45 Athanasius of Nazarba, for instance, U.11, 18.1–3. *Pantōn estin ho huios* can be found in Origen (de princ. IV.4.8, 360.2), but too much should not be made of this, as it is a concessive remark in the inconclusive discussion of a hypothetical question.

46 E.g. II.71–2, 297A–301A.

47 Opitz, U.4b, 8.2–3 (note the gloss *hōs kai panta*, 'just like everything else', which Arius would of course, have repudiated), U.14, 21.7–22.3.

48 I.37–52, on the exegesis of Phil. 2.9–10, and Ps. 45.7–8.

49 Hall (1982); cf. n.40 above.

50 The very end of A (v) parallels 5.29; which encourages the speculation that the earlier part of A (v) is Athanasius' interpretation.

51 Opitz, U.8, 16.6–7; cf. Eusebius of Caesarea, eccl. theol. I.8, 66.21–3 and I.12, 70.26–72.37. This is, among other things, a way of stressing that the Son is 'not as one among the creatures'.

52 Opitz, ibid. 16.9–10.

53 I.B.2, pp. 64–5.

54 S.36, assuming (with A (vii)) that *heautou* is not a slip for *autou* on the part of some early copyist.

55 Williams in Gregg (1985), p. 8; cf. below, II.B.1, pp. 120, 122 on a parallel in Philo, and III.B, pp. 200–3, 209–12, on a possible Plotinian background.

56 Stead (1978), pp. 37–8, also suggests an alternative, taking the line to mean 'Using the power by which *divinity* can see . . .' But I cannot imagine *ho theos* having this generalized sense.

57 Hippolytus, refutatio VII.20, 195.24, 197.16: the non-existent God transcends even what is named as *arrētos*, being incapable of being *any* name.

58 See, e.g., Irenaeus, adv. haer. I.1.4 (Harvey, p. 21). For the idea that *katalēpsis* of God is unattainable by the human mind, cf. Origen, excerpta in psalmos 77.31 (PG 17, 141B), Eusebius, praep. ev. VII.12, 386.12–13.

59 See the rejection in Book VI of the *Apostolic Constitutions* (ed. Funk, 1895, p. 325) of the gnostic view that God is *agnōstos* and *alektos;* and cf. Williams in Gregg (1985), p. 18.

60 As does Gwatkin (1900), pp. 20–1, and cf. pp. 273–4; followed in some degree by Pollard (1970), pp. 123, 143–4, 316.

61 Opitz, U.17, 33.1–5.

62 Following Epiphanius, haer. 69.12.1, 162.6ff; see Lorenz (1978), p. 68, and cf. Simonetti (1965), pp. 32–7, on Arius' probable interpretation of Prov. 8:22, and its indebtedness to Dionysius of Alexandria. Simonetti proposes (p. 36) that Arius' intensification of the subordinationist elements of the tradition grew out of his philosophical concerns, and that 'he saw in Prov. 8:22ff the scriptural *point d'appui* that would allow him to treat the Son as a mere creature' (pp. 36–7). I suspect that this a bit of an oversimplification; it is much qualified in Simonetti's later studies.

63 Gregg and Groh (1981), pp. 3, 7–12, Kannengiesser (1982), 1–5 and passim.

64 (1971), p. 151.

65 For a fine discussion of how this issue remains central in modern theology, see Kelsey (1975), especially chs. 2, 5 and 8.

66 Opitz, U.14, 20.7–11.
67 Chs. 26ff; whether or not this work is from Athanasius' hand (Kannengiesser (1983) argues that it is not), the texts were obviously under discussion.
68 con. Ar. I.46–52; cf. Opitz, U.14, 22.1–3, for Alexander's allusion to the controversial use of this text.
69 I.37, PG 26, 89AB.
70 10, Opitz 9.7–8.
71 Opitz, U.14, 21.16, where it is the first text quoted.
72 Opitz, U.8, 17.1–2.
73 Opitz, U.6, 13.17–18.
74 It appears in *hē philarchos* (Opitz, U.14, 24.31) and *henos sōmatos* (Opitz, U.4b, 9.1–3), and recurs in de decr. 13 (Opitz 11.34–5) and 21 (Opitz 18.11–13); here too it is associated with John 8:42.
75 de decr. 26 (Opitz 23.5–7).
76 Abramowski (1982); see below, p. 151 and n. 292.
77 Opitz, U.11, 18.3–4; on the hundred sheep as the totality of rational creatures, cf. Origen, in Gen. hom. II.5, 34.12–24; Methodius, symp. III.5–6, 32.1–33.16, seems to assume a similar interpretation to Origen's, but uses the passage rather differently. Both plainly distinguish between the Logos as shepherd and the rational creation.
78 de syn. 18 (Opitz 246.1–21), con. Ar. II.37, 38 (PG 26, 225C–228C).
79 This may be why they do not receive the same extended treatment in con. Ar. as do other passages.
80 (1971), pp. 153–4.
81 Opitz, U.14, 27.16–17.
82 con. Ar. I.58, PG 26.133BC.
83 *kreittōn* – the same word used by Arius himself in S.27, and a common appellation for the supreme God.
84 adv. Arium I.7, 202–4.
85 con. Ar. I.37–45.
86 Ibid. 53–64, and II.1–10.
87 Ibid. II. 11–18.
88 Ibid. 61–7.
89 This interpretation owes a great deal to Newman's sharp distinction between Alexandrian allegory and Antiochene literalism (above, pp. 3–4); Simonetti (1971), pp. 319–23, is justifiably critical of the way in which this antithesis still exerts a stranglehold on Arian studies; see above, p. 17, and II.C.1, passim. For a recent judgment, see also Wallace-Hadrill (1982), p. 29.
90 Above, n.77.
91 See, e.g., Origen, de princ. II.11.2, 186.1–3, for the idea of the literal sense of scriptural prophecy in particular as 'Jewish'.

92 con. Ar. I.37, PG 26, 88BC.

93 *Ekklēsiastikē dianoia;* cf. ibid., 44, PG 26, 101C; a certain reading is recommended as being more 'ecclesiastical' than the Arian interpretation.

94 Opitz, U.14.

95 E.g., con. Ar. II.23–24, PG 26, 193C–197B.

96 Ibid. II.41, 233A–236A; cf. the use of a similar argument in ep. I ad Ser., 29–30, PG 26, 597B–600C.

97 As in the case of prayer to the Logos in Origen's scheme; see de oratione XV.1–XVI.1, 333.26–336.20.

98 Kannengiesser (1982), pp. 39–40.

99 Opitz, U.6, 12.3.

100 'God is *pneuma*' was evidently such a statement in the intellectual climate of the early third century, given that *pneuma* was, for the Stoics, the designation of a material reality: hence Origen's discussion of this proposition in de princ. I.1 passim, 16–27, arguing that the context of Scripture as a whole makes it plain that *pneuma* means 'what is not *sōma*'.

101 On the fusion of scriptural idiom with classical philosophical conventions concerning the divine, Pannenberg (1971) is of great interest; note in particular pp. 134–40, 173–83.

102 In de spir. sancto, XXVII.66, PG 32, 188A–192C.

103 The attempt to draw out the implications of scriptural witness to the free and incorporeal nature of God with the help of philosophical tools is, of course, central to the whole Alexandrian tradition. II.B.1, below, explores the tensions that result in the case of Philo.

104 The relation of father and son could be seen as an example of 'emanation', *aporroia*, in virtue of its being a transmission of *ousia;* see Dörrie (1976), pp. 73, 77.

105 (1982), pp. 38–9.

106 See, for example, con. Ar. I.14–16, 26–29, II.2.

107 On Athanasius' refusal to oppose nature and freedom in God, see Meijering (1974/1975:1) and (1974/1975:2) esp, pp, 105–6 of the latter.

108 con. Ar. I.37 (PG 26, 88C–89B) and 49 (113A–116A).

109 (1981), esp. chs. 1 to 3.

110 Gregg and Groh (1981) are not always exact about this; see, e.g., pp. 59 ('the condition of humans'), 90 ('among the *men* incapable of perceiving the Deity') – despite the more careful statements of, e.g., pp. 19–24, 81–7.

111 Cf. the con. Ar. paraphrase of the *Thalia*, A(vi).

112 Whereas Athanasius, con. Ar. I.46 (PG 26, 105C–108C) insists on taking the genitive *sou* as objective, so that the text refers to those

who *participate in* Christ. On the fluidity of the term *metochē* at this period, see below III.C.

113 Cf. Williams (1983), pp. 77–8, 80; (1985:1), pp. 11–12, 22–3.

114 con. Ar. I.35–45, esp. 38 (PG 26, 89B–92B).

115 Opitz, U.4b, 8.7–10.

116 For examples of this technique, see Stead (1976), pp. 133–5. Stead dubs this *reductio retorta:* 'it saddles the opponent with the very proposition which he regards as evidently false' (134).

117 Opitz, U.14, 25.11–12.

118 See, for example, the remark in Epiphanius, haer. 64.4, 410.5–6.

119 E.g. Pollard (1970), Wiles (1962), Simonetti (1971); see below, II.C.1, and n.89 above.

120 Above all, Simonetti, whose 1971 article is of major significance; cf. Simonetti (1975), p. 20.

121 The accusation of 'illogicality' levelled at Arius by Gwatkin and Pollard among others should be laid to rest once and for all. One of the virtues of Kannengiesser (1982) is the author's insistence on Arius' rigour and individuality of thought (and consequent isolation); see, e.g., pp. 11, 35–40.

B ALEXANDRIA AND THE LEGACY OF ORIGEN

1 Wolfson (1956), p. 585.

2 See, e.g., Justin, apol. sec. VI.6, dial. LXI.1, LXII.4, Tatian, orat. 5, Athenagoras, suppl. 10.

3 Wolfson (1956), p. 582, (1948), vol. 1, pp. 231–4, 247–52, on the Logos as a discrete entity over against God.

4 Possibly implied by e.g., Gen. I.4, where the Logos is the 'original *sphragis* (seal)'; but cf. n.15 below. There is more mileage in texts about 'mediation', like that quoted in n.6, below.

5 E.g. agr. 12.51, conf. 28.146–7, leg. all. III.61.175, imm. 6.31, somn. I.37.215.

6 heres 42.206: the Logos is *mesos tōn akrōn*, between God and creatures.

7 Somn. I.39.228–30, 41.238–41, leg. all. III.73.207–8; *deuteros theos* in qu. Gen. 62. See Sandmel (1979), p. 92.

8 In the con. Ar. *Thalia* paraphrase A(iii).

9 opif. 4.16.

10 Ibid. 6.24: again we find the Logos called *sphragis.*

11 One might compare Aquinas' doctrine that the divine ideas depend for their plurality on the plurality of concretely possible beings (ST I.15.2).

12 leg. all. III.31.96.

13 Note the denial in opif. 6.23 of the presence of a 'counsellor' beside God in creation.
14 leg. all. III.31.96.
15 opif. 5.20: the plan previously 'impressed as a seal' in the maker's mind is now to be realized. *Sphragis* does not necessarily mean anything outside the divine mind.
16 E.g., heres 42.205–6.
17 E.g., cher. 5.16–17.
18 somn. I.41.241.
19 Talbert (1976).
20 Sandmel (1979), p. 94.
21 See Louth (1981), pp. 29ff, on the significance for Philo of meditation on Scripture.
22 imm. 12.57.
23 somn. I.11.62.
24 cher. 9.27.
25 Abr. 24.120ff.
26 Louth (1981), p. 28, referring also to fuga 101.
27 qu. Ex. II.68; cf. perhaps heres 38.188, on the Logos as that which makes all things cohere by filling them with his *ousia*.
28 heres 42.205–6.
29 migr. 1.4–6; cf. leg. all. III.61.175.
30 somn. I.11.65–6.
31 leg. all. III.31.96, 33.100.
32 leg. all. III.33.100; cf. imm. 24.110.
33 leg. all. III.62.177.
34 post. 5.15.
35 See Louth (1981), pp. 29–35.
36 somn. I.10.60.
37 leg. all. I.29.91–30.92.
38 somn., loc. cit.; mut. 2.8; cf. cher. 20.65, 33.116–18.
39 spec. leg. 1.47; cf. imm. 12.62, 17.78–81.
40 mut. 2.15.
41 leg. all. III.73.206.
42 Abr. 24.120–3; cf. mut. 2.11–17, 27, etc.
43 For 'God' as *genikōtatos*, see leg. all. II.21.86.
44 Above, n.7.
45 Abr. 24.120.
46 E.g. plant. 20.86, implicitly deriving *theos* from *tithēmi*. Unsurprisingly, there are other derivations used elsewhere.
47 Abr. 24.122; cf. leg. all.II.1.3.
48 On the inevitable duality of logos, see gig. 11.52.
49 heres 35.172.

50   qu. Ex. II.68; cf. cont. 1.2, praem. et poen. 6.40.

51   opif. 15.35, leg. all. I.8.19, conf. 28.146.

52   On which, see Goodenough (1935), pp. 35–8.

53   See Parm. 141E: the one 'in no way partakes of *ousia*'. This statement, of course, has a primarily dialectical function: the *Parmenides* demonstrates the equal impossibility of saying that the One 'exists' *and* of saying that it does not. It is beyond being in the sense that existence-questions make no sense when asked about it.

54   opif. 5.21.

55   leg. all. I.2.2, 8.20, opif. 7.26–28, imm. 6.31–32, sacrif. 18.65; see Sorabji (1983), pp. 203–9, for a full discussion of Philo's views on this question. Whether there is time before the existence of the *ordered* cosmos is far from clear in Philo; but he does not believe in eternal matter, as far as we can tell, and the implication is that some sort of time begins as matter is created. On the whole issue, see III.A, below.

56   decal. 12.58.

57   Above, pp. 105–6.

58   Compare Arius' alleged *akribōs* (A(vii)) with the *ēkribōse* of mut. 2.14.

59   See Part III, passim; cf. Smith in Blumenthal and Markus (1981) for a helpful survey of how this problem is posed for Plotinus.

60   Wittgenstein (1966), pp. 30–1.

61   Völker (1952), pp. 93–6, minimizes the importance of the apophatic element; Lossky (1974), pp. 18–23, 33–5, allows it a significant place, but considers it to be insufficiently consistently worked out; Osborn (1957), pp. 184–6, and (1981), pp. 45–50, defends Clement's seriousness and consistency as a follower of the *via negativa*.

62   strom. II.16, 152.19–23.

63   Ibid. II.2, 115.22–3.

64   Ibid. II.2, 116.4–5.

65   Ibid. V.12, 380.25. The parallels with Philo are clear, and are listed in Stählin's notes on this and other passages cited.

66   Ibid. V.12, 381.2–3.

67   Ibid. V.12, 380.10–12, 381.7–8.

68   Ibid. V.12, 380.12–14.

69   Ibid. II.3, 118.11–119.3.

70   Ibid. VI.18, 517.22–3.

71   Ibid. 517.28ff; for *theodidaktos*, cf. quis dives 20, 172.28.

72   Ibid. VII.2, 6.8–28.

73   Ibid. VII.2, 7.9–11, 20–2.

74   Ibid. VII.2, 8.10–16.

75   Ibid. VII.2, 8.17; cf. ibid. 3.10, 18.

76   Ibid. VII.2, 8.18.

77 The high priestly image again probably relates to Philo primarily, rather than to the scriptural *Hebrews*.
78 protr. 12.120, 84.30.
79 strom. VII.3, 12.21–2; on 'becoming *logos*', cf. exc. ex Theod. 27, 116.11.
80 Ibid. VII.3, 12.23–4.
81 Ibid. VII.3, 10.16.
82 Ibid. V.10, 370.16–21; see Camelot (1945), pp. 110–12, on the range of meaning of *katalēpsis*.
83 strom. V.3, 336.1–14, perhaps IV. 25, 317.11.
84 Ibid. IV.25, 318.1.
85 Ibid. IV.25, 318.24–319.2; on the Plotinian parallels, see Lilla (1971), pp. 206–7.
86 Osborn (1957), p. 43, prefers the latter; the word in question can also mean 'twined' or 'plaited' together, as strands in a cord.
87 strom. IV.25, 317.22–4.
88 Ibid. V.14, 387.21–388.4.
89 paid. I.71.1, 131.18–19.
90 Ibid. I.62.4, 127.5–6.
91 Ibid. V.11, 374.4–20; the technique is paralleled in Albinus' *epitomē*, X.4–5.
92 Sandmel (1979), p. 95.
93 protr. 11.111, 79.5.
94 Ibid. 10.91, 67.24.
95 strom. II.16, 152.17ff.
96 protr. chs. 6 and 7 passim; the theme is equally pervasive in strom. I and II.
97 protr. 1.6–7, 7.14–8.1.
98 Ibid. 1.8, 9.10–11.
99 Ibid. chs. 10 and 11, passim.
100 And cf. Goodenough (1935), p. 102.
101 For references, see above, II.B.1, n.2.
102 Osborn (1981), p. 242, rightly argues against Lilla (1971) that Clement's main works do not give a clear two– or three-stage doctrine of the Logos' 'emergence'.
103 19.2, 112.30–31, cf. 113.8, if we follow Bunsen and Sagnard's reading of *huios* here, and do not accept Casey's retention of *logos* as it stands in the ms.
104 The aorist participle (*energēsas*) in the original suggests this translation rather than 'when he acted through the prophets'.
105 112.27–113.9.
106 Notably Zahn (1884); see Duckworth and Osborn (1985), pp. 77–83, for a good discussion, building on the seminal study of Casey (1924).

107 bibl. 109; in Stählin's edition of Clement, with other fragments of the *Hypotyposes*, 202.16–22.
108 adumb. 211.15–16; *secundum substantiam* probably represents *kath'hupostasin*, i.e. 'really and truly' as opposed to 'notionally'.
109 Thalia, A(iv), S.23.
110 (1978), p. 103.
111 exc. ex Theod. 10–11, 109.16–110.22.
112 Ibid. 7, 108.1–14.
113 Discussed at length in 59–61 of the work, 126.17–127.25.
114 Ibid. 8, 108.20–2.
115 Ibid. 4, 106.17–21.
116 Ibid. 19, 113.1–7, 20, 113.15–17; but note too the clear distinction drawn between the Logos and the *prōtoktistoi* in 10 and 12 (109.16–110.7 and 110.23–4).
117 Ibid. 7, 108.13–14.
118 Ibid. 15, 112.1–3.
119 Alexander of Alexandria, Opitz, U.14, 27.5–6, assumes that Valentinian emanationism is materialistic; Arius probably makes the same assumption in U.6, 12.10ff. Cf. nn.126 and 127 below.
120 exc. ex Theod. 2, 106.6–7.
121 Ibid. 6, 107.17–25.
122 Ibid. 41, 119.17–18.
123 Ibid. 2–3, 105.14–106.12; cf. Casey's introduction to his edition (1934), pp. 25–6.
124 On I Jn., adumb. 211.6–7.
125 Thalia, S.34 and 39.
126 Opitz, U.6, 12.10–12.
127 Opitz, U.14, 27.6.
128 See Williams in Gregg (1985), pp. 4–6 and nn.18–28, and Lorenz (1978), pp. 119–22.
129 See Stählin's index, p. 730B; an example at strom. I.18, 57.9.
130 strom. VII.16, 73.16–17.
131 Ibid. VI.18, 517.28; cf. n.71, above.
132 E.g. ibid. V.10, 369.28.
133 quis dives 23, 175.4–11.
134 376.7, 378.2.
135 Stählin's index, p. 341.
136 E.g. strom. III.8, 224.19, VI.14, 486.12.
137 Ibid. VI.17, 515.2.
138 Lorenz (1978), p. 122.
139 Lorenz (1978) and (1983), Simonetti (1971), (1973) and (1980), Barnard (1970) and (1972), and Hanson (1972) represent some of the more significant currents in the debate. Lorenz (1978), pp. 31–6,

is worth consulting for an overview of some of this material. A valuable essay by Hanson formed part of the proceedings of the fourth Origen Colloquium at Innsbruck in 1985; these proceedings are due to be published as *Origeniana Quarta*, in the Innsbrucker Theologische Studien, 1987.

140 Eusebius, con. Marc. I.4.19ff, 757–61.

141 In fact this is not one of Origen's preferred terms: two possible uses of *hupothesis* for 'subject' (hom. Jer. XIV.14, 120.18, and fr. III in Lam. 236.20) are far from convincing in this respect. On the origins and meaning of *hupostasis* terminology, A. H. B. Logan's study, also forthcoming in *Origeniana Quarta*, is excellent, correcting as it does, in some respects, Dörrie (1955).

142 73.14.

143 See, e.g., Alexander of Aphrodisias, in Arist. Met., 230.36; several patristic instances of this opposition in PGL 1454, B.6. Cf. n.150, below.

144 229.21–230.4.

145 Cf. Clement in protr. 12.120, 84.30 (above, p. 125 and n.78).

146 in Mt. 17.14, 624.11–16.

147 334.4–5.

148 65.16.

149 65.8–9.

150 X.37, 212.8–19.

151 This is the conclusion of Hanson (1972) and Simonetti (1965), p. 125, n.76. Stead (1977), pp. 211–13, is, rather surprisingly, less sceptical.

152 This purports to be an extract from a commentary on Hebrews; the text is printed in Lommatzsch V.299 and XXIV.357. Cf. fr. IX in Jo., 490.20–1, for an apparent use of *ek tēs ousias tou patros;* but these words are obviously the gloss of the anthologist.

153 Lommatzsch, 353–5. Nautin (1977), p. 150, assumes that the whole list of charges has been redrafted by Rufinus from the original list of 15 preserved by Photius, bibl. 117.

154 I.e. *agenētos* or *agennētos;* compare the texts quoted in ch. III of the *Defence*, ibid. 328, to clear Origen of the charge of teaching two *archai*.

155 Or 'all rule and power as an inheritance'; the mss differ slightly.

156 So Westcott (1889, p. 168), commenting on the idea of *klēronomia* in Hebrews, suggested, referring to Aristotle's *Politics* V.8.

157 Lommatzsch, 357.11–12.

158 Ibid. 359.1–9. The Wisdom text appears elsewhere in Origen, notably in de princ. I.2.5, 33.8–34.7.

159 351.4–11.

160 249.4–13.

161 240.29–250.3.

162 XX.20, 352.33, XX.24, 358.15, 18.

163 Cf. de princ. I.2.6, 35.9–15.

164 249.9–10; this sounds like a familiar and quasi-technical definition of *homoousios*.

165 (1968), p. 11.

166 Lommatzsch, 359.1–2.

167 I am not completely convinced by Nautin's account of this (1977; pp. 150–3), I believe – as I shall argue in what follows – that there is a plausible context for these charges in the era of Pamphilus and that the distortion comes in Rufinus' handling of them. The fact that the *responsiones* do not at present correspond to the charges strongly suggests that this is the point at which Rufinus' hand is evident. As to Photius' fifteen charges, their exact source is obscure. Since Photius *distinguishes* the work containing this list from Pamphilus' defence (Nautin's argument for disregarding the distinction – pp. 112–13 – is very weak), it may well be that it is actually a composition of the sixth century or later: several of the charges would fit well into the intellectual climate before and after the second Council of Constantinople, but would be rather unexpected in the early fourth century.

168 Lommatzsch, 354.1–4.

169 As, e.g., in the Commentary on John II.2, 54.12–55.8.

170 Did Rufinus have in mind the fact that Dionysius of Alexandria claimed, according to Athanasius (below, n.303), to have used the *aporroia* metaphor to underline the absolute inseparability of Father and Son, and had done so in the work in which he accepted the legitimacy of the *homoousios?*

171 E.g. by Stead (1977), pp. 213–14.

172 We have no means at all of dating the Hebrews commentary, which is only evidenced in Pamphilus; see Nautin (1977), p. 240, n.63, suggesting that our citations come from the *homilies* on Hebrews mentioned elsewhere.

173 Cf. Methodius' argument against the possibility of two first principles in de autex V, 157.6–159.4.

174 Cf. de princ. I.1.3, 18.20–19.10: many agents 'participate' in the *ars* of medicine, but no one supposes they all share some material thing.

175 in Jo. I.16, 20.15.

176 Very clearly stated in hom. Jer. IX.4, 70.3–28; see also de princ. I.1.9, 40.11, IV.4.1, 350.15–16, in Jo. I. 29, 37.2–12, II.1, 53.14–24.

177 For alleged parallels in Origen to this phrase, see the Hebrews fragment in Lommatzsch, XXIV.328, and Athanasius, de decr. 27, Opitz 23.24–5; also a fragment on Romans, Lommatzsch VI.22–3, which is the most suspect of these texts.

178 Ibid. 40.12–41.7; on the senses of *archē*, see in Jo. I.16–18, 20.1–23.11.

179 de princ. I.1.9, 41.11–12; cf. in Jo. X.37, 212.16–19, a passage using this argument to underline the distinction of the Son from the Father.

180 de princ. loc. cit. 41.11–43.4.

181 Athanasius, con. Ar. I.20–2, II.2, III.3–6, etc.

182 de princ. I.2.6, 35.9ff.

183 Ibid. I.2.6, 35.4 and 16, I.2.9, 40.7–8.

184 Ibid. praef. 8–9, 14.14–15.27, and I.1, passim.

185 Ibid. I.2.12, 45.10–15.

186 in Jo. I.16, 20.1–21.2; cf. ibid. XX.34, 372.27–373.19 for *gnōsis* and *agapē* as the characteristics of sonship. de oratione throughout presupposes the same model; see especially chs. I, X, XV, XXII.

187 E.g. in Jo XXXII.28 and 29.

188 See ref. in n.179 above.

189 E.g. de princ. I.3.8, 61.13–20.

190 Implied by. e.g., in Jo. I.19, 23.18–24, I.25, 30.33–31.6, I.39, 43.16–33 etc.

191 in Jo. I.20, 24.23–4.

192 See the strong statement of in Jo. 13.25, 259.14.22: the Father transcends the Son and the Spirit more than they excel other beings. But this and similar passages are partly conditioned by the need to rebut the gnostic doctrine that the redeemer is *above* the creator (cf. VI.39).

193 in Mt. XV.10, 375.20–376.13, and perhaps con. Cels. V.11, 12.9–11.

194 According to the *syllabus errorum* in Photius, bibl. 117; see Nautin (1977), pp. 120–2 on this issue, and cf. n.167 above on the difficulty of dating or locating the charge.

195 de princ. IV.4.8, 360.1–7.

196 E.g. in Jo. I.16, 20.15–23.

197 XXXII.28 and 29, 473–5.

198 Ibid. 473.28–474.1, 475.16–25. The argument is very subtly nuanced: the Father's self-contemplation seems to remain greater than the Son can contain, yet the Son certainly has the maximum possible share in it.

199 con. Cels. VII.38, 188.11–12.

200 Below, III.B.

201 de princ. IV.4.1, 349.11, is ambiguous, in so far as *ek thelēmatos* just might mean that the Son *expresses* the Father's will, as in I.2.9.

202 I.2.9.

203 40.16–41.3.

204 XIII.35, 260.29–261.29.

205 Ibid. 260.33–4.

206 Ibid. 261.11.

207 Ibid. 261.25–8.

208 Ibid. 261.28–9.

209 Cf. above, p. 125.
210 IV.4.1, 349.13; though the word sits oddly among the other titles here given to Wisdom. There may be an adjective missing (*teleion*, as in Opitz, U.6?). See Abramowski (1982), pp. 266–8, for a full discussion, proposing that the Son is called *ktisma* in so far as he contains the ideal forms of creatures. Cf. also Lowry (1938).
211 V.37, 41.23.
212 Above all, Jerome and Justinian; see Koetschau's introduction to his edition of de princ. for details, and his notes on pp. 10, 35, and 349.
213 By M. Harl, in a further paper forthcoming in *Origeniana Quarta*.
214 Possibly in Mt XIII.20, 234.16–237.23, ibid. XV.27, 429–33. The case for a precise terminological distinction is not, I think, wholly conclusive.
215 II.96, 169.18–170.17.
216 Ibid. 170.5–7.
217 Ibid. III.1.24, 243.1–244.9.
218 349.3–10.
219 See Lorenz (1978), p. 71 for references to Theognostus and Gregory Thaumaturgus as denying that the Son is *ex nihilo*.
220 in Jo. I.17, 22.9–13, 19–26.
221 Ibid. 22.14–18; de princ. I.1.4, 9.13–14, is ambiguous. *Creavit atque composuit* may reflect a distinction in the Greek between *ektise* and *ekosmēse*; cf. above, n.213.
222 II.2, 55.4–8.
223 I.3.6, 57.1–5; but this really says no more than that creation participates in God through the Son.
224 Lommatzsch XIII.134.19–20.
225 schol. in Apoc. 20 (TU 38, p. 29).
226 The authenticity of this fragment is uncertain, but the correspondence with the *ousia-metousia* antithesis of sel. in Ps. reinforces its claims somewhat.
227 Lorenz (1978), p. 77.
228 I.2.10, 44.17ff.
229 in Jo. II.2, 54.29–55.4.
230 Above, n.193.
231 Cf. e.g., the text from in Jo. X.37 cited in n.179, above, and passages like de princ. I.3.8, n.189, above.
232 Origen does not mention Sabellius by name, but the polemic against 'monarchianism' in the John commentary is everywhere apparent.
233 Cf. above, II.B.1, n.2.
234 con. Cels. VIII.26, 242.24–29; cf. in Jo. XIX.5, 303.12–304.29, commenting on John 20:17 ('my Father and your Father, my God and your God'), which is also alluded to in the con. Cels. passage.

235 In addition to the text quoted in the preceding note, de oratione XV is the *locus classicus* for this; cf. also con. Cels. VIII.13, 230.21–6.

236 E.g. con. Ar. I.41, 42, 61; II.23, 24.

237 Lorenz (1978), p. 163, notes the 'liturgical' sound of the familiar *ischuros theos;* but this is very speculative.

238 (1978), pp. 211–24.

239 de princ. II.6.3, 142.10.

240 Ibid. 142.10.

241 This may be a slip; it is hard to see how *christos* could properly be a title of the Word himself, especially in the light of in Jo. I.28, 35.14–28, with its application of the 'anointing' of Ps. 45:8 to the human soul of Jesus alone.

242 de princ. II.6.3, 143.4–6.

243 Ibid. II.6.4, 143.24–144.17, and 145.24–27. Cf. in Jo. I.28, as in the preceding note.

244 de princ. II.6.5, 144.21–145.4.

245 Ibid. II.6.6, 145.7–13.

246 Ibid. 145.19–20.

247 VI.79, 150.25–151.5. Note the reference here to the possibility of many *christoi* coming into existence by union with the primary *christos.*

248 As above, n.242.

249 In addition to II.6.4, see IV.4.4, 354.11–13.

250 Ibid. IV.4.5, 355.15–356.5.

251 Ibid. IV.4.4, 354.26–355.10.

252 in Jo. I.28, 35.16–21.

253 Thalia, 5.24–5.

254 This is the burden of the sophisticated Christological discussion of de princ. on the need to pass beyond the fleshly Jesus to the pre-incarnate Logos (de princ. II.6, esp. 3–6. Cf. con. Cels. VI.68, 138.11–17).

255 con. Cels. VI.79; n.247, above.

256 (1978), pp. 211–19, 223–4.

257 in Jo. II.31, 88.6–89.21.

258 S.31.

259 Opitz, U.6, 13.1.

260 As classically in the *Ascension of Isaiah* 10.7–31, Charlesworth (1985), vol. 2, pp. 173–4; cf. Talbert (1976), and Smith (1968/1978) on the *Prayer of Joseph.*

261 From the hymn to the Mother of God in the Liturgy of St John Chrysostom (*Axion estin hōs alēthōs . . .*).

262 Ch. IV, section ii; pp. 143–4 in the 1878 edn.

263 It has been noted – e.g. by Torrance (1975), pp. 139–214, esp. pp. 203–4 – that the denial of Christ's role as priest and intercessor

is tacitly Apollinarian, and that certain features not only of Mariology, but of soteriology and sacramental theology, owe their ambiguous development to this heresy.

264 Talbert (1976); cf. Segal (1977), ch. 12, Heyward (1979).
265 E.g. Justin, dial. 56 and 63, Irenaeus, dem. 47, adv. haer. III.6.1 (Harvey, vol. II p. 21), IV. 55.1 (ibid. p. 265) Cyprian, test. II.6; it is purely and simply a proof-text on the uniquely exalted status of Christ. Frequently v.8 is taken (as by Irenaeus) to mean, 'Therefore, O God, your God has anointed you'.
266 As in Jewish-Christian debate from Paul, through Justin's Dialogue, to Origen himself; see de Lange (1976), esp. ch. 9.
267 The use of *archē* and *epinoia* in the Thalia is an obvious example; for other parallels, see Williams in Gregg (1985), pp. 4–6, and nn.9–21.
268 Harnack (1897), vol. 3, pp. 95–9.
269 Loofs (1893), p. 142.
270 H. Crouzel, LThK VII, 1233–5, usefully enumerates the different sorts of 'Origenist' controversy that arose between the third and the sixth centuries, relating as they do to a variety of theological issues.
271 Bienert (1978), p. 8.
272 Ibid. pp. 16–18.
273 See above, II.B.3, nn.153, 167.
274 de decr. 27, Opitz 23.19ff. This passage suggest that Origen's reputation is already under a cloud as far as many are concerned; by calling him *philoponos*, 'conscientious', Athanasius reinforces his point that, as Origen is careful to state a whole range of possible solutions to a question while he is exploring it, he must never be quoted out of context. The anti-Nicenes were evidently already quarrying Origen's works for polemical purposes.
275 Peter of Alexandria, Eustathius of Antioch, Methodius (assuming him to have been a bishop) are all critical of aspects of Origen's thought, but none of them anathematizes him totally and without qualification; i.e. they may believe him to have been *wrong*, but do not treat him as a heretic *sans phrase*.
276 Op. cit. pp. 24–5, 222–3.
277 Eusebius, h.e. VI.26, 580.10–15. Heraclas, a former pupil and then assistant of Origen, succeeded Origen in the catechetical school, and so was probably more acceptable to Demetrius; and as bishop he took no steps to lure Origen back from Palestine. Cf. Trigg (1983), pp. 206–8, on the conflicts between the two men.
278 Op. cit. p. 222; cf. pp. 187–93 on Dionysius' involvement in the controversy over schismatic baptism, and his appeal to the Syro-Palestinians for support.
279 de sent. dionysii, 9, Opitz 52.8–9.

280 h.e. VII.26, 700.15–16; see Bienert (1978), p. 205.

281 Eusebius, ibid. 700.21–2.

282 de sent. Dionysii 4, Opitz 48.20–3.

283 Athanasius, de decr. 26, Opitz 22.1–23.16.

284 Ibid. 22.3–4.

285 Ibid. 19–20.

286 Ibid. 25–7 (cf. 17 and 23.6).

287 Ibid. 20–5.

288 Ibid. 23.1–4.

289 Ibid. 23.7–8.

290 Opitz 22.12–13; cf. Abramowski (1982), p. 246. Feltoe, in his edition of Dionysius, notes the evidence for a later variety of Marcionism teaching three divine principles (p. 179).

291 h.e. VII.26, 700.16–18. Athanasius' wording in de sent. Dionysii 13, Opitz 55.20, suggests two treatises, though 14 (Opitz 56.33) has commonly been taken as meaning that one work only is involved, *elenchos kai apologia*. Matters are further complicated by a reference in 18 (Opitz 60.9) to 'the third book', and in 23 (Opitz 63.12) to the 'fourth'. There may have been two bipartite works, or something similar, 'bound up' as one; and, in any case, the title or titles need not go back to Dionysius himself.

292 Abramowski (1982), who also questions the authenticity of the quotation from Dionysius of Rome in de decr. 26. *Prima facie*, this is unlikely (why should anyone *invent* so complex and embarrassing a controversy?); but a fuller consideration would need the kind of careful and extended stylistic and lexical analyses for which I have no space here.

293 Opitz 53.12–54.4.

294 Ibid. 54.5–11.

295 Ibid. 54.22ff.

296 E.g. con. Ar. II.44–50 (cf. ibid. 10–12), 52–3, 56: Wisdom comes to be able to call herself a creature 'for the sake of' creatures, i.e. becomes incarnate in the divine economy of redemption.

297 de sent. Dionysii 20 and 21, Opitz 61.17–62.14.

298 Ibid. 62.6.

299 Though con. Ar. II.4, for example, grants that *poieō* at least can mean 'beget' in some scriptural contexts.

300 Ibid. 15, Opitz 57.4–19.

301 Ibid. 57.15–16; 17, 58.19–20.

302 Ibid. 18, Opitz 59.8–13.

303 Ibid. 23, Opitz 63.7–11: immanent and expressed *logos* are 'each in the other, while remaining different from each other; they are one while still being two'.

325

304 Ibid. 63.12–64.2.

305 Ibid. 25, Opitz 65.5–12.

306 Bienert (1978), p. 221, Orbe (1958), pp. 617–21.

307 See, e.g., con. Ar. I.14–21, 28–9, III.4–6, etc.

308 Some have seen a hint of this doctrine in a fragment attributed to Dionysius in a letter of Athanasius of Nazarba, published and discussed in Bardy (1936), pp. 207–9. The text survives in rather peculiar Latin, and Opitz (1937) and Abramowski (1982) have attempted retroversions. But it is not completely clear that we have anything like a verbatim quotation from Dionysius. The alleged extract runs: *ita pater quidem pater et non filius; non quia factus est, sed quia est; non ex aliquid, sed in se permanens. Filius autem et non pater; non quia erat, sed quia factus est; non de se, sed es eo qui eum fecit, filii dignitatem sortitus est.* The last phrase is quite alien to anything we know of Dionysius. The repeated *quia*'s may represent a Greek *hoti*, indicating reported speech of fragmentary citation. I suggest that the opening phrase is from Athanasius, paraphrasing Dionysius, and what follows explicates this. Dionysius agrees that the Father is not the Son, for '(he does not say) that the Father is "made", but that he "exists, not from any other source but abiding in himself"': *[legei gar] ouch' hoti gegonen all'hoti [aei] estin, ouk ek tinos all' en* (or *eph'*) *heautou menōn.* Nor is the Son the Father, for (Dionysius says) not that "he always was" but "he came into being, not of his own accord but out of the one who made him"': *ouch' hoti ēn, all'hoti gegonen, ouk ex heautou, all' ek tou poiēsantos auton.*' Dionysius' point would be the denial that the Son had eternal *self-subsistent* being alongside the Father.

309 See the texts published by Bienert (1973), and discussed by him in (1978), pp. 119–20, where he notes that Origen's own view on this is not absolutely clear by any means.

310 Bienert (1973), p. 309.

311 PG 87, 221B.

312 Peter is described as sharing the views of Clement, Dionysius and Methodius, among others, on this matter.

313 Bienert (1973), p. 311. Cf. the brief passage from a homily 'on the non-pre-existence of the soul' ascribed to Peter, Pitra, *Analecta Sacra* IV (1883), pp. 193–4.

314 The Syriac fragments were collected and published by Pitra, op. cit. pp. 189–93, and are summarized in Radford (1908), pp. 76–82.

315 Ibid. pp. 81–2.

316 Despite Bienert's remarks (1978), p. 198.

317 Above, nn.153, 167.

318 The last three in the list, dealing with final punishment, the soul's independence and the idea of transmigration.

319 So Photius alleges, bibl. 106, Routh (1846), p. 413.1. Gregory of Nyssa also preserved a quotation or recollection from Theognostus, teaching that the Son was brought into being when God decided to create the world (ibid. p. 412.6–9); so Athanasius accuses Arius of teaching (in the Thalia paraphrase of con. Ar. I, A(iii); above, p. 100).

320 Routh, 412.23–413.1.

321 Ibid. 411.1–11 (= de decr. 25, Opitz 21.1–6); note the denial that the Son is *ek mē ontōn*. This may be a sign of post-Nicene tinkering, but if it were, we should expect *ex ouk ontōn*.

322 Diekamp (1902), p. 483, 1.2; Radford (1908), pp. 21–2.

323 Diekamp (1902), p. 483, 11.15–24; Radford (1908), pp. 25–6. Note also the stress (Diekamp, p. 483, 1.17) on there being 'one Word and one Wisdom'.

324 Routh, op. cit. p. 430.9–10 (again from Photius, bibl 119).

325 Ibid. p. 430.19–21.

326 Radford, op. cit. p. 53.

327 E.g. conf. 146; see Smith (1968/1978), pp. 37–40, for a very full list of relevant texts.

328 in Jo. II.31, 88.23–89.2.

329 Opitz, U.14, 22.22.

330 Ibid. 22.16, 23.14, 30–1.

331 Ibid. 23.29.

332 Ibid. 23.23–4.

333 Ibid. 24.4–6; cf. 25.24–6 and 27.18–19.

334 Ibid. 22.7.

335 Ibid. 25.23 (*oude tas tē(i) hupostasei duo phuseis mian einai saphēnizōn*); it is not clear whether *hupostasei* should be taken with *phuseis* or with *mian* – a vivid illustration of the ambiguity of *hupostasis* at this period.

336 Ibid. 21.11–22, and 24.24–25.7.

337 Ibid. 26.27; cf. Origen, con. Celsum III.34.

338 Ibid. 27.15–16.

339 Ibid. 27.13–17.

340 Ibid. 22.15–19, and 23.6–11; cf. 24.8–11, 27.8–10.

341 Ibid. 27.5.

342 Ibid. 27.5–6: the Son is not generated 'in any bodily way – by splitting off, or by the emanation of distinct levels of reality, as Sabellius and Valentinus teach'.

C THEOLOGY OUTSIDE EGYPT

1 Cf. II.A, n.89, above

2 Newman (1876), pp. 1–24.

3　II.14–17 (pp. 50–4 in Grant's edition).

4　See below, p. 160, for the possibility that one fragment of Paul's represents a Christological exegesis of one of the royal psalms.

5　His objection (e.g. de engastrimytho 21–2, PG 18, 656A–670A) is to the turning of *all* scriptural narrative into allegory of 'fable'. Some of his exegetical fragments (PG 18, 675–92) show standard features of 'spiritual' interpretation.

6　See Wallace-Hadrill (1982), pp. 29–35, for some useful observations, though I am not wholly persuaded by his account of the purpose of Lucian's method in editing Scripture.

7　Meijering (1968) gives a generally very balanced account of the continuities and discontinuities between Athanasius and his Alexandrian precursors. As so often in the patristic period, Origen provides a vocabulary and a quarry of arguments, but not a systematic hermeneutical or theological framework.

8　ad Autol. II.15 (Grant, p. 52).

9　Ibid. II.22 (Grant, pp. 62–4).

10　de syn. 81, PL 10, 534B.

11　de syn. 45, Opitz 269.37–270.26.

12　Hilary, de syn., loc. cit.

13　Discussed at length in Loofs (1924), pp. 147–64, 209–11.

14　See de Riedmatten (1952), pp. 106–7, for this point.

15　de Riedmatten (1952), fragments 36 and 37, pp. 156–8. Cf. Loofs (1924), PP. 203–7, on this question.

16　Bardy (1929), pp. 440–1, on the possibility that Paul used the term *organon*, 'instrument', for the Word. On the parallels with Theophilus, see Loofs (1924), pp.207, 303–9, and Bardy (1929), p. 434.

17　Op. cit. p. 110.

18　In other words, we cannot safely conclude that he was a Sabellian in any simple sense. On Paul's probable concern for strict monotheism, see Loofs (1924), pp. 203–11. cf. Bardy (1929), pp. 448–53, for a critical assessment of Loofs' account, giving more weight to the genuine element of trinitarian pluralism in Paul's thought.

19　de Riedmatten (1952), fragment 26, p. 153.

20　Ibid. fragments 8 and 9, p. 138, and 25, p. 153; cf. fragments 31, p. 155, and 36, p. 157.

21　Ibid. fragment 26, p. 153.

22　Ibid. cf. fragments 6, p. 137, 8, p. 138, 25–7, p. 153, and the phrase from the lost *logoi pros Sabinon* describing Christ as 'anointed by the Holy Spirit' (*tō(i) hagiō(i) pneumati christheis*), printed in Loofs (1924), p. 339, and Bardy (1929), p. 186 (no. IV).

23　Above, p. 145. Eustathius also discussed this text (PG 18, 685B–688B).

24 This possible allusion is not discussed by Loofs or Bardy. It is worth noting that the 'letter of the six bishops' (a document of questionable authenticity, it must be admitted) uses Ps. 45:7–8 as earlier writers do, to prove Christ's divinity (see Bardy (1929), p. 14, for the text). Was Paul responding directly to this?

25 Printed in Bardy (1929), p. 54; Bardy sees no objection to accepting the substantial authenticity of this passage.

26 Bardy (1929), p. 187 (no. VI). This again comes from the *pros Sabinon*.

27 The *pros Sabinon* texts survive in late and unreliable florilegia; Bardy (1929), pp. 187–96, notes the reasons for doubting their authenticity, unconvinced by Loofs (1924), pp. 283–93, who offers some criteria for sorting out authentic Paulinian fragments from their obviously fraudulent settings, and his text (p. 339) demonstrates how such fragments might be restored. Norris (1984) is sceptical of the reliability of *everything* not found in Eusebius, which is rather drastic; but some of his arguments are vulnerable. On pp. 57–8, he suggests that Paul's 'adoptionism' was a polemical retrojection of Arian adoptionism (i.e. he accepts the thesis of Gregg and Groh). But if Arian adoptionism is largely a myth, this case will not stand; and I suspect that fragments with a degree of exegetical significance have a fair chance of being authentic, since the fabrication *ex nihilo* of heterodox interpretations of Scripture is not common as a polemical technique.

28 Above, pp. 108–9, 113ff.

29 (1980), pp. 457–9.

30 Above, II.A, n.116.

31 God's *idios logos;* see Stead (1978), pp. 38–9 and Williams (1983), pp. 58–62.

32 Opitz, U.146, 25.12–13.

33 Loofs (1924), pp. 183–6.

34 Bardy (1936), p. 55.

35 Above, pp. 183–8 and n.6 to I.C.

36 Bardy (1923), p. 401. In the completely revised version of 1929 Bardy abandons his earlier conclusion and confesses himself undecided ((1929), pp. 384–5).

37 Ibid. p. 411; cf. Wallace-Hadrill (1982), p. 83.

38 Bardy (1936), pp. 58–9.

39 Loofs (1924), p. 185.

40 So much is implied by canon XIX of Nicaea (Mansi, 676D–677A).

41 Epiphanius, ancoratus 33, 42.20–4, reports that 'Lucian and all the Lucianists deny that the Son of God took on a *psychē*', with the result that they ascribe human *pathos* directly to the Word.

42 Newman (1876), pp. 7–8, Robertson (1892), p. xxviii; cf. Bardy (1936), pp. 48–9.

43 de vir. inl. 77, PL 23, 685C.
44 h.e. III.5, 106.30–107.3.
45 h.e. IX.6, 813.13–815.17.
46 Some of them displayed in the comparative tabulations of Lorenz (1978), pp. 182–90 and 193–5. For the text, see Athanasius, de syn. 23, Opitz 249.11–250–4; in Appendix (a) below.
47 Opitz, U.18, 36–41 (not in Lorenz; see (d) in the Appendix to this volume).
48 Opitz, U.30, 64.
49 Collected in Bardy (1936), pp. 341–57; note especially fragment XXI, p. 349.
50 See Bardy (1936), pp. 129–30, no.72 (not in Lorenz).
51 Opitz, U.22, 43.9–25.
52 The grammatical structure in Asterius, fragment XXI, is different, but the sequence of titles is the same, with the addition of *theos:* 'For, says Asterius, the Father who generated the only-begotten Son and firstborn of all creation from himself (*ex autou*) is other [than the Son], the only one [who generated] the only one, the perfect [who generated] the perfect . . . God who generated God, the identical image of the substance, the will, the glory and the power [of his own being]'. Bardy adduces further allusions from the literature. In the text of Gregory Thaumaturgus, we have 'the only one from the only one, God from God, imprint and image of the godhead . . . the invisible of the invisible, the incorruptible of the incorruptible, the eternal of the eternal'.
53 de syn. 23, Opitz 249.17–18.
54 Ibid. 249.15–16; cf. 5.24–6.
55 de syn. 23, Opitz 249.26–9; cf. Opitz, U.30, 64.9–14.
56 Lorenz (1978), pp. 190 and 194–5; cf. Opitz, U.18, 39.3 and 15 (Syr.), 3 and 17 (Gr.).
57 de syn. 23, Opitz 249.16–17.
58 Opitz, U.6, 12.9
59 (1936), pp. 94–119.
60 h.e. II.15, 25.25–7.
61 Philostorgius records the *diadochē* of Lucian's pupils from the master to Aetius: in h.e. III.15, 44.9–46.12, Aetius is described as student and protégé of several Lucianists, especially Antony of Tarsus, who was particularly close to the martyr.
62 As in Origen; cf. pp. 132ff. above.
63 Reproduced in Bardy (1936), pp. 134–49, as well as in Rufinus (above, n.45).
64 Bardy (1936), p. 138, n.17. This similarity is touched upon in

Lorenz's discussion of the points of contact between Lactantius and Arius, (1978), p. 159.

65   Bardy (1936), pp. 140–3. It should not be *too* readily assumed that 'clothed in flesh' implies belief in the absence of a human soul, though it may well be that Lucian so believed.

66   Ibid. pp. 145–8.

67   (1936), p. 134.

68   de vir. inl. 77, PL 23, 685C.

69   Bardy, p. 143; cf. Eusebius, h.e. IX.5.1, 810.8ff.

70   Despite Lorenz's assertion (1978), p. 198, there is no evidence of adoptionism in the text.

71   Above, IB.

72   Philostorgius, h.e. II.3, 14.3–5.

73   See Williams (1983), p. 71; and cf. Luibheíd (1981), pp. 33–4, and Barnes (1981), pp. 186 and 188.

74   S.25.

75   de syn. 22, Opitz 248.29–32.

76   See Williams in Gregg (1985), pp. 13–15.

77   As was shown in the case of Athanasius of Nazarba, above, pp. 108–9.

78   See above, II.A, p. 108, and n.77 for similarities in their exegesis of the parable of the good shepherd; and Methodius' fragment on Jonah, printed by Bonwetsch as de res. II.25, 380.16–382.15, has clear echoes of Origen. Cf. Patterson (1976), p. 165, n.1, on allegory in Methodius, and Bonwetsch (1903), pp. 148–54.

79   Both are concerned to combat any form of gnostic determinism, and both set high store by asceticism and virginity, as marks of the dignity of human free will. For a survey of parallels, see Bonwetsch (1903), pp. 168–9.

80   de creatis VI, 497.8–20.

81   Ibid. IV-V, 496.13–497.7.

82   de res. I.27.1–28.1, 254.6–257.2, assumes that Methodius' Origenian opponents are committed to the idea of eternally and independently existing matter awaiting 'adornment' from God. The same view is attacked at several points in de autex. and the fragments of de creatis.

83   de res. I.3.8, 223.21ff may suggest this connection between dualist heresy and philosophy; cf. I.27.1–28.1, 254.7–257.2, as Patterson (1976), p. 162, suggests.

84   de autex. V, 157.6–159.4. The argument is evidently a conventional one, familiar to Christians with some philosophical education: a rather cruder form of it appears in a fragment of Dionysius of Alexandria preserved in Eusebius, praer. ev. VII.19, and published by Feltoe as part of Dionysius' reply to Dionysius of Rome (which seems unlikely); see Feltoe, pp. 183.6–14, for the relevant passage.

85 On the body as *sunergos* with the soul, not a 'fetter' upon it, de res. I.31–34, 54; on the problem of evil in the will and the will's restoration, de res. I.43 and 60, and II.2–6 (a discussion of Rom.7, of considerable interest).

86 Below, pp. 186–8.

87 (1982), pp. 917–18, 920.

88 symp. III.4, 30.19, VII.1, 71.12.

89 symp. VIII.9, 91.4–17; directed against a gnostic Christology in which a celestial Christ descends upon Jesus at his baptism, making him Son. For Methodius, Jesus incarnates one who is already and eternally Son; the Son is not the *result* of a fusion between heavenly Christ and earthly Jesus.

90 Ibid. 91.11.

91 de creatis XI, 499.13–15.

92 symp. VIII.1, 71.15–17.

93 Patterson (1982), pp. 916–19, discusses this at length.

94 In the strict modern sense; see Stead (1964), pp. 26–7, and III.A below.

95 Not only those listed in U.1, but also perhaps expressions like *homoousios* and *idios tēs tou patros ousias* applied to the Son; see Williams (1983), pp. 57–66.

96 Opitz, U.1, 2.1.

97 Opitz, U.14b, 20.8–9.

98 Luibhéid (1981) minimizes Eusebius' 'Arianism', Barnes (1981) stresses it (see, e.g., p. 265: 'it is an Arian orthodoxy which Eusebius represents as the accepted teaching of the Church' in the eccl. theol.).

99 Op. cit., e.g., pp. 5 and 26.

100 Ibid. pp. 31–3; cf. Williams (1983), p. 71.

101 h.e. I.2.3, 12.4–5, dem. ev. IV.3, 152.20–154.24, 15.15, 175.12–33 (note the references to Ps. 45), V.4.9, 225.6–14, eccl. theol. I.2, 63.21–26, II.17, 120.28–121.18.

102 Luibhéid (1981), pp. 50–1, does not bring this out sufficiently clearly.

103 dem. ev. IV.6.3, 158.29–159.10, 15.15, 175.22–23, 15.19, 176.23–7.

104 Ibid. IV.3, 152.20–154.24.

105 Opitz, U.3, 4–6.

106 (1981), pp. 36–7, 43–4.

107 dem. ev. IV.3.13, 154.11–24.

108 Ibid. IV.5.13, 157.35–158.5, IV.6.2, 158.22–9, etc.

109 See the discussion of creation in ST I.46.1 and 2, and cf. de potentia III.14.8 ad 8.

110 dem. ev. V.1.15, 212.23–6: 'the *genesis* of the Son is one thing, the creation that takes place through the Son is something else'.

111 Opitz, U.7, 14–15.

112 dem. ev. V.1.15, loc. cit.
113 Opitz, U.7, 15.2–6.
114 Williams (1985), pp. 134–5.
115 eccl. theol. I.20, 87.34–5; and cf. dem. ev. VII.1.23, 24, 302.2–15 and X.8.74, 485.16–21.
116 This seems to be the controversial point of the text quoted in the preceding note.
117 Stead (1982), pp. 246–7.
118 Lommatzsch, 373.13–374.2; cf. 398–405, on the soul in general.
119 This seems to be implied in Eusebius' comments on Ps. 68, for example; see Stead (1982), pp. 241–2.
120 Cf. ref. in n.115 above.

CONCLUSION

1 On the question of God's 'idleness' before creation, see Sorabji (1983), esp. pp. 249–52. The point about the essential simultaneity of the existence of Father and Son is reflected in many ways in the history of Christian theology and spirituality, perhaps most notably in Meister Eckhart's language about the eternal coincidence of silence (absolute potentiality) and speech (the action of the Word) in the divine life. Such language is in part adumbrated in the trinitarian thought of Marius Victorinus in the fourth century; see below, n.3 to IIID, and, for a general discussion of this issue, pp. 239–45 of the Postscript.
2 The major contrast between the credal texts associated with Arius himself and the whole tradition of theology stemming from Origen, as well as the Lucianist approach; compare the use of *eikōn* in Appendix (a), (c) and (d), and note its absence in (b) and (g).
3 Is.1.2 is a favourite, quoted by Eusebius of Nicomedia, Opitz, U.8, 17.1ff. Athanasius makes it clear that it was a regular part of the controversial arsenal of anti-Nicenes (see, e.g., con.Ar.I.37, PG 26,89AB).

ART III ARIUS AND PHILOSOPHY

CREATION AND BEGINNING

1 Sorabji (1983), p. 276.
2 Origen knows Numenius, according to Porphyry as quoted by

Eusebius (h.e. VI.19.8, 560.12) and Jerome, ep. 70.4 (PL 22.667); Eusebius preserved several important fragments of Atticus in prep. ev. XV.4.1–139, 350–78 (those in XV.6, 359–63, are most pertinent here); Methodius is almost certainly aware of contemporary discussions of time (see below); and Athanasius, who knew Eusebius' praep. ev., will have been familiar with some such discussions through this medium (see Meijering (1968), pp. 165–6).

3 See Guthrie (1978), pp. 258–9, on whether *all* form is contained in the *autozōon* or only some (the forms of living creatures in our cosmos).

4 de caelo I.10ff; see Sorabji (1983), pp. 277–8.

5 Timaeus 41A.

6 de caelo I.12, 281b.25f.

7 Ibid. 281b.2–282a.25.

8 So Sorabji (1983) argues, p. 278.

9 Sorabji (1983), pp. 279–83, discusses a number of passages.

10 I.10, 279b.32–280a.11.

11 Taurus (ap. Philoponus, aet. VI.8, 145–7) argued in the second century AD for a non-literal reading of the Timaeus. Whittaker (1981), pp. 58–9, notes that Phaedrus 245C (on the soul as uncreated) was used to support such a reading. Philoponus' great work attacking the notion of the eternity of the world is planned as a refutation of Proclus' case for a creation without beginning, and Proclus' commentary on the Timaeus contains criticisms of writers like Plutarch and Atticus, who read the Timaeus in a more simply 'creationist' way. See Proclus, in Timaeum I.276–7, 381–2, for the view of these earlier writers that the moment of creation was preceded by 'disorderly motion'.

12 Op. cit. p. 299; the whole of his discussion on time and creation (pp. 299–305) is of great value.

13 See the important studies by Vlastos in Allen (1965). Sorabji (1983), p. 274, has reservations about this interpretation.

14 Atticus, frs. 22 and 24, pp. 74 and 75.

15 Ibid. fr. 20, pp. 73–4.

16 Ibid. fr. 19, p. 73.

17 fr. 52, p. 95.6–14.

18 Metaphysics 12.17, 1072a.

19 Sorabji (1983), pp. 282–3.

20 Ibid. p. 310, n.16 for references.

21 Porphyry criticizes Atticus for implying a plurality of *archai*. See fr. 51 of Porphyry in Platonis Timaeum, p. 34.9ff.

22 See Rist (1967), pp. 117–19.

23 Enneads 2.4.4.

24 Ibid. 2.4.5 (and cf. O'Brien in Blumenthal and Markus (1981), p. 111, on 2.9.3, for a clear account of this argument).

25 Ibid. 2.4.8.
26 fr. 51 in Timaeum, p. 34.11–14; cf. Enneads 2.4.2.
27 Enneads 4.8.6.
28 Ibid. 5.2.1, 5.4.2, 5.5 passim, 5.9.5, etc.
29 5.2.1.
30 Metaphysics 12.7, 1072a.
31 See Sorabji (1983), p. 247, n.70.
32 Cf. Metaphysics 12.2–3, 1069b–1070a.
33 Metaphysics 12.6, 1071b; cf. Physics 4.11, 219b.
34 Sorabji (1983), pp. 247–8, argues that Aristotle could conceive of new
    forms emerging 'out of nothing', and might have been able to make
    some sense of matter coming into being from nothing; Alexander
    of Aphrodisias and Philoponus both utilize the point about forms.
    However, the emergence of *absolute* novelty, the universe rather than
    nothing, is still, I think, incapable of being accommodated in Aris-
    totle's terminology. It certainly could not be called a 'making', at
    any rate, and I am not sure that the appearance of novel form could
    have been seen as a 'creation' by Aristotle. But the issue is a complex
    one, and Sorabji's case is skilful and attractive.
35 prov. 1, opif. 7.27.
36 See Whittaker in Blumenthal and Markus (1981) on Plutarch's
    appeal to Christians.
37 Above, n.2, for references.
38 See above, pp. 168–70, and cf. the passage from Dionysius of Alexan-
    dria referred to in II.C.2, n.84.
39 E.g. de princ. I, praef. 4, 15.13–15, with its two distinct terms for
    'creation' *might* be thus read, as might in Jo. I.19, 23.17–24.10 (a
    notoriously difficult and certainly corrupt passage), and several other
    passages in the Commentary.
40 Cf. Plotinus' far more sophisticated views on the rational structuring
    principle in individuals; there is some discussion of this complex point
    in Rist (1967), pp. 86–88, 110–111.
41 Above, pp. 121–2.
42 (1976), p. 336, esp. n.1.
43 (1976), p. 165, n.1; cf. Patterson (1982), p. 917.
44 de res. II.25, 380.19–382.15.
45 See ch. 21 of Sorabji (1983), on Zeno.
46 Timaeus 37DE, 39A-D.
47 V, 158.6–9.
48 Their nuances are slightly different, but Methodius uses them inter-
    changeably in de res. II.25, 382.3–6. Cf. Philoponus, who prefers
    diastasis (e.g. aet. IV.4, 64.22–6, IV.14, 95.23–7), but can use *diastēma*
    in much the same sense (ibid., V.4, 115.1–11).

49   de creatis IV, 469.13–31.

50   e.g. aet. IV.59–102, esp. 64–5.

51   ST I.45.2 ad 2; de potentia III.3.

52   As Eusebius clearly did, for instance, given his interest in the 'minority' Platonist tradition that held to the idea of a moment of generation for the cosmos (praep. ev. XV).

53   Opitz U.14, 22.16.

54   Ibid. 23.14–19.

55   Ibid. 23.19–20.

56   Opitz, U.1, 1.2.

57   *atomos* may mean an instant in time; but (as the discussion following in the text will, I hope, make clear) I am not sure that Arius would have wanted to say that the Father is prior to the Son by an ordinary interval of time, and would have accordingly opted for the more general sense of the word.

58   Opitz, U.1, 3.2.

59   Ibid. 3.3.

60   498.24–30. Once again, the language of Dionysius of Alexandria shows some parallels: he speaks of God's decision to create matter 'according to his wisdom, impressing on it the manifold and comprehensively varied structure and model of his creative power' (Feltoe, pp. 184.12–14).

61   Timaeus 28A–29C, 30C–31B.

62   e.g. opif. 4.16; see above, p. 117.

63   Cf. III.B, below.

64   See in particular in Jo. I.19 and 20.

65   de creatis 499.14–15.

66   S.19.

67   (1964), p. 19.

68   gig. 11.52 (rationality, *logos*, when expressed, is a *duas* – of thought and sound – and therefore offers no stable knowledge); imm. 18.82–4 (distinguishing God's 'monadic' utterance from the dyadic process of speech in human beings, in which high and low pitch, or the mixture of breath and air, are harmonized into a composite unity). Neither of these passages seems to qualify very significantly the derogatory association of *duas*, and neither is especially illuminating theologically.

69   fr. 8, p. 68; much the closest parallel to Arius – the *duas* sits by (presumably) the first god, containing the intelligibilia and making sensation possible in creation.

70   fr. 16, p. 57.

71   fr. 52, p. 95.5–19.

72   Preserved in Iamblichus, Theologoumena Arithmeticae.

73   Ibid. 9.

74   Ibid. 8.
75   By *chusis*, emanation; ibid. 8.
76   Ibid.
77   Ibid.
78   Metaphysics 1.6, 987b–988a.
79   Anatolius/Iamblichus, op. cit. 5–6, 14.
80   Enneads, 2.4, passim.
81   Armstrong (1980), pp. 249, 256–7.
82   In his note to the Loeb text, p. 26, n.1.
83   Enneads 5.1.6, 5.1.7; cf. 5.9.2, 6.7.15–18, etc.
84   Ibid. 5.16.
85   Ibid.
86   Ibid. 6.6.12, 6.6.14.
87   Op. cit. 13–14.
88   Ibid. 6.
89   Ibid.
90   Iamblichus, fr. 53 in Timaeum, p. 160.
91   Ibid. fr. 54, p. 162.
92   Dillon (1973), pp. 30–3.
93   In a paper on 'Causality in Plato and Origen', forthcoming in *Origeniana Quarta*.
94   Cf. the discussion of Enneads 5.2.4 in the next section.
95   Op. cit. 6.
96   Rist (1981), pp. 166–7.
97   Ibid., esp. pp. 178–90.
98   Grant (1971/1983).
99   Indeed, he is willing to use *nous* as a suitable analogue for God (de princ. I.1.6); God is, in a sense, *nous*, though he also transcends it (con. Cels. VII.38). See also Williams, forthcoming in *Origeniana Quarta*.
100 *Apostolic Constitutions*, VI.11.1; cf. Williams in Gregg (1985), p. 18.
101 See e.g. con. Ar. I.14–21, III.60–3.
102 Cf. Sorabji (1983), p. 318, on differences between Platonists and Christians on the role of will in creation.
103 Cf. the view ascribed by Philostorgius (h.e. II.15, 25.22–5) to Theognis of Nicaea, that the Father can be so called because he has the eternal *dunamis* to beget (even if not eternally realized). He may have had Aristotle, Metaphysics 5.15 in mind; see Lorenz (1983), pp. 27–8.
104 Benz (1932) remains a fascinating and valuable study of the role played by concepts of will in the Arian controversy; see esp. the description of will in the Enneads, pp. 289–309, and the concluding chapter, pp. 414–21 on the Arian understanding of will as

'functional', contrasted with the Catholic view of God's nature *as will*. Cf. also Stead (1985) on this area.

B INTELLECT AND BEYOND

1 This may go back to Antiochus of Ascalon in the first century BC; see Merlan in Armstrong (1980), pp. 54–5.
2 See ch. IX, esp. 1 and 3, of his *epitome;* Merlan, p. 66.
3 fr. 12 (pp. 70–1); see Williams, *Origeniana Quarta.*
4 Atticus, fr. 18 (p. 73); from Proclus, in Timaeum I.271–2.
5 Ep. VII, 341CD, Timaeus, 28C.
6 Cf. also the 'negative theology' of Albinus (above II.B.2, n. 91) for the idea that the first principle is to be known by the total thinking away of particular determinations or attributes.
7 Enneads, 5.4.2.
8 Ibid. 5.3.1.
9 Ibid. 5.3.5.
10 Ibid. 5.3.1.
11 Ibid. 5.3.5.
12 Ibid. 5.3.6.
13 Ibid. 5.3.8.
14 12.9, 1074b.
15 Enneads, 5.3.10.
16 Ibid. 5.3.17: 'my soul labours still harder . . .' The imagery of this passage – concepts emerging from the agonizing birth-pangs of the mind – is striking and moving.
17 Ibid. 5.3.11.
18 Accepting, with Armstrong (Loeb edn, p. 110, n.1), Igal's emendation, *aei de endeomenos,* 'eternally falling short'; *nous* both grasps and fails to reach the One.
19 Ibid. 5.3.17 (cf. Augustine in Conf. VII.10 and IX.10).
20 Ibid. 5.3.12; cf. 5.3.15, 6.9.6.
21 Ibid. 5.3.13.
22 Ibid. 5.3.14.
23 Ibid. 5.3.7.
24 See the classical exposition of Gregory of Nyssa by Daniélou (1944), esp. pp. 291–307; and cf. Mühlenberg (1966) and Williams (1979), pp. 52–62.
25 In Armstrong (1980), p. 142; this does not mean that Philo is responsible for this notion (see n.1, above).
26 Above, p. 119.
27 As is implied by his view of the ideal forms and his doctrine of the

nous as God's image in us; see e.g. opif. 23.69, for God as *nous* of all things.

28 leg. all. I.29.91ff, somn. I.10.60; see above, II.B.1, p. 120.

29 See above, IIB.4, n.327.

30 On God as creator of matter, see esp. prov. 1 and 2, and the full discussion in Sorabji (1983), pp. 203–9.

31 strom. IV.25, 320.18ff.

32 in Jo. I.38, 49.5ff.

33 Above, pp. 136, 140–1.

34 Above, pp. 126, 139.

35 VII.38, 188.11–14, VIII.38, 253.19–20.

36 *epitome* X.5 (pp. 60/61).

37 in Jo. I.17, 19, 27, 34, II.2, etc.

38 Both may owe something in this respect to their common teacher, Ammonius Saccas; see Williams, *Origeniana Quarta*.

39 E.g. Enneads 5.5.12 (Loeb edn, p. 192). The One as Good is even spoken of as exercising *will* in this passage.

40 According to Photius' catalogue of charges, bibl. 117.

41 de princ. IV.4.8, 359.16–19, 360.1–7.

42 I.27, 34.19–31.

43 II.23, 80.12–15.

44 XXXII.28 and 29, 473.10–475.33.

45 474.1–3.

46 (1977), pp. 134–44, 150–3.

47 Above, II.B.3, n.167.

48 The point is noted in *henos sōmatos* (Opitz, U.4b, 8.2–6).

49 Above, pp. 63, 165.

50 Men such as Athanasius of Nazarba, Leontius of Antioch and Antony of Tarsus, all close to Lucian, played a significant role in training Aetius: see Kopecek (1979), vo. 1, pp. 68–73. The Origenian Paulinus also taught the young Aetius (ibid. 63–5; Philostorgius, h.e. III.15, 45.9–12, 27–32).

51 Syntagmation, Part II, 12–16; Kopecek (1979), vol. 1, pp. 266–7.

52 Cf. above, II.B.1, p. 107, and n.59; IIC.1, n.100.

53 E.g. con. Ar. I.59, II.81, 82.

54 See especially Or. XXVIII (the second of the five 'Theological' Discourses).

55 In the contra Eunomium, especially Book II.

56 Cf. Williams (1979), pp. 52–62.

57 E.g. Gregory of Nyssa, de vita Moysis, PG 44, 376C–377B; for *theologia* in this sense, ibid. 373D–376A.

58 Ibid. 381B–384B; even here, the straightforward Philonic tradition of understanding the heavenly tabernacle as the Logos, continuing the

world of forms, is qualified by a more 'personalist' Christian idea of the Word as embracing and animating the world of spiritual agents. Cf. Daniélou's n.2 on p. 225 of his edn.

59   See Rist (1981), pp. 192–3, 195–220, on the error of identifying any more than the slightest genuine influence of Plotinus upon Basil and the other Cappadocians.

60   Cf. Athanasius, con. Ar. II.2, 149B–152B, for the classical statement of the principle that God's will as creative must reflect a nature that is by definition not 'sterile'.

61   See the remarks on Philo, above II.B.1, pp. 119–20.

62   Hence the remark of Pseudo-Dionysius that God is neither *monas* nor *trias* in our usual sense of the words (*hē pros hēmōn*): de div. nom. 13, PG 3, 980D–981A.

63   (1982), pp. 36–8.

64   Ibid. p. 36.

65   Ibid. pp. 33–4.

66   Ibid. p. 38.

67   (1981), passim.

68   5.14–15.

69   A(vii).

70   (1978), p. 37.

71   I use the masculine pronoun for the One and the neuter for *nous* for the sake of clarity; in the Greek, 'the One', of course, is neuter and *nous* masculine – and the genitive of both is the same, so that the meaning of the passage is not always clear. The translation follows what seems the most natural sense, but should not be regarded as unchallengeable.

72   Enneads, 5.3.7.

73   Kannengiesser (1982), pp. 33 and 38, contrasts this with Origen, de princ. II.4.3, 130–1.

74   In the Loeb edition of Plotinus' text, n.1, pp. 92–3.

75   Enneads, 5.3.4.

76   Ibid. 5.3.8.

77   Ibid. 5.3.16.

78   Ibid. 5.3.17.

79   Taking 'the power by which God himself can see' as meaning God's power to see or know *himself*, and rejecting, as we surely must (see above, II.A, n.56), the suggestion that *ho theos* could here mean '*a god*'.

80   (1982), pp. 38–40.

C ANALOGY AND PARTICIPATION

1   Allen (1960/1965) and Bigger (1968) are important studies of the
    Platonic background but a satisfactory extended study of the concept
    in classical and patristic thought is still lacking. Normann (1978) is
    disappointing on the philosophical side.
2   As Annas (1981), p. 217, reminds us, it is misleading to speak as
    though Plato had a single 'doctrine' or 'theory' of forms.
3   132E–133A.
4   E.g. Geach (1956/1965).
5   Bigger (1968), p. 74.
6   Parmenides, 131A-E.
7   (1960/1961), pp. 48–51.
8   Ibid. p. 50.
9   Bigger (1968), pp. 89–90.
10 Ibid. pp. 74–5.
11 Metaphysics 1.9, 991a20; Booth (1983), p. 219, speaks of Aristotle's
    'ironic' us of participation language.
12 E.g. Alexander of Aphrodisias, in Arist. Met. 90–5.
13 Ibid., 84.1, 101.3.
14 Porphyry, *eisagōgē*, 22.9–10.
15 Alexander, op. cit. 94.8ff; cf. 126.
16 Aristotle, Categories 1.1a; cf. Alexander, op. cit. p. 241. For a full
    discussion of Aristotle's views in the categories and elsewhere, see
    Owens (1978), pp. 107–35.
17 Categories 1.1a; see Anton (1968) and (1969/1971) on this expression,
    its background and its interpretation in later commentators.
    (1969/1971), pp. 571–4, explains Porphyry's misunderstanding of it
    in terms of the quite distinct question of homonymous *individuals* of
    a single species.
18 in Arist. Cat. 65.21–66.21.
19 Though these are not Porphyry's own examples.
20 Metaphysics 4.2, 1003aff.
21 Porphyry, in Arist. Cat. 66.15–21, Aristotle, Metaphysics 4.2.1003a;
    see Owens (1978), pp. 118–22.
22 The question must remain open as to whether Allen (art. cit. p. 58,
    n.1) is right to assimilate what he argues to be Plato's theory of
    predication in respect of forms so closely to Aristotle's *pros hen* equi-
    vocity: the latter does not necessarily involve *ontological* dependence,
    as does talk about the 'derivative designation' of particulars in
    relation to forms.
23 6.508A–509B.

24 The sun not only gives light (so that things can be seen), it is the source of life and growth in the material world.

25 E.g. 144A, though, as with any quotation from the Parmenides, this cannot be taken as the simple statement of a position; cf. Aristotle's account of Plato on number in Metaphysics 13, esp. 6–7.

26 Republic 509B, Parmenides 141E onwards, bearing in mind the cautions of the preceding note.

27 See Rist (1967), pp. 22–4.

28 Ibid. p. 23.

29 Ibid. p. 24.

30 The Parmenides shows (among other things) the logical problems raised by leaving the definition of *to hen* in such terms; the brilliant dialectical elaboration of c. 140 onwards shows the impossibility of defining the One as not-other, *a* being in itself.

31 Republic 6.509D–7.535A.

32 *Platonika zētēmata* 2, 1002c, quoted by Dörrie in Blumenthal and Markus (1981), p. 41.

33 Plutarch, adv. Colot. 15, 1115e, Dörrie in Blumenthal and Markus (1981), p. 42; cf. Numenius, frs. 16, 19, 20.

34 See, e.g., Booth (1983), ch. 2, and Armstrong (1980), p. 248.

35 Lloyd, in Armstrong (1980), p. 321.

36 Albinus, *epitomē* X passim, esp. 4; cf. Celsus in Origen, con. Cels. VII.42, 192.22–193.3. See Lilla (1971), pp. 221–3, for further parallels.

37 Albinus, *epitomē* X.5; Clement of Alexandria, strom. V.11.71.2–3, 374.4–20. Cf. above, II.B.2, pp. 125–6, 130 and n.91.

38 Albinus, *epitomē* X.5.

39 See Booth (1983), p. 83.

40 See Wallis (1972), pp. 106, 110–11, for the probabilities as to what Porphyry taught.

41 The latter two may also appear as *metechomenos* (participated) and *kata methexin* or *en schesei* (in participation, in relation); see Dillon (1973), p. 33.

42 See Williams (1983), pp. 63–5.

43 Above, III.A, p. 195.

44 Opitz, U.6, 12.11; cf. 13.18 for 'a portion of a *homoousios* compound'. For *homoousios* designating a compound of different substances, see Iamblichus, de mysteriis, III.21.150.9.

45 S.16.

46 A(viii).

47 Opitz, U.8, 16.3–4.

48 de autex. V, 157.6ff. For the attacks of Arius and others, see Opitz, U.1, 2.10; 3, 4–5, passim; 6, 13.10–12, 7, 15.3–6.

49 S. 8–9.
50 fr. 19, p. 59.
51 E.g., eccl. theol. I.2, 63.25, II.17, 121.15, h.e. I.3.13, 34.9–10.
52 (1981), pp. 165–70.
53 S.3–4.
54 E.g. Porphyry, *eisagōgē* 12.15ff; see Williams (1983), pp. 58–62.
55 E.g. Porphyry, de abstinentia I.19.1, p. 56.
56 Cf. possibly Numenius, fr. 16, p. 57.
57 The real and significant elements of 'grace' in Plotinus' system might be thought of as revelation, in a sense, but they are in no way linked with text or history.
58 Opitz, U.4b, 7.21–8.2.
59 con. Ar. I.5, 6, 9; II.37–38, III.15, 24, etc.
60 Thus Alexander, Opitz, U.4b, 7.23.
61 Athanasius, ad ep. Aeg. 12, PG 25, 565A, con. Ar. II.37, PG 26, 225A.
62 Athanasius, con. Ar. I.9, PG 26, 29C. For the equivalence of all these terms as (apparently) assumed by Athanasius, see Williams (1983), pp. 76–7.
63 See, e.g. Porphyry's discussion of equivocity, above, n.18.
64 But, as noted above (II.A, p. 113 and n.112), he or his supporters seem to have opted in exegesis for a sense of *metochoi* agreeable to the neo-Aristotelian and Porphyrian account of *metochē* as a 'horizontal', not a 'vertical' relation.
65 S.24.
66 See above, II.A.
67 S.16–17.
68 S.25.
69 S.29, and perhaps 23.
70 A(iv).
71 Opitz, U.6, 12.9–10, 13.6.
72 S.31.
73 S.4.
74 Cf. Williams (1983), p. 78.
75 See esp. Lossky (1974), chs. 1 and 2, on the tensions in Greek patristic thought between the apophatic impulse and the desire to affirm real and truthful knowledge of God produced by grace.
76 Despite the still-prevalent misunderstandings of the Thomist understanding of analogy, this is not Aquinas' own view (for a valuable and controversial discussion of this, see Burrell (1979)); Scotus comes closer to the idea of analogy as based on *resemblance*, as Gilson (1952), pp.101–2, indicates.
77 Chs. 58–67; once again, I am obliged here to bracket the question

lately raised of the authenticity of this work. On the theological point here, see Florovsky (1962/1975), pp. 57–60, Meijering (1974/1975:1) and (1974/1975:2).

78 con. Ar. III.62, PG 26, 453C–456A.

79 Ibid. 65, PG 26, 460B.

80 Ibid. 60, PG 26, 448C–449A; 65, PG 26, 460BC.

81 E.g. ibid. 61, PG 26, 452B–453A; cf. Origen's analogy of mind and will for Father and Son (above, p. 141).

82 con. Ar. III.65, PG 26, 461A – an obvious reminiscence, but not a direct quotation.

83 Ibid. 66, PG 26, 464A-C; and II.2, PG 26, 149B–152B for a still clearer statement. Cf. above, III.B, n.60, and Meijering (1973/1975) and (1974/1975:1), esp. pp. 7–11, an excellent discussion.

D CONCLUSION

1 Whether or not the con. Gentes and de inc. are pre-Nicene (on the question of dating, see Kannengiesser (1970)), they undoubtedly represent an 'archaic' style of theology, in which the concept of the perfect *eikōn* of the transcendent God is crucial.

2 Above, I.A, p. 31; cf. III.B.

3 The great contribution of Marius Victorinus in the Arian debates is to utilize very freely the language of the Father as primordial indeterminacy, pure *esse*, even *pre-esse*, while insisting that this is an abstraction in itself since it only *is* and is *known* in its eternal procession into *vivere;* for an admirable introduction to his trinitarian theology, see Henry (1950). Passages from the adv. Arrium which illustrate this point include I.13 (esp. CSEL, pp. 72–3), 31 (esp. p. 111), 42–3 (pp. 130–4), 63 (esp. pp. 165–6), III.7–9 (pp. 202–7), IV.21 (pp. 256–8).

POSTSCRIPT (THEOLOGICAL)

1 In the preface to his adversus Arrium, Candidi ep. II.1 and 2, CSEL 83, 49–53.

2 h.e. II.2, 13.6–10.

3 Athanasius, con. Ar. I.2 and 3, seems to imply that it was not unknown for Nicenes to be called 'Athanasians' by their opponents, cf. Augustine, op. imperf. 1.75, CSEL 85, pp. 91.36–7, and the case noted by Bauer (1972), p. 21.

4 See Kopecek (1985), pp. 172–5, on the deep concern of 'neo-

Arianism' with God's gift of the true and secure knowledge of his being.

5 As reported in chs. 29 and 30 of Athanasius' de syn.

6 The phrase is Florovsky's (1961), p. 172.

7 See MacKinnon (1975/1979) and Ericksen (1985) on the effect of all these pressures.

8 Sykes (1984) offers an impressive and nuanced discussion of the problems of continuity and identity; see, in particular, chs. 1, 2 and 10.

9 In creation *and* incarnation, for Athanasius: he is not a 'Barthian' in this respect, but believes God can be truly, if imperfectly, known through the rational order of the world.

10 Bell (1924), pp. 53ff., 62.

11 See, e.g., con. Ar. II.19, 20, 67–69, 72.

12 Ibid. II.67.

13 Ibid. II.21–2.

14 Ibid. II.67–8.

15 Ibid. II.68.

16 Ibid. Adam in Paradise receives grace only *exōthen*, but in the new covenant it is 'fitted on to' (*sunērmosmenēn*) the body (PG 26, 292C).

17 See, e.g., the long quotation from Eusebius of Emesa in Theodoret's Eranistes III (PG 83, 312C–317A). If the homilies ascribed to Asterius the Sophist, published by Richard in 1956 are indeed from his hand, we have further confirmation; but the correctness of the attribution remains doubtful.

18 The example of father and son is used by Aristotle (Metaphysics 5.15) to illustrate the relation of agent to patient as it arises in consequence of a temporal event (begetting); he is followed by Alexander of Aphrodisias (in Arist. Met. 406.7–10). Some such assumption was obviously shared by Arius. See Williams (1983), pp. 72–3, for further details.

19 Cf. above, III.C, n.83.

20 For the Cappadocians, the Father is *pēgē* and *aitia* of the divine life – see, e.g. Gregory of Nyssa, ad Abl., PG 45, 128C, de orat. dom. 3, PG 46, 1109B, Basil, de spir. sancto 21, PG 32, 105C, etc.

21 Cf. Milbank (1986), for some well-aimed criticisms of recent Trinitarian theology as translating the divine fatherhood into a non-relational 'surplus' of personhood, a primitive 'self-positing subject' prior to relation (pp. 217–22); the philosophical ambivalence of such a translation is fully explored in this important essay.

22 I.e. even though that relation cannot be said to be definitive or constitutive for what it is to be God (the error of 'process theology'), there can be no words for what it is to be God that are not bound

to what God is for the world. The Byzantine distinction of God's *ousia* from his *energeiai* arises originally from the desire to secure this point, though it does so only by an awkward methodological abstracting of nature from action.

23 MacKinnon (1976), p. 104.

24 For a brilliant exposition of this, see McCabe (1985); 'The eternal life of Jesus as such could not precede, follow or be simultaneous with his human life. There is no story of God "before" the story of Jesus. This point would not, of course, be grasped by those for whom God is an inhabitant of the universe, subject to experience and to history' (p. 474).

25 For a very suggestive – though sketchy – recent discussion of how the Nicene faith is to be understood in terms of certain continuing and irreducible 'regulative principles' of Christian commitment, *see* Lindbeck (1984), pp. 92–6.

26 Laeuchli (1968) is an interesting case in point: Nicene orthodoxy is seen as (more or less) an epiphenomenon of an age obsessed with social and political unity and taking monarchical principles for granted. The trinitarian church is the Constantinian church, a church forgetful of its eschatological roots. 'The trinitarian doctrine is an ancient case of analogy [*analogia entis*, in the most pejorative sense]. Its *Sitz-im-Leben* is the dramatic breakthrough in antiquity from a mythical to a metaphysical epoch, and its life is drawn from the hierarchical political structure of the *imperium* initially a reality secured on hostile pagan foundations and subsequently established in terms of a Christian optimism' (p. 230). The Nicene church is essentially totalitarian (p. 232). Hence, Laeuchli argues, the tensions arising for a contemporary theology that takes up a trinitarian position: the target of this is Barth, whose anti-totalitarian stance Laeuchli sees as compromised by his Nicene commitment. As historical analysis, this is simplistic (the parallels with Leach (1983) are worth noting); and the contemporary critique rests on an agressively uncritical theological and political pluralism. But the points made or implied about both imperial power in the Church and the power involved in episcopally-enforced orthodoxy are worth pondering: cf. above, pp. 86–91.

APPENDIX 1: ARIUS SINCE 1987

1 A magisterial survey of the whole of the fourth-century controversy, completed just before Hanson's death. For some detailed comments, see R. Williams (1992).

2 For surveys, see, e.g., Kannengiesser (1982:1), Ritter (1990). Barnes

and Williams (1993) is a good collection of essays building on the researches of the 1980s. Barnes and Williams also contributed two important essays to Ayres and Jones (1998), navigating the borders between historical scholarship and theological interpretation with great skill, and questioning both a historically positivist approach to doctrinal history (including the fashion for analysis in primarily political terms) and a naïve narrative of conceptual development.

3 See, for example, D. Williams (1995), M. R. Barnes (1993).

4 Outstanding here is Brakke (1995).

5 Some thoughts on this in R. Williams (1993:1) and R. Williams (1997).

6 E.g., E. Clark (1992), Lyman (1994), Widdicombe (1994).

7 See Lyman (1993). Hanson (1988) still attempts to identify a theological core of 'Arianism', finding it in the articulation of a religious need for a suffering God (pp. 109–22); this certainly throws into relief a theme found especially in some western non-Nicene writers, but there is much here that would not have shocked a Nicene. And the problem remains that the saviour in non-Nicene theologies is not strictly *God*. In any case, the presupposition that there must be an essential core only works if you think there is a single movement of some kind; the most we can say is that some critics of Nicaea worried that the *homoousios* imperilled the reality of Jesus' salvific sufferings.

8 See, for an exhaustive account, J. C. D. Clark (1985), ch. 5.

9 Cf. Lindbeck (1984), ch. 5.

10 Cf. above, pp. 109–13.

11 Forthcoming 2001, Leominster and Notre Dame.

12 T. D. Barnes (1978), particularly pp. 59–60.

13 In the first part of Martin (1989:1); the second, pp. 320–33, deals with the literary development of the narrative of Arius' death, tracing how this is partly modelled on the narrative of Arius' earlier condemnation and designed also to show how God's judgement supersedes the decision of a human synodical (or even imperial) court.

14 Richard Vaggione, in a review article full of constructive criticism in the *Toronto Journal of Theology* 5 (1989), pp. 63–87, notes the circularity of some argumentation, especially (p. 77) with regard to the implications in redating the early documents in the controversy for our understanding of Arius' relation to the Lucianists. He allows that the method is not necessarily illegitimate, but leaves us with an unclarity as to some of the criteria for the selection and privileging of particular kinds of evidence. Incidentally, on the question of Arius and the Lucianists, Hanns Christof Brennecke (1993) offers a detailed study which reinforces doubts as to whether Arius can be said to have any real intellectual common ground with the majority of Lucian's pupils,

given what we know from fourth-century sources about them (which is quite a lot).

15 Gregg (1989), esp. pp. 252ff.

16 Lyman (1989), p. 495, n.8.

17 Ibid., pp. 497–503, dealing with the anti-Manichaean work of Alexander of Lycopolis, probably a non-Christian, but not un-informed about Christianity, and the dialogue between 'Archelaus' and 'Manes' contained in the *Acta Archelai*, a very important quarry for anti-Manichaean material.

18 She allows that the material in the *Acta* suggests not an adoptionist but 'an inchoate two-nature model at best' (p. 501): my point precisely. Note the verbal parallels between 34, 49 and 50 of the *Acta* and, e.g., fragments 12, 19, 23 and 66 of Eustathius in M. Spanneut's edition (Lille 1948).

19 Lorenz (1980), p. 163.

20 R. Williams (1993:2).

21 Strutwolf (1999), pp. 187ff.

22 Hanson (1988), pp. 91–4.

23 T. D. Barnes (1993) (like his earlier work on Constantine and Eusebius, a magisterial work of historical reconstruction), p. 245, n.50.

24 See Widdicombe (1994) for a full exploration of this theme.

25 See, for example, Virginia Burrus, 'Athanasius and Newman on Arians and Jews', due to appear in StP XXXIV.

26 For some brief and programmatic reflections on this, see R. Williams (1993:3).

APPENDIX 2: CREDAL DOCUMENTS

(a)   The 'Creed of Lucian of Antioch'

1 Note the careful distinction between the Father *from* whom creation originates and the Word *through* whom it comes to be as it is; cf. Methodius' view of the distinction of roles, above III.A, p. 190.

2 Col. 1:15.

3 John 1:2.

4 John 1:1.

5 John 1:3.

6 Col. 1:17.

7 1 Tim. 2:5.

8 Alluding to Heb. 3:1.

9 Alluding to Heb. 12:2, where Christ is the *archēgos* of our faith.

10 John 6:38.

11 An unusual expansion of the credal affirmation about the Spirit, and likely therefore to be original to Lucian's circle; the mention of *para-klēsis* anchors it in the thought of the fourth gospel, and the stress on

the Spirit's work of sanctification (rather than the more usual references to the inspiration of the prophets and others) is unique to this text.

12 Matt. 28:19.

13 The repeated *alēthōs* reinforces the anti-Sabellian – more specifically, anti-Marcellan – concerns of the Antiochene Council of 341. This explanatory phrase must belong to the period of the council itself.

14 The association of distinction in *hupostasis* and distinction in *doxa* is paralleled in the *Thalia* (n.16).

15 For quite a close parallel, see Origen, con. Cels. VIII.12,229. 32–230.2.

(b)   The statement of faith of Arius

1 Opitz' punctuation suggests taking 'glories' with 'receiving from the Father'; but this leaves the phrase *sunupostēsantos autō(i)tou patros* as a bit of a puzzle. Arius would not have countenanced the idea that Father and Son 'coexisted' in the sense that term possessed in the debates of the day; the whole of the rest of the creed rules out such a reading. If 'the Father coexisting with him' is not possible, the alternative 'making the Son exist alongside him' is not much better, as there is no explicit object for the verb. It is probably best to move Opitz' comma back, and to take *doxas* as the object for *sunopostēsantos*.

2 Alluding to Heb. 1:2; cf. II.B.3 above (pp. 133–4) for Origen's views on this text.

3 Probably referring to Matt. 11:27. The rest of the verse was, of course, a favourite text for Arius' opponents, as U.14 shows.

4 Rom. 11:36.

5 Ps. 110:3.

6 John 10:28.

7 For the sense of *homoousios* as designating a compound substance that can be resolved into its constituents, see Williams (1983), pp. 63–4, esp. n.39. The earlier *meros homoousion* in this text may be a misreading of the *meros homoousiou* here – or vice versa, of course, though this is less likely.

(c)   The orthodox faith according to Alexander

1 The most solid common ground between Arius and Alexander (and Athanasius too, for that matter) is this attack on the monism or modalism of gnostic and Sabellian groups (as understood by Catholic controversialists).

2   Isa. 53:8.

3   Matt. 11:27, slightly modified; not a variant text, but a catechetical gloss.

4   *Aparallaktos eikōn,* as in 'Lucian's' creed and the writings of Asterius the Sophist.

5   A difficult phrase to render with precision; the sense seems to be that the *essential,* constitutive attributes of the archetype must be reproduced in the *eikōn.*

6   John 14:28.

7   Heb. 1:3.

8   One of the several locutions in this letter suggesting that it was composed as a circular.

9   A – deliberately? – bold and paradoxical expression, in the light of the agreed doctrine that the Son's *archē* is the Father.

10   Reading *kinēsan,* with a minority of mss, rather than *kainisan.* This gives a better sense, but remains doubtful. If the majority reading stands, we should translate, 'who renewed, or recreated, the holy men . . .'

11   John 16:33.

12   An allusion to 1 Cor. 15:20.

13   One of the earliest recorded uses of the term *theotokos* for the Virgin. All the evidence points to Alexandria as the place of origin of this title.

14   Heb. 1:3.

(d)   The creed of the Synod of Antioch, 325.

1   The similarity to Arius' appeal in the *Thalia* to the *theodidaktoi* is striking.

2   Matt. 11:27 – apparently quoted from the familiar text, not in Alexander's version.

3   '*Sole* image' gives notices of the clear differentiation of the Son from all other *gennēmata* that will be spelt out further on in the confession.

4   The slight hesitation over the words *ek tou patros* no doubt shows a recognition that Airus' objection to such language had to be met by allowing that the expression was in some respects improper.

5   *Thesei* (and its Syriac counterpart) can mean 'adoption' as well as 'convention'; but the context seems to demand a contrast between two ways of talking. The Son might be called so by a Sabellian, for instance, in a 'conventional' sense, that is, in a manner of speaking, not as describing some authentic and essential aspect of the second Person's existence. This is not, n.b., a simple literal/metaphorical distinction: the early Christian theologians knew that 'Son' was not

a literal term, but its metaphorical character did not mean that there was any *arbitrary* element in its use; it is not used by human agreement only, 'by stipulation' (which is perhaps the most accurate rendering of *thesei* in this context).

6 Alluding to Heb. 1:3.

7 A fusion of Heb. 1:3 and Matt. 26:64, both of them dependent on Dan. 7:13.

8 The text may be defective here. The Syriac repeats the same word ('he is/was and he is/was and he is light'); Schwartz takes this to represent a Greek original reading *hoti ēn kai hoti estin kai hoti phōs estin*, 'he was and he is and he is light'. Possibly, however, another title originally stood in the text (e.g. 'he is/was, and he is wisdom/life/power, and he is light'); or else there is a dittograph, and we should take it as simply 'he existed eternally and he is light'. The vagaries of Semitic translations of Greek tenses make it impossible to be certain.

(e) The creed of Eusebius of Caesarea

1 He claims to have received the faith from his predecessors in the see, from his own baptismal instruction and from Scripture (U.22, 43.5–6).

2 Eusebius is elsewhere rather cautious about this image; see above, II.C.2, p. 172.

3 Opitz' punctuation is again faulty; no new sentence begins here.

4 The emphasis is on the *abiding* independent existence of the three hypostases – that characteristically anti-Sabellian concern of traditionalists in the eastern Mediterranean.

5 Matt. 28:19, also quoted by 'Lucian'.

(f) The creed of Nicaea

1 *Ek tou patros* turned out to be a phrase that the supporters of Arius could accept in a very carefully generalized sense; hence the need for the gloss that follows, *ek tes ousias tou patros*.

2 A challenge to the Origenian restriction of *alēthinos* to the Father, and the seed of a wholesale revision of hierarchical accounts of the Trinity as previously developed.

3 The reference to the Spirit is hardly enough to constitute a third 'article'; and the total absence of any mention of the Church is strange, given the relatively developed treatment of it in the Alexandrian confession.

(g)   The confession of Arius and Euzoius

1   Who claim also to speak for 'all who are with us' – either others sharing their exile, perhaps other clerics in the inferior orders of ministry, as the text suggests, or else their supporters in general.
2   See above, p. 308 for the difficulties over whether to read *gegenēmenon*, 'made' or 'produced', rather than *gegennēmenon*, 'begotten'.
3   This reflects the willingness of Airus' party at Nicaea to accept *ek tou patros* in the sense in which *everything* could be said to be 'from' or 'out of' the Father.
4   Matt. 28:19 used as Eusebius uses it in (e).
5   Or: 'if we do not accept that the Father, the Son and the Holy Spirit exist *alēthōs*', i.e. as really distinct entities.

Abbreviations

AnalBoll	*Analecta Bollandiana*
AJAHist	*American Journal of Ancient History*
Byz	*Byzantion*
ByZ	*Byzantinische Zeitschrift*
ChH	*Church History* (American Society of Church History)
CRAI	*Comptes rendues des séances de l'académie des inscriptions et belles lettres* (Paris)
DACL	*Dictionnaire d'archéologie chrétienne et de liturgie*, Paris, 1903–53
DHGE	*Dictionnaire d'histoire et de géographie ecclésiastiques*, Paris, 1912–
HSCP	*Harvard Studies in Classical Philology*
HThR	*Harvard Theological Review*
JAC.E	*Jahrbuch für Antike und Christentum, Ergänzungsband*
JEH	*Journal of Ecclesiastical History*
JHP	*Journal of the History of Philosophy*
JJP	*Journal of Juristic Papyrology*
JThS	*Journal of Theological Studies*, 1899–1949
JThS, n.s.	*Journal of Theological Studies* (new series, 1950–)
LThK	*Lexikon für Theologie und Kirche*, Freiburg, 1957–65
NAKG	*Nederlands archief voor kerkgeschiednis*
NedThT	*Nederlands theologisch tijdschrift*
NTS	*New Testament Studies* (Cambridge)
OrChP	*Orientalia Christiana Periodica*
Pauly-Wissowa	*Paulys Real-Encyclopädie der classischen Altertumswissenschaft*, Stuttgart, 1894–1980
PGL	Patristic Greek Lexicon (Oxford, 1961)
PRE	*Real-Encyklopädie für protestantische Theologie und Kirche*, 3rd edn, Leipzig, 1896–1913
RAC	*Reallexikon für Antike und Christentum*, Stuttgart, 1950–
RHPR	*Revue d'histoire et de philosophie religieuses*
RSLR	*Rivista di storia e letteratura religiosa*
RSR	*Recherches de science religieuse*
RevSR	*Revue des sciences religieuses*
SJT	*Scottish Journal of Theology*

Abbreviations

StP	*Studia patristica. Papers presented to the international conference on patristic studies*
TRE	*Theologische Realenzyklopädie*
TU	*Texte und Untersuchungen zur Geschichte der altchristlichen Literatur*
ThLZ	*Theologische Literaturzeitung*
ThQ	*Theologische Quartalschrift* (Tübingen)
ThStKr	*Theologische Studien und Kritiken*
ThZ	*Theologische Zeitschrift* (Basle)
VC	*Vigilae Christianae*
ZKG	*Zeitschrift für Kirchengeschichte*
ZNTW	*Zeitschrift für die neutestamentaliche Wissenschaft und die Kunde der älteren Kirche*

Bibliography

(This list only works directly referred to in the text and notes, and does not aim to be a comprehensive guide to the very extensive and growing body of literature in Arian studies. Barnes (1981) has an excellent bibliography, and Gregg (1985) provides a basic list of modern works – not without a few inaccuracies, but a most useful survey of an enormous field.)

Abramowski, Luise (1975), 'Die Synode von Antiochien 324/5 und ihr Symbol', ZKG 86, pp. 356–66.

(1976:1), 'Das Bekenntnis des Gregor Thaumaturgus bei Gregor von Nyssa und das Problem seiner Echtheit,' ZKG 87, pp. 145–66.

(1976:2), '*diadochē* und *orthos logos* bei Hegesipp', ZKG 87, pp. 321–7.

(1982), 'Dionys von Rom (†268) und Dionys von Alexandrien (†264/5) in den Arianischen Streitigkeiten des 4. Jahrhunderts', ZKG 93, pp. 240–72.

Achelis, H. (PRE), 'Melitius von Lykopolis', PRE (3rd edn), vol. 12, pp. 558–62.

Allen, R. E. (ed.) 1965), *Studies in Plato's Metaphysics*, London.

(1960/1965), 'Participation and Predication in Plato's Middle Dialogues', Allen, pp. 43–60.

Annas, Julia (1981), *An Introduction to Plato's Republic*, Oxford.

Anton, John P. (1981), 'Aristotle's Doctrine of *Homonyma* in the *Categories* and its Platonic Antecedents', JHP 6, pp. 315–26.

(1971) (ed.), *Essays in Ancient Greek Philosophy*, Albany.

(1969/1971), 'Ancient Interpretation of Aristotle's Doctrine of *Homonyma*', Anton, pp. 569–92.

Armstrong, A. H. (1980) (ed.), *The Cambridge History of Later Greek and Early Mediaeval Philosophy*, 3rd edn, Cambridge.

Ayres, Lewis, and Jones, Gareth (eds) (1998), *Christian Origins. Theology, Rhetoric and Community*, London and New York.

Bardy, Gustave (1923), *Paul de Samosate. Etude Historique*, Louvain.

(1926), 'Saint Alexandre d'Alexandrie a-t-il connu la "Thalia" d'Arius?', RevSR 6, pp. 527–32.

(1929) *Paul de Samosate. Etudé historique*, 2nd edn (extensively rev.), Louvain.

(1936) *Recherches sur Saint Lucien d'Antioche et son école*, Paris.

(1937) 'Aux origines de l'École d'Alexandrie', RSR 27, pp. 65–90.

Barnard, Leslie W. (1970), 'The Antecedents of Arius', VC 24, pp. 172–88.

(1972), 'What was Arius' Philosophy?', ThZ 28, pp. 110–17.

Barnes, Michel R. (1993), 'The Arians of Book V and the Genre of *De trinitate*', JThS, n.s. 44, pp. 185–95.

(1998), 'The fourth century as trinitarian canon', Ayres and Jones, pp. 47–67.

and Williams, Daniel H. (eds) (1993), *Arianism After Arius. Essays on the Development of the Fourth Century Trinitarian Conflicts*, Edinburgh.

Barnes, Timothy D. (1976), 'Sossianus Hierocles and the Antecedents of the Great Persecution', HSCP 80, pp. 239–52.

(1978), 'Emperor and Bishops, AD 324–344: Some Problems', AJAHist 3, pp. 53–75.

(1981), *Constantine and Eusebius*, Cambridge, Mass.

(1982), *The New Empire of Diocletian and Constantine*, Cambridge, Mass.

(1986), 'Angel of Light or Mystic Initiate? The Problem of the *Life of Antony*', JthS, n.s. 37, pp. 353–68.

(1993), *Athanasius and Constantius. Theology and Politics in the Constantinian Empire*, Cambridge, Mass.

(1976) and (1978) also in T. D. Barnes, *Early Christianity and the Roman Empire*, London, 1984.

Barns, J. W. B., and Chadwick, Henry (1973), 'A Letter Ascribed to Peter of Alexandria', JThS, n.s. 24, pp. 443–55. See also Reymond.

Battifol, P. (1898), 'Sozomène et Sabinos', ByZ 7, pp. 265–84.

(1901), 'La Synodikon de S. Athanase', ByZ 10, pp. 128–43.

Bauer, Walter (1972), *Orthodoxy and Heresy in Earliest Christianity*, ed. R. A. Kraft and G. Krodel, London.

Bell, H. Idris (1924), *Jews and Christians in Egypt*, London.

Benz, Ernst (1932), *Marius Victorinus und die Entwicklung der abendländischen Willensmetaphysik*, Stuttgart.

Bienert, Wolfgang (1973), 'Neue Fragmente des Dionysius und des Petrus von Alexandrien aus Cod. Vatop. 236', *Kleronomia* 5, pp. 308–14.

(1978), *Dionysius von Alexandrien. Zur Frage des Origenismus im Dritten Jahrhundert*, Berlin.

Bigger, C. (1968), *Participation. A Platonic Inquiry*, Baton Rouge.

Blumenthal, H., and Markus, R. A. (eds) (1981), *Neoplatonism and Early Christian Thought. Essays in Honour of A. H. Armstrong*, London.

Bonwetsch, N. (1903), *Die Theologie des Methodius von Olympus*, Göttingen.

Booth, Edward (1983), *Aristotelian Aporetic Ontology in Islamic and Christian Thinkers*, Cambridge.

Boularand, Éphrem (1972), *L'Hérésie d'Arius et la 'Foi' de Nicée*, 2 vols., Paris.

Bibliography

Brakke, David (1995), *Athanasius and the Politics of Asceticism*, Oxford.

Brennecke, Hans Christof (1993), 'Lukian von Antiochien in der Geschichte des ariansichen Streites', Brennecke, Grasmück and Markschies, pp. 170–92.

Grasmück, Ernst Ludwig, and Markschies, Christoph (eds) (1993), *Logos. Festschrift für Luise Abramowski*, Berlin/New York.

Broek, van den, Roelof (1986), 'Jewish and Platonic Speculation in Early Alexandrian Theology: Eugnostus, Philo, Valentinus, and Origen', Pearson and Goehring, pp. 190–203.

Brown, Peter (1980), *The Philosopher and Society in Late Antiquity* (Colloquy 34 of the Center for Hermeneutical Studies in Hellenistic and Modern Culture), Berkeley.

Burrell, David (1979), *Aquinas, God and Action*, London.

Calderini, A. (1935), *Dizionario dei nomi geografici e topografici dell'Egitto Greco-Romano*, vol. 1, fasc. 1, Cairo.

Calderone, S. (1962), *Costantino e il cattolicesimo I*, Florence.

Camelot, Thomas (1945), *Foi et gnose. Introduction à l'étude de la connaissance mystique chez Clément d'Alexandrie*, Paris.

Campenhausen, H. von (1951), 'Lehrerreihen und Bischofsreihen im 2. Jahrhundert', *In Memoriam Ernst Loymeyer*, ed. W. Schmauch, Stuttgart, pp. 240–9.

(1969), *Ecclesiastical Authority and Spiritual Power in the Church of the First Three Centuries*, London.

Casey, R. P. (1924), 'Clement and the Two Divine Logoi', JThS 25, pp. 43–56.

Cave, William (1683), *Ecclesiastici: or, the History of the Lives, Acts, Death and Writings of the Most Eminent Fathers of the Church*, London.

Chadwick, Henry (1948), 'The Fall of Eustathius of Antioch', JThS, o.s. 49, pp. 27–35.

(1958), 'Ossius of Cordova and the Presidency of the Council of Antioch', JThS, n.s. 9, pp. 292–304.

(1960), 'Faith and Order at the Council of Nicaea: A Note on the Background of the Sixth Canon', HThR 53, pp. 171–95.

(1980), *The Role of the Christian Bishop in Ancient Society* (Colloquy 35 of the Center for Hermeneutical Studies in Hellenistic and Modern Culture), Berkeley.

(1958) and (1960) also in Henry Chadwick, *History and Thought of the Early Church*, London, 1982. See also Barns.

Charlesworth, J. H. (ed.) (1983), *The Old Testament Pseudepigrapha*, 2 vols, London.

Clark, Elizabeth (1992), *The Origenist Controversy. The Cultural-Construction of an Early Christian Debate*, Princeton.

Clark, J. C. D. (1985), *English Society 1688–1832*, Cambridge.

Clercq, Victor C. de (1954), *Ossius of Cordova. A Contribution to the History of the Constantinian Period* (CUA Studies in Christian Antiquity 13), Washington.

Cox, Patricia (1983), *Biography in Late Antiquity: a Quest for the Holy Man*, Berkeley.

Crouzel, Henri (LThK), 'Origenes IV. Origenist Streitigkeiten', LThK, vol. 7, cols 1233–5.

Daniélou, Jean (1944), *Platonisme et thélogie mystique. Doctrine spirituelle de Saint Grégoire de Nysse*, Paris.

Devos, P. (1965), 'Une passion grecque inédite de Saint Pierre d'Alexandrie et sa traduction par Anastase le Bibliothécaire', Analboll 85, pp. 157–87.

Diekamp, F. (1902), 'Ein neues Fragment aus den Hypotyposen des Alexandriner Theognost', ThQ 84, pp. 481–4.

Dillon, John M. (1973), *Iamblichi Chalcidiensis in Platonis Dialogos Commentariorum Fragmenta*, ed. with translation and commentary (Philosophia Antiqua 23), Leiden.

Dörrie, Heinrich (1955), Hypostasis: Wort und Bedeutungsgeschichte, Göttingen.

    (1976), 'EMANATION. Ein unphilosophischen Wort in spätantiken Denken', *Platonica Minora*, Munich, pp. 70–86.

    (1981) '*Formula Analogiae:* An Exploration of a Theme in Hellenistic and Imperial Platonism', Blumenthal and Markus, pp. 33–49.

Duckworth, Colin, and Osborn, Eric (1985), 'Clement of Alexandria's *Hypotyposeis:* A French Eighteenth-Century Sighting', JThS, n.s. 36, pp. 67–83.

Elliger, Walter (1931), 'Bemerkungen zur Theologie des Arius', ThStKr 103, pp. 244–51.

Ericksen, Robert P. (1985), *Theologians Under Hitler. Gerhard Kittel, Paul Althaus and Emmanuel Hirsch*, New Haven and London.

Fabian, Johannes (1983), *Time and the Other. How Anthropology Makes its Object*, New York.

Feidas, Vlasios (1973), *To Kollouthianon Schisma kai hai archai tou Areianismou*, Athens.

Flesseman-van Leer, Ellen (1954), *Tradition and Scripture in the Early Church*, Assen.

Florovsky, Georges V. (1961), 'St Gregory Palamas and the Tradition of the Fathers', Sobornost, series 4, no. 4, pp. 165–76.

    (1962), 'St Athanasius' Concept of Creation', StP VI (TU 81, 1962), pp. 36–57.

Frend, W. H. C. (1974), 'Athanasius as an Egyptian Christian leader in the fourth century', New College Bulletin (Edinburgh), 8, pp. 20–37; = no. XVI in W. H. C. Frend, *Religion Popular and Unpopular in the Early Christian Centuries*, London, 1976.

Geach, Peter (1956/1965), 'The Third Man Again', Allen, pp. 265–77.

Bibliography

Gilson, Étienne (1952), *Jean Duns Scot. Introduction à ses positions fondamentales*, Paris.

Glucker, John (1978), *Antiochus and the Late Academy*, Göttingen.

Goodenough, Erwin R. (1935), *By Light, Light: The Mystic Gospel of Hellenistic Judaism*, New Haven.

Grant, Robert M. (1971), 'Early Alexandrian Christianity', ChH 40, pp. 133–44, and R. M. Grant, *Christian Beginnings: Apocalypse to History*, London, 1983.

— (1980), *Eusebius as Church Historian*, Oxford.

Gregg, Robert C. (1980) (tr. and introd.), *Athanasius: The Life of Antony and the Letter to Marcellus*, New York.

— (1989), Review of Rowan Williams' *Arius: Heresy and Traditions*, JThS, n.s. 40, pp. 247–54.

— and Groh, Dennis E. (1981), *Early Arianism: A View of Salvation*, London and Philadelphia.

— (ed.) (1985), *Arianism. Historical and Theological Reassessments*, Cambridge, Mass. (Philadelphia Pastristic Foundations).

See also Wiles.

Guthrie, W. K. C. (1978), *A History of Greek Philosophy V. The Later Plato and the Academy*, Cambridge.

Gwatkin, H. M. (1900), *Studies of Arianism Chiefly Referring to the Character and Chronology of the Reaction which Followed the Council of Nicaea*, 2nd edn. Cambridge.

— (1906), *The Knowledge of God and its Historical Development* (2 vols), Edinburgh.

Halkin, F. (1963), 'L'"Apologie" du martyr Philéas de Thmuis (Papyrus Bodmer XX) et les actes latins de Philéas et Philoromus', AnalBoll 81, pp. 5–27.

Hall, S. G. (1982), Review of Gregg and Groh (1981), *King's Theological Review*, 5 (1982), p. 28.

— (1985), 'The *Thalia* of Airus in Athanasius' Accounts', Gregg, pp. 37–58.

Hanson, R. P. C. (1962), *Tradition in the Early Church*, London.

— (1972), 'Did Origen apply the Word Homoousios to the Son?', *Epektasis. Mélanges patristiques offerts au cardinal Jean Daniélou*, ed. J. Fontaine and C. Kannengiesser, Paris, pp. 292–303.

— (1985), 'The Arian Doctrine of the Incarnation', Gregg, pp. 181–217.

— (1988), *The Search for the Christian Doctrine of God*, Edinburgh.

Hardy, E. R. (1952), *Christian Egypt: Church and People*, New York.

Harnack, Adolf von (1894), *Lehrbuch der Dogmengeschichte*, 4th edn, vols I and II, Tübingen, 1909.

— (1897), (1898), *History of Dogma*, vols III and IV, tr. E. B. Speirs and J. Millar, London, Edinburgh and Oxford.

Henry, Patrick (1982), 'Why is Contemporary Scholarship so Enamoured of Ancient Heretics?', StP XVII, Part One, pp. 123–26.

Henry, Paul (1950), 'The *Adversus Arium* of Marius Victorinus, the First

359

Systematic Exposition of the Doctrine of the Trinity', JThS, n.s. 1, pp. 42–55.

Hernández, G. Fernández (1984), 'El cisma meleciano en la iglesia egipcia', Gerion (Madrid), 2, pp. 155–80.

Hertling, L. von (1956), 'Studi storiei antoniani negli ultimi trent' anni', Steidle, pp. 13–34.

Heussi, Karl (1936), *Der Ursprung des Mönchtums*, Tübingen.

Heyward, C. T. R. (1979), 'The Holy Name of the God of Moses and the Prologue of St John's Gospel', NTS 25, pp. 16–32.

Honigmann, E. (1939), 'La liste originale des Pères de Nicée, Byz 14, pp. 17–76.

(1953), 'Basileus of Amasea', E. Honigmann, *Patristic Studies* (Studi e Testi 173), Vatican.

Hornschuh, M. (1960), 'Das Leben des Origenes und die Entstehung der alexandrinischen Schule', ZKG 71, pp. 1–25, 193–214.

Javierre, A. M. (1963), *El tema literario de la sucesion. Prolegómenos para el estudio de la sucesion apostolica*, Zurich.

Kannengiesser, Charles (1970), 'La date de l'Apologie d'Athanase Contre les Païens et Sur l'Incarnation due Verbe', RSR 58, pp. 383–428.

(1971), 'Où et quand Arius composa-t-il la *Thalie?*', *Kyriakon: Festchrift Johannes Quasten*, ed. P. Granfield and J. A. Jungmann, Münster, vol. 1, pp. 346–51.

(1982:1), 'Bulletin de théologie patristique. 2ème section: crise arienne', RSR 70, pp. 597–612.

(1982), *Holy Scripture and Hellenistic Hermeneutics in Alexandrian Christology: the Arian Crisis* (Colloquy 41 of the Center for Hermeneutical Studies in Hellenistic and Modern Culture), Berkeley.

(1983), *Athanase d'Alexandrie, évêque et ecrivain. Une lecture des traités 'Contre les Ariens'*, Paris.

(1984), 'Les "blasphèmes d'Arius" (Athanase d'Alexandrie, *de synodis* 15: un écrit neo-Arien', *Mémorial André-Jean Festugière. Antiquité Païenne et Chrétienne* (Cahiers d'Orientalisme X), ed. E. Lucchesi and H. D. Saffrey, Geneva, pp. 143–51.

(1985), 'The Blasphemies of Arius: Athanasius of Alexandria *De Synodis* 15', Gregg, pp. 59–78.

Kelsey, David H. (1975), *The Uses of Scripture in Recent Theology*, London.

Kemp, Eric (1955), 'Bishops and Presbyters in Alexandria', JEH 6, pp. 125–42.

Kettler, F. H. (1936), 'Der melitianische Streit in Ägypten', ZNTW 35, pp. 155–93.

Klijn, A. F. J. (1986), 'Jewish Christology in Egypt', Pearson and Goehring, pp. 161–75.

Kopecek, Thomas A. (1979), *A History of Neo-Arianism* (2 vols), Cambridge, Mass. (Philadelphia Patristic Foundation).

(1982), 'Professor Charles Kannengiesser's View of the Arian Crisis: A Critique and Counter-Proposal', Kannengiesser, pp. 51–68.

(1985), 'Neo-Arian Religion: The Evidence of the *Apostolic Constitutions*', Gregg, pp. 153–80.

Laeuchli, Samuel (1968), 'Das "Vierte Jahrhundert" in Karl Barths Prolegomena', *Theologie zwischen Gestern und Morgen. Interpretationen und Anfragen zum Werk Karl Barths*, ed. W. Dantine and K. Lüthi, Munich.

Lange, N. de (1976), *Origen and the Jews*, Cambridge.

Leach, Edmund (1983), 'Melchisedech and the Emperor: icons of subversion and orthodoxy', *Structuralist Interpretations of Biblical Myth*, ed. E. Leach and D. A. Aycock, London, pp. 67–88.

Leclercq, Henri (DACL), 'Alexandrie (Archéologie)', DACL, vol. 1, cols 1098–1182.

Lewis, Naphtali (1983), *Life in Egypt Under Roman Rule*, Oxford.

Lilla, Salvatore R. C. (1971), *Clement of Alexandria. A Study in Christian Platonism and Gnosticism*, Oxford.

Lindbeck, George A. (1984), *The Nature of Doctrine: Religion and Theology in a Postliberal Age*, London.

Loeschke, Gerhard (1910), 'Zur Chronologie der beiden grossen antiarianischen Schrieben des Alexander von Alexandrien', ZKG 31, pp. 548–6.

Loofs, Friedrich (1893), *Leitfaden zum Studien der Dogmengeschichte*, 3rd edn, Halle.

(1924), *Paulus von Samosata. Eine Untersuchung zur Altkirchlichen Literatur- und Dogmen-geschichte* (Tu 14.3), Leipzig.

Loose, Uta (1990), 'Zur Chronologie des arianischen Streites', ZKG 101, pp. 88–92.

Lorenz, Rudolf (1978), *'Arius judaizans?' Untersuchungen zur dogmengeschichtlichen Einordnung des Arius*, Göttingen.

(TRE), 'Eustathius von Antiochien', TRE, vol. 10, pp. 543–6.

(1980), *'Arius, judaizans'? Untersuchungen zur dogmengeschichtlichen Einordnung des Arius*, Gottingen.

(1983), 'Die Christusseele im Arianischen Streit. Nebst einigen Bemerkungen zur Quellenkritik des Arius und zur Glaubwürdigkeit des Athanasius', ZKG 94, pp. 1–51.

Lossky, Vladimir (1974), *In the Image and Likeness of God*, New York.

Louth, Andrew (1981), *The Origins of the Christian Mystical Tradition. From Plato to Denys*, Oxford.

Lowry, Charles W. (1938), 'Did Origen Style the Son a *ktisma?*', JThS 39, pp. 39–42.

Luibhéid, Colm (1981), *Eusebius of Caesarea and the Arian Crisis*, Galway.

(1982), *The Council of Nicaea*, Galway.

(1983), 'The Alleged Second Session of the Council of Nicaea', JEH 34, pp. 165–74.

361

Lyman, Rebecca (1989), 'Arians and Manichees on Christ', JThS, n.s. 40, pp. 493–503.

(1993), 'A Topography of Heresy: Mapping the Rhetorical Creation of Arianism', Barnes and Williams, pp. 45–62.

(1994), *Christology and Cosmology. Models of Divine Activity in Origen, Eusebius and Athanasius*, Oxford.

MacKinnon, Donald (1975/1979), 'Tillich, Frege, Kittel: Some Reflections on a Dark Theme', Donald MacKinnon, *Explorations in Theology*, London, 1979, pp. 129–37.

(1976), 'The Relation of the Doctrines of the Incarnation and the Trinity', *Creation, Christ and Culture. Studies in Honour of T. F. Torrance*, ed. Richard McKinney, Edinburgh, pp. 92–107.

Marrou, Henri-Irénée (1973), 'L'arianisme comme phénomène alexandrin', CRAI, pp. 533–42.

Martin, Annik (1989:1), 'Le fil d'Arius: 325–335', *Revue d'histoire ecclésiastique* LXXXIV, pp. 297–333.

(1989:2), 'Les relations entre Arius et Mélitios dans la tradition alexandrine', JThS, n.s. 40, pp. 401–13.

McCabe, Herbert (1985), 'The Involvement of God', New Blackfriars 66, pp. 464–76.

(1996), *Athanase d'Alexandrie et e'église d'Egypt au iv Siècle (c328–373)*, Rome.

McGill, Arthur C. (1982), *Suffering: A Test of Theological Method*, Philadelphia.

Meijering, E. P. (1968), *Orthodoxy and Platonism in Athanasius*, Leiden.

(1973/1975), 'The Doctrine of the Will and of the Trinity in the Orations of Gregory of Nazianzus', NedThT 27 (1973), pp. 224–34, and in Meijering (1975), pp. 103–13.

(1974/1975:1), 'ΕΝ ΠΟΤΕ ΗΟΤΙ ΟΥΚ ΕΝ ΗΟ ΗΥΙΟΣ. A discussion on Time and Eternity', VC 28 (1974), pp. 161–68, and in Meijering (1975), pp. 81–8.

(1974/1975:2), 'Athanasius on the Father as the Origin of the Son', NAKG 55 (1974), pp. 1–14, and in Meijering (1975), pp. 89–102.

(1975), *God, Being, History: Studies in Patristic Philosophy*, Amsterdam and Oxford, 1975.

Meinardus, Otto F. A. (1970), 'An Examination of the Traditions pertaining to the Relics of St Mark', OrChP 36, pp. 348–76.

Metzler, Karin (1991), 'Ein Beitrag zur Rekonstruktion der "Thalia" des Arius', *Ariana et Athanasiana: Studien zur Überlieferung und zu philologischen Problemen der Werke des Athanasius von Alexandrien*, Karin Metzler and Frank Simon, Opladen, pp. 13–45.

Milbank, John (1986), 'The Second Difference: For a Trinitarianism Without Reserve', Modern Theology 2, pp. 213–34.

Molland, Einar (1954/1970), 'La développement de l'idée de succession apostolique', RHPR 34 (1954), pp. 1–29, and E. Molland, *Opuscula Patristica*, Oslo, pp. 181–206.

Mönnich, C. (1950), 'De Achtergrond van de arianse Christologie', NedThT 4, pp. 378–412.

Mühlenberg, Ekkehard (1966), *Die Unendlichkeit Gottes bei Gregor von Nyssa*, Göttingen.

Müller, Guido (1952), *Lexicon Athanasianum*, Berlin.

Nautin, Pierre (1949), 'Deux interpolations orthodoxes dans une lettre d'Arius', AnalBoll 67, pp. 131–41.

(1961), *Lettres et écrivains chrétiens des II⁰ et III⁰ siecles*, Paris.

(1977), *Origène: sa vie et son oeuvre* (Christianisme antique I), Paris.

Newman, John Henry (1833), *The Arians of the Fourth Century*, London.

(1842) *Select Treatises of St Athanasius in Controversy with the Arians*, 2 vols, Oxford.

(1876), *The Arians of the Fourth Century*, 4th edn, London.

(1878), *An Essay on the Development of Christian Doctrine*, 2nd edn, London.

Nockles, Peter (1994), *The Oxford Movement in Context. Anglican High Churchmanship, 1760–1857*, Cambridge.

Noel, Conrad (1909), *Socialism and Church Tradition*, London.

Normann, Friedrich (1978), *Teilhabe. Ein Schlüsselwort der Vätertheologie*, Münster.

Norris, F. W. (1984), 'Paul of Samosata: *Procurator Ducenarius*', JThS, n.s. 35, pp. 50–70.

O'Brien, D. (1981), 'Plotinus and the Gnostics on the Generation of Matter', Blumenthal and Markus, pp. 108–23.

Opitz, Hans-Georg (1934), 'Die Zeitfolge des arianischen Streites von den Anfängen bis zum Jahr 328', ZNTW 33, pp. 131–59.

(1937), 'Dionys von Alexandrien und die Libyer', *Quantulacumque Studies Presented to Kirsopp Lake*, London.

Orbe, A. (1958), *Hacia la primera teologia de la procesion del Verbo*, Rome.

Osborn, Eric (1957), *The Philosophy of Clement of Alexandria*, Cambridge.

(1981), *The Beginning of Christian Philosophy*, Cambridge.

(1984), 'Arian Obedience: Scouting for Theologians' (review of Gregg and Groh (1981), *Prudentia*, 16 (1984), pp. 51–6.

See also Duckworth.

Otis, B. (1976), 'Gregory of Nyssa and the Cappadocian Concept of Time', Stp XIV (TU 117), pp. 327–52.

Owens, Joseph (1978), *The Doctrine of Being in the Aristotelean Metaphysics. A Study in the Greek Background of Mediaeval Thought* (3rd edn, rev.), Toronto.

Pagels, Elaine (1978), 'Visions, Appearances and Apostolic Authority: Gnostic and Orthodox Traditions', *Gnosis. Festschrift für Hans Jonas*, ed. Barbara Aland, Göttingen, pp. 415–30.

(1980), *The Gnostic Gospels*, London.

Pannenberg, Wolfhart (1971), 'The Appropriation of the Philosophical Concept of God as a Dogmatic Problem of Early Christian Theology', W. Pannenberg, *Basic Questions in Theology*, II, London, pp. 119–83.

Patsavos, Elia I. (1973), *Hē eisodos eis ton klēron kata tous pente prōtous aiōnas*, Athens.

Patterson, Lloyd G. (1976), '*De libero arbitrio* and Methodius' Attack on Origen', StP XIV (TU 117), pp. 160–6.

(1982), 'Methodius, Origen and the Arian Dispute', StP XVII, Part Two, pp. 912–23.

Pearson, Birger (1986), 'Earliest Christianity in Egypt: Some Observations', Pearson and Goehring, pp. 132–59.

and Goehring, James (eds) (1986), *The Roots of Egyptian Christianity*, Philadelphia.

Peterson, E. A. (1935), *Der Monotheismus als politisches Problem*, Leipzig.

Pollard. T. E. (1970), *Johannine Christology and the Early Church* (SNTS Monograph Series 13), Cambridge.

Prestige, G. L. (1940), *Fathers and Heretics. Six Studies in Dogmatic Faith, with Prologue and Epilogue*, London.

Radford, L. B. (1908), *Three Teachers of Alexandria. Theognostus, Pierius and Peter. A Study in the Early History of Origenism and Anti-Origenism*, Cambridge.

Reymond, E. A. E., and Barns, J. W. B. (1973), *Four Martyrdoms from the Pierpont Morgan Coptic Codices*, Oxford.

Riedmatten, Henri de (1952), *Les actes du procès de Paul de Samosate* (Paradosis 6), Fribourg.

Rist, J. M. (1967), *Plotinus. The Road to Reality*, Cambridge.

(1981), 'Basil's "Neoplatonism". Its Background and Nature', *Basil of Caesarea: Christian, Humanist, Ascetic*, ed. P. J. Fedwick, Toronto, pp. 139–222.

Ritter, A.-M. (1990), '*Arius redivivus?* Ein Jahrzwölft Ari(anism)usforschung', *Theologische Rundschau*, xxx.

Rius Camps, J. (1968), 'Comunicabilidad de-la naturaleza de Dios segun Origenes I', OrChP 34, pp. 1–37.

Robertson, Archibald (1892), *St Athanasius. Select Works and Letters*, ed. with prolegomena, etc. (NPNF 4), Oxford.

Rousseau, Philip (1978), *Ascetics, Authority and the Church in the Age of Jerome and Cassian*, Oxford.

Routh, M. J. (1846), *Reliquiae sacrae*, vol. III, Oxford.

Sanders, E. P. (ed.) (1980), *Jewish and Christian Self-Definition* vol. I, *The Shaping of Christianity in the Second and Third Centuries*, London.

Sandmel, Samuel (1979), *Philo of Alexandria: an Introduction*, New York.

Schmidt, Carl (1901), *Fragmente einer Schrift des Märtyrerbischofs Petrus von Alexandrien* TU (NS) 5.4b, Leipzig.

Schneemelcher, Wilhelm (1954), 'Zur chonologie des arianischen Streites', ThLZ 79, pp. 393–400.

Schoedel, William R. (1980) 'Theological Norms and Social Perspectives in Ignatius of Antioch', Sanders, pp. 30–56.

Schubart, W. (RAC), 'Alexandria', RAC, vol. 1, cols 271–83.

Bibliography

Schwartz, Eduard (1905:1), 'Die Quellen über den melitianischen Streit', Nachrichten von der königlichen Gesellschaft der Wissenschaften zu Göttingen, 1905, pp. 164–7; = E. Schwartz, *Gesammelte Schriften. Bd. 3. Zur Geschichte des Athanasius*, Berlin, 1959, pp. 87–116.

(1905:2), 'Die Dokumente des arianischen Streites bis 325', Nachrichten . . . 1905, pp. 257–99; = *Gesammelte Schriften. Bd 3* . . . pp. 117–68.

(1911), 'Von Nicaea bis zu Konstantins Tod', Nachrichten . . . , 1911, pp. 367–426; = *Gesammelte Schriften. Bd 3* . . . pp. 188–264.

Seeck, O. (1896), 'Untersuchungen zur Geschichte des Nicänischen Konzils', ZKG 17, pp. 1–76, 319–62.

Segal, Alan F. (1977), *Two Powers in Heaven. Early Rabbinic Reports about Christianity and Gnosticism*, Leiden.

Simonetti, Manlio (1965), *Studi sull' arianesimo*, Rome.

(1971), 'Le origini deil' Arianesimo', RSLR 7, pp. 317–30.

(1975), *La crisi ariana nel IV secolo*, Rome.

(1980), Review of Lorenz (1978), RSLR 16, pp. 455–60.

(1983), Review of Gregg and Groh (1981), RSLR 18, pp. 304–6.

Smith, Jonathan Z. (1968/1978), 'The Prayer of Joseph', J. Z. Smith, *Map is Not Territory. Studies in the History of Religions*, Leiden, 1978.

Smith, Morton (1973), *Clement of Alexandria and a Secret Gospel of Mark*, Cambridge, Mass.

Sorabji, Richard (1983), *Time, Creation and the Continuum. Theories in Antiquity and the Early Middle Ages*, London.

Spanneut, Michel (DHGE), 'Eustathe d'Antioche', DHGE 16, cols 13–23.

Stead, G. C. (1964), 'The Platonism of Arius', JThS, n.s. 15, pp. 14–31.

(1973), ' "Eusebius" and the Council of Nicaea', JThS, n.s. 24, pp. 85–100.

(1976), 'Rhetorical Method in Athanasius', VC 30, pp. 121–37.

(1977), *Divine Substance*, Oxford.

(1978), 'The *Thalia* of Arius and the Testimony of Athanasius,' JThS, n.s. 29, pp. 20–52.

(1983), 'The Freedom of the Will and the Arian Controversy', *Platonismus und Christentum. Festschrift für Heinrich Dörrie*, ed. H.-D. Blume and F. Mann (JAC.E. 10), Münster, pp. 245–57.

(1988), 'Athanasius's Earliest Written Work', JThS, n.s. 39, pp. 76–91.

(1997), 'Was Arius a Neoplatonist?', StP XXXIII, pp. 39–52.

(1964), (1973), (1976), (1978), (1983) also in Christopher Stead, *Substance and Illusion in the Christian Fathers*, London, 1985.

Steidle, Basilius (1956), ' "Homo Dei Antonius". Zum Bild des "Mannes Gottes" im alten Mönchtum', B. Steidle, ed., *Antonius Magnus Eremita, 356/1956*, Studia Anselmiae 38, Rome, pp. 148–200.

Strutwolf, Holger (1999), *Die Trinitätstheologie und Christologie des Euseb von Caesarea. Eine dogmengeschichtliche Untersuchung seiner Platonismusrezeption und Wirkungsgeschichte*, Gottingen.

Sykes, S. W. (1985), *The Identity of Christianity*, London.

Talbert, Charles H. (1976), 'The Myth of a Descending-Ascending Redeemer in Mediterranean Antiquity', NTS 22, pp. 418–40.

Telfer, W. R. (1936), 'Arius Takes Refuge in Nicomedia', JThS 37, pp. 60–3.

(1943), 'The Codex Verona LX (58)', HThR 36, pp. 169–246.

(1946), 'When Did the Arian Controversy Begin?', JThS 47., pp. 129–42.

(1949), 'St Peter of Alexandria and Arius', AnalBoll 67, pp. 117–30.

(1952), 'Episcopal Succession in Egypt', JEH 3, pp. 1–13.

(1955), 'Meletius of Lycopolis and Episcopal Succession in Egypt', HThR 48, pp. 227–37.

(1962), *The Office of a Bishop*, London.

Thomas, Stephen (1991), *Newman and Heresy*, Cambridge.

Torrance, T. F. (1975), *Theology in Reconciliation: Essays towards Evangelical and Catholic Unity in East and West*, London.

Trigg, Joseph W. (1983), *Origen. The Bible and Philosophy in the Third-century Church*, London.

Tuilier, A. (1982), 'Les évangélistes et les docteurs de la primitive église et les origines de l'École (*didaskaleion*) d'Alexandrie', StP XVII, Part Two, pp. 738–49.

Vaggione, R. P. (2000), *Eunomius of Cyzicus and the Nicene Revolution*, Oxford.

Vallée, Gérard (1980), 'Theological and Non-Theological Motives in Irenaeus' Refutation of the Gnostics', Sanders, pp. 174–85.

Vandersleyen, C. (1961), 'La date de la préfecture de Sossianus Hiéroclès en Égypte (à propos de P. Cairo-Boak 57049)', JJP 13, pp. 109–22.

Vlastos, Gregory (1939/1965), 'The Disorderly Motion in the *Timaeus*', Allen (1965), pp. 379–99.

(1964/1965), 'Creation in the *Timaeus*: is it a Fiction?', Allen (1965), pp. 401–19.

Völker, W. (1952), *Der wahre Gnostiker nach Clemens Alexandrinus*, Berlin and Leipzig.

Wallace-Hadrill, D. S. (1982), *Christian Antioch. A study of early Christian thought in the East*, Cambridge.

Wallis. R. T. (1972), *Neoplatonism*, London.

West, M. L. (1982), 'The Metre of Arius' *Thalia*', JThs, n.s. 33, pp. 98–105.

Westcott, B. F. (1889), *The Epistle to the Hebrews. The Greek Text with Notes and Essays*, London.

Whittaker, J. (1981), 'Plutarch, Platonism and Christianity', Blumenthal and Markus, pp. 50–63.

Widdicombe, Peter (1994), *The Fatherhood of God from Origen to Athanasius*, Oxford.

Wiles, M. F. (1962), 'In Defence of Arius', JThS, n.s. 13, pp. 339–47, and *Working Papers in Doctrine*, London, 1976, pp. 28–37.

(1967), *The Making of Christian Doctrine*, Cambridge.

(1985) with R. C. Gregg, 'Asterius: A New Chapter in the History of Arianism', Gregg, pp. 111–51.

(1996), *Archetypal Heresy. Arianism through the Centuries*, Oxford.

Wilken, Robert P. (1971), *The Myth of Christian Beginnings*, New York.

Williams, Daniel H. (1995), *Ambrose of Milan and the End of the Arian-Nicene Conflicts*, Oxford.

(1998), 'Constantine, Nicaea and the "fall" of the Church', Ayres and Jones, pp. 117–36.

Williams, Rowan (1979), *The Wound of Knowledge. Christian Sprituality from the New Testament to St John of the Cross*, London.

(1983), 'The Logic of Arianism', JThS, n.s. 34, pp. 56–81.

(1985:1), 'The Quest of the Historical *Thalia*', Gregg, pp. 1–35.

(1985:2), 'Origen on the Soul of Jesus', *Origeniana Tertia*, ed. R. P. C. Hanson, Rome, pp. 131–7.

(1986), 'Arius and the Melitian Schism', JThS, n.s. 37, pp. 35–52.

(1990), 'Newman's *Arians* and the Question of Method in Doctrinal History', *Newman After a Hundred Years*, ed. Ian Ker and Alan G. Hill, pp. 263–85.

(1992), 'R. P. C. Hanson, *The Search for the Christian Doctrine of God*: Article Review', SJT 45, pp. 110–11.

(1993:1), 'Baptism and the Arian Controversy', Barnes and Williams, pp. 149–80.

(1993:2), '*Damnosa haereditas*: Pamphilus' Apology and the reputation of Origen', Brennecke, Grasmück and Markschies, pp. 151–169.

(1993:3), 'The Nicene Heritage', *The Christian Understanding of God*, ed. James M. Byrne, Dublin, pp. 45–8.

(1997), 'Angels Unawares: Heavenly Liturgy and Earthly Theology in Alexandria', StP XXX, pp. 350–63.

Wittgenstein, Ludwig (1970), *Lectures and Conversations on Aesthetics, Psychology and Religious Beliefs*, Oxford.

Wolfson, H. A. (1948), *Philo*, vol. 2, Cambridge, Mass.

(1956), *The Philosophy of the Church Fathers*, vol. 1, Cambridge, Mass.

Zahn, Theodor (1884), *Forschugen zur Geschichte des neutestamentlichen Kanons und der altkirchlichen Literatur. III. Theil: Supplementum Clementinum*, Erlangen.

Zizioulas, John (1985), *Being as Communion. Studies in Personhood and the Church*, New York and London.

CLASSICAL AND PATRISTIC TEXTS

(a)

Plato and *Aristotle* are referred to and quoted according to the standard texts (Oxford Classical Texts, Loeb Classical Library): note that references to Aristotle's Metaphysics follow the numerical, not the alphabetical, convention.

Bibliography

References to *Philo* follow the Loeb edition, except for the *de providentia*, for which see the edition of M. Hadas-Lebel, Paris, 1973.

References to *Plotinus* generally follow the text of Henry and Schwyzer, Paris and Brussels, 1953–; use is also made of what has so far appeared of the Loeb edition, edited by A. H. Armstrong, Cambridge, Mass., 1966–.

For other writers:

Albinus, Epitome, ed. P. Louis, Paris (Collection Budé), 1945.

Alexander of Aphrodisias, in Aristotelis metaphysica, ed. M. Hayduck, Berlin, 1891, (CAG 1).

Anatolius, see *Iamblichus, Theologoumena arithmeticae*.

Atticus, Fragments, ed. E. des Places, Paris (Collection Budé), 1977.

Iamblichus, de mysteriis (Les mystères d'Égypte), ed. E. des Places, Paris (Collection Budé), 1966.

  Theologoumena arithmeticae, ed. V. de Falco, Stuttgart (Teubner), 1975.

  In Platonis Dialogos, see Bibliography, Dillon, John M. (1973).

Numenius, Fragments, ed. E. des Places, Paris (Collection Budé), 1973.

Philoponus, de aeternitate mundi contra Proclum, ed. H. Rabe, Leipzig (Teubner), 1899.

Porphyry, Eisagoge, ed. A. Busse, Berlin, 1877 (CAG IV.1).

  in Aristotelis categorias, ed. A. Busse, Berlin, 1887 (CAG IV.1).

  de abstinentia (De l'abstinence), 2 vols, ed. J. Bouffartigue and M. Patillon, Paris (Collection Budé), 1977, 1979.

  in Platonis Timaeum, ed. A. R. Sodano, Naples, 1964.

Proclus, in Platonis Timaeum, ed. E. Diehl, 3 vols, Leipzig, 1903, 1904, 1906 (cf. also the tr. by A. J. Festugière, 3 vols, Paris, 1966, 1967, 1968).

(b)

Patristic references to J.-P. Migne, *Patrologia Graeca* and *Patrologia Latina*, are by volume and column number (e.g. PG 26, 24B).

The following authors are quoted according to the editions in the Berlin Corpus (GCS: *Die Griechischen Christlichen Schriftsteller der Ersten Drei Jahrhunderte*) with the exceptions noted:

Clement of Alexandria (see also below), *Epiphanius, Eusebius of Caesarea, Methodius, Origen* (see also below), *Philostorgius, Sozomen, Theodoret (historia ecclesiastica)*. Reference is given by title, chapter or section number, page and line numbers (e.g Origen, in Jo. I.16, [p.] 20. [lines] 15–23).

The editions of *Clement's excerpta ex Thodoto* by R. P. Casey (London, 1934), and F. Sagnard, Paris (Sources chrétiennes), 1948, have also been used.

Works by *Origen* not published in GCS follow the text of Lommatzsch, and are referred to by volume and page number (e.g. Lommatzsch XXIV. 357). *Pamphilus' Defence of Origen* is also quoted from Lommatzsch's text.

Dionysius of Alexandria is for the most part quoted as he appears in the texts of Athanasius; but reference is also made to the edition of his works by C. L. Feltoe (Cambridge, 1904).

There exists no complete modern edition of *Athanaasius*; where texts are available in H.-G. Opitz' edition (*Athanasius Werke*, II.1, Berlin/Leipzig, 1934/1941), they have been quoted accordingly (chapter or section number, followed by 'Opitz' and page and line numbers, e.g. de syn. 15, Opitz 242.1–6). Otherwise references are to the Benedictine edition as printed in Migne.

Opitz is also used for the primary texts of the controversy to 333 (*Athanasius Werke*, III.1: *Urkunden zur Geschichte des Arianischen Streites*, Berlin/Leipzig, 1935; quoted as 'Opitz, U', with document, page and line numbers, e.g. Opitz, U.14, 19.11–20.19.

Irenaeus is quoted following W. W. Harvey's edition (2 vols, Cambridge, 1857).

Referencs to *Theophilus of Antioch* follow R. M. Grant's edition of the *ad Autolycum* (Oxford, 1970).

Latin texts are generally quoted from editions in CSEL (*Corpus Scriptorum Eccliesiasticorum Latinorum*) by section, page (and, where appropriate, line) numbers (e.g. Victorinus, adv. Arrium, I.13, CSEL, pp. 72–3); otherwise, Migne is followed.

Index of Names

(Page numbers in square brackets indicate that the reference occurs in a note)